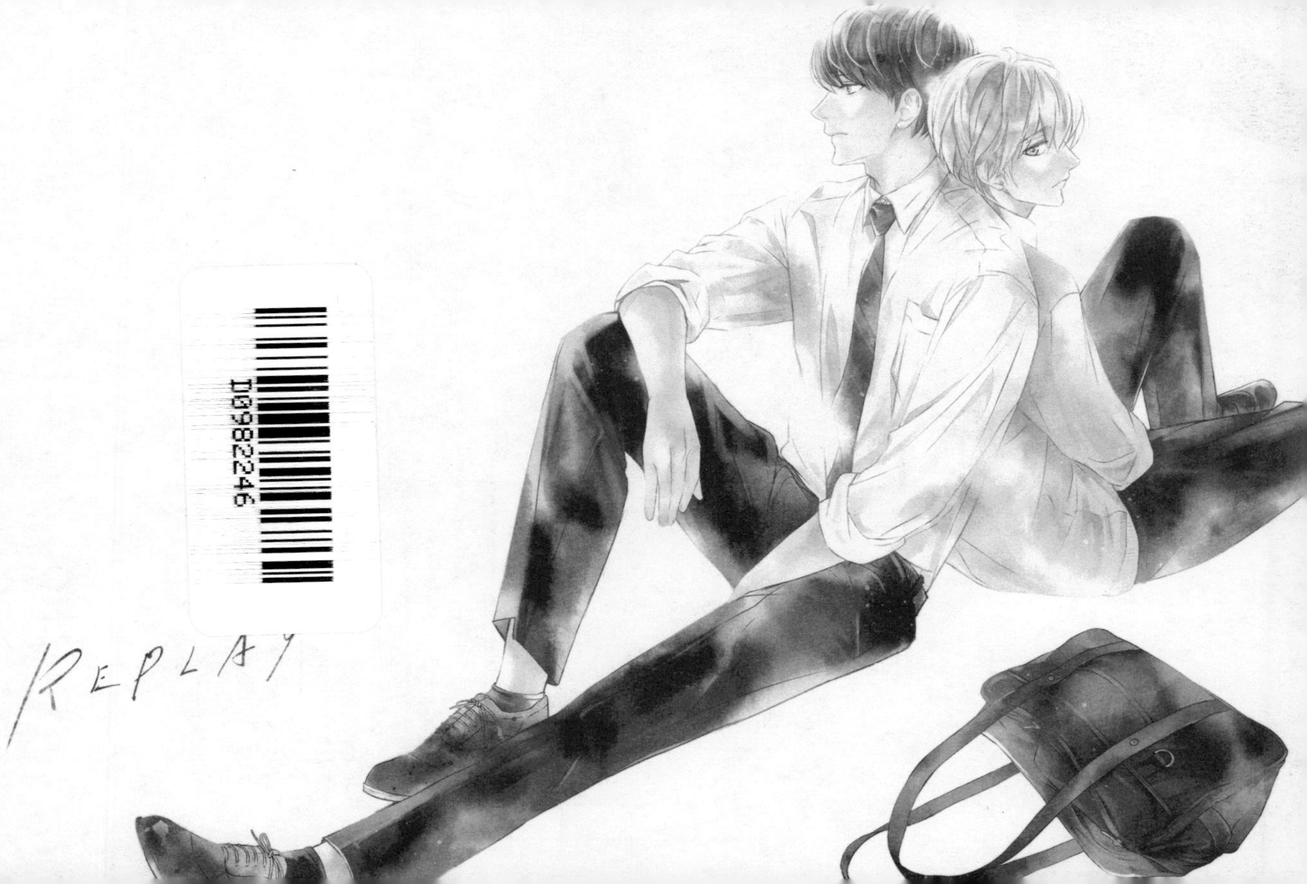
REPLAY

BIRZ COMICS LYNX COLLECTION

# CONTENTS

REPLAY

presented by
SAKI TSUKAHARA

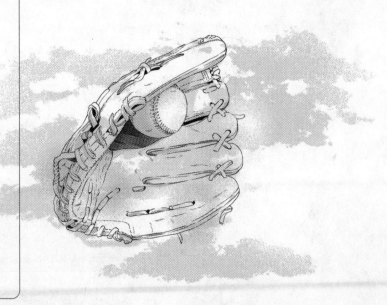

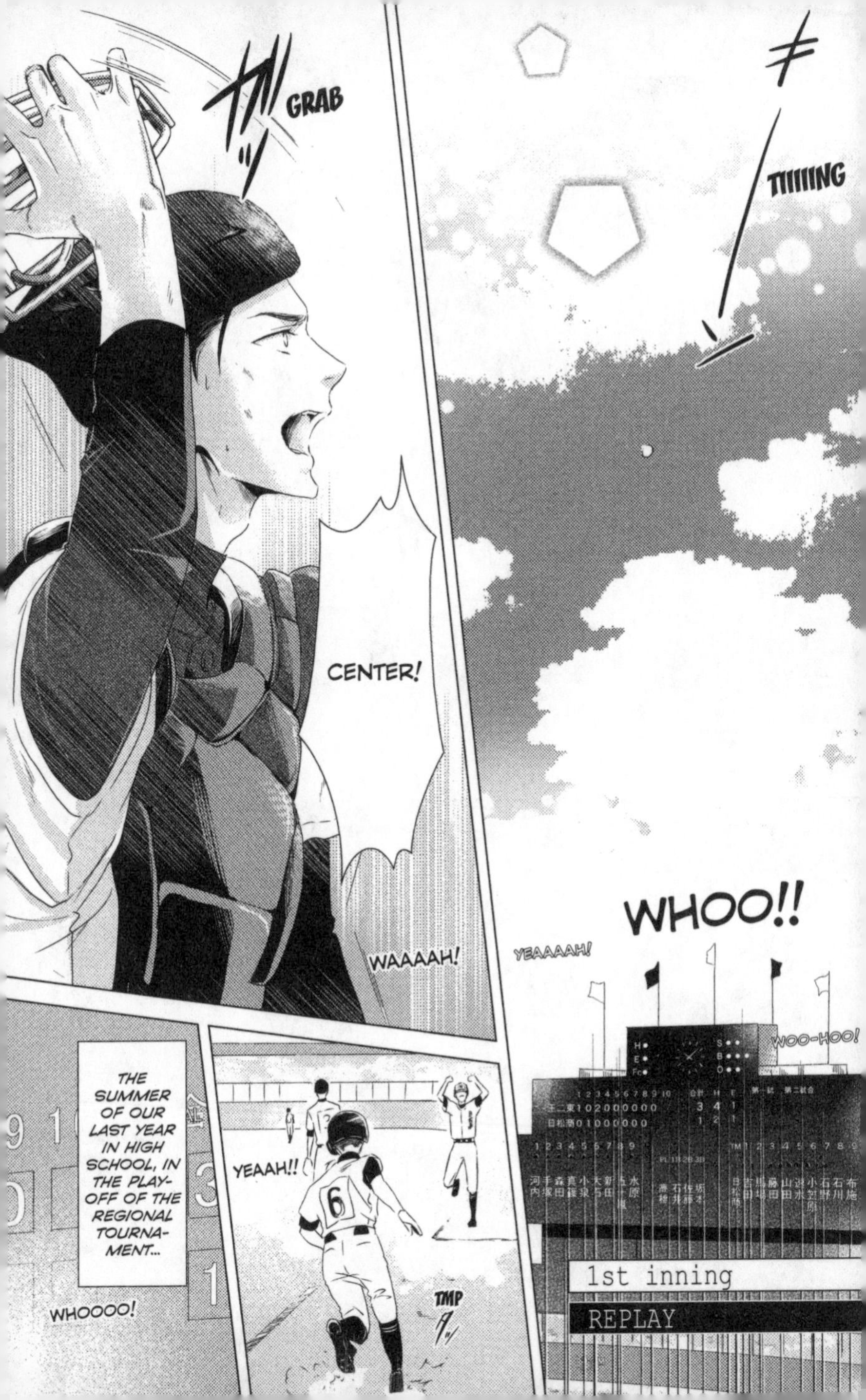
TIIIIING
WHOO!!
YEAAAAH!
WOO-HOO!
1st inning
REPLAY
GRAB
CENTER!
WAAAAH!
YEAAH!!
TMP
THE SUMMER OF OUR LAST YEAR IN HIGH SCHOOL, IN THE PLAY-OFF OF THE REGIONAL TOURNA-MENT...
WHOOOO!

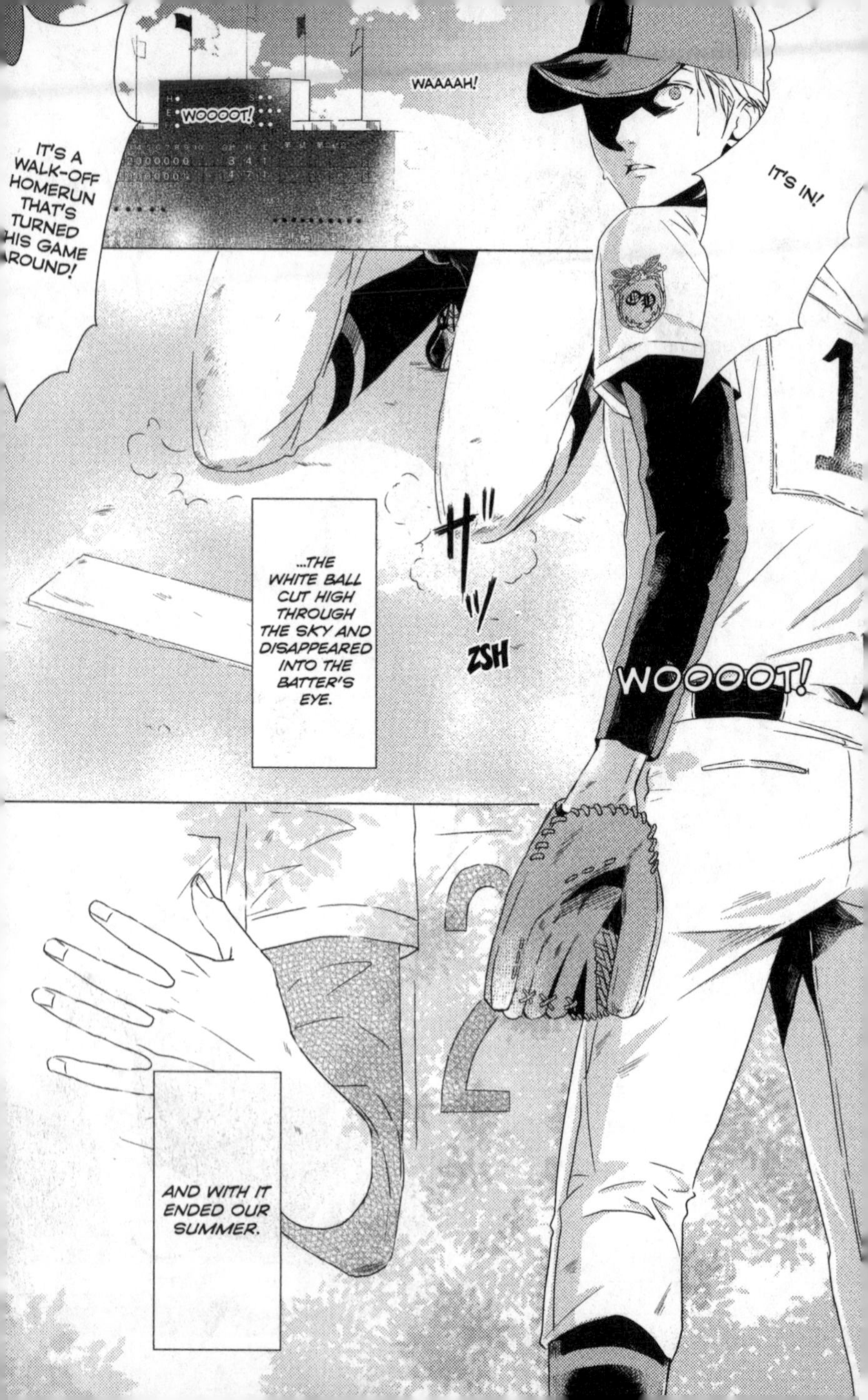

IT'S IN!
WAAAAH!
WOOOOT!
WOOOOT!
IT'S A WALK-OFF HOMERUN THAT'S TURNED HIS GAME AROUND!
ZSH
...THE WHITE BALL CUT HIGH THROUGH THE SKY AND DISAPPEARED INTO THE BATTER'S EYE.
AND WITH IT ENDED OUR SUMMER.

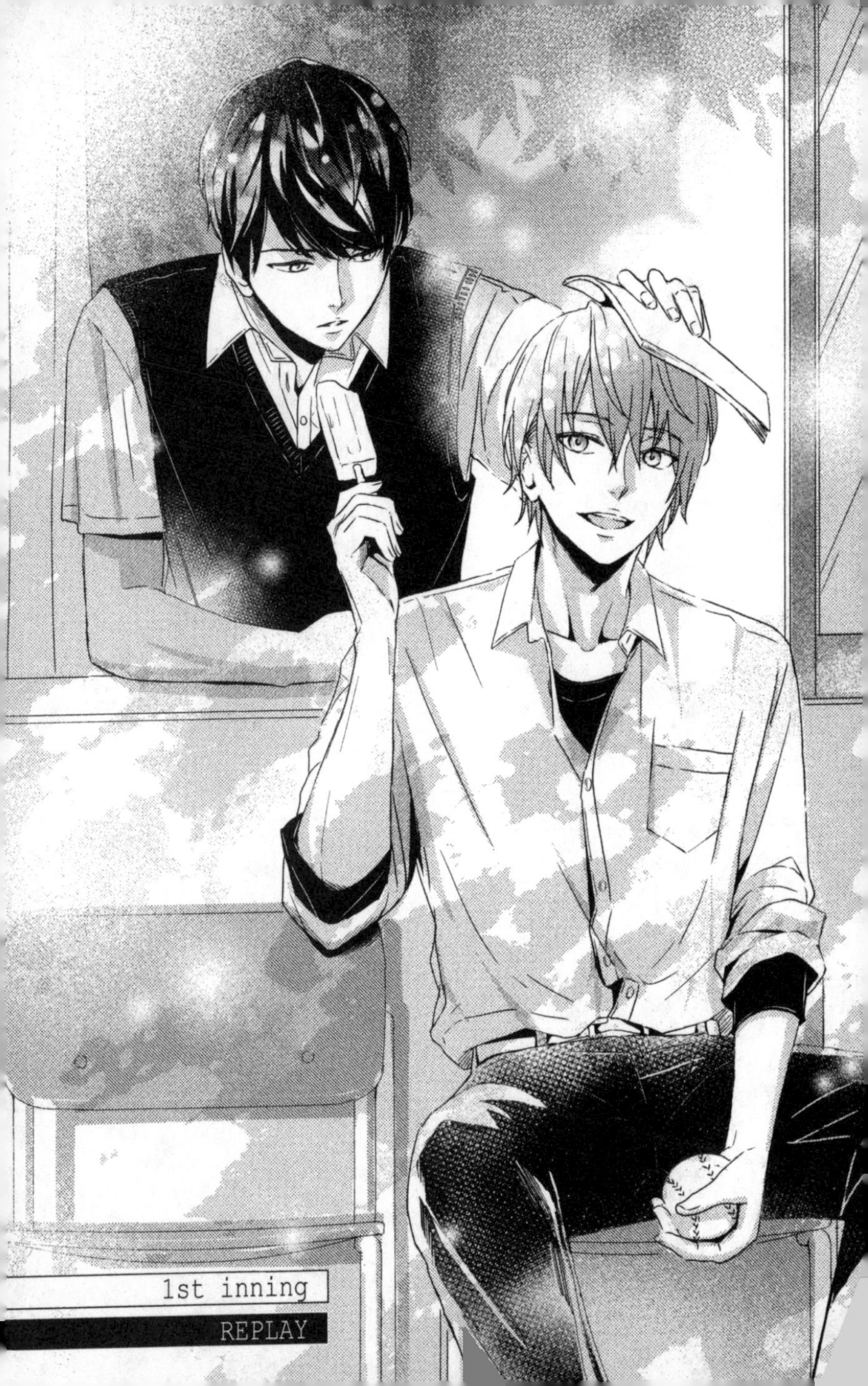
1st inning
REPLAY

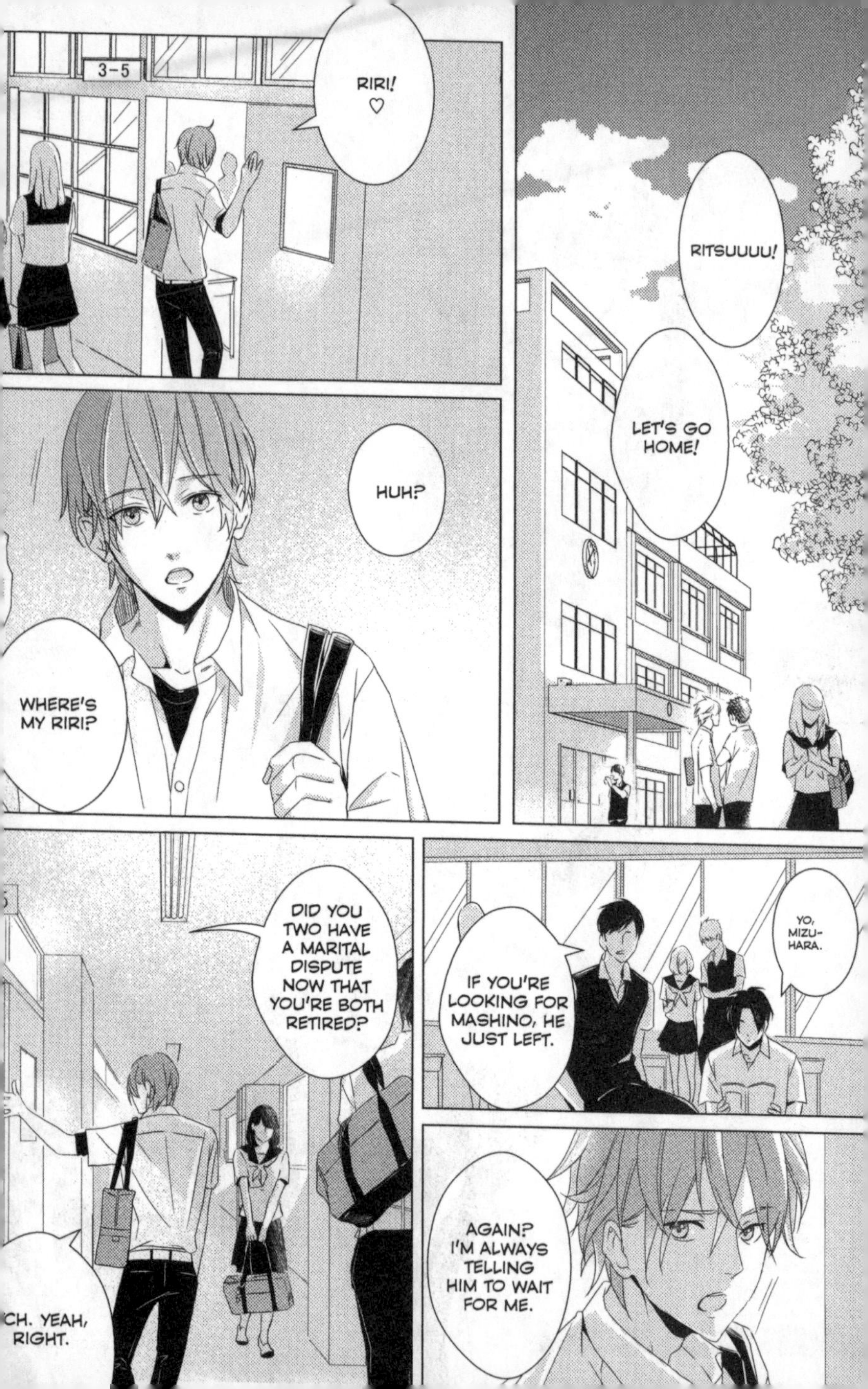
RITSUUUU!
LET'S GO HOME!
RIRI! ♡
HUH?
WHERE'S MY RIRI?
YO, MIZU-HARA.
IF YOU'RE LOOKING FOR MASHINO, HE JUST LEFT.
AGAIN? I'M ALWAYS TELLING HIM TO WAIT FOR ME.
DID YOU TWO HAVE A MARITAL DISPUTE NOW THAT YOU'RE BOTH RETIRED?
CH. YEAH, RIGHT.

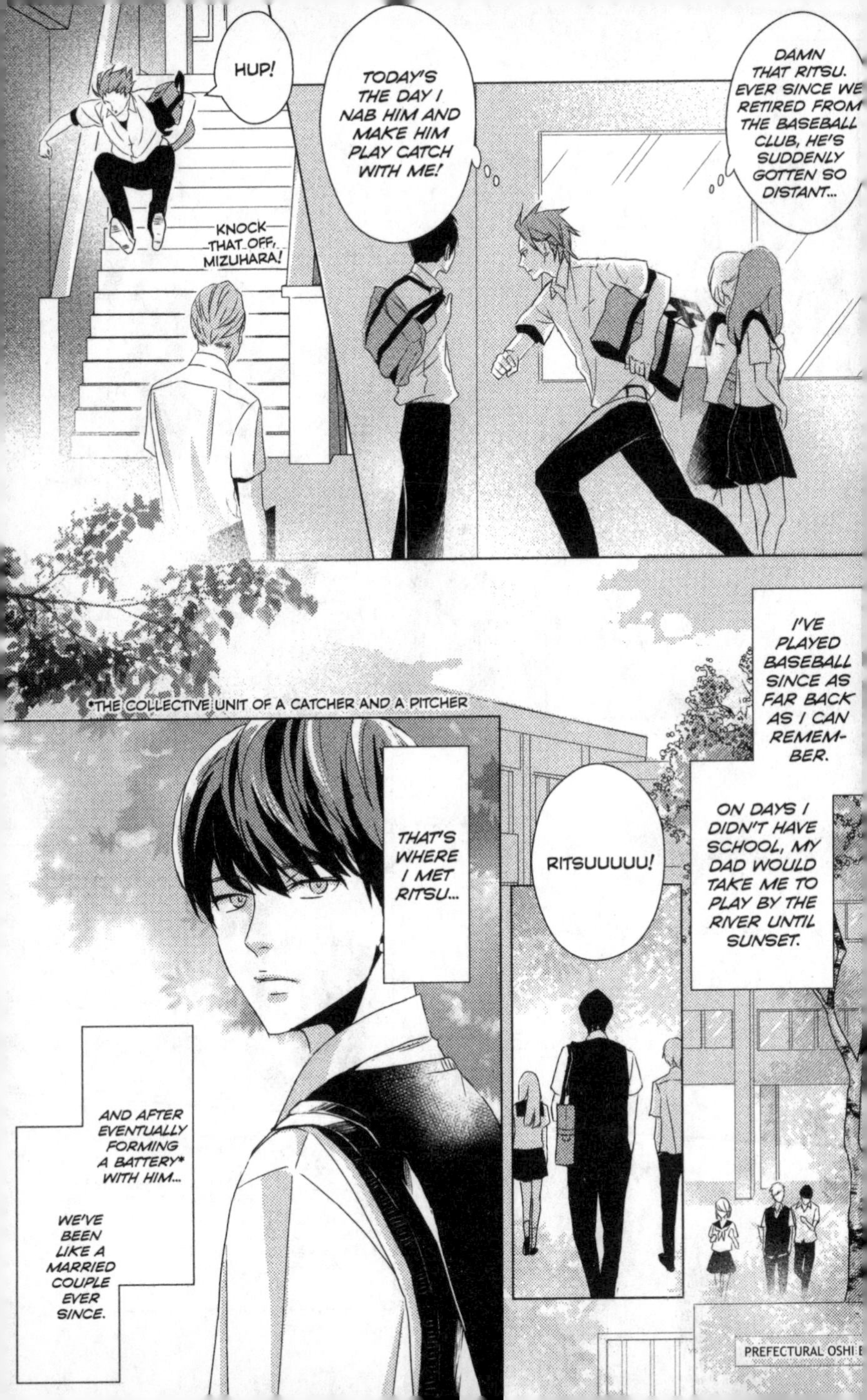
DAMN THAT RITSU. EVER SINCE WE RETIRED FROM THE BASEBALL CLUB, HE'S SUDDENLY GOTTEN SO DISTANT...
TODAY'S THE DAY I NAB HIM AND MAKE HIM PLAY CATCH WITH ME!
HUP!
KNOCK THAT OFF, MIZUHARA!
I'VE PLAYED BASEBALL SINCE AS FAR BACK AS I CAN REMEMBER.
ON DAYS I DIDN'T HAVE SCHOOL, MY DAD WOULD TAKE ME TO PLAY BY THE RIVER UNTIL SUNSET.
RITSUUUUUU!
PREFECTURAL OSHI
THAT'S WHERE I MET RITSU...
AND AFTER EVENTUALLY FORMING A BATTERY* WITH HIM...
WE'VE BEEN LIKE A MARRIED COUPLE EVER SINCE.
*THE COLLECTIVE UNIT OF A CATCHER AND A PITCHER

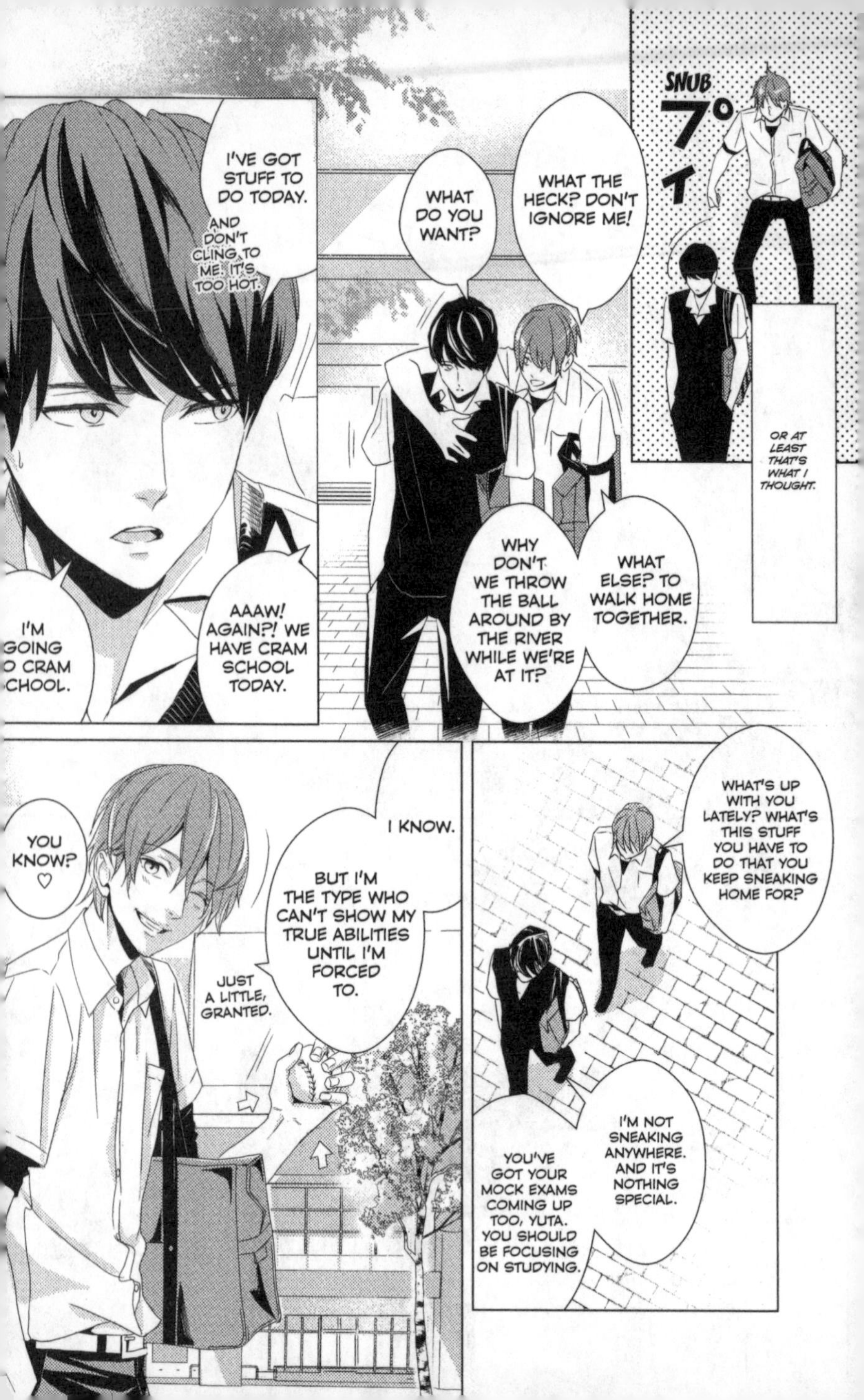
SNUB
7°
OR AT LEAST THAT'S WHAT I THOUGHT.
WHAT THE HECK? DON'T IGNORE ME!
WHAT DO YOU WANT?
WHAT ELSE? TO WALK HOME TOGETHER.
WHY DON'T WE THROW THE BALL AROUND BY THE RIVER WHILE WE'RE AT IT?
I'VE GOT STUFF TO DO TODAY.
AND DON'T CLING TO ME. IT'S TOO HOT.
AAAW! AGAIN?! WE HAVE CRAM SCHOOL TODAY.
I'M GOING O CRAM CHOOL.
WHAT'S UP WITH YOU LATELY? WHAT'S THIS STUFF YOU HAVE TO DO THAT YOU KEEP SNEAKING HOME FOR?
I'M NOT SNEAKING ANYWHERE. AND IT'S NOTHING SPECIAL.
YOU'VE GOT YOUR MOCK EXAMS COMING UP TOO, YUTA. YOU SHOULD BE FOCUSING ON STUDYING.
I KNOW.
BUT I'M THE TYPE WHO CAN'T SHOW MY TRUE ABILITIES UNTIL I'M FORCED TO.
JUST A LITTLE, GRANTED.
YOU KNOW? ♡

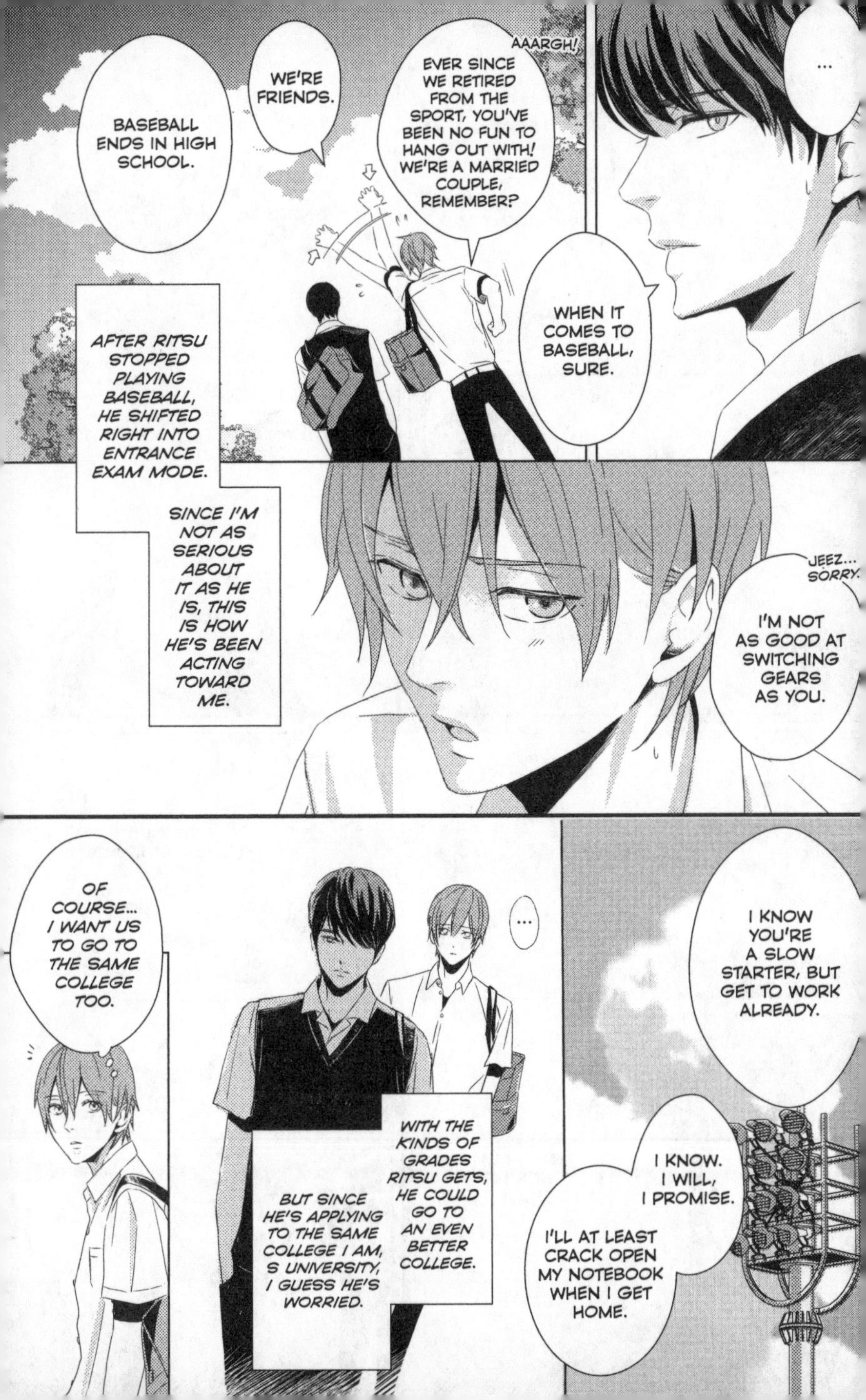
...
WHEN IT COMES TO BASEBALL, SURE.
AAARGH!
EVER SINCE WE RETIRED FROM THE SPORT, YOU'VE BEEN NO FUN TO HANG OUT WITH! WE'RE A MARRIED COUPLE, REMEMBER?
WE'RE FRIENDS.
BASEBALL ENDS IN HIGH SCHOOL.
AFTER RITSU STOPPED PLAYING BASEBALL, HE SHIFTED RIGHT INTO ENTRANCE EXAM MODE.
JEEZ... SORRY.
I'M NOT AS GOOD AT SWITCHING GEARS AS YOU.
SINCE I'M NOT AS SERIOUS ABOUT IT AS HE IS, THIS IS HOW HE'S BEEN ACTING TOWARD ME.
I KNOW YOU'RE A SLOW STARTER, BUT GET TO WORK ALREADY.
I KNOW. I WILL, I PROMISE.
I'LL AT LEAST CRACK OPEN MY NOTEBOOK WHEN I GET HOME.
...
WITH THE KINDS OF GRADES RITSU GETS, HE COULD GO TO AN EVEN BETTER COLLEGE.
BUT SINCE HE'S APPLYING TO THE SAME COLLEGE I AM, S UNIVERSITY, I GUESS HE'S WORRIED.
OF COURSE... I WANT US TO GO TO THE SAME COLLEGE TOO.

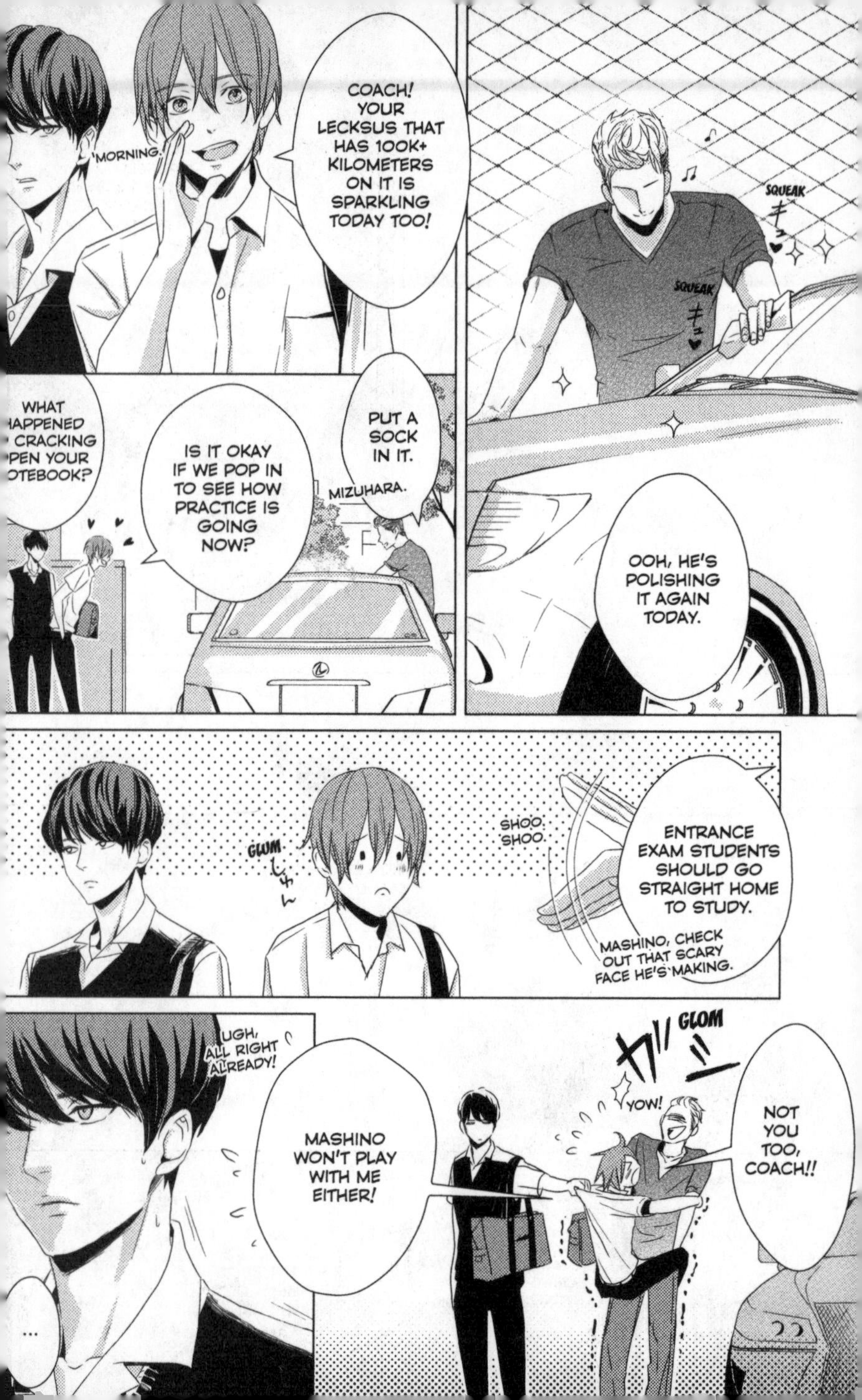

SQUEAK
SQUEAK
OOH, HE'S POLISHING IT AGAIN TODAY.
COACH! YOUR LECKSUS THAT HAS 100K+ KILOMETERS ON IT IS SPARKLING TODAY TOO!
'MORNING.
PUT A SOCK IN IT.
MIZUHARA.
IS IT OKAY IF WE POP IN TO SEE HOW PRACTICE IS GOING NOW?
WHAT
IAPPENED
CRACKING
PEN YOUR
OTEBOOK?
ENTRANCE EXAM STUDENTS SHOULD GO STRAIGHT HOME TO STUDY.
SHOO SHOO
MASHINO, CHECK OUT THAT SCARY FACE HE'S MAKING.
GLUM
NOT YOU TOO, COACH!!
GLOM
YOW!
MASHINO WON'T PLAY WITH ME EITHER!
UGH, ALL RIGHT ALREADY!
...

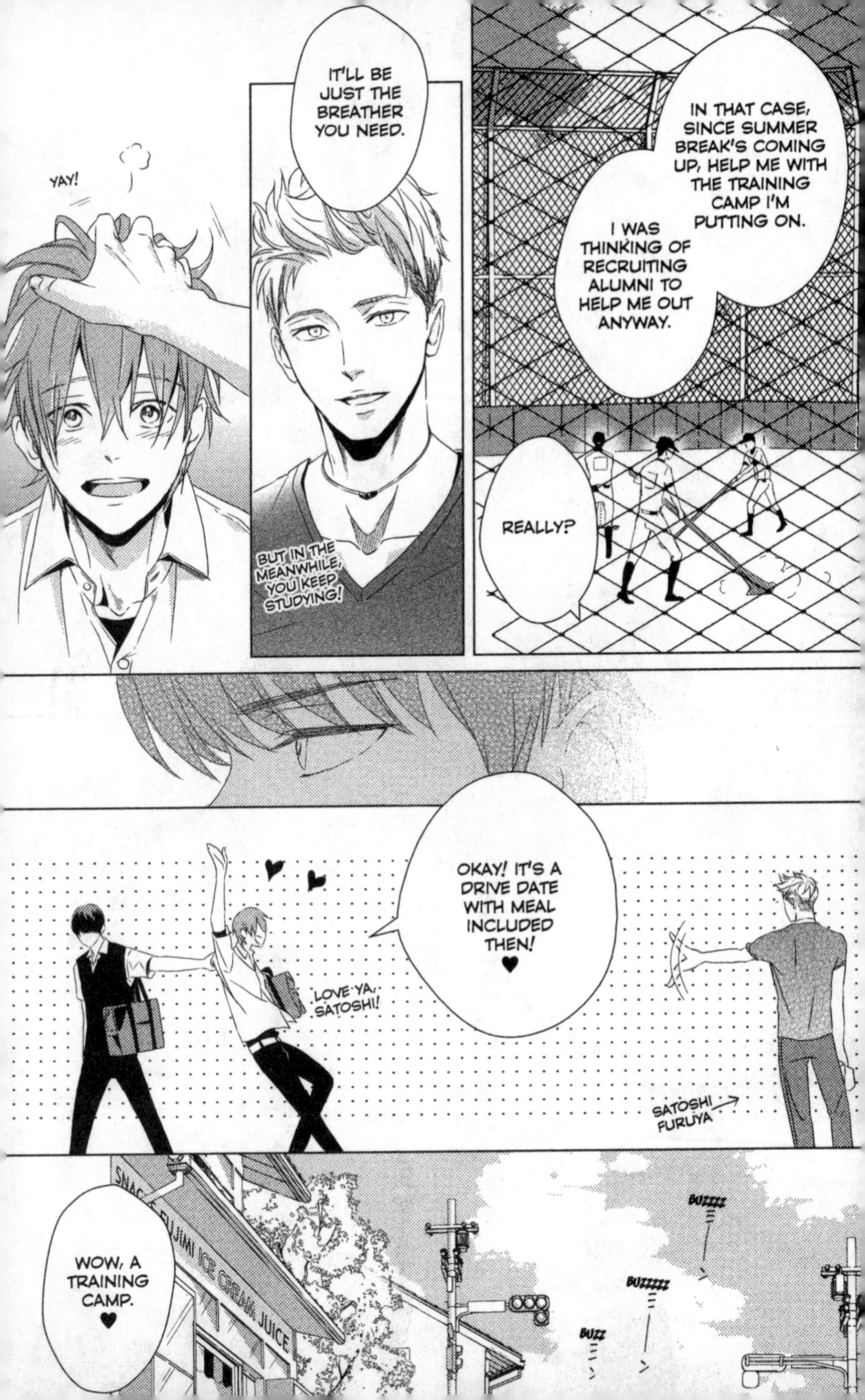
IN THAT CASE, SINCE SUMMER BREAK'S COMING UP, HELP ME WITH THE TRAINING CAMP I'M PUTTING ON.
I WAS THINKING OF RECRUITING ALUMNI TO HELP ME OUT ANYWAY.
REALLY?
IT'LL BE JUST THE BREATHER YOU NEED.
BUT IN THE MEANWHILE, YOU KEEP STUDYING!
YAY!
SATOSHI FURUYA
OKAY! IT'S A DRIVE DATE WITH MEAL INCLUDED THEN! ♥
LOVE YA, SATOSHI!
BUZZZZ
BUZZZZZ
BUZZ
ICE CREAM JUICE
WOW, A TRAINING CAMP. ♥

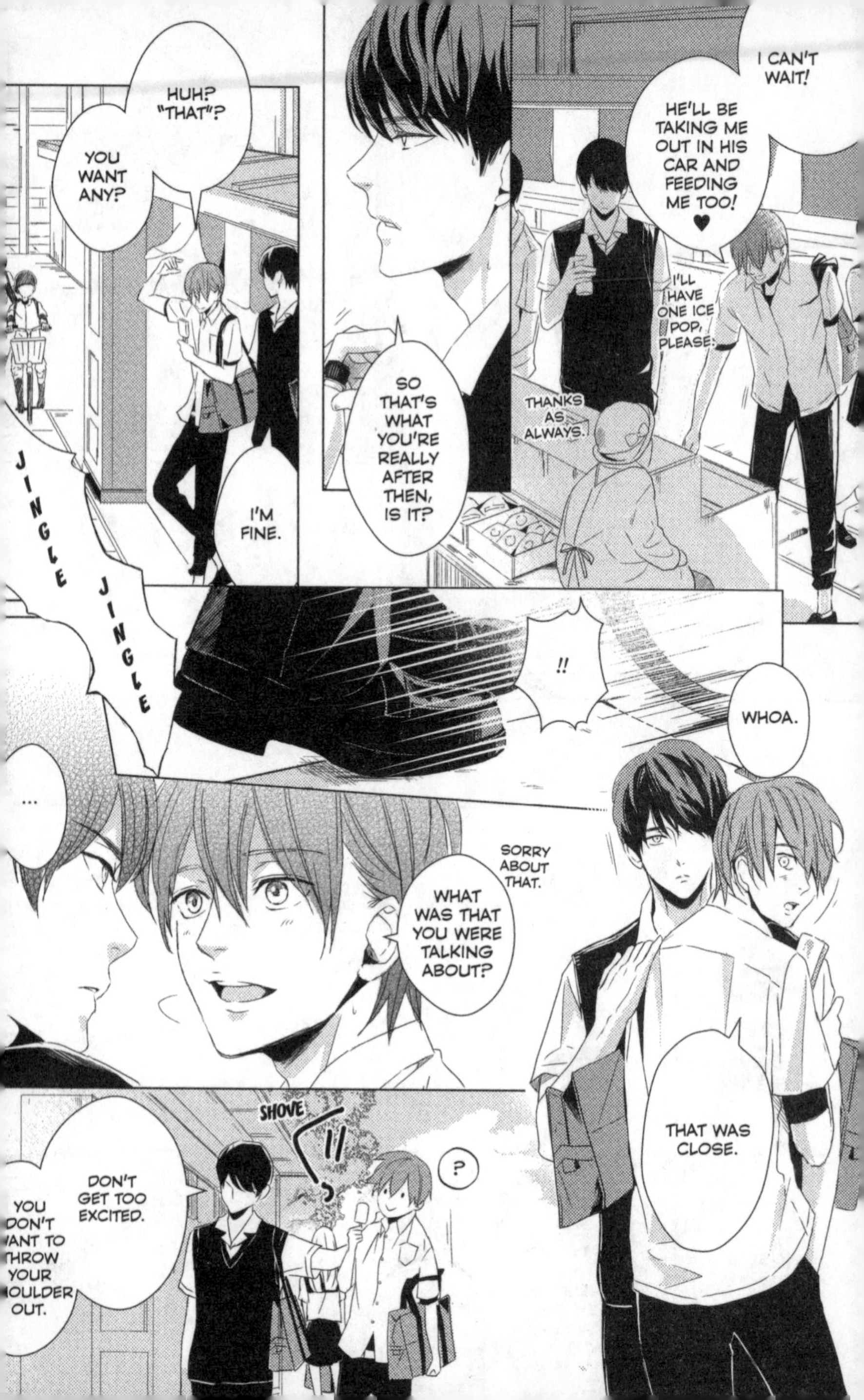
I CAN'T WAIT!
HE'LL BE TAKING ME OUT IN HIS CAR AND FEEDING ME TOO! ♥
I'LL HAVE ONE ICE POP, PLEASE.
THANKS AS ALWAYS.
SO THAT'S WHAT YOU'RE REALLY AFTER THEN, IS IT?
HUH? "THAT"?
YOU WANT ANY?
I'M FINE.
JINGLE
JINGLE
WHOA.
THAT WAS CLOSE.
!!
...
SORRY ABOUT THAT.
WHAT WAS THAT YOU WERE TALKING ABOUT?
?
SHOVE
!!
DON'T GET TOO EXCITED.
YOU DON'T ANT TO THROW YOUR OULDER OUT.

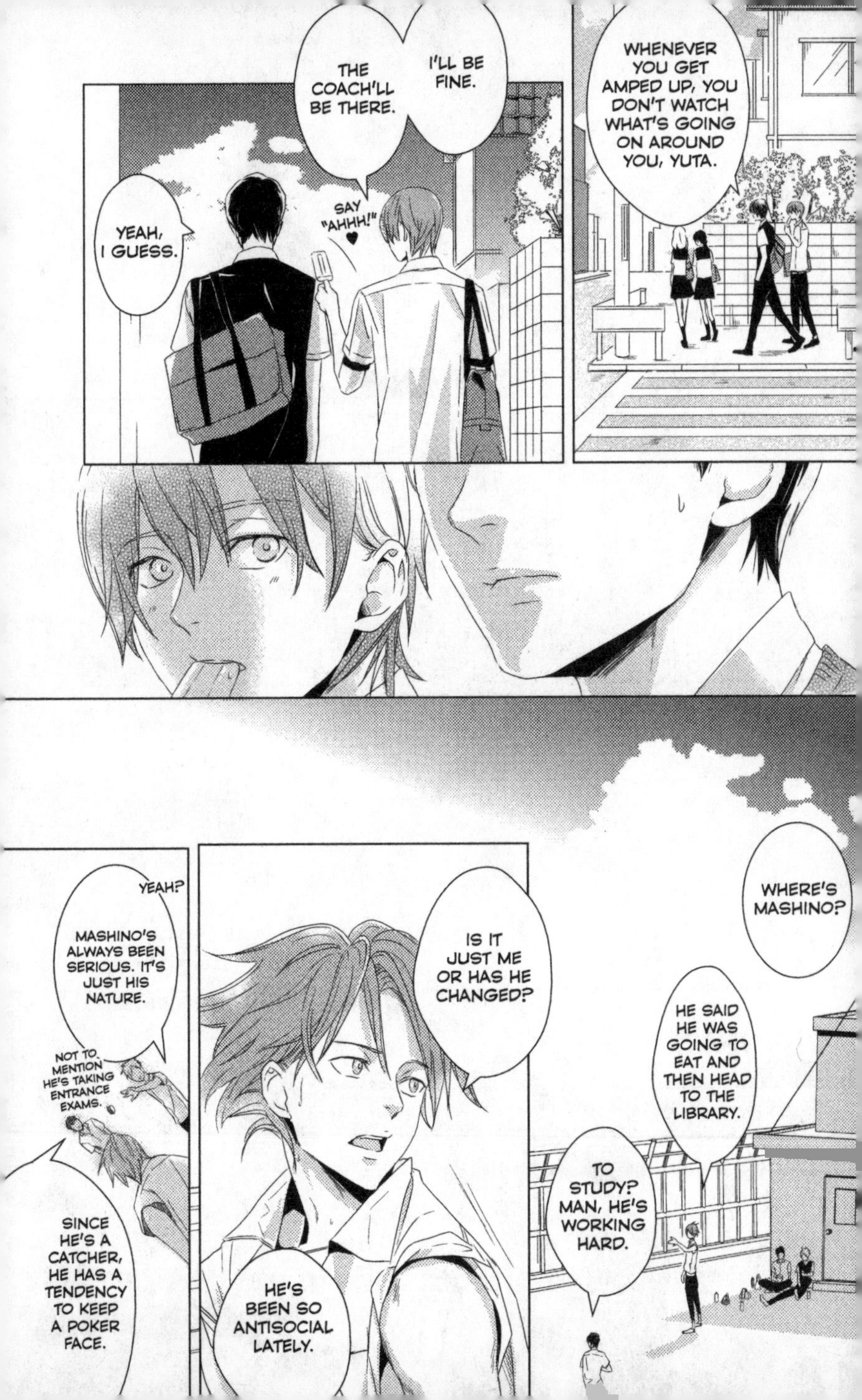
WHENEVER YOU GET AMPED UP, YOU DON'T WATCH WHAT'S GOING ON AROUND YOU, YUTA.
I'LL BE FINE.
THE COACH'LL BE THERE.
SAY "AHHH!" ♥
YEAH, I GUESS.
WHERE'S MASHINO?
HE SAID HE WAS GOING TO EAT AND THEN HEAD TO THE LIBRARY.
TO STUDY? MAN, HE'S WORKING HARD.
IS IT JUST ME OR HAS HE CHANGED?
HE'S BEEN SO ANTISOCIAL LATELY.
YEAH?
MASHINO'S ALWAYS BEEN SERIOUS. IT'S JUST HIS NATURE.
NOT TO MENTION HE'S TAKING ENTRANCE EXAMS.
SINCE HE'S A CATCHER, HE HAS A TENDENCY TO KEEP A POKER FACE.

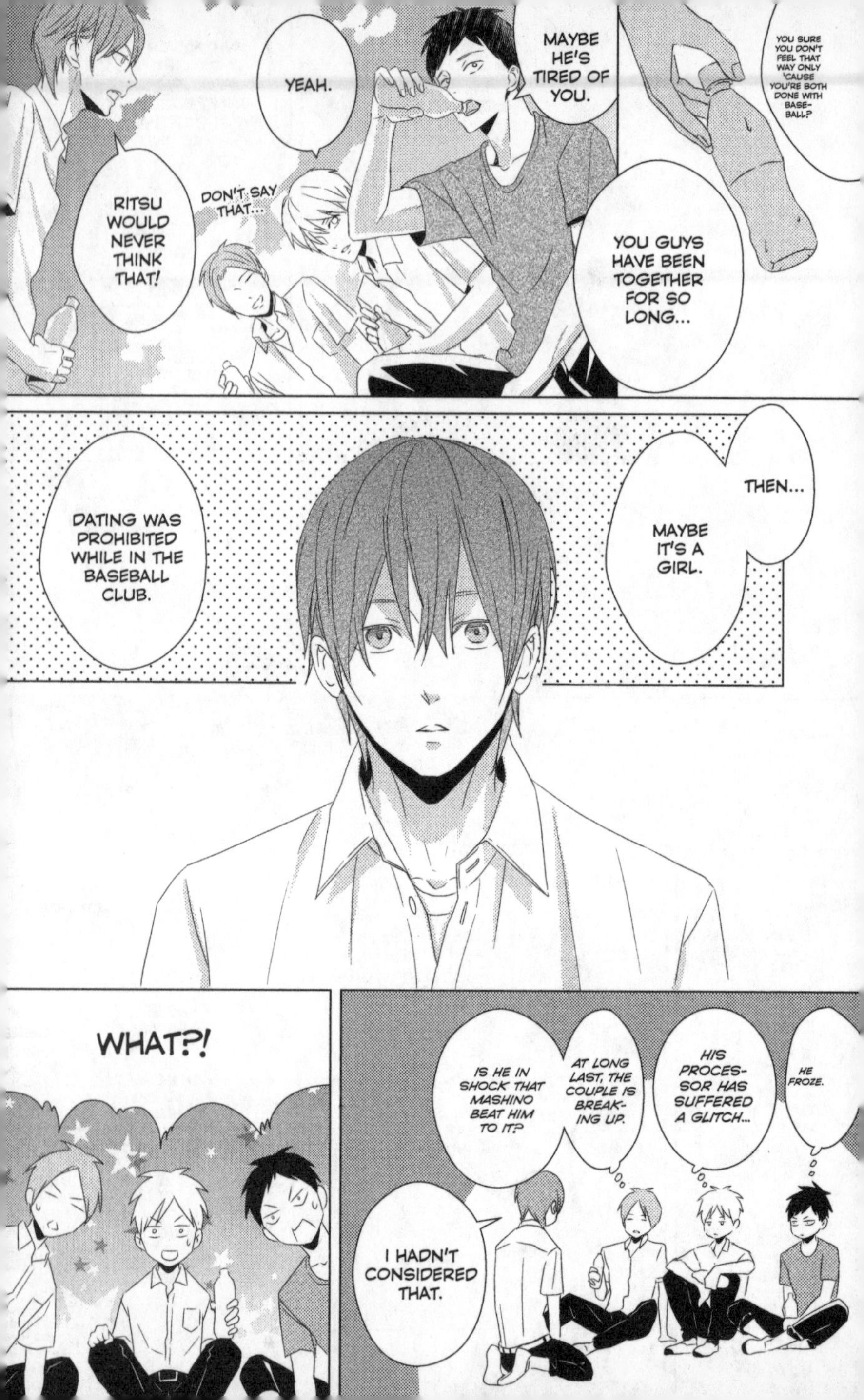
YOU SURE YOU DON'T FEEL THAT WAY ONLY 'CAUSE YOU'RE BOTH DONE WITH BASE-BALL?
MAYBE HE'S TIRED OF YOU.
YEAH.
YOU GUYS HAVE BEEN TOGETHER FOR SO LONG...
DON'T SAY THAT...
RITSU WOULD NEVER THINK THAT!
THEN...
MAYBE IT'S A GIRL.
DATING WAS PROHIBITED WHILE IN THE BASEBALL CLUB.
HE FROZE.
HIS PROCES-SOR HAS SUFFERED A GLITCH...
AT LONG LAST, THE COUPLE IS BREAK-ING UP.
IS HE IN SHOCK THAT MASHINO BEAT HIM TO IT?
I HADN'T CONSIDERED THAT.
WHAT?!

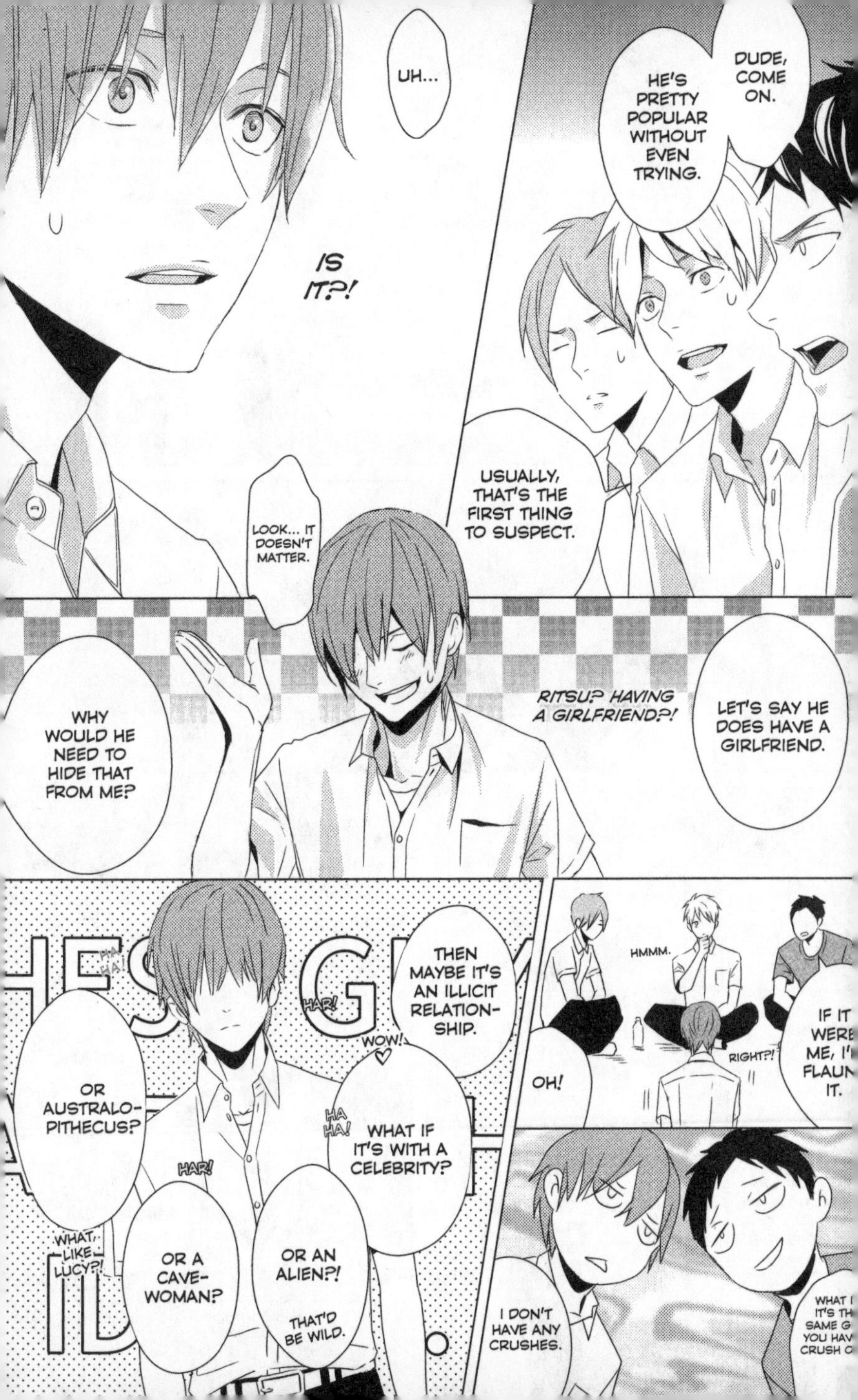
DUDE, COME ON.
HE'S PRETTY POPULAR WITHOUT EVEN TRYING.
USUALLY, THAT'S THE FIRST THING TO SUSPECT.
UH...
IS IT?!
LET'S SAY HE DOES HAVE A GIRLFRIEND.
RITSU? HAVING A GIRLFRIEND?!
LOOK... IT DOESN'T MATTER.
WHY WOULD HE NEED TO HIDE THAT FROM ME?
IF IT WERE ME, I' FLAUN IT.
HMMM.
RIGHT?!
OH!
WHAT I IT'S TH SAME G YOU HAV CRUSH O
I DON'T HAVE ANY CRUSHES.
THEN MAYBE IT'S AN ILLICIT RELATION-SHIP.
WOW! ♥
HA HA!
HAR!
WHAT IF IT'S WITH A CELEBRITY?
HA HA!
OR AUSTRALO-PITHECUS?
WHAT, LIKE LUCY?!
HAR!
OR AN ALIEN?!
THAT'D BE WILD.
OR A CAVE-WOMAN?

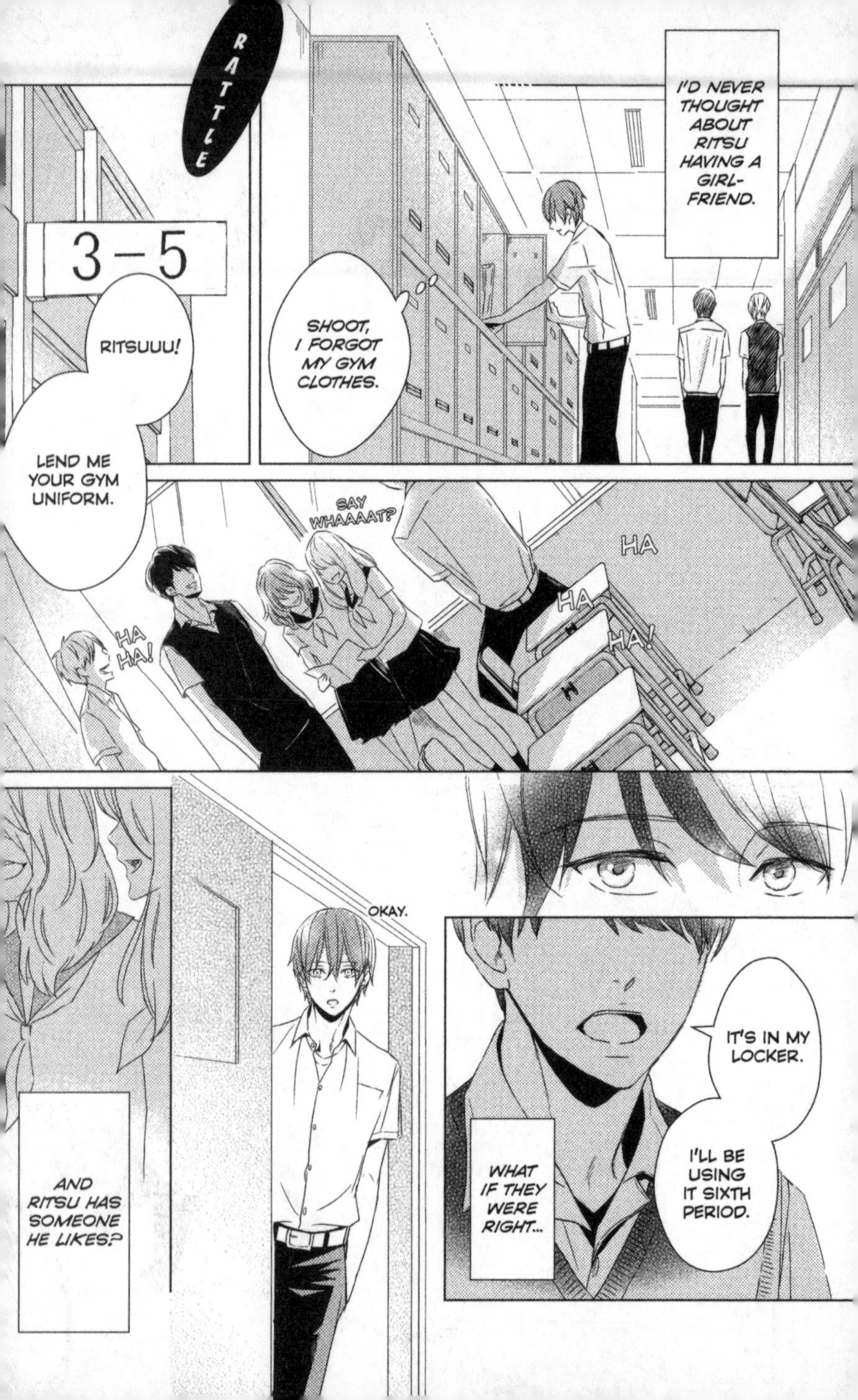
I'D NEVER THOUGHT ABOUT RITSU HAVING A GIRL-FRIEND.
RATTLE
SHOOT, I FORGOT MY GYM CLOTHES.
3-5
RITSUUU!
LEND ME YOUR GYM UNIFORM.
HA HA HA!
SAY WHAAAAT?
HA HA!
IT'S IN MY LOCKER.
I'LL BE USING IT SIXTH PERIOD.
WHAT IF THEY WERE RIGHT...
OKAY.
AND RITSU HAS SOMEONE HE LIKES?

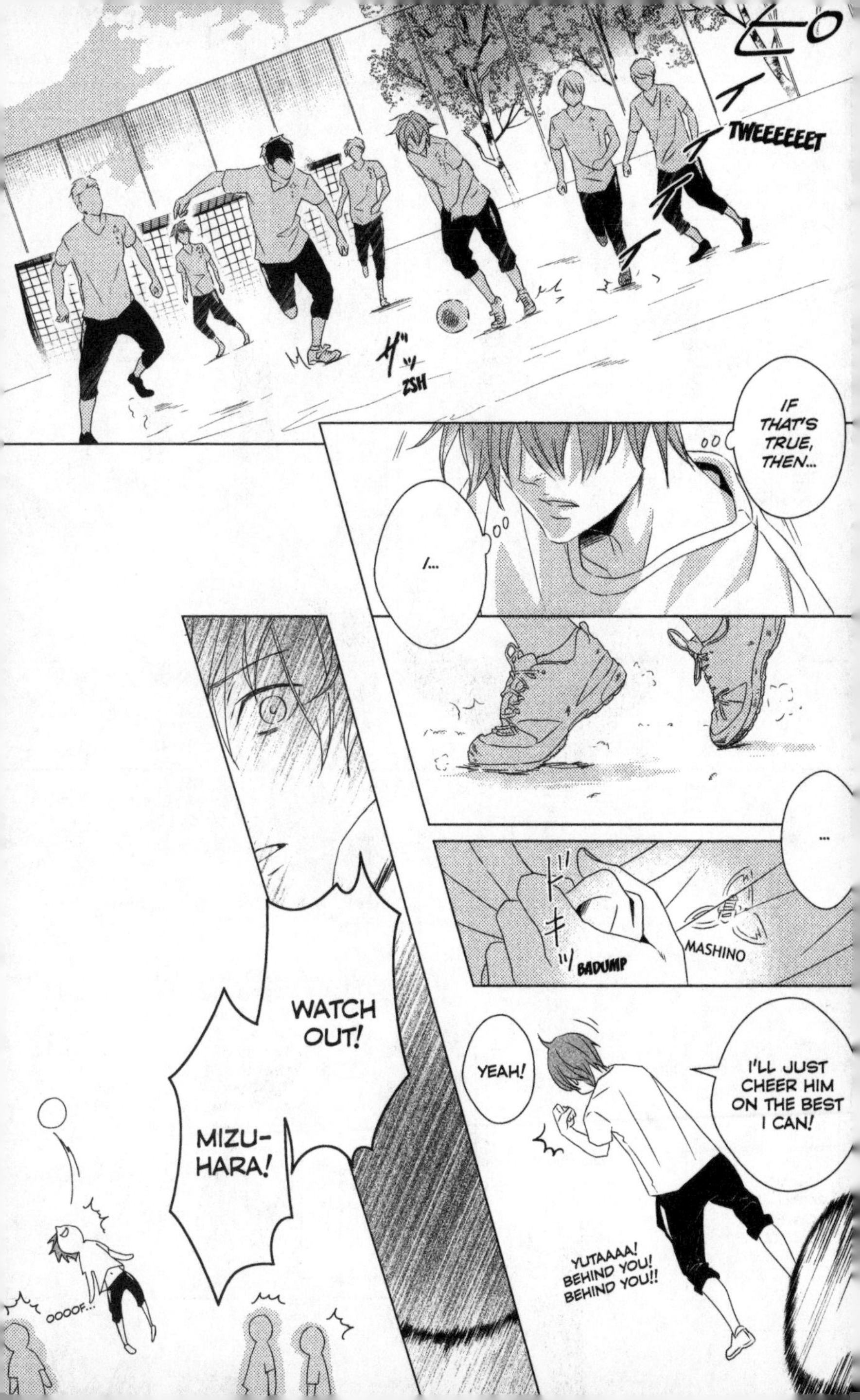
TWEEEEEET
ZSH
IF THAT'S TRUE, THEN...
I...
...
BADUMP
MASHINO
I'LL JUST CHEER HIM ON THE BEST I CAN!
YEAH!
YUTAAAA! BEHIND YOU! BEHIND YOU!!
WATCH OUT!
MIZU-HARA!
OOOOF...

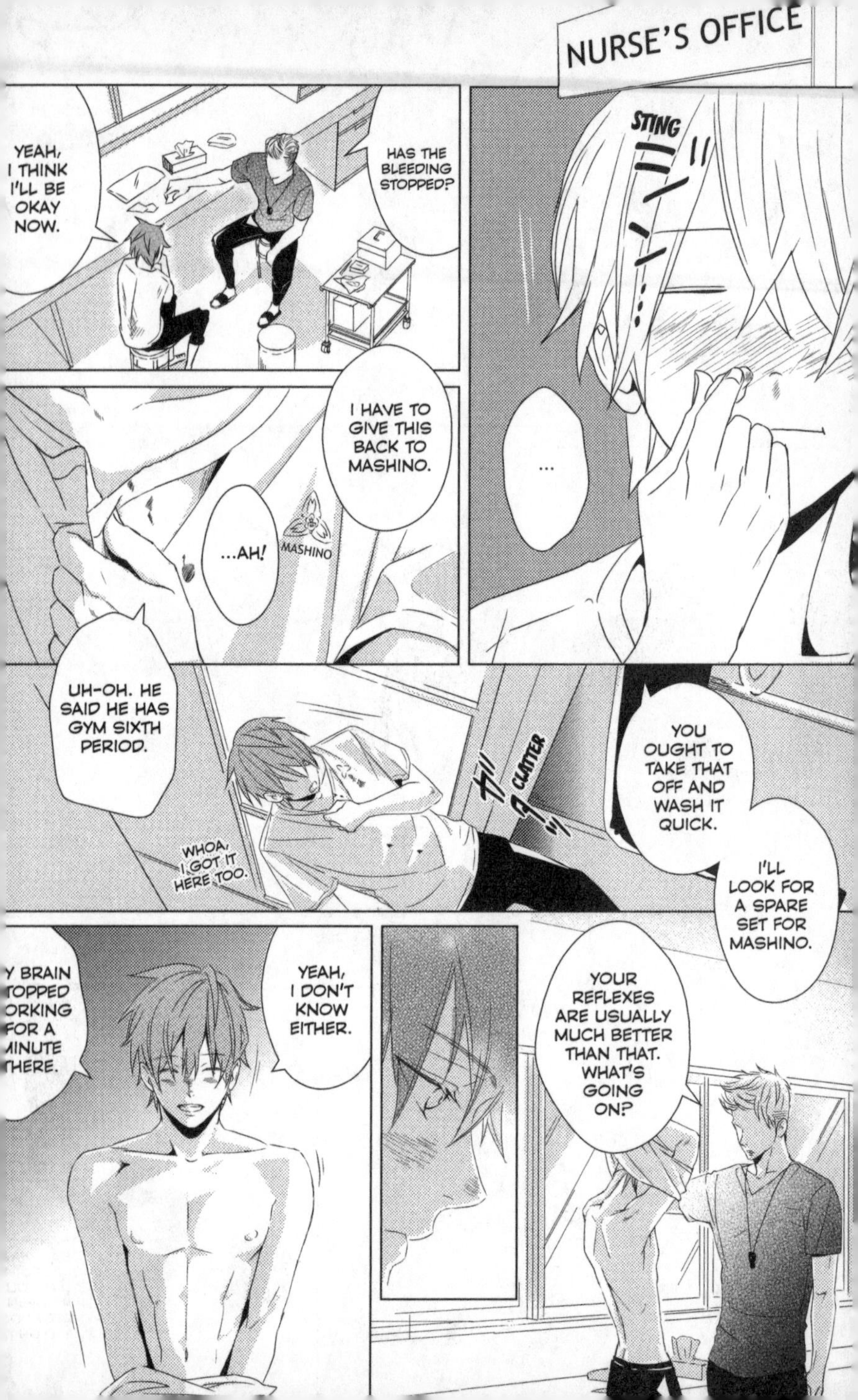
NURSE'S OFFICE
STING
...
HAS THE BLEEDING STOPPED?
YEAH, I THINK I'LL BE OKAY NOW.
I HAVE TO GIVE THIS BACK TO MASHINO.
MASHINO
...AH!
UH-OH. HE SAID HE HAS GYM SIXTH PERIOD.
YOU OUGHT TO TAKE THAT OFF AND WASH IT QUICK.
I'LL LOOK FOR A SPARE SET FOR MASHINO.
CLATTER
WHOA, I GOT IT HERE TOO.
YOUR REFLEXES ARE USUALLY MUCH BETTER THAN THAT. WHAT'S GOING ON?
YEAH, I DON'T KNOW EITHER.
Y BRAIN TOPPED ORKING FOR A MINUTE THERE.

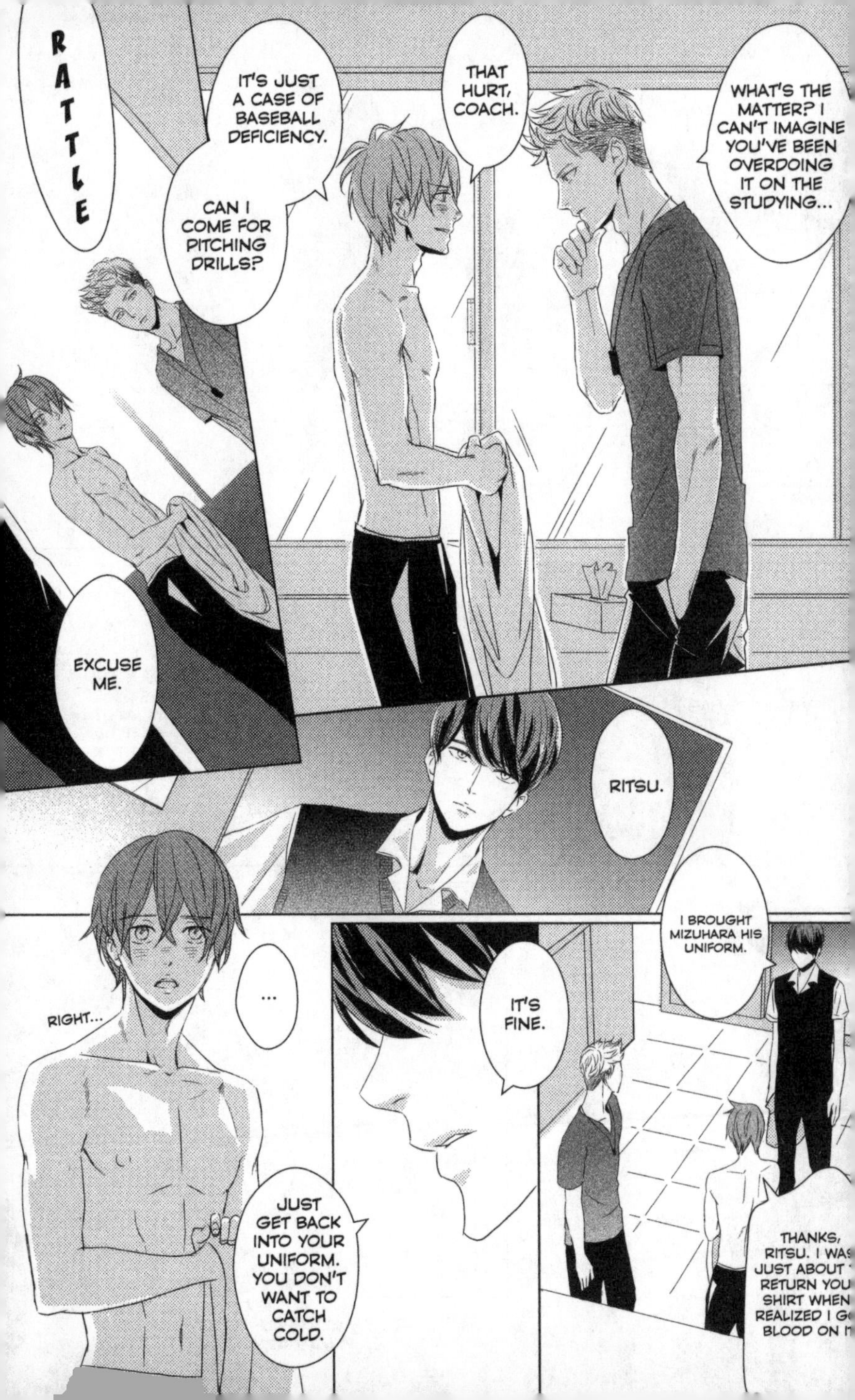
WHAT'S THE MATTER? I CAN'T IMAGINE YOU'VE BEEN OVERDOING IT ON THE STUDYING...
THAT HURT, COACH.
IT'S JUST A CASE OF BASEBALL DEFICIENCY.
CAN I COME FOR PITCHING DRILLS?
RATTLE
EXCUSE ME.
RITSU.
I BROUGHT MIZUHARA HIS UNIFORM.
THANKS, RITSU. I WAS JUST ABOUT T RETURN YOU SHIRT WHEN REALIZED I GO BLOOD ON IT
IT'S FINE.
JUST GET BACK INTO YOUR UNIFORM. YOU DON'T WANT TO CATCH COLD.
...
RIGHT...

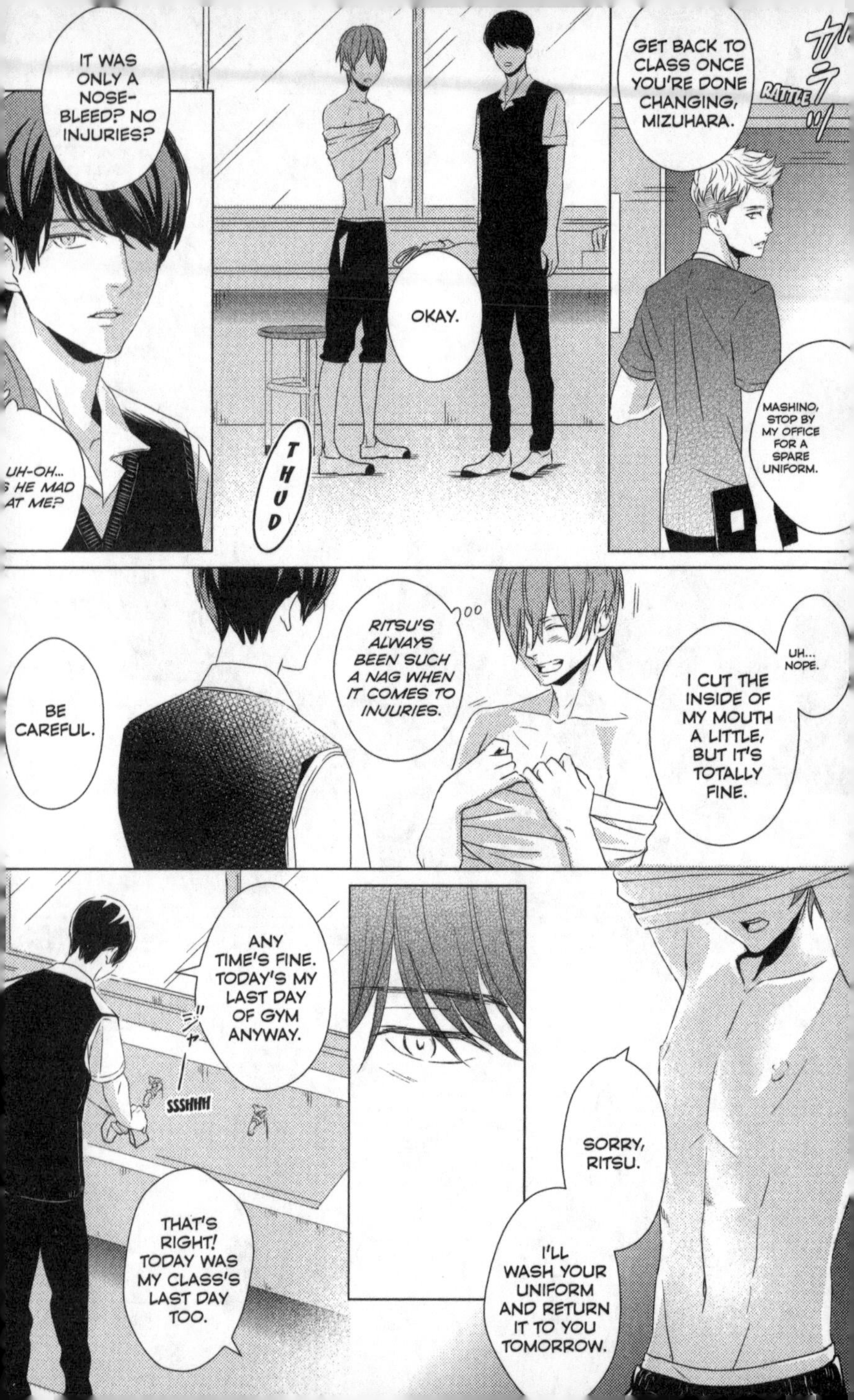
RATTLE
GET BACK TO CLASS ONCE YOU'RE DONE CHANGING, MIZUHARA.
MASHINO, STOP BY MY OFFICE FOR A SPARE UNIFORM.
OKAY.
THUD
IT WAS ONLY A NOSE-BLEED? NO INJURIES?
UH-OH... S HE MAD AT ME?
UH... NOPE.
I CUT THE INSIDE OF MY MOUTH A LITTLE, BUT IT'S TOTALLY FINE.
RITSU'S ALWAYS BEEN SUCH A NAG WHEN IT COMES TO INJURIES.
BE CAREFUL.
SORRY, RITSU.
I'LL WASH YOUR UNIFORM AND RETURN IT TO YOU TOMORROW.
ANY TIME'S FINE. TODAY'S MY LAST DAY OF GYM ANYWAY.
SSSHHH
THAT'S RIGHT! TODAY WAS MY CLASS'S LAST DAY TOO.

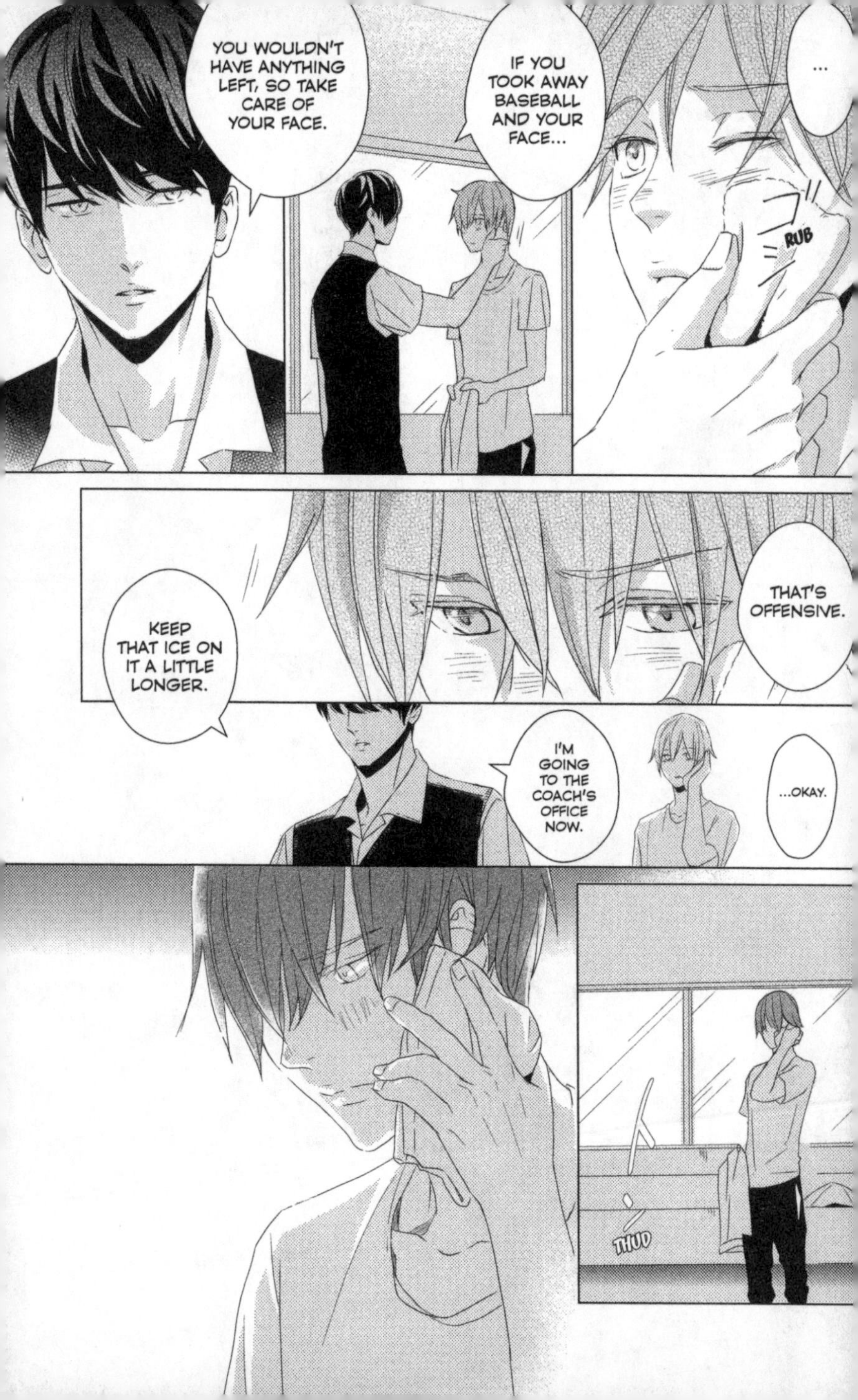
...
RUB
IF YOU TOOK AWAY BASEBALL AND YOUR FACE...
YOU WOULDN'T HAVE ANYTHING LEFT, SO TAKE CARE OF YOUR FACE.
THAT'S OFFENSIVE.
KEEP THAT ICE ON IT A LITTLE LONGER.
I'M GOING TO THE COACH'S OFFICE NOW.
...OKAY.
THUD

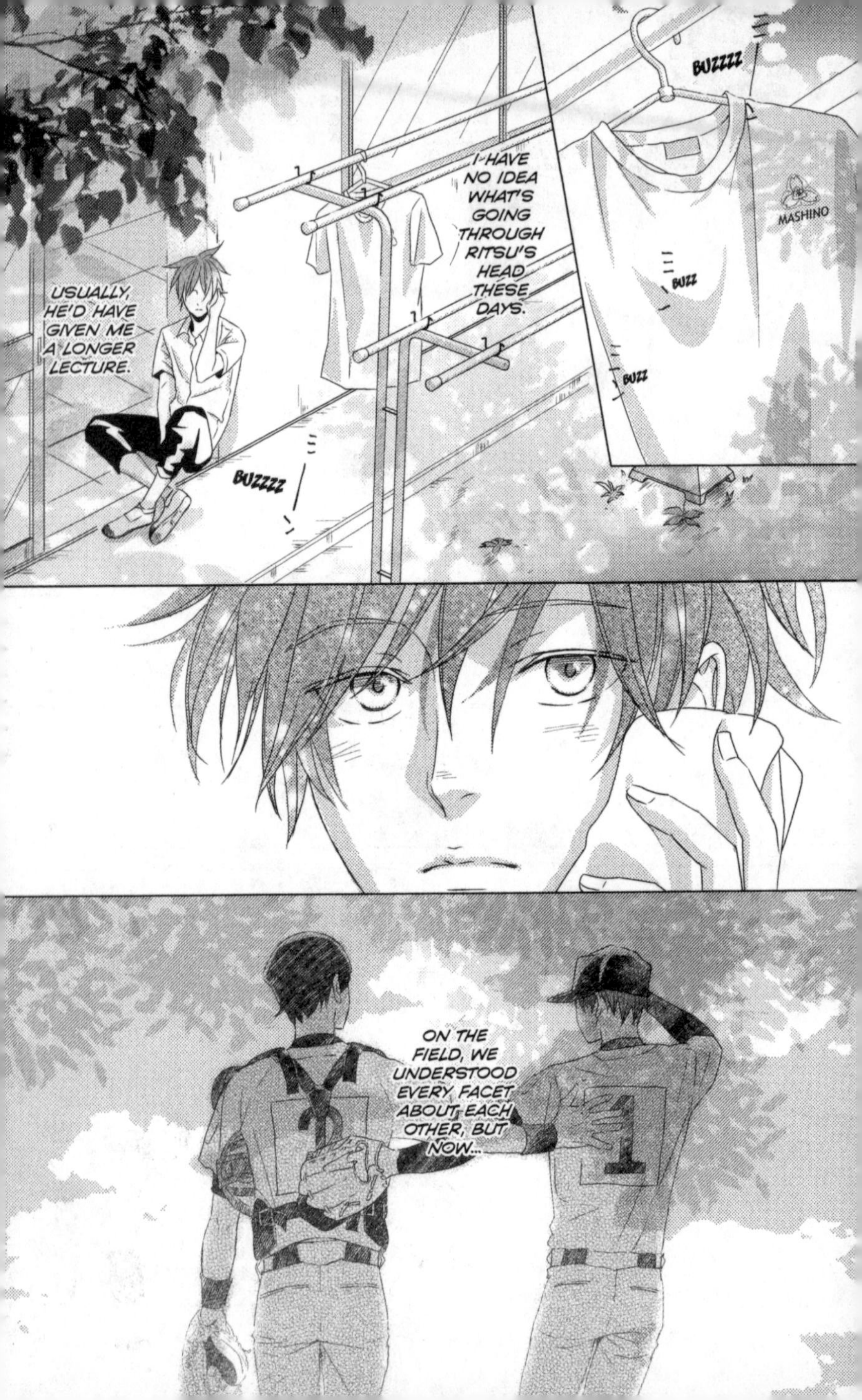

BUZZZZZ
MASHINO
BUZZ
BUZZ
I HAVE NO IDEA WHAT'S GOING THROUGH RITSU'S HEAD THESE DAYS.
USUALLY, HE'D HAVE GIVEN ME A LONGER LECTURE.
BUZZZZZ
ON THE FIELD, WE UNDERSTOOD EVERY FACET ABOUT EACH OTHER, BUT NOW...

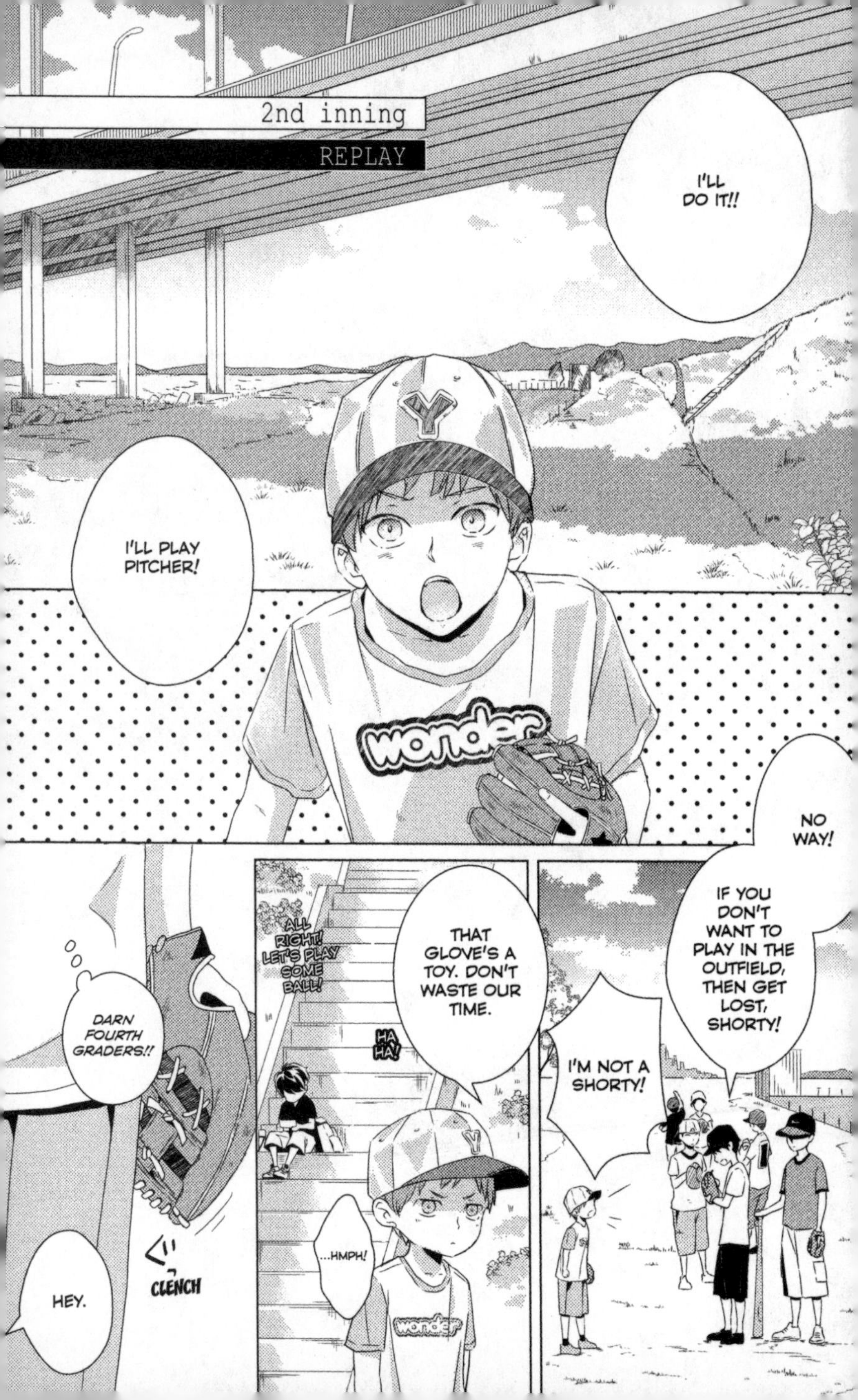
2nd inning
REPLAY
I'LL DO IT!!
I'LL PLAY PITCHER!
NO WAY!
IF YOU DON'T WANT TO PLAY IN THE OUTFIELD, THEN GET LOST, SHORTY!
I'M NOT A SHORTY!
THAT GLOVE'S A TOY. DON'T WASTE OUR TIME.
ALL RIGHT! LET'S PLAY SOME BALL!
HA HA!
...HMPH!
DARN FOURTH GRADERS!!
CLENCH
HEY.

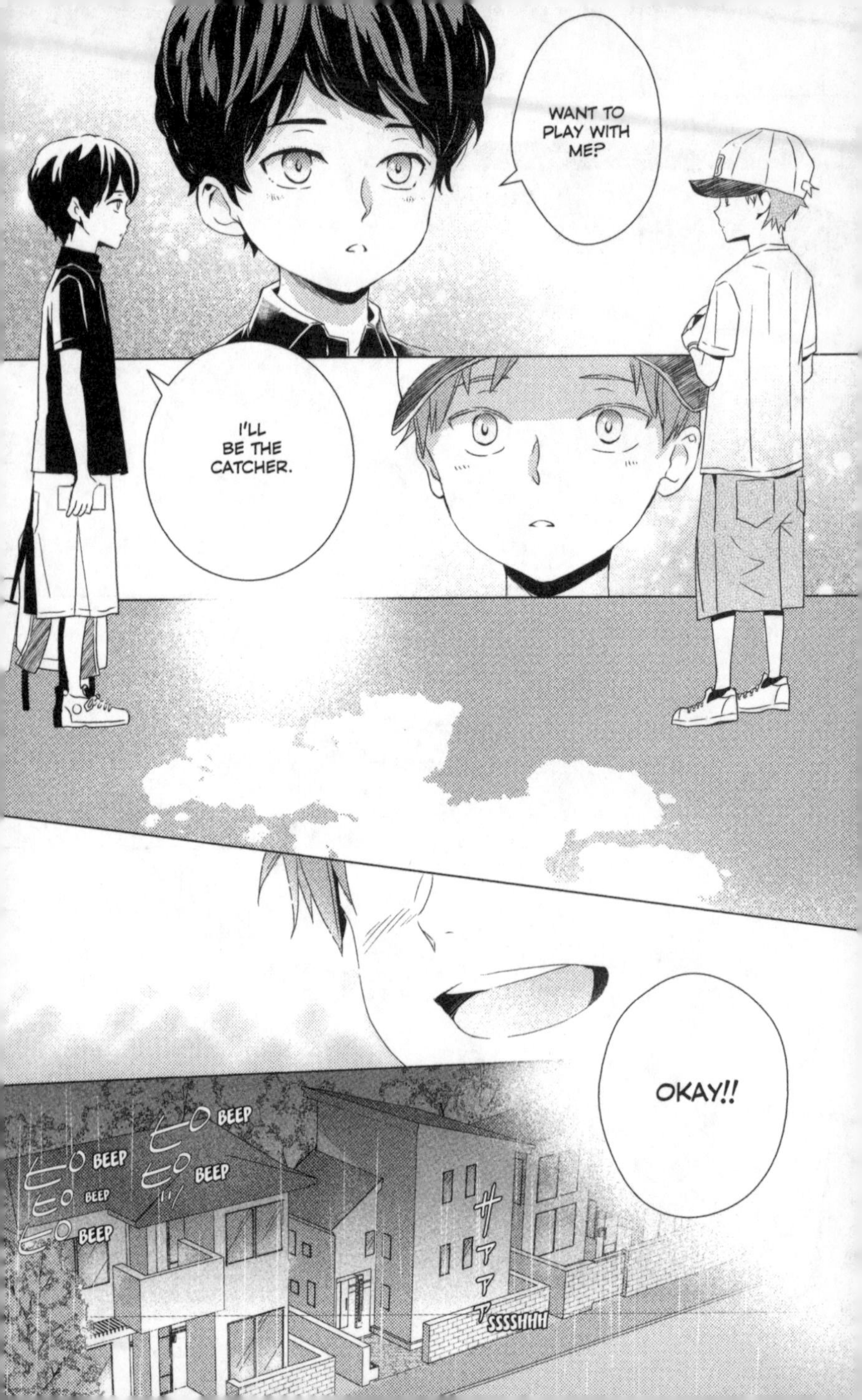
WANT TO PLAY WITH ME?
I'LL BE THE CATCHER.
OKAY!!
SSSSHHH
BEEP
BEEP
BEEP
BEEP
BEEP

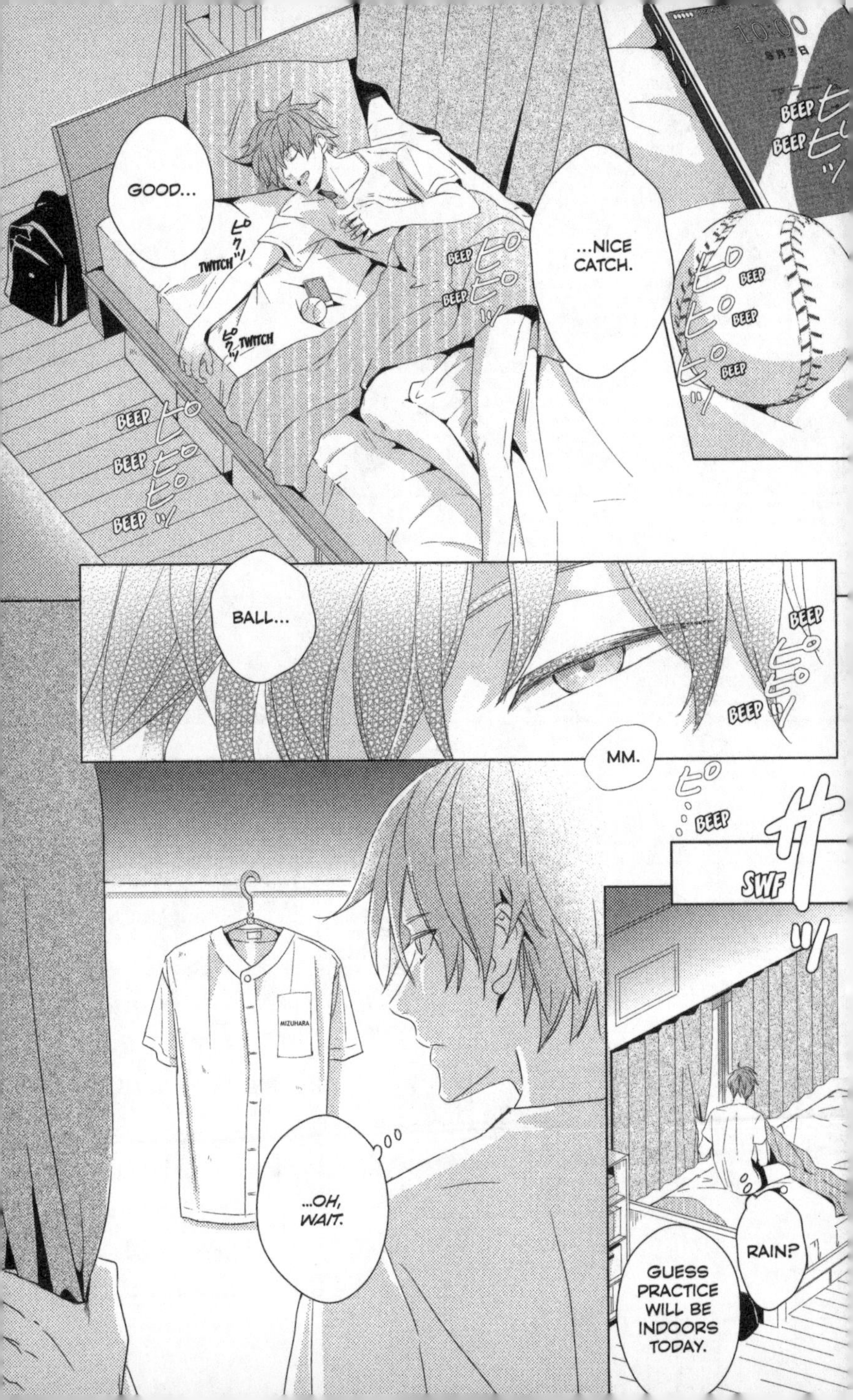
BEEP
BEEP
BEEP
BEEP
BEEP
GOOD...
...NICE CATCH.
TWITCH
TWITCH
BEEP
BEEP
BEEP
BEEP
BEEP
BEEP
BEEP
BALL...
MM.
BEEP
SWF
RAIN?
GUESS PRACTICE WILL BE INDOORS TODAY.
MIZUHARA
...OH, WAIT.

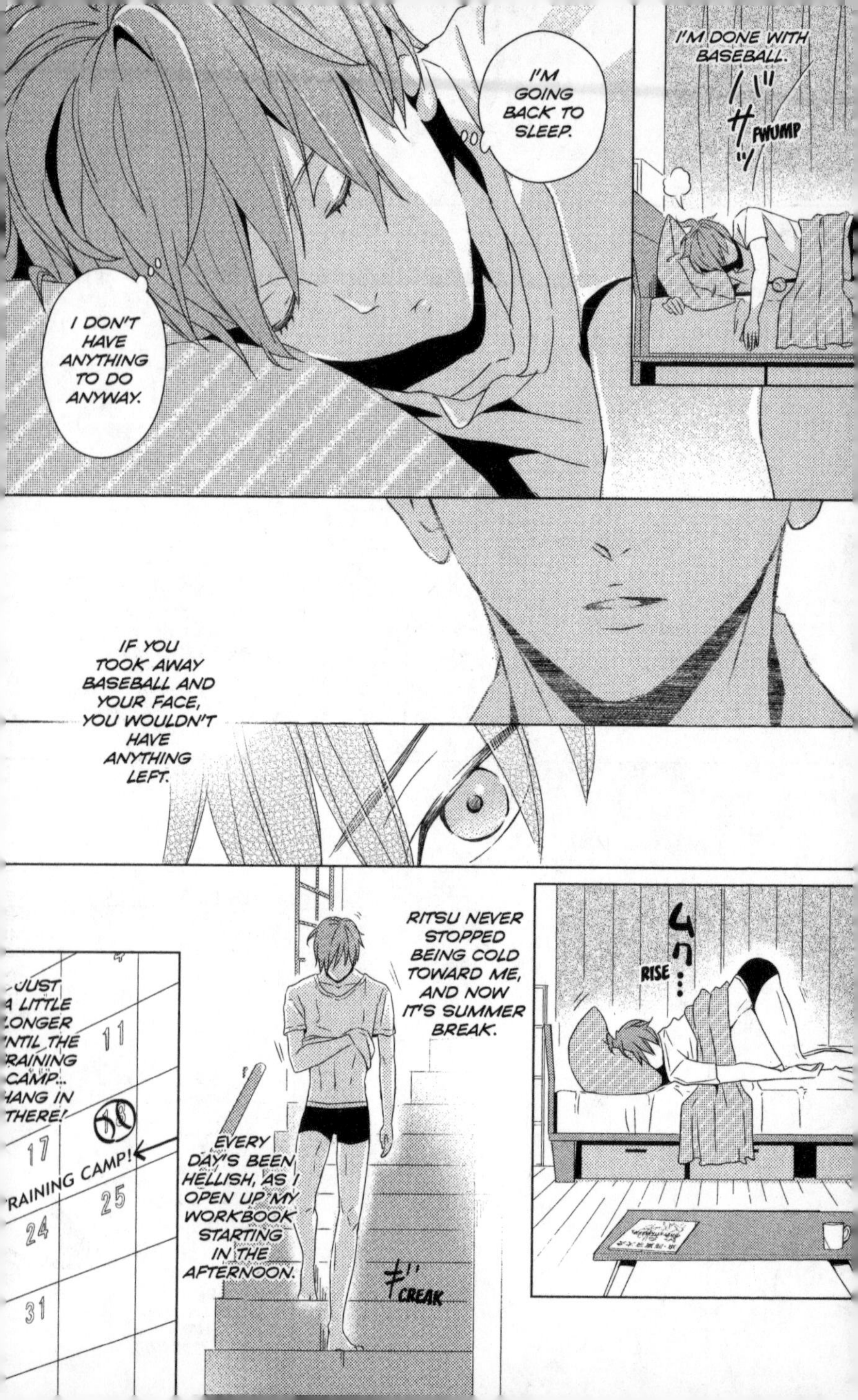
I'M DONE WITH BASEBALL.
バサッ PWUMP
I'M GOING BACK TO SLEEP.
I DON'T HAVE ANYTHING TO DO ANYWAY.
IF YOU TOOK AWAY BASEBALL AND YOUR FACE, YOU WOULDN'T HAVE ANYTHING LEFT.
ムク… RISE
RITSU NEVER STOPPED BEING COLD TOWARD ME, AND NOW IT'S SUMMER BREAK.
EVERY DAY'S BEEN HELLISH, AS I OPEN UP MY WORKBOOK STARTING IN THE AFTERNOON.
ギ CREAK
JUST A LITTLE LONGER NTIL THE RAINING CAMP... HANG IN THERE!
4
11
17
RAINING CAMP!
25
24
31

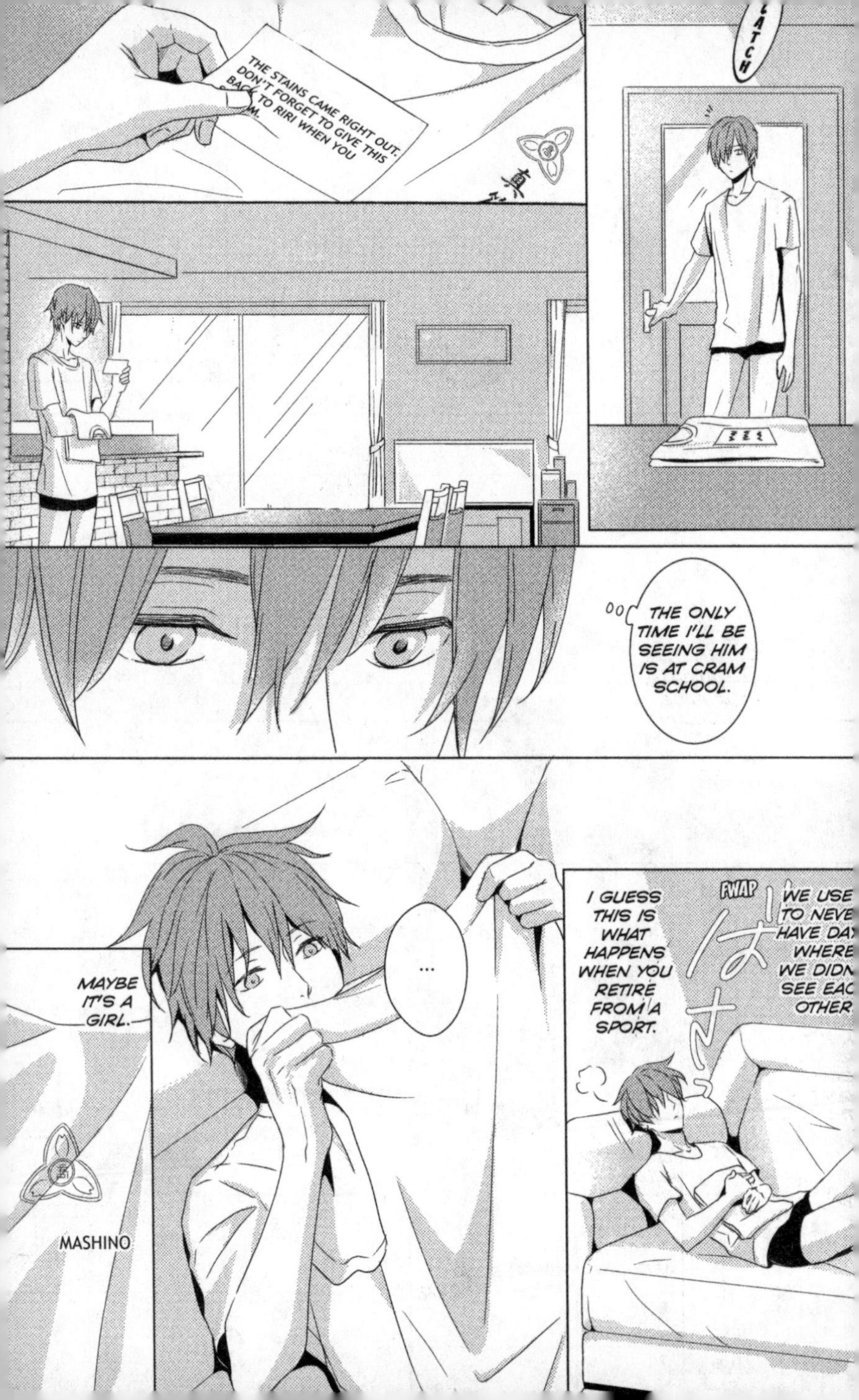
CATCH
THE STAINS CAME RIGHT OUT. DON'T FORGET TO GIVE THIS BACK TO RIRI WHEN YOU
THE ONLY TIME I'LL BE SEEING HIM IS AT CRAM SCHOOL.
FWAP
WE USE TO NEVE HAVE DAY WHERE WE DIDN SEE EAC OTHER
I GUESS THIS IS WHAT HAPPENS WHEN YOU RETIRE FROM A SPORT.
...
MAYBE IT'S A GIRL.
MASHINO

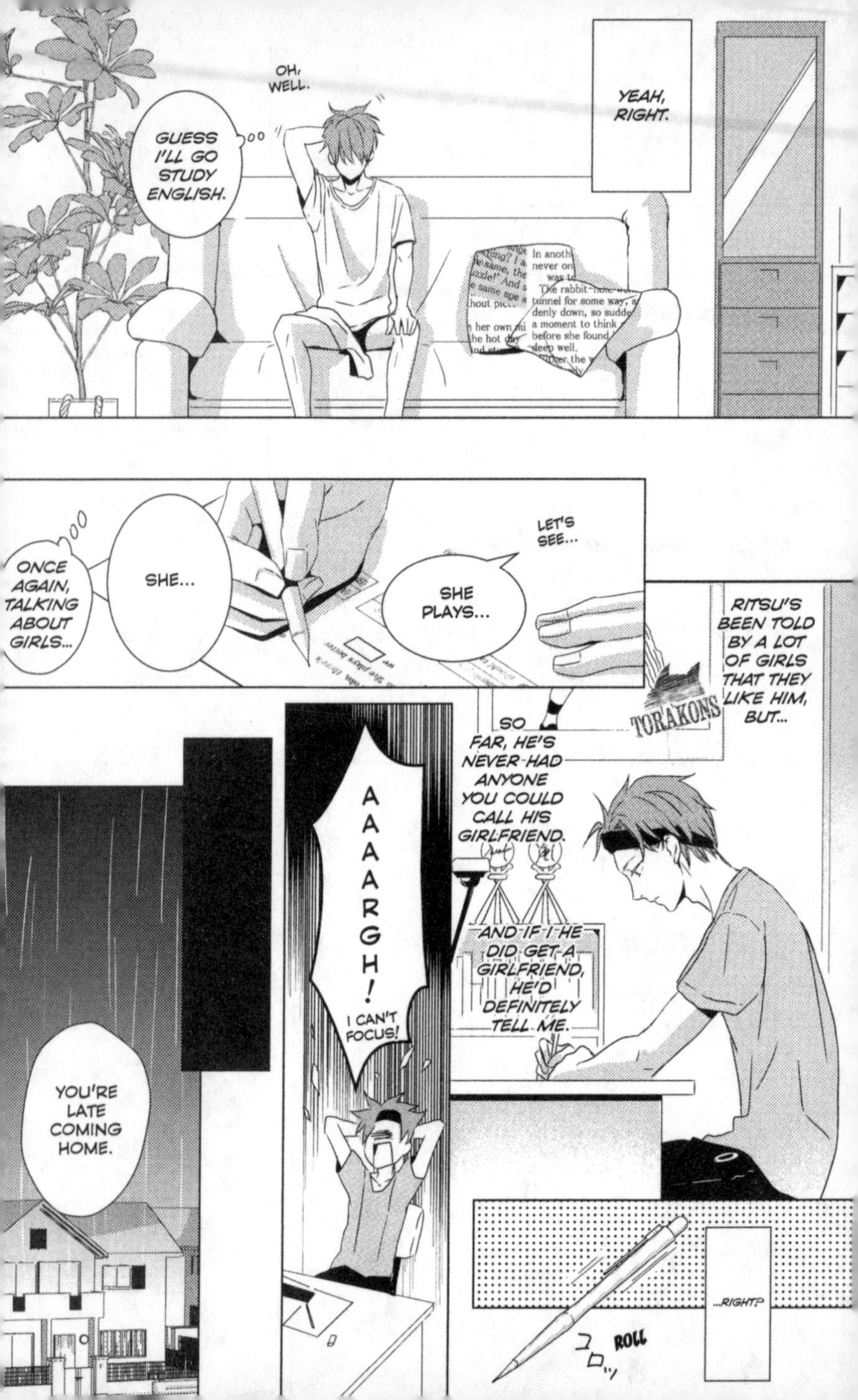
YEAH, RIGHT.
OH, WELL.
GUESS I'LL GO STUDY ENGLISH.
LET'S SEE...
SHE PLAYS...
SHE...
ONCE AGAIN, TALKING ABOUT GIRLS...
RITSU'S BEEN TOLD BY A LOT OF GIRLS THAT THEY LIKE HIM, BUT...
TORAKONS
SO FAR, HE'S NEVER HAD ANYONE YOU COULD CALL HIS GIRLFRIEND.
AND IF HE DID GET A GIRLFRIEND, HE'D DEFINITELY TELL ME.
...RIGHT?
ROLL
AAAARGH!
I CAN'T FOCUS!
YOU'RE LATE COMING HOME.

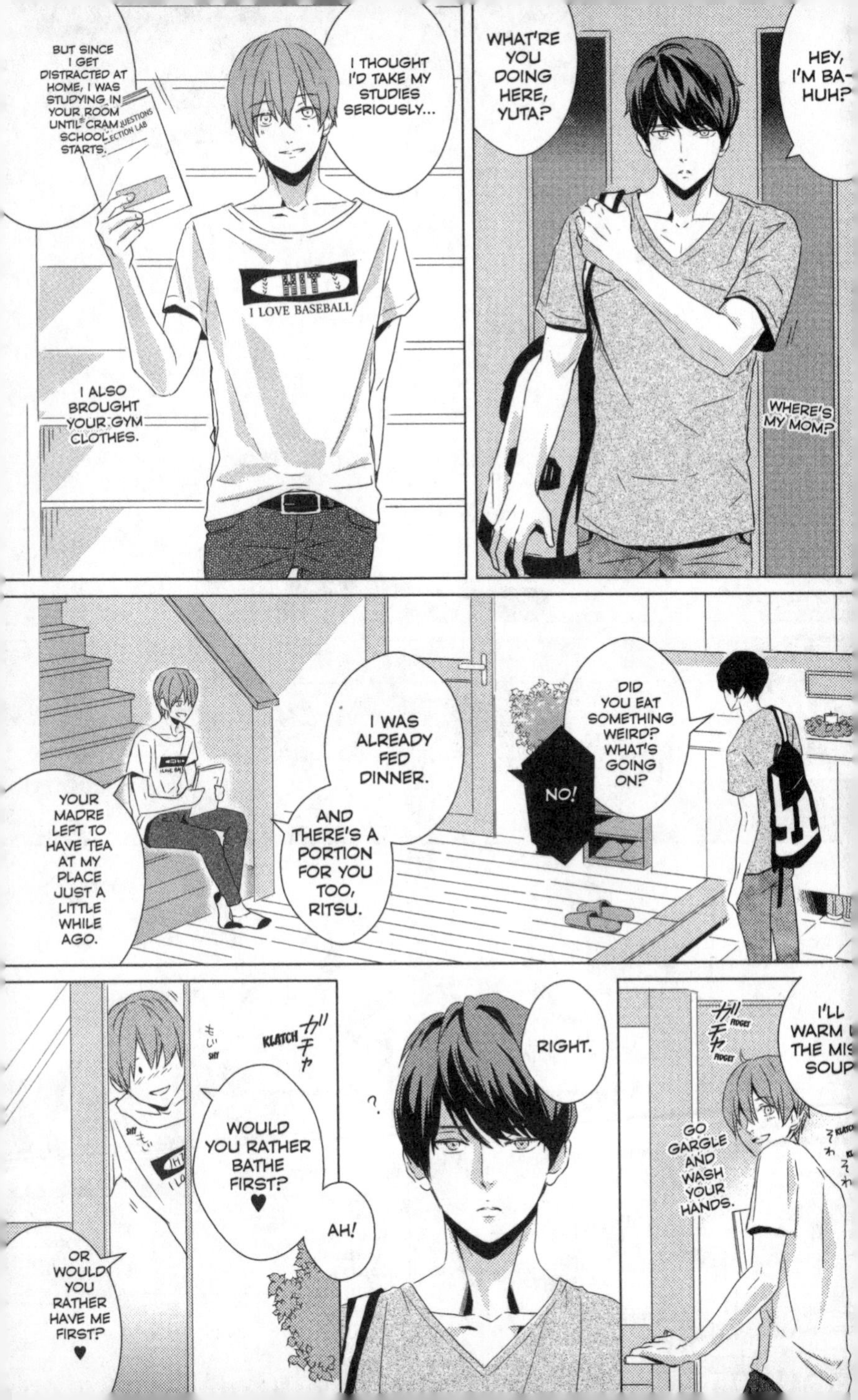
HEY, I'M BA- HUH?
WHAT'RE YOU DOING HERE, YUTA?
WHERE'S MY MOM?
I THOUGHT I'D TAKE MY STUDIES SERIOUSLY...
BUT SINCE I GET DISTRACTED AT HOME, I WAS STUDYING IN YOUR ROOM UNTIL CRAM SCHOOL STARTS.
I LOVE BASEBALL
I ALSO BROUGHT YOUR GYM CLOTHES.
DID YOU EAT SOMETHING WEIRD? WHAT'S GOING ON?
NO!
I WAS ALREADY FED DINNER.
AND THERE'S A PORTION FOR YOU TOO, RITSU.
YOUR MADRE LEFT TO HAVE TEA AT MY PLACE JUST A LITTLE WHILE AGO.
I'LL WARM
THE MIS
SOUP
FIDGET
FIDGET
GO GARGLE AND WASH YOUR HANDS.
KLATCH
RIGHT.
?
KLATCH
SHY
SHY
WOULD YOU RATHER BATHE FIRST? ♥
AH!
OR WOULD YOU RATHER HAVE ME FIRST? ♥

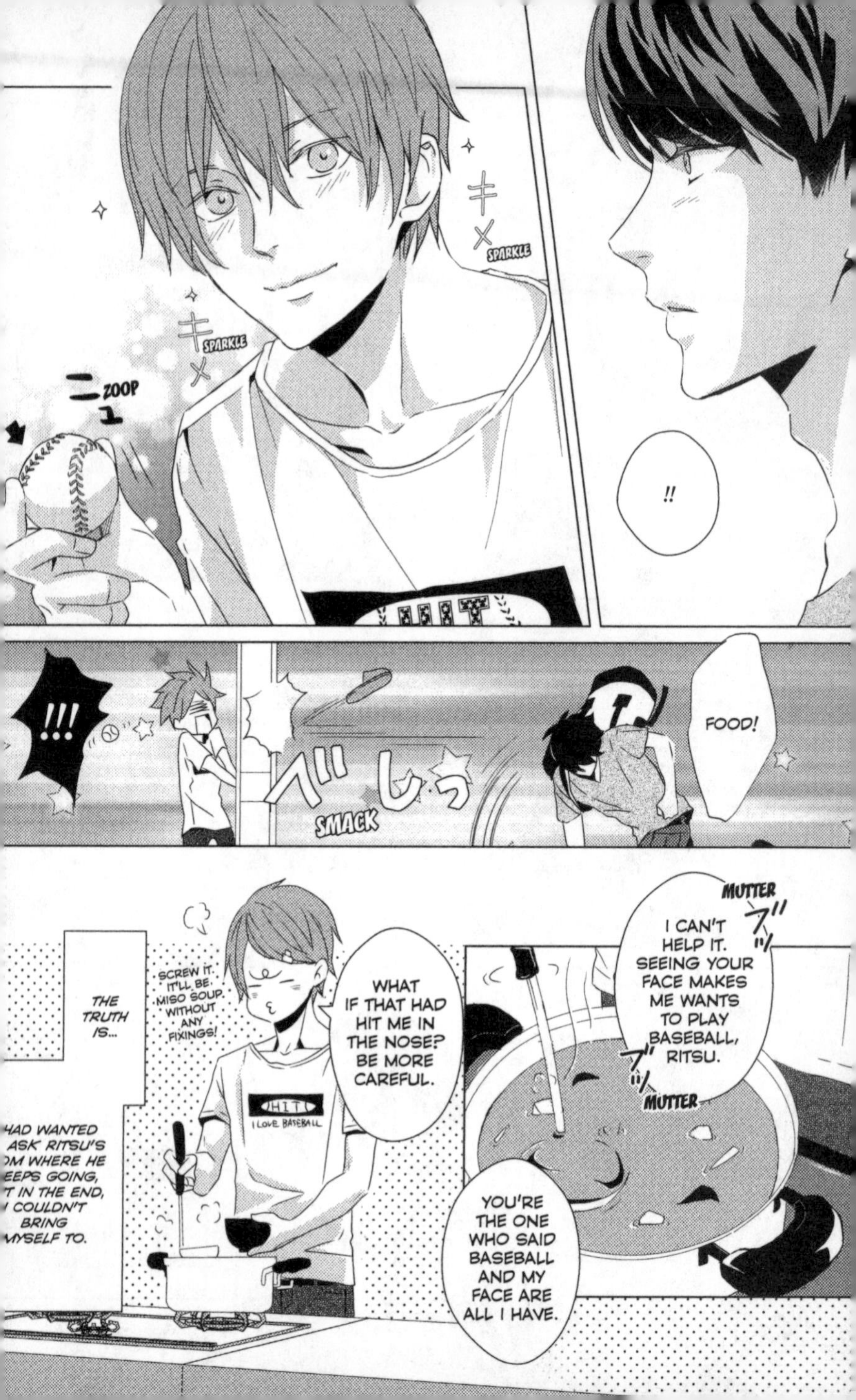
!!
SPARKLE
SPARKLE
ZOOP
FOOD!
SMACK
!!!
MUTTER
I CAN'T HELP IT. SEEING YOUR FACE MAKES ME WANTS TO PLAY BASEBALL, RITSU.
MUTTER
YOU'RE THE ONE WHO SAID BASEBALL AND MY FACE ARE ALL I HAVE.
WHAT IF THAT HAD HIT ME IN THE NOSE? BE MORE CAREFUL.
SCREW IT. IT'LL BE MISO SOUP WITHOUT ANY FIXINGS!
HIT
I LOVE BASEBALL
THE TRUTH IS...
HAD WANTED ASK RITSU'S OM WHERE HE EEPS GOING, T IN THE END, COULDN'T BRING MYSELF TO.

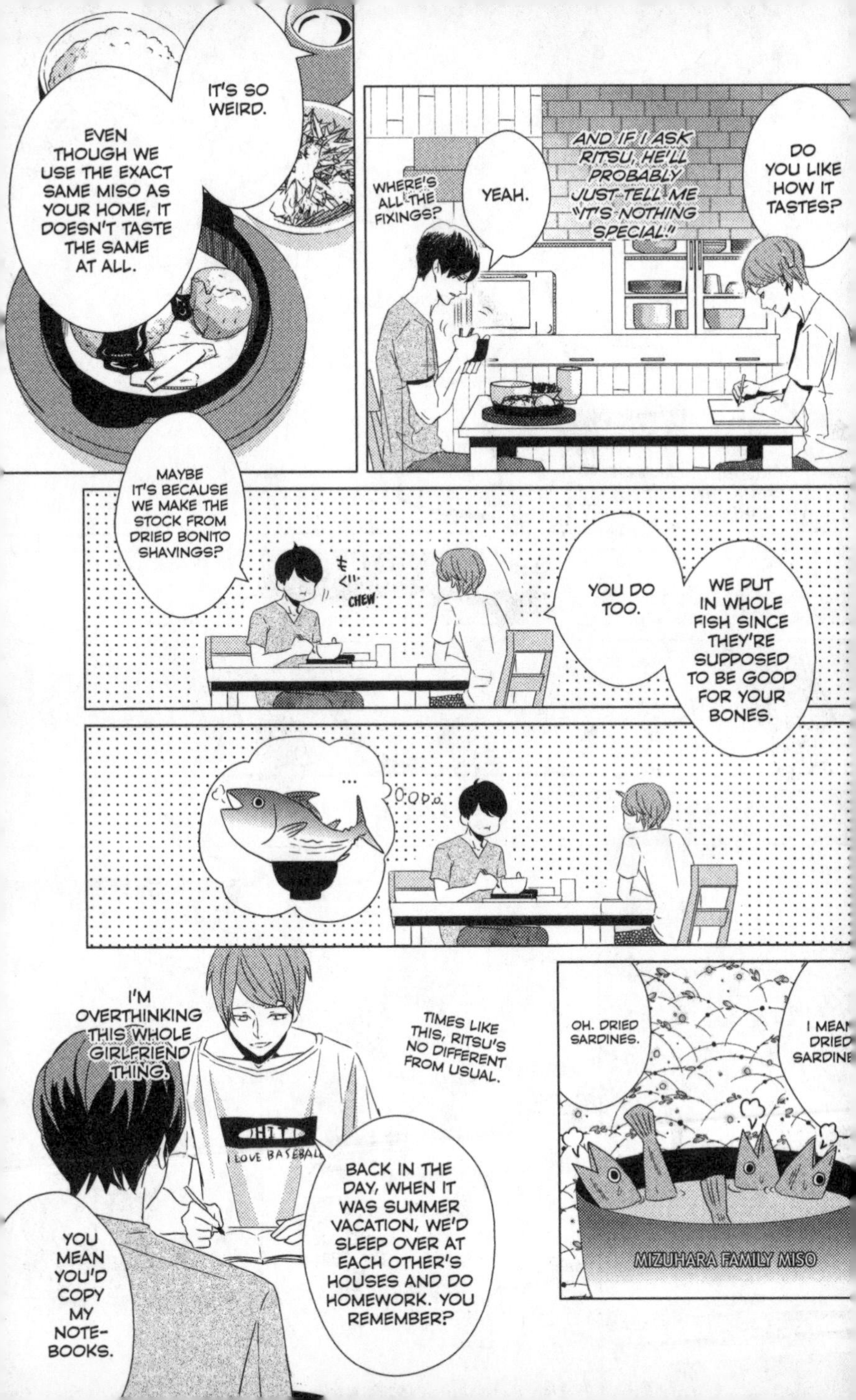
DO YOU LIKE HOW IT TASTES?
AND IF I ASK RITSU, HE'LL PROBABLY JUST TELL ME "IT'S NOTHING SPECIAL."
YEAH.
WHERE'S ALL THE FIXINGS?
IT'S SO WEIRD.
EVEN THOUGH WE USE THE EXACT SAME MISO AS YOUR HOME, IT DOESN'T TASTE THE SAME AT ALL.
MAYBE IT'S BECAUSE WE MAKE THE STOCK FROM DRIED BONITO SHAVINGS?
CHEW
YOU DO TOO.
WE PUT IN WHOLE FISH SINCE THEY'RE SUPPOSED TO BE GOOD FOR YOUR BONES.
...
I MEAN DRIED SARDINE
OH. DRIED SARDINES.
MIZUHARA FAMILY MISO
TIMES LIKE THIS, RITSU'S NO DIFFERENT FROM USUAL.
I'M OVERTHINKING THIS WHOLE GIRLFRIEND THING.
I LOVE BASEBAL
BACK IN THE DAY, WHEN IT WAS SUMMER VACATION, WE'D SLEEP OVER AT EACH OTHER'S HOUSES AND DO HOMEWORK. YOU REMEMBER?
YOU MEAN YOU'D COPY MY NOTEBOOKS.

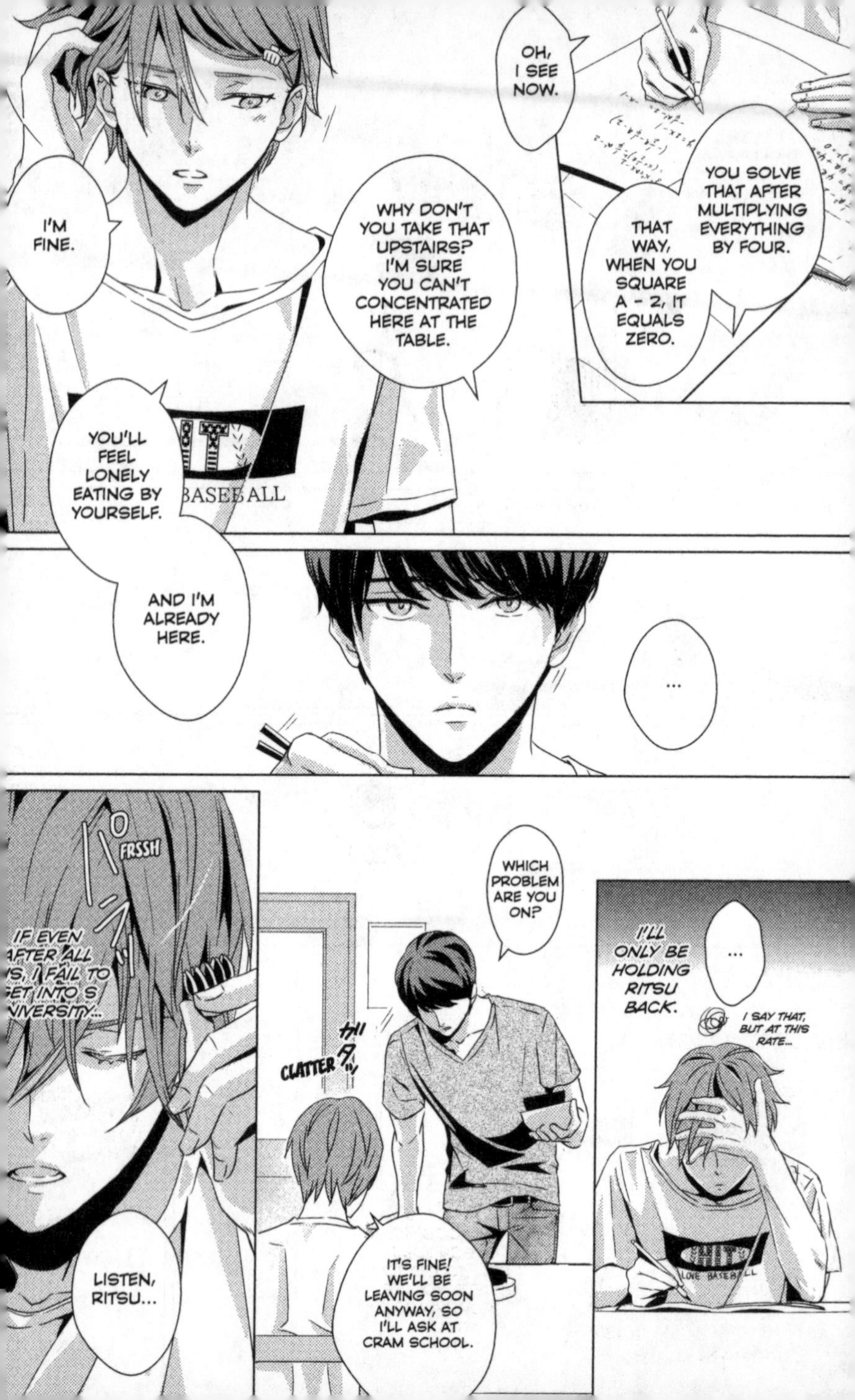
OH, I SEE NOW.
YOU SOLVE THAT AFTER MULTIPLYING EVERYTHING BY FOUR.
THAT WAY, WHEN YOU SQUARE A - 2, IT EQUALS ZERO.
WHY DON'T YOU TAKE THAT UPSTAIRS? I'M SURE YOU CAN'T CONCENTRATED HERE AT THE TABLE.
I'M FINE.
BASEBALL
YOU'LL FEEL LONELY EATING BY YOURSELF.
AND I'M ALREADY HERE.
...
...
I'LL ONLY BE HOLDING RITSU BACK.
I SAY THAT, BUT AT THIS RATE...
WHICH PROBLEM ARE YOU ON?
CLATTER
IT'S FINE! WE'LL BE LEAVING SOON ANYWAY, SO I'LL ASK AT CRAM SCHOOL.
FRSSH
IF EVEN AFTER ALL S, I FAIL TO GET INTO S UNIVERSITY...
LISTEN, RITSU...

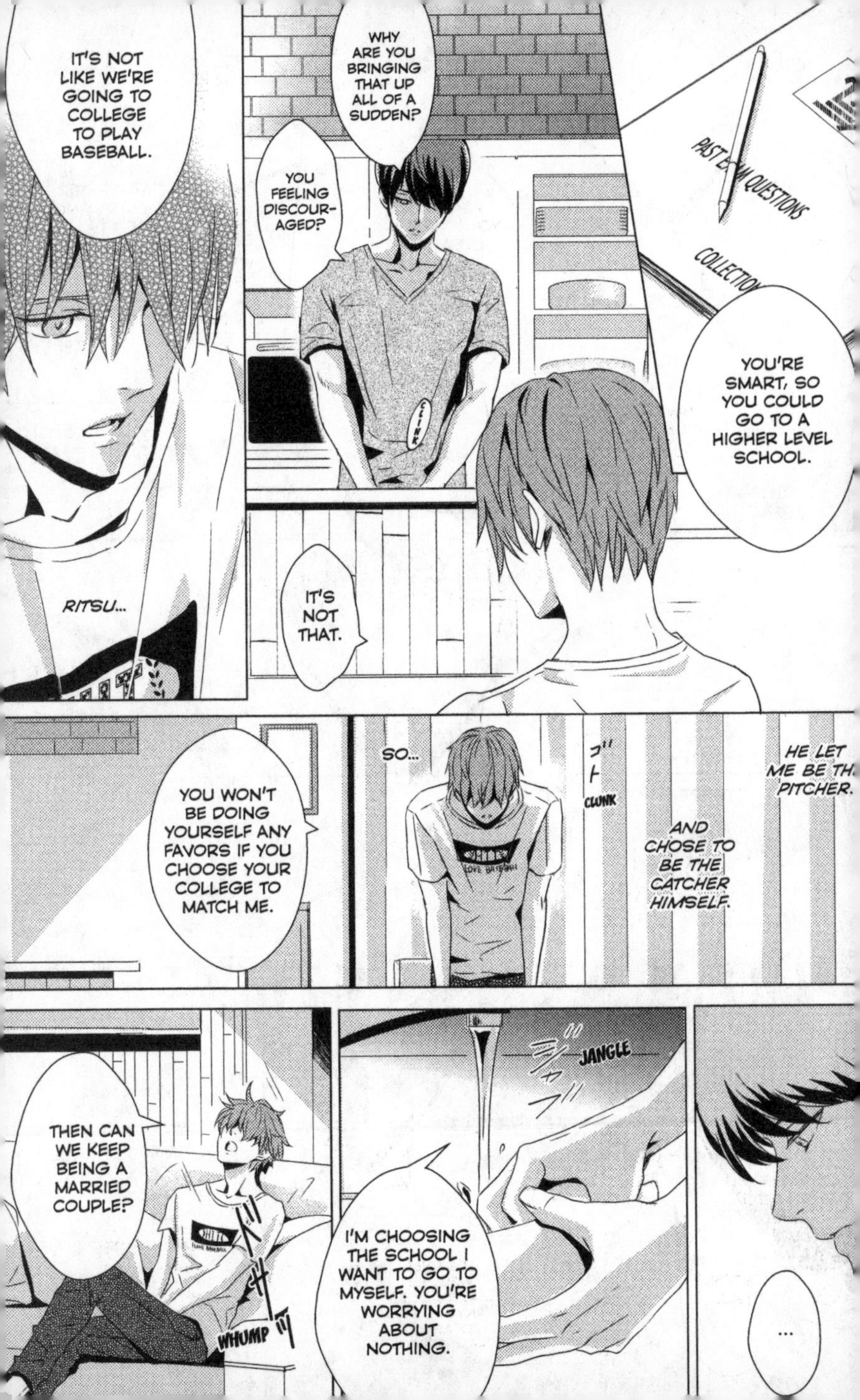
PAST EXAM QUESTIONS
COLLECTION
YOU'RE SMART, SO YOU COULD GO TO A HIGHER LEVEL SCHOOL.
IT'S NOT THAT.
WHY ARE YOU BRINGING THAT UP ALL OF A SUDDEN?
YOU FEELING DISCOURAGED?
CLINK
IT'S NOT LIKE WE'RE GOING TO COLLEGE TO PLAY BASEBALL.
RITSU...
HE LET ME BE TH PITCHER.
AND CHOSE TO BE THE CATCHER HIMSELF.
ゴト
CLUNK
SO...
YOU WON'T BE DOING YOURSELF ANY FAVORS IF YOU CHOOSE YOUR COLLEGE TO MATCH ME.
...
JANGLE
I'M CHOOSING THE SCHOOL I WANT TO GO TO MYSELF. YOU'RE WORRYING ABOUT NOTHING.
THEN CAN WE KEEP BEING A MARRIED COUPLE?
WHUMP

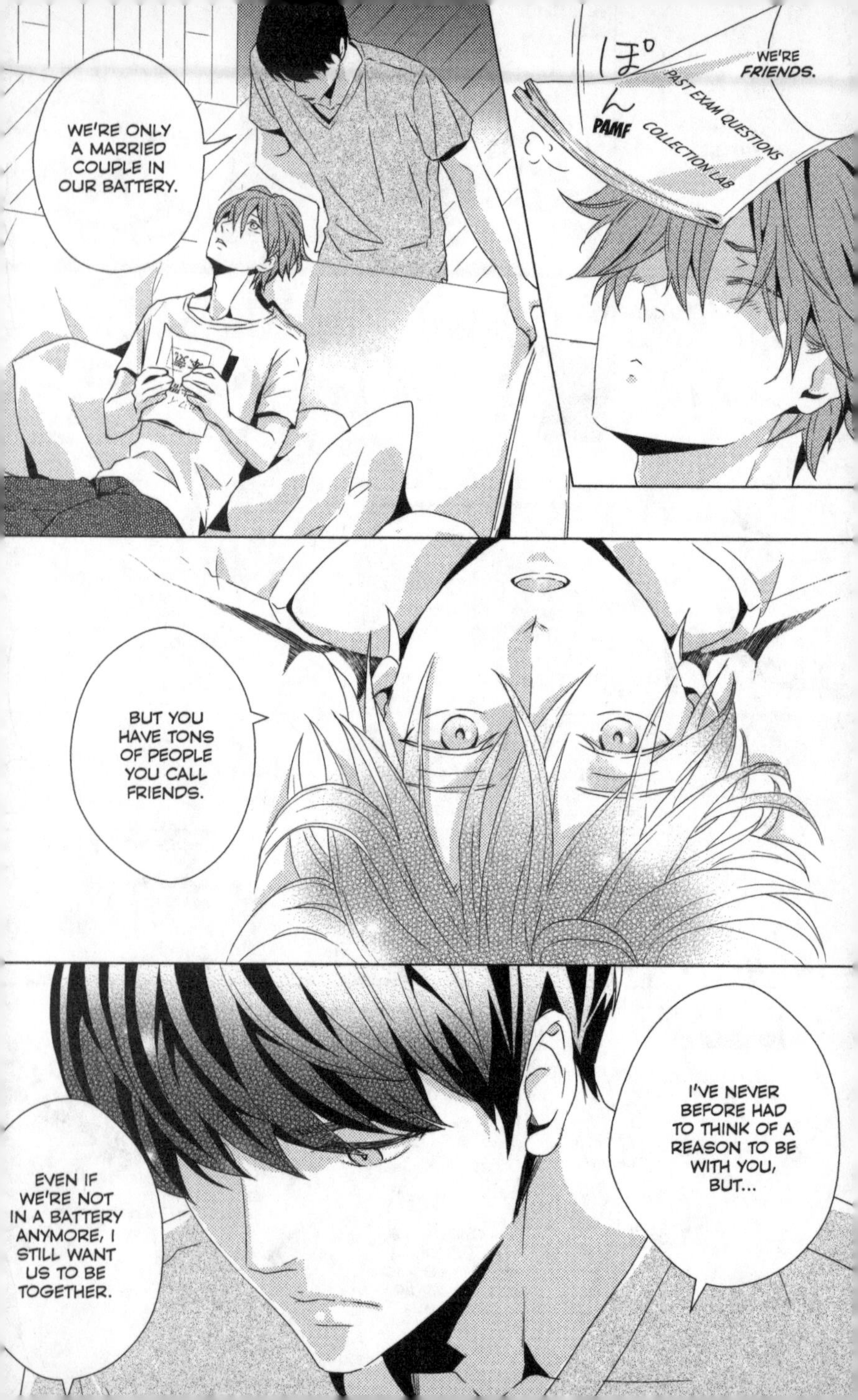
WE'RE FRIENDS.
PAST EXAM QUESTIONS
COLLECTION LAB
ぽん
PAMF
WE'RE ONLY A MARRIED COUPLE IN OUR BATTERY.
BUT YOU HAVE TONS OF PEOPLE YOU CALL FRIENDS.
I'VE NEVER BEFORE HAD TO THINK OF A REASON TO BE WITH YOU, BUT...
EVEN IF WE'RE NOT IN A BATTERY ANYMORE, I STILL WANT US TO BE TOGETHER.

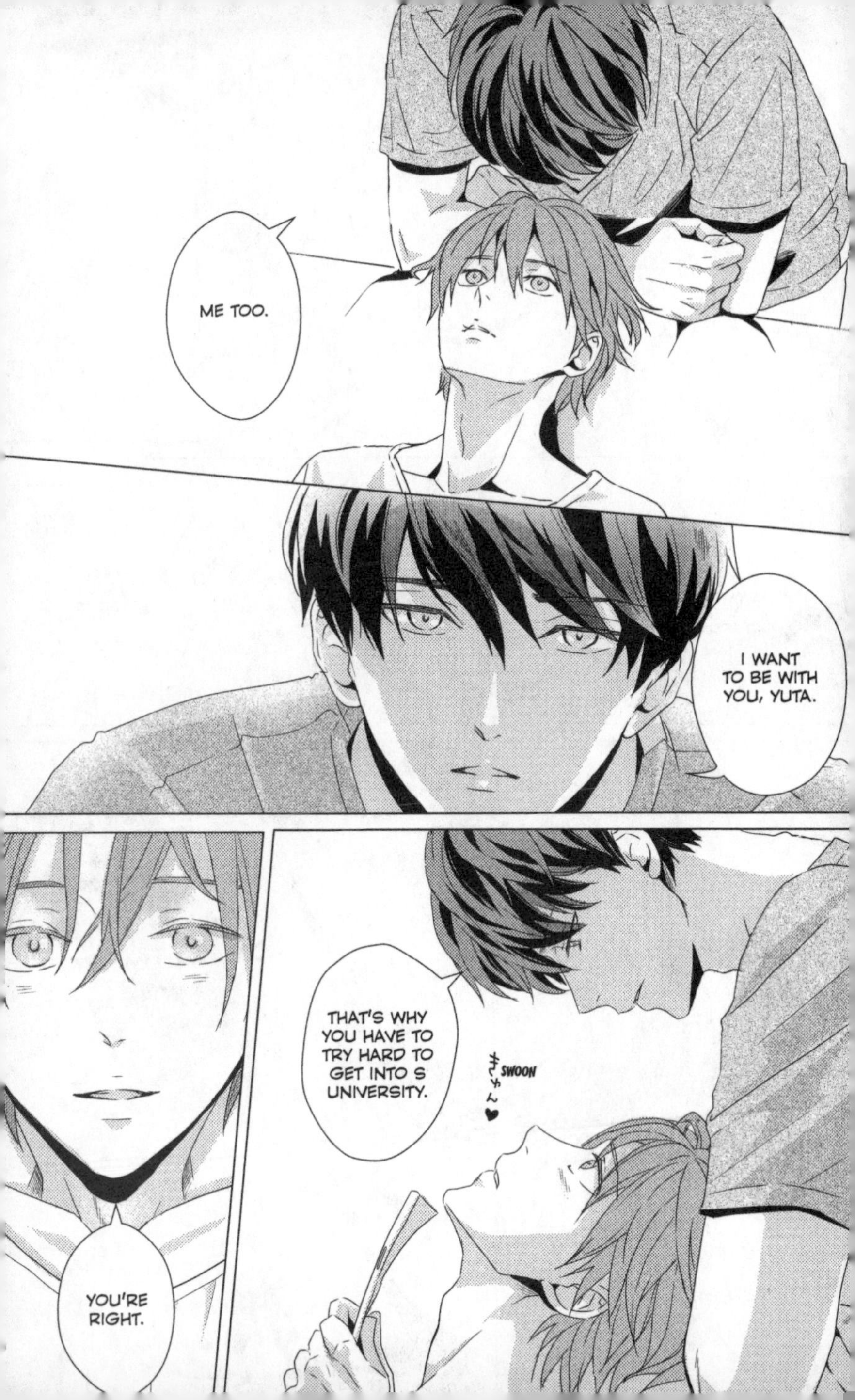
ME TOO.
I WANT TO BE WITH YOU, YUTA.
THAT'S WHY YOU HAVE TO TRY HARD TO GET INTO S UNIVERSITY.
きゅん♥
SWOON
YOU'RE RIGHT.

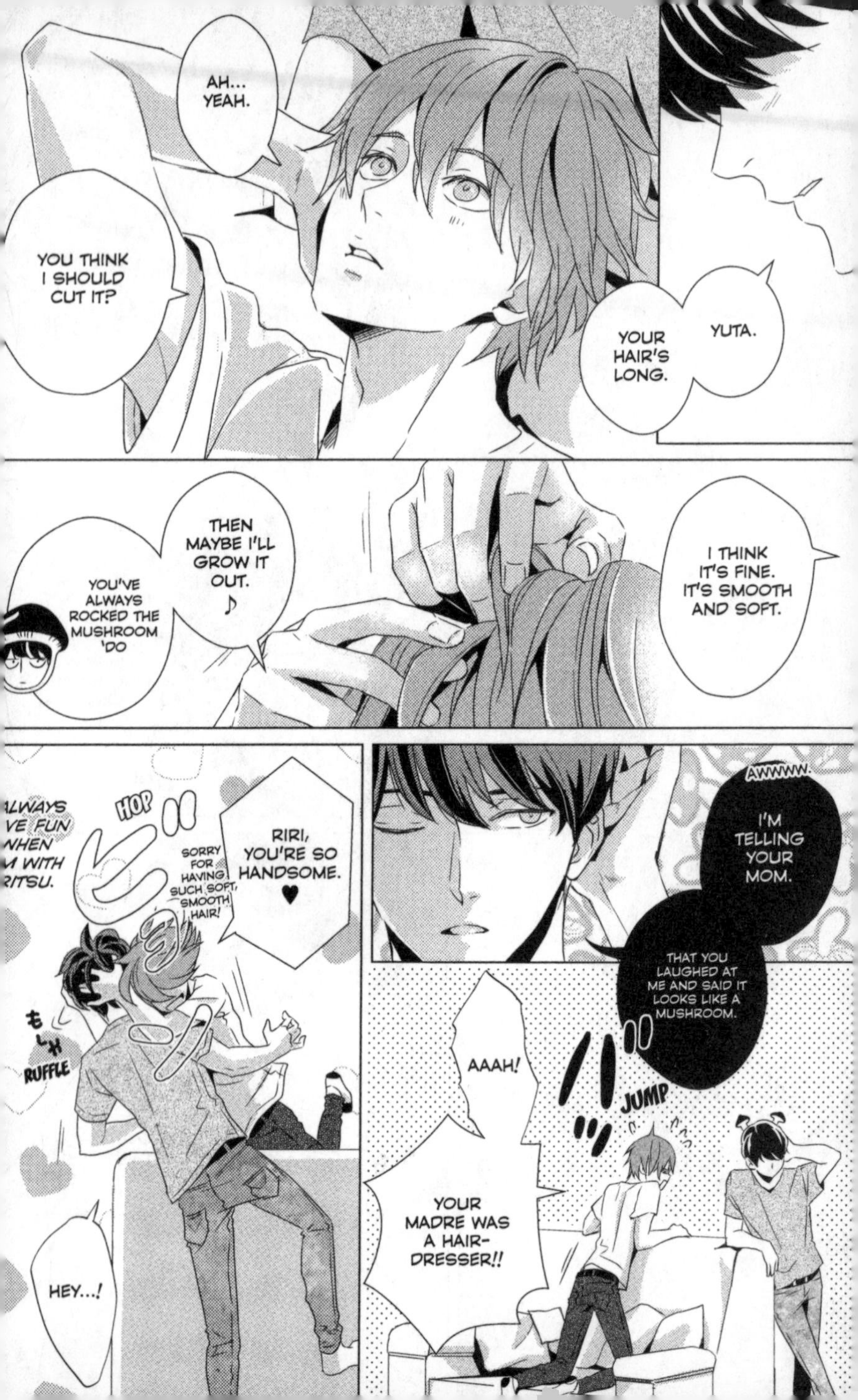
YUTA.
YOUR HAIR'S LONG.
AH... YEAH.
YOU THINK I SHOULD CUT IT?
I THINK IT'S FINE. IT'S SMOOTH AND SOFT.
THEN MAYBE I'LL GROW IT OUT. ♪
YOU'VE ALWAYS ROCKED THE MUSHROOM 'DO
AWWWW.
I'M TELLING YOUR MOM.
THAT YOU LAUGHED AT ME AND SAID IT LOOKS LIKE A MUSHROOM.
JUMP
AAAH!
YOUR MADRE WAS A HAIR-DRESSER!!
RIRI, YOU'RE SO HANDSOME. ♥
SORRY FOR HAVING SUCH SOFT, SMOOTH HAIR!
HOP
LWAYS VE FUN WHEN M WITH RITSU.
RUFFLE
HEY...!

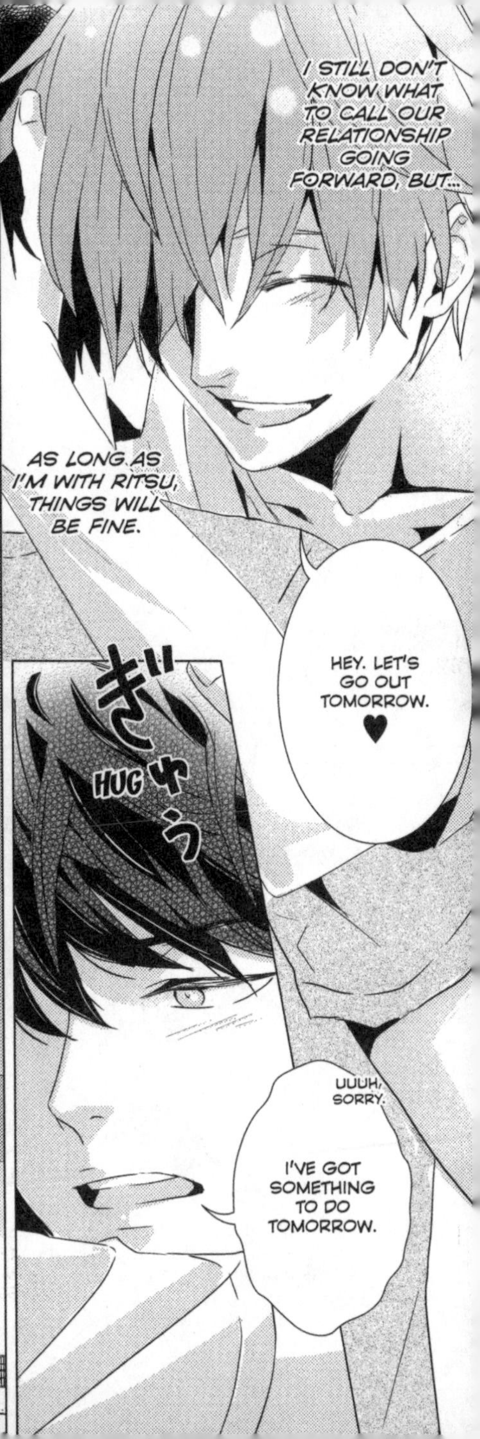
I STILL DON'T KNOW WHAT TO CALL OUR RELATIONSHIP GOING FORWARD, BUT...
AS LONG AS I'M WITH RITSU, THINGS WILL BE FINE.
HEY. LET'S GO OUT TOMORROW. ♥
ぎゅう
HUG
UUUH, SORRY.
I'VE GOT SOMETHING TO DO TOMORROW.
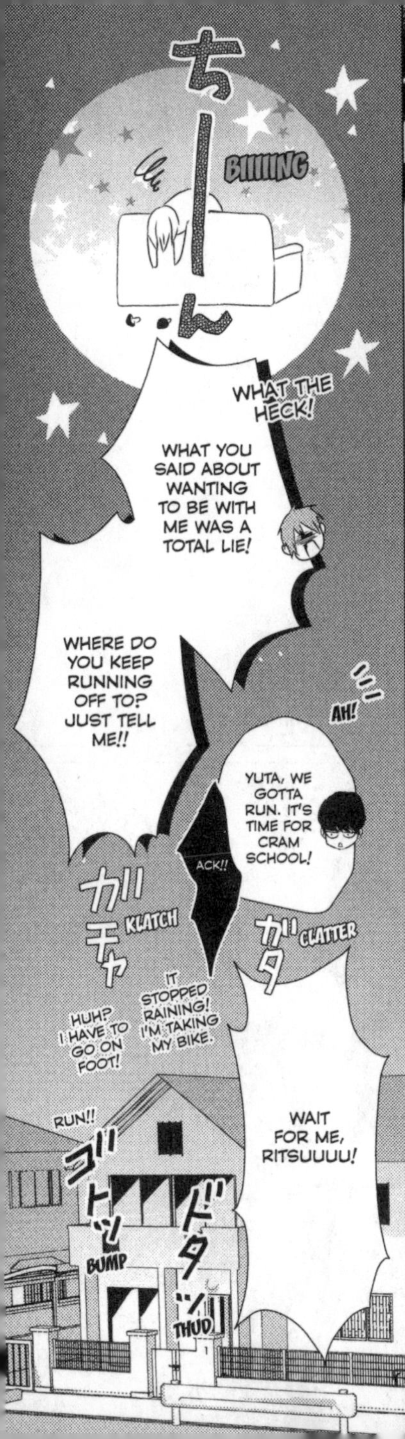
ちーん
BIIIIING
WHAT THE HECK!
WHAT YOU SAID ABOUT WANTING TO BE WITH ME WAS A TOTAL LIE!
WHERE DO YOU KEEP RUNNING OFF TO? JUST TELL ME!!
AH!
YUTA, WE GOTTA RUN. IT'S TIME FOR CRAM SCHOOL!
ACK!!
カチャ
KLATCH
ガタ
CLATTER
IT STOPPED RAINING! I'M TAKING MY BIKE.
HUH? I HAVE TO GO ON FOOT!
WAIT FOR ME, RITSUUUU!
RUN!!
ゴトッ
BUMP
ドタッ
THUD

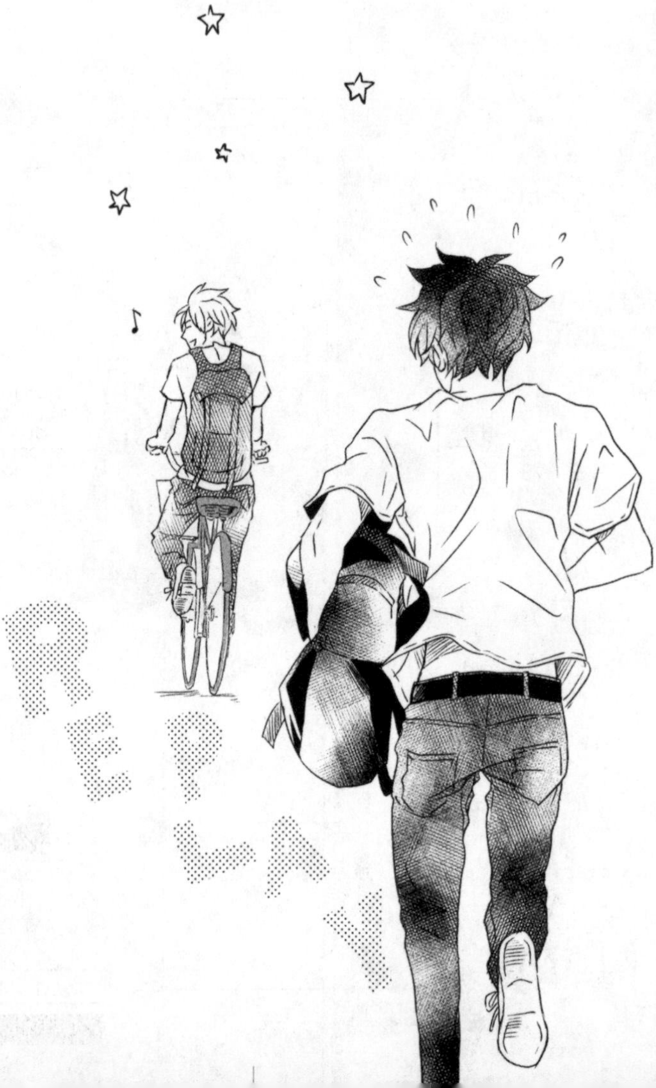
REPLAY

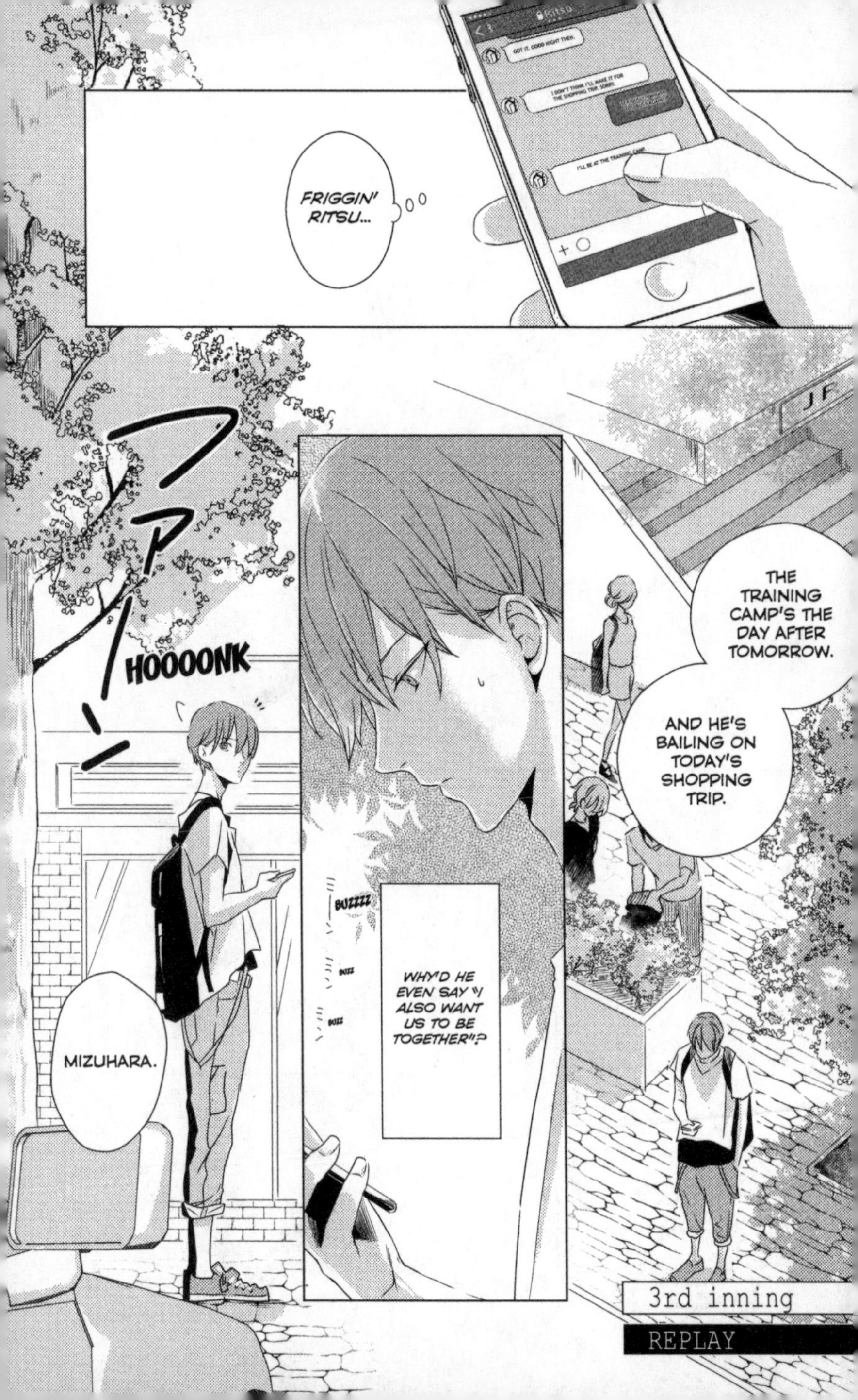
Ritsu
GOT IT. GOOD NIGHT THEN.
I DON'T THINK I'LL MAKE IT FOR THE SHOPPING TRIP. SORRY.
I'LL BE AT THE TRAINING CAMP.
FRIGGIN' RITSU...
THE TRAINING CAMP'S THE DAY AFTER TOMORROW.
AND HE'S BAILING ON TODAY'S SHOPPING TRIP.
3rd inning
REPLAY
BUZZZZ
BUZZ
BUZZ
WHY'D HE EVEN SAY "I ALSO WANT US TO BE TOGETHER"?
HOOOONK
MIZUHARA.

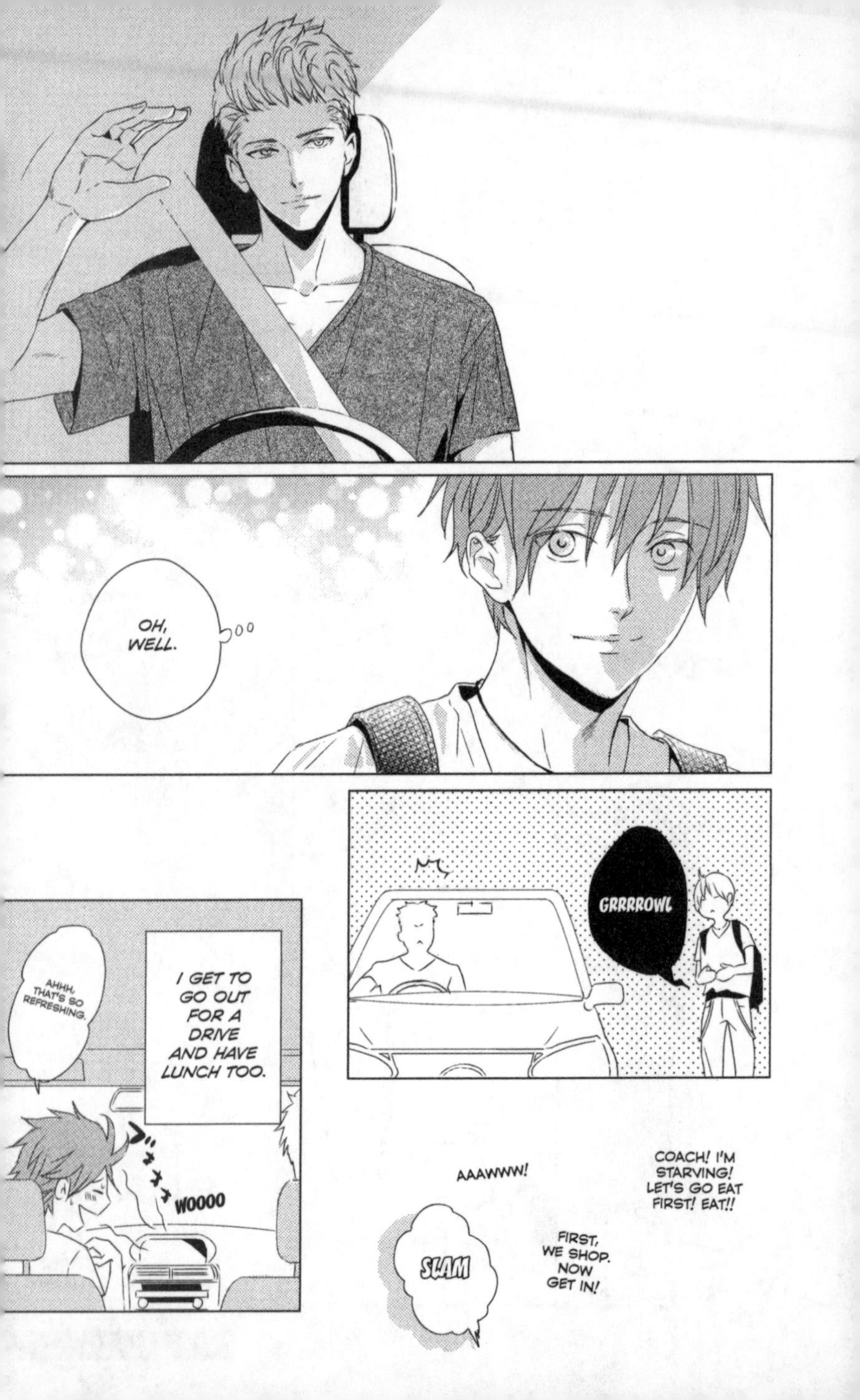
OH, WELL.
GRRRROWL
COACH! I'M STARVING! LET'S GO EAT FIRST! EAT!!
AAAWWW!
FIRST, WE SHOP. NOW GET IN!
SLAM
I GET TO GO OUT FOR A DRIVE AND HAVE LUNCH TOO.
AHHH, THAT'S SO REFRESHING.
WOOOO

## 3rd inning

## REPLAY

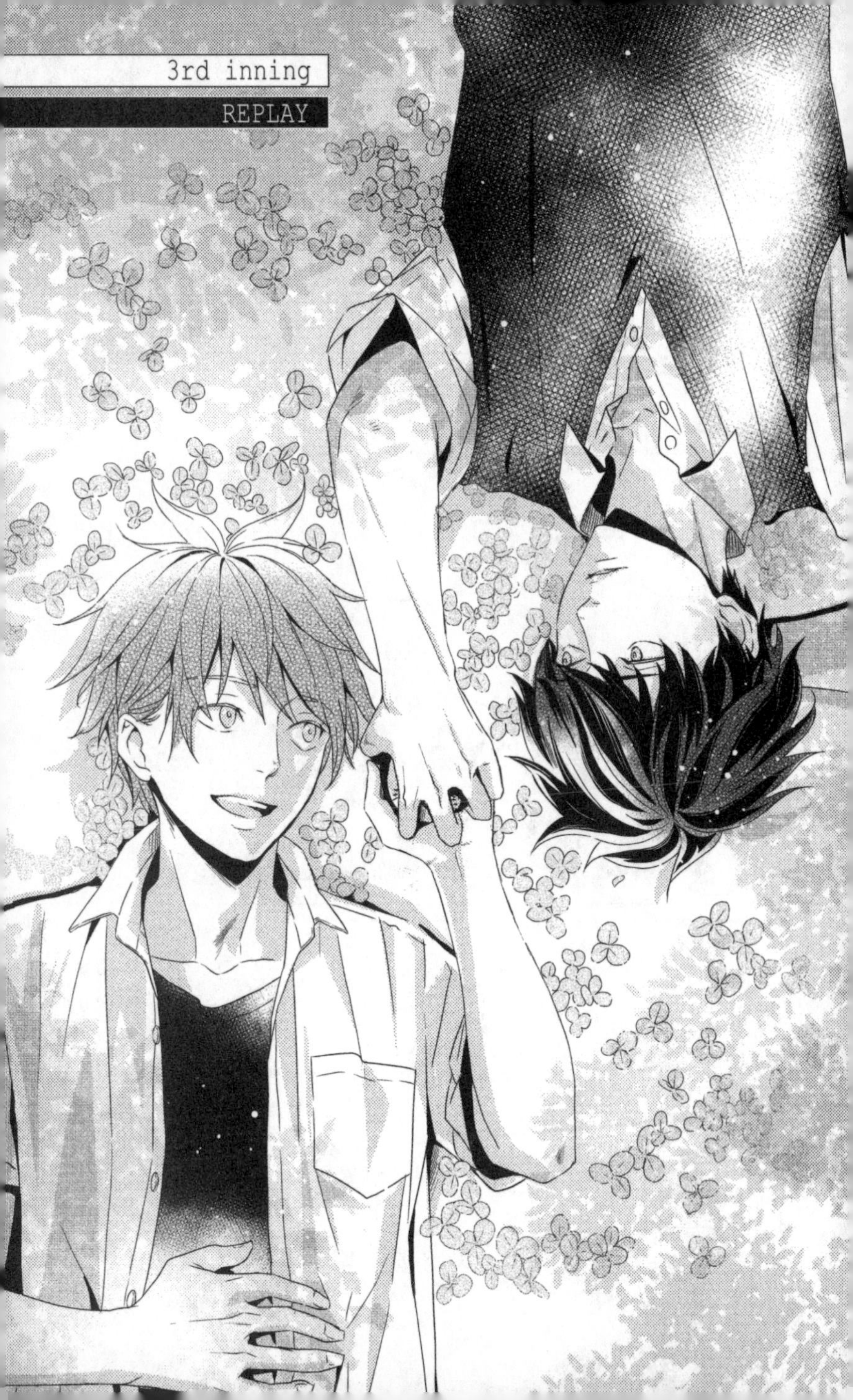

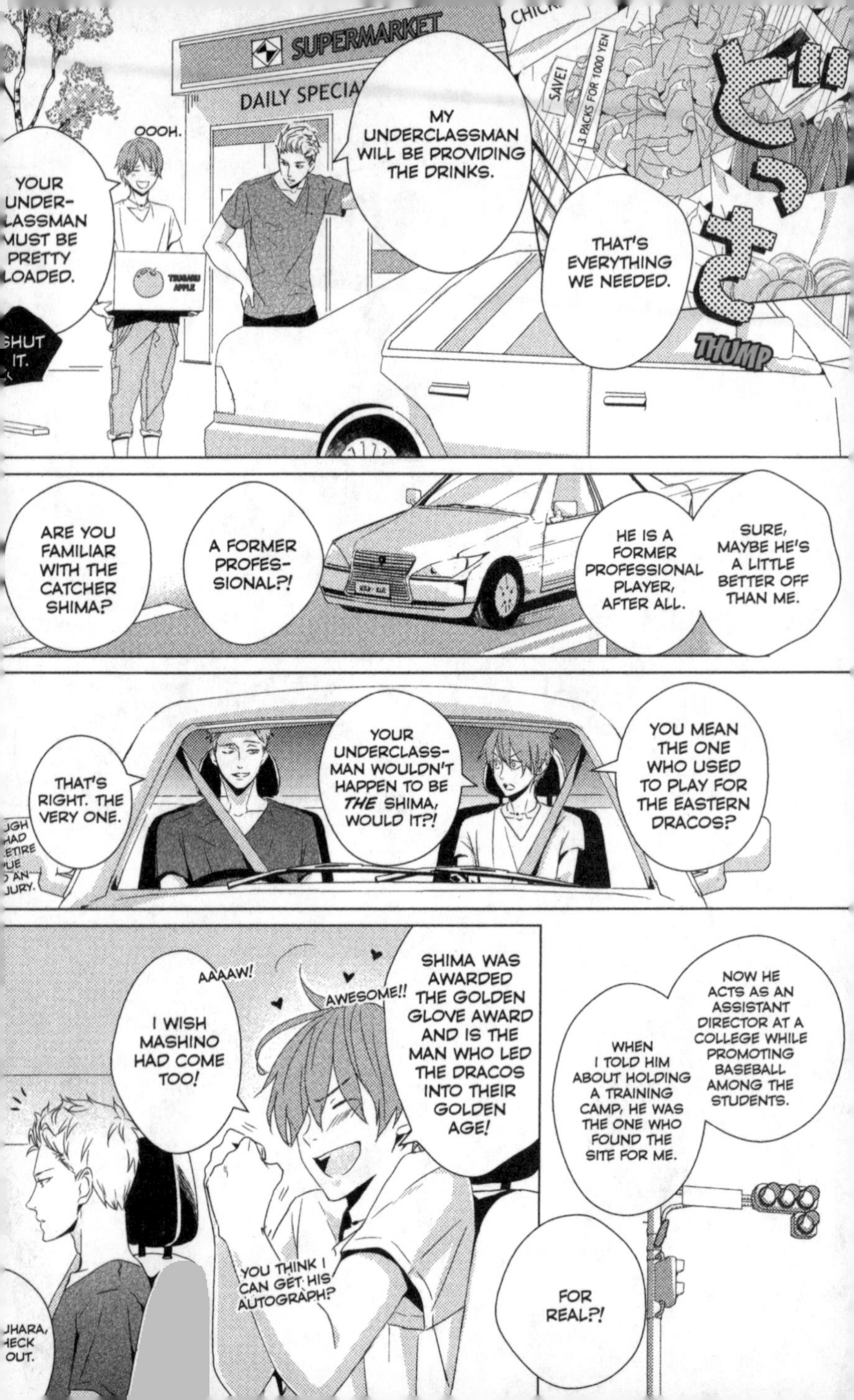

どさっ
SAVE!
3 PACKS FOR 1000 YEN
THAT'S EVERYTHING WE NEEDED.
THUMP
SUPERMARKET
DAILY SPECIA
MY UNDERCLASSMAN WILL BE PROVIDING THE DRINKS.
OOOH.
YOUR UNDER-CLASSMAN MUST BE PRETTY LOADED.
SHUT IT.
SURE, MAYBE HE'S A LITTLE BETTER OFF THAN ME.
HE IS A FORMER PROFESSIONAL PLAYER, AFTER ALL.
A FORMER PROFES-SIONAL?!
ARE YOU FAMILIAR WITH THE CATCHER SHIMA?
YOU MEAN THE ONE WHO USED TO PLAY FOR THE EASTERN DRACOS?
YOUR UNDERCLASS-MAN WOULDN'T HAPPEN TO BE *THE* SHIMA, WOULD IT?!
THAT'S RIGHT. THE VERY ONE.
NOW HE ACTS AS AN ASSISTANT DIRECTOR AT A COLLEGE WHILE PROMOTING BASEBALL AMONG THE STUDENTS.
WHEN I TOLD HIM ABOUT HOLDING A TRAINING CAMP, HE WAS THE ONE WHO FOUND THE SITE FOR ME.
FOR REAL?!
SHIMA WAS AWARDED THE GOLDEN GLOVE AWARD AND IS THE MAN WHO LED THE DRACOS INTO THEIR GOLDEN AGE!
AWESOME!!
AAAAW!
I WISH MASHINO HAD COME TOO!
YOU THINK I CAN GET HIS AUTOGRAPH?

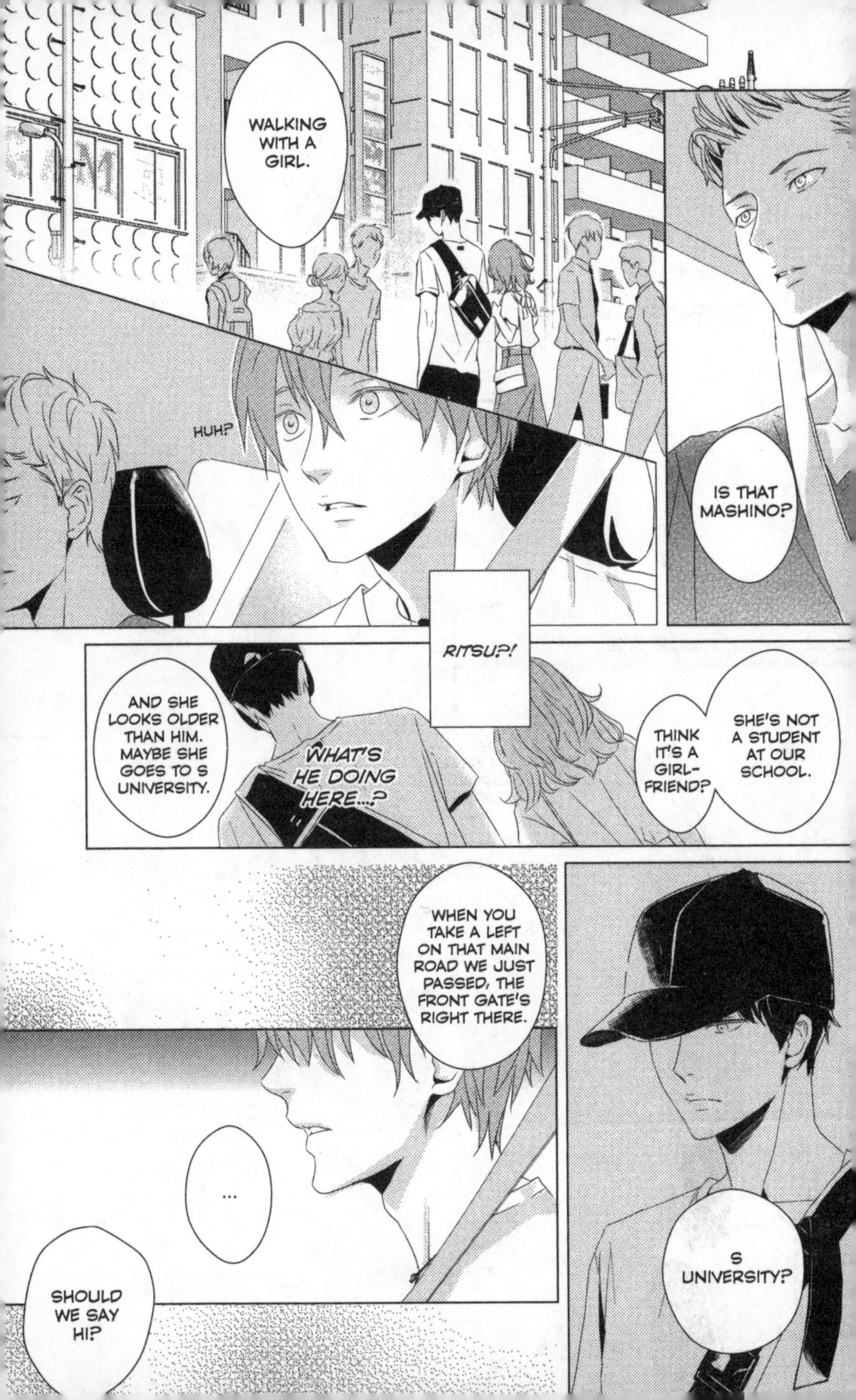
IS THAT MASHINO?
WALKING WITH A GIRL.
HUH?
RITSU?!
SHE'S NOT A STUDENT AT OUR SCHOOL.
THINK IT'S A GIRL-FRIEND?
WHAT'S HE DOING HERE...?
AND SHE LOOKS OLDER THAN HIM. MAYBE SHE GOES TO S UNIVERSITY.
S UNIVERSITY?
WHEN YOU TAKE A LEFT ON THAT MAIN ROAD WE JUST PASSED, THE FRONT GATE'S RIGHT THERE.
...
SHOULD WE SAY HI?

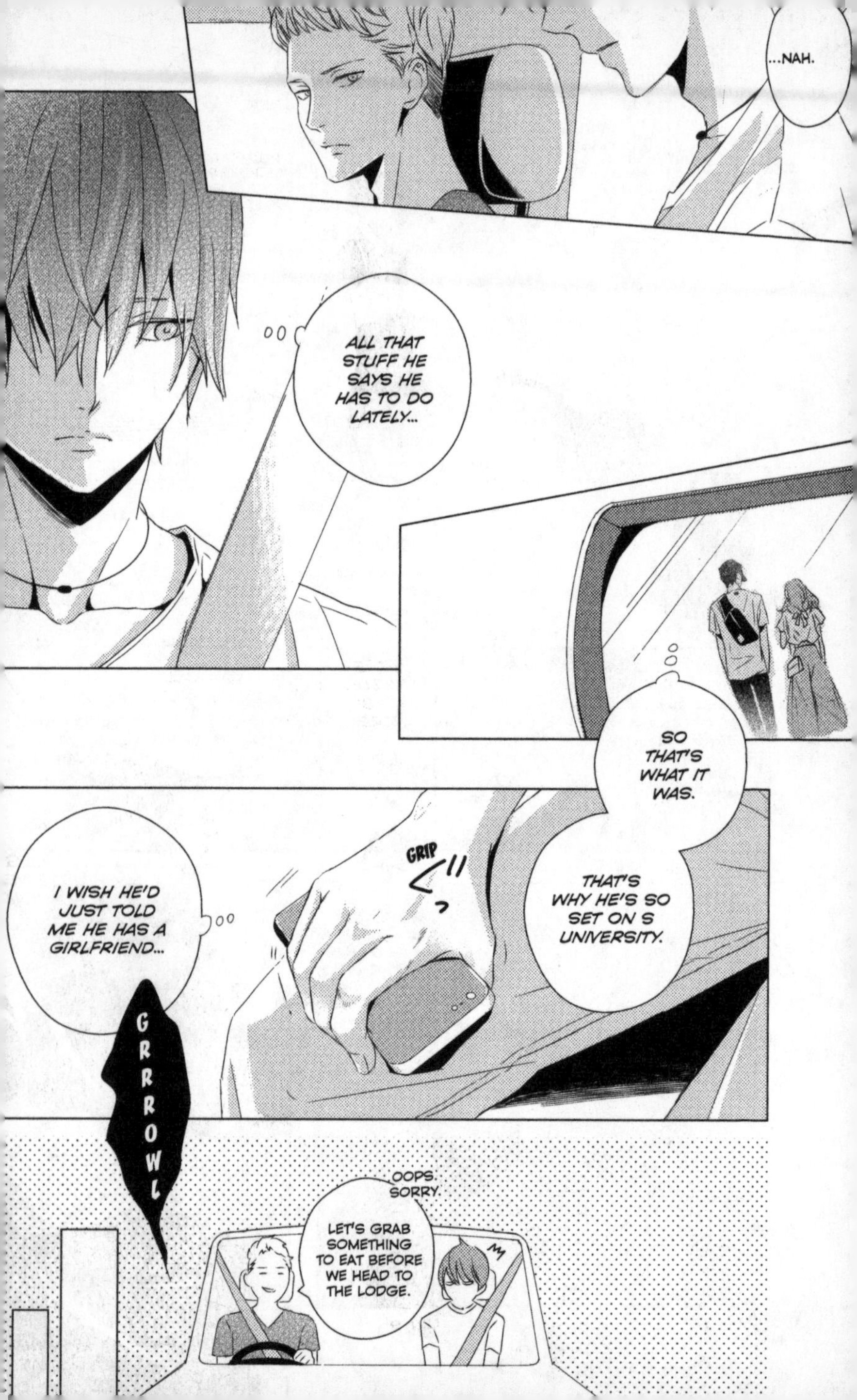
...NAH.
ALL THAT STUFF HE SAYS HE HAS TO DO LATELY...
SO THAT'S WHAT IT WAS.
THAT'S WHY HE'S SO SET ON S UNIVERSITY.
GRIP
I WISH HE'D JUST TOLD ME HE HAS A GIRLFRIEND...
GRRROWL
OOPS. SORRY.
LET'S GRAB SOMETHING TO EAT BEFORE WE HEAD TO THE LODGE.

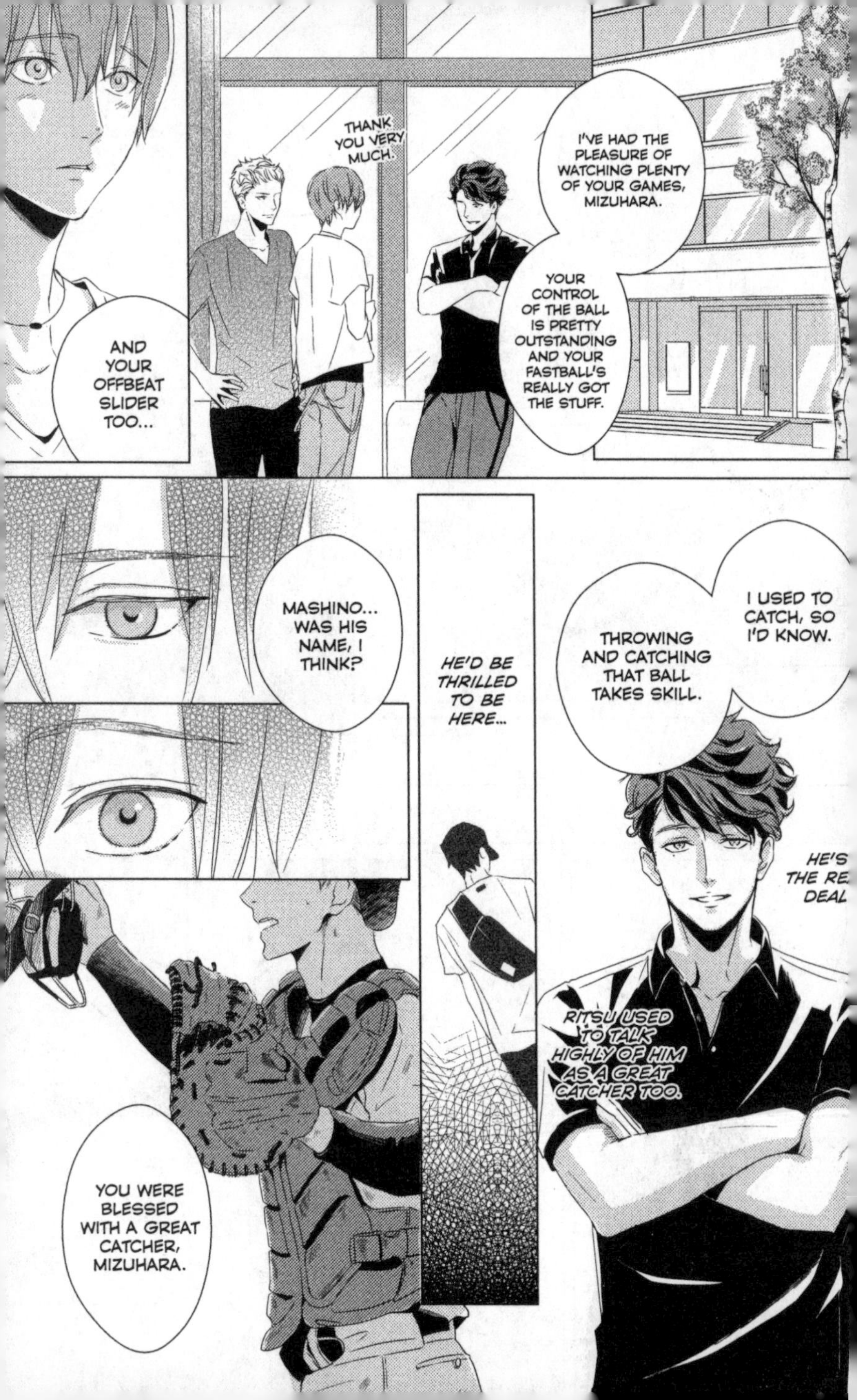
I'VE HAD THE PLEASURE OF WATCHING PLENTY OF YOUR GAMES, MIZUHARA.
YOUR CONTROL OF THE BALL IS PRETTY OUTSTANDING AND YOUR FASTBALL'S REALLY GOT THE STUFF.
THANK YOU VERY MUCH.
AND YOUR OFFBEAT SLIDER TOO...
I USED TO CATCH, SO I'D KNOW.
THROWING AND CATCHING THAT BALL TAKES SKILL.
HE'S THE RE DEAL
RITSU USED TO TALK HIGHLY OF HIM AS A GREAT CATCHER TOO.
HE'D BE THRILLED TO BE HERE...
MASHINO... WAS HIS NAME, I THINK?
YOU WERE BLESSED WITH A GREAT CATCHER, MIZUHARA.

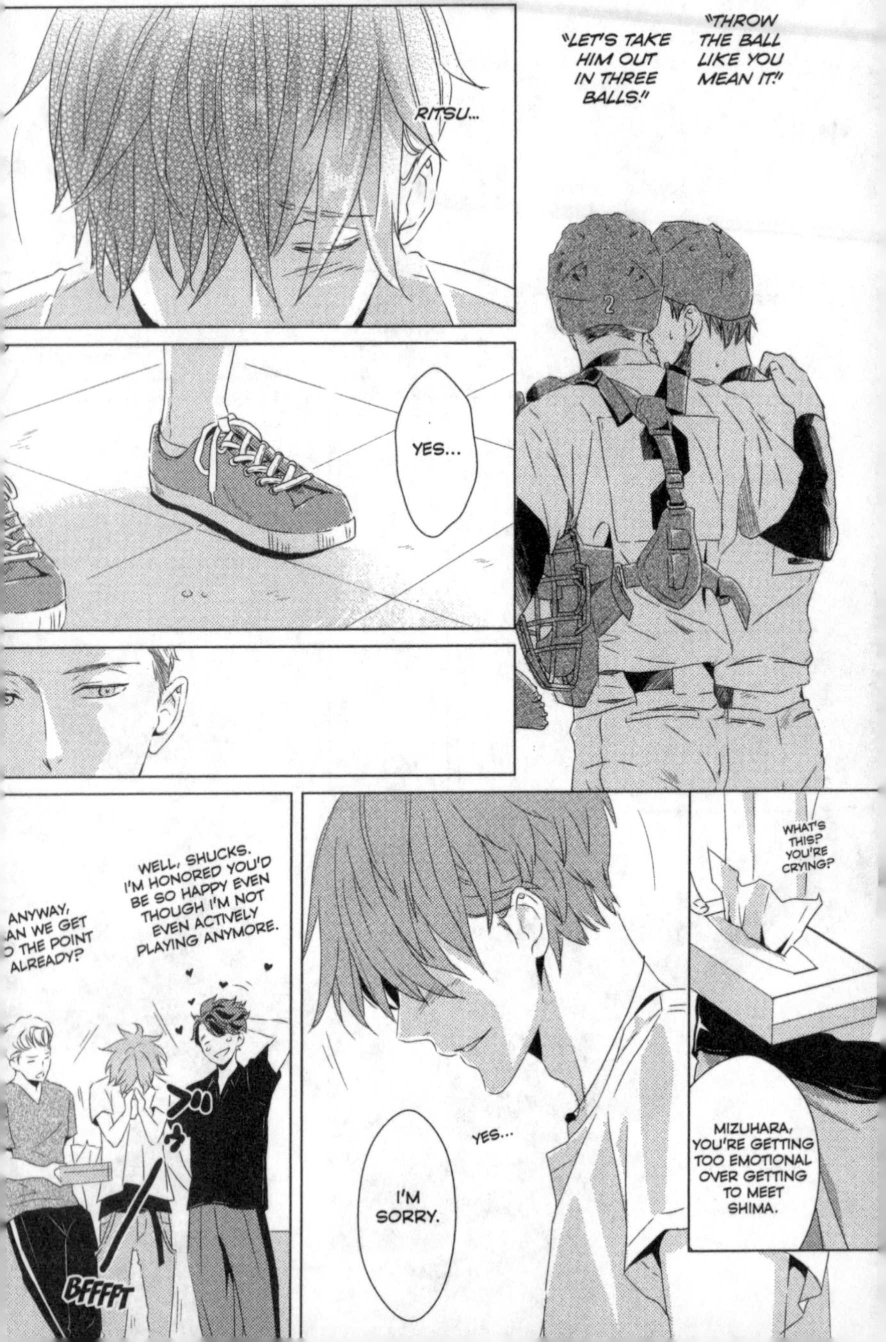
"THROW THE BALL LIKE YOU MEAN IT!"
"LET'S TAKE HIM OUT IN THREE BALLS."
RITSU...
YES...
WHAT'S THIS? YOU'RE CRYING?
MIZUHARA, YOU'RE GETTING TOO EMOTIONAL OVER GETTING TO MEET SHIMA.
YES...
I'M SORRY.
WELL, SHUCKS. I'M HONORED YOU'D BE SO HAPPY EVEN THOUGH I'M NOT EVEN ACTIVELY PLAYING ANYMORE.
ANYWAY, AN WE GET O THE POINT ALREADY?
BFFFPT

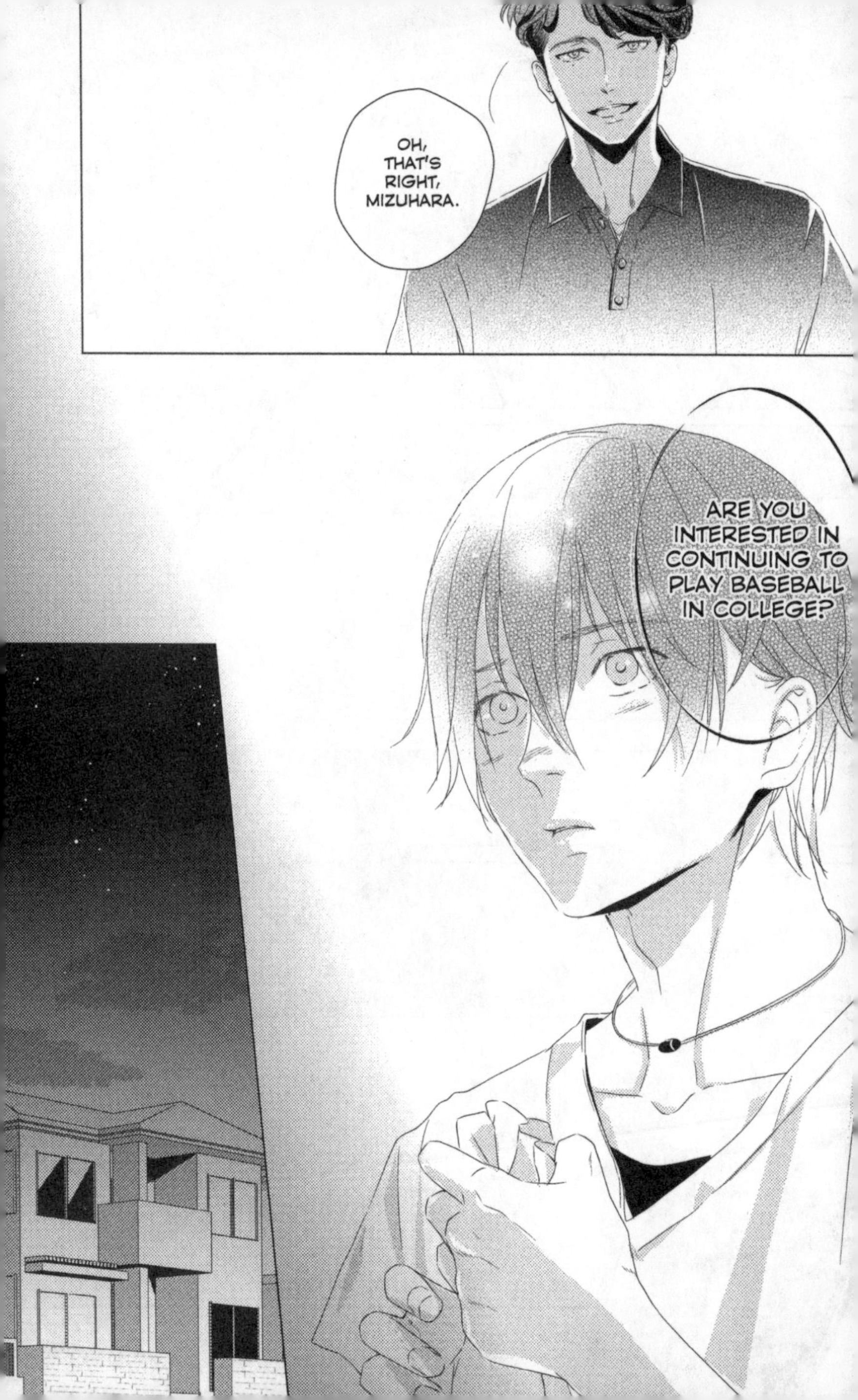
OH, THAT'S RIGHT, MIZUHARA.
ARE YOU INTERESTED IN CONTINUING TO PLAY BASEBALL IN COLLEGE?

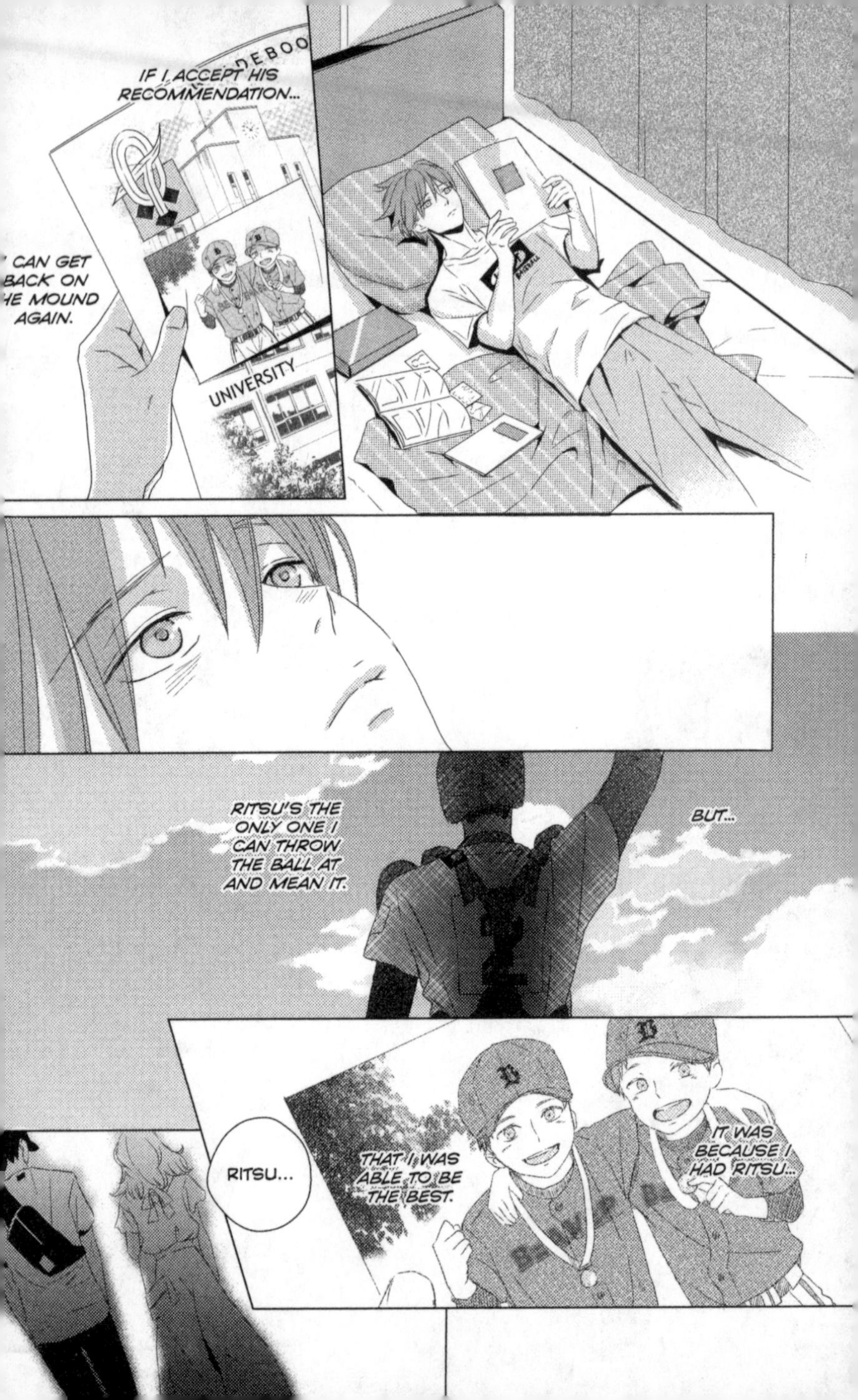
DEBOO
IF I ACCEPT HIS RECOMMENDATION...
UNIVERSITY
CAN GET BACK ON HE MOUND AGAIN.
BUT...
RITSU'S THE ONLY ONE I CAN THROW THE BALL AT AND MEAN IT.
IT WAS BECAUSE I HAD RITSU...
THAT I WAS ABLE TO BE THE BEST.
RITSU...

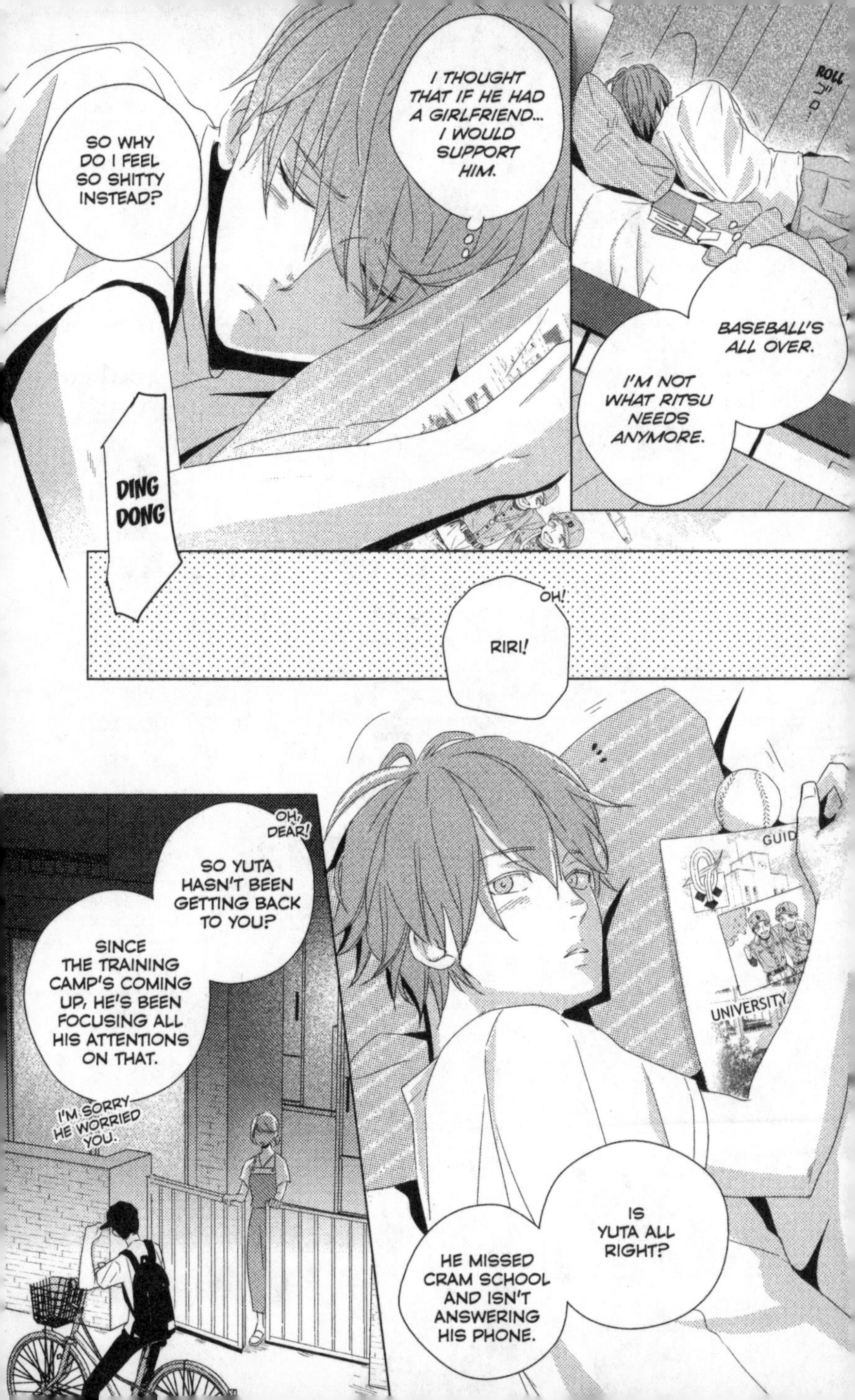
ROLL
BASEBALL'S ALL OVER.
I'M NOT WHAT RITSU NEEDS ANYMORE.
I THOUGHT THAT IF HE HAD A GIRLFRIEND... I WOULD SUPPORT HIM.
SO WHY DO I FEEL SO SHITTY INSTEAD?
DING DONG
OH!
RIRI!
IS YUTA ALL RIGHT?
HE MISSED CRAM SCHOOL AND ISN'T ANSWERING HIS PHONE.
UNIVERSITY
OH, DEAR!
SO YUTA HASN'T BEEN GETTING BACK TO YOU?
SINCE THE TRAINING CAMP'S COMING UP, HE'S BEEN FOCUSING ALL HIS ATTENTIONS ON THAT.
I'M SORRY HE WORRIED YOU.

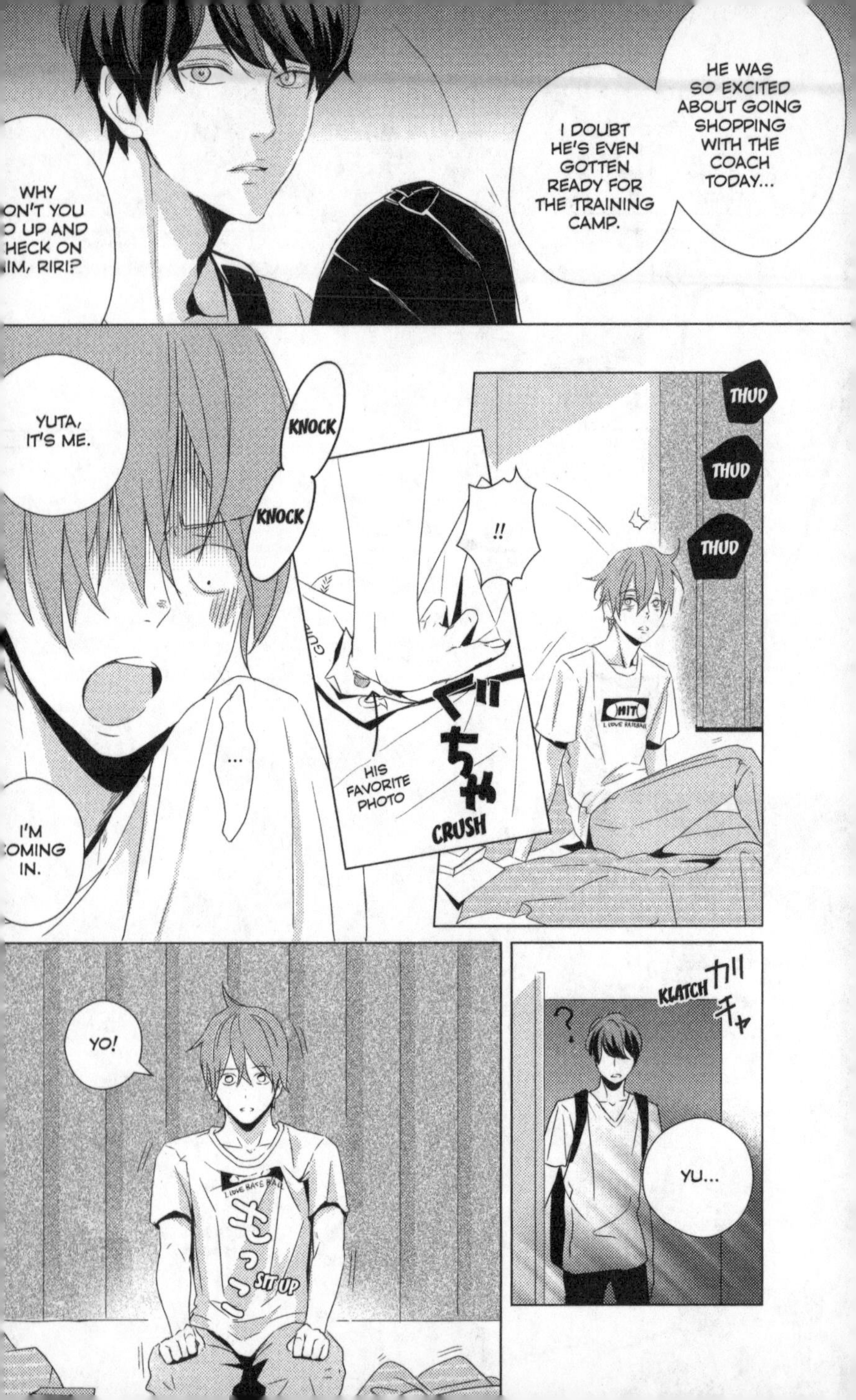

HE WAS SO EXCITED ABOUT GOING SHOPPING WITH THE COACH TODAY...
I DOUBT HE'S EVEN GOTTEN READY FOR THE TRAINING CAMP.
WHY ON'T YOU O UP AND HECK ON IM, RIRI?
THUD
THUD
THUD
!!
ぐちゃ
CRUSH
HIS FAVORITE PHOTO
KNOCK
KNOCK
YUTA, IT'S ME.
...
I'M OMING IN.
KLATCH
?
YU...
YO!
SIT UP

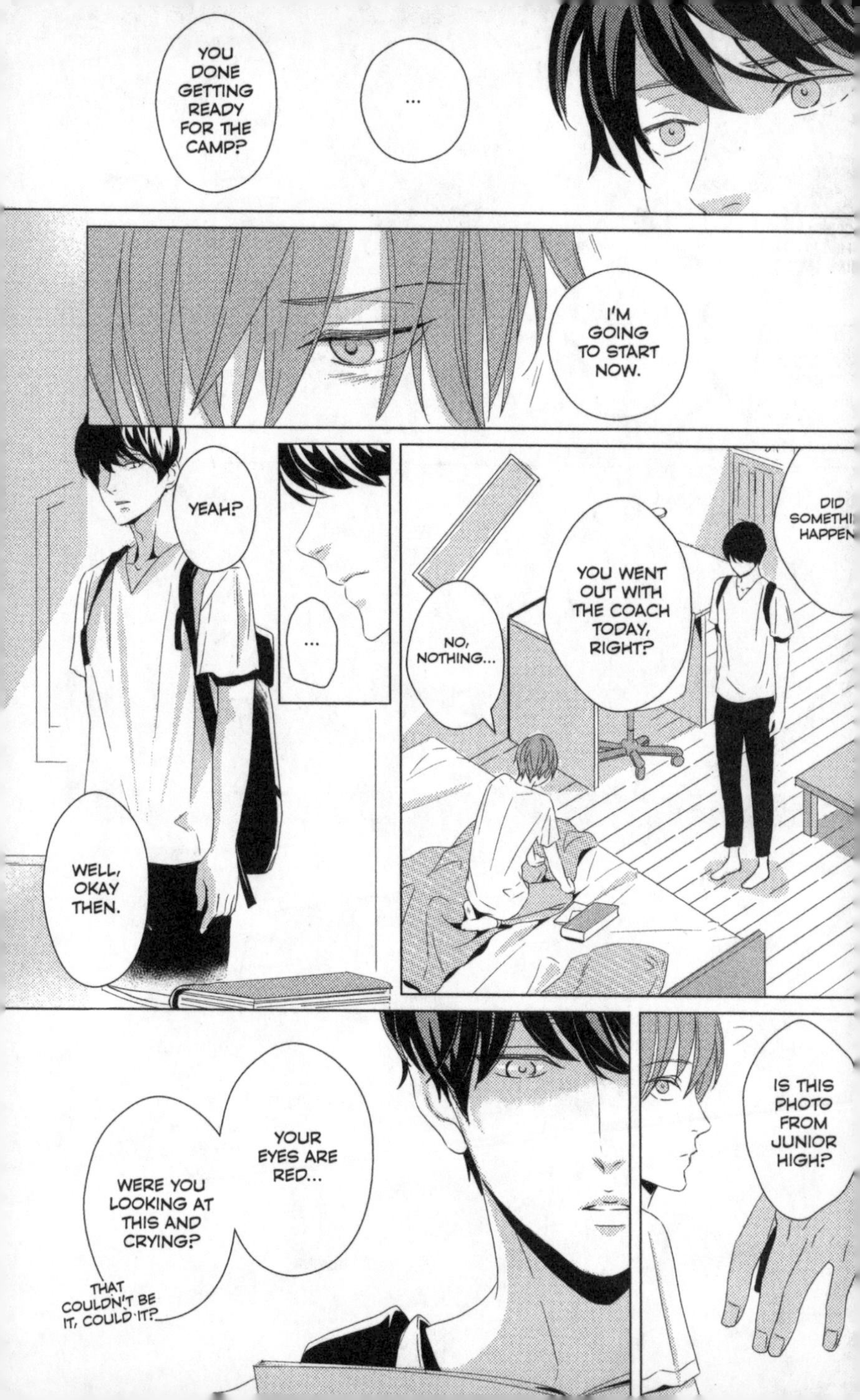
...
YOU DONE GETTING READY FOR THE CAMP?
I'M GOING TO START NOW.
DID SOMETHI HAPPEN
YOU WENT OUT WITH THE COACH TODAY, RIGHT?
NO, NOTHING...
...
YEAH?
WELL, OKAY THEN.
IS THIS PHOTO FROM JUNIOR HIGH?
YOUR EYES ARE RED...
WERE YOU LOOKING AT THIS AND CRYING?
THAT COULDN'T BE IT, COULD IT?

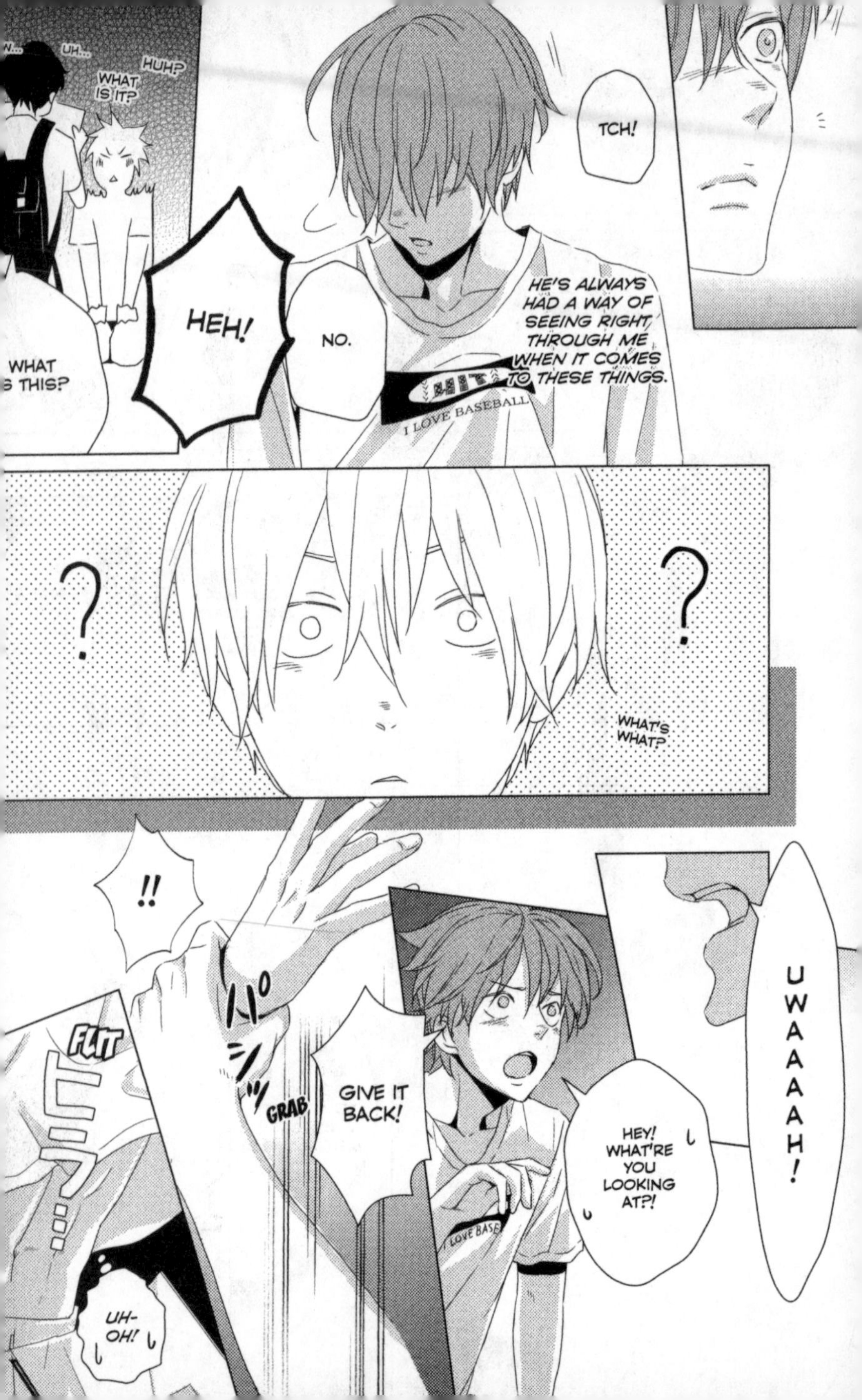
TCH!
HE'S ALWAYS HAD A WAY OF SEEING RIGHT THROUGH ME WHEN IT COMES TO THESE THINGS.
NO.
HEH!
I LOVE BASEBALL
HUH?
UH...
W...
WHAT IS IT?
WHAT
S THIS?
?
?
WHAT'S WHAT?
UWAAAAAH!
HEY! WHAT'RE YOU LOOKING AT?!
GIVE IT BACK!
I LOVE BASE
!!
GRAB
FLIT
UH-OH!

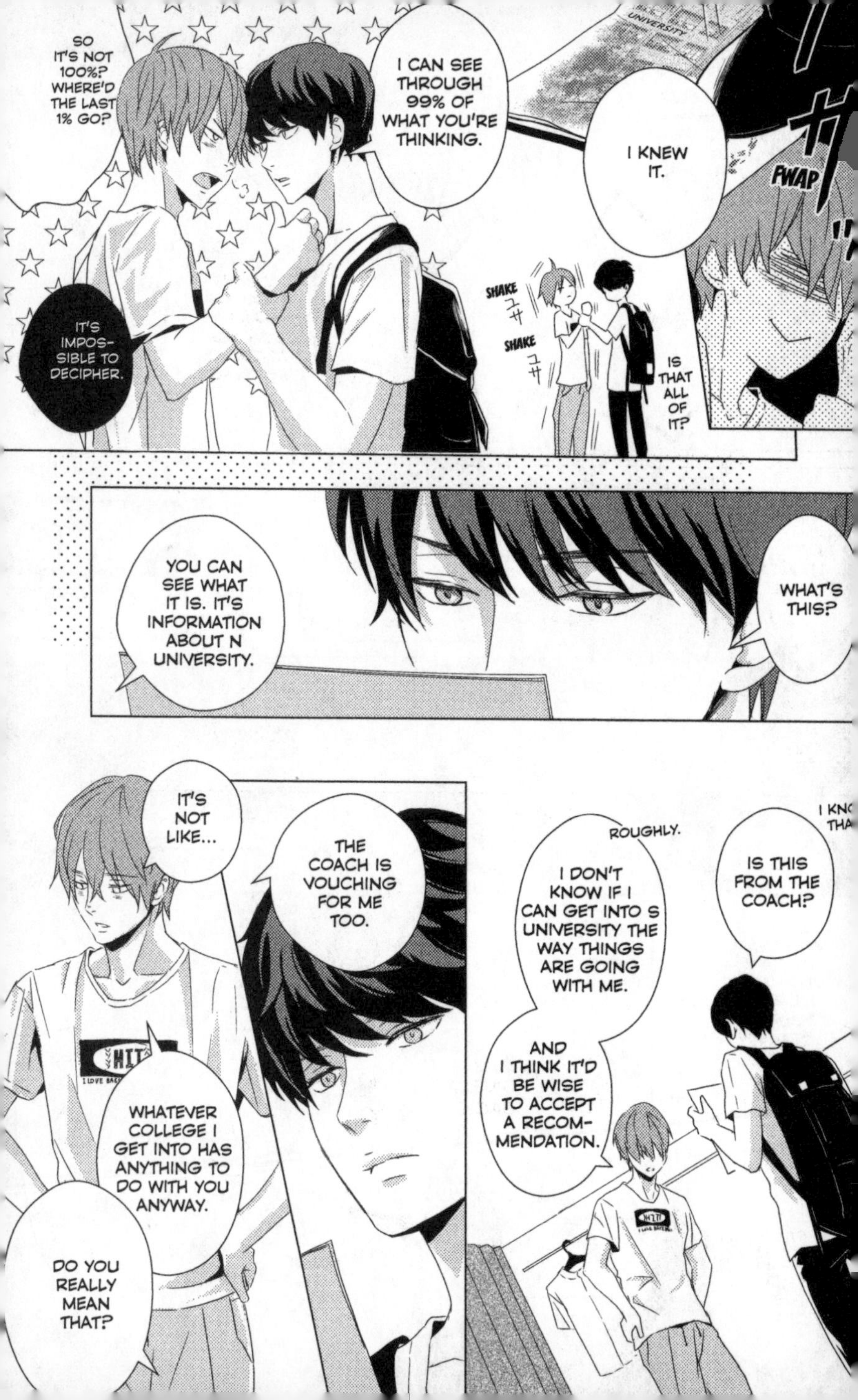
PWAP
I KNEW IT.
SHAKE
SHAKE
IS THAT ALL OF IT?
I CAN SEE THROUGH 99% OF WHAT YOU'RE THINKING.
SO IT'S NOT 100%? WHERE'D THE LAST 1% GO?
IT'S IMPOS-SIBLE TO DECIPHER.
WHAT'S THIS?
YOU CAN SEE WHAT IT IS. IT'S INFORMATION ABOUT N UNIVERSITY.
IS THIS FROM THE COACH?
ROUGHLY.
I DON'T KNOW IF I CAN GET INTO S UNIVERSITY THE WAY THINGS ARE GOING WITH ME.
AND I THINK IT'D BE WISE TO ACCEPT A RECOM-MENDATION.
THE COACH IS VOUCHING FOR ME TOO.
IT'S NOT LIKE...
WHATEVER COLLEGE I GET INTO HAS ANYTHING TO DO WITH YOU ANYWAY.
DO YOU REALLY MEAN THAT?

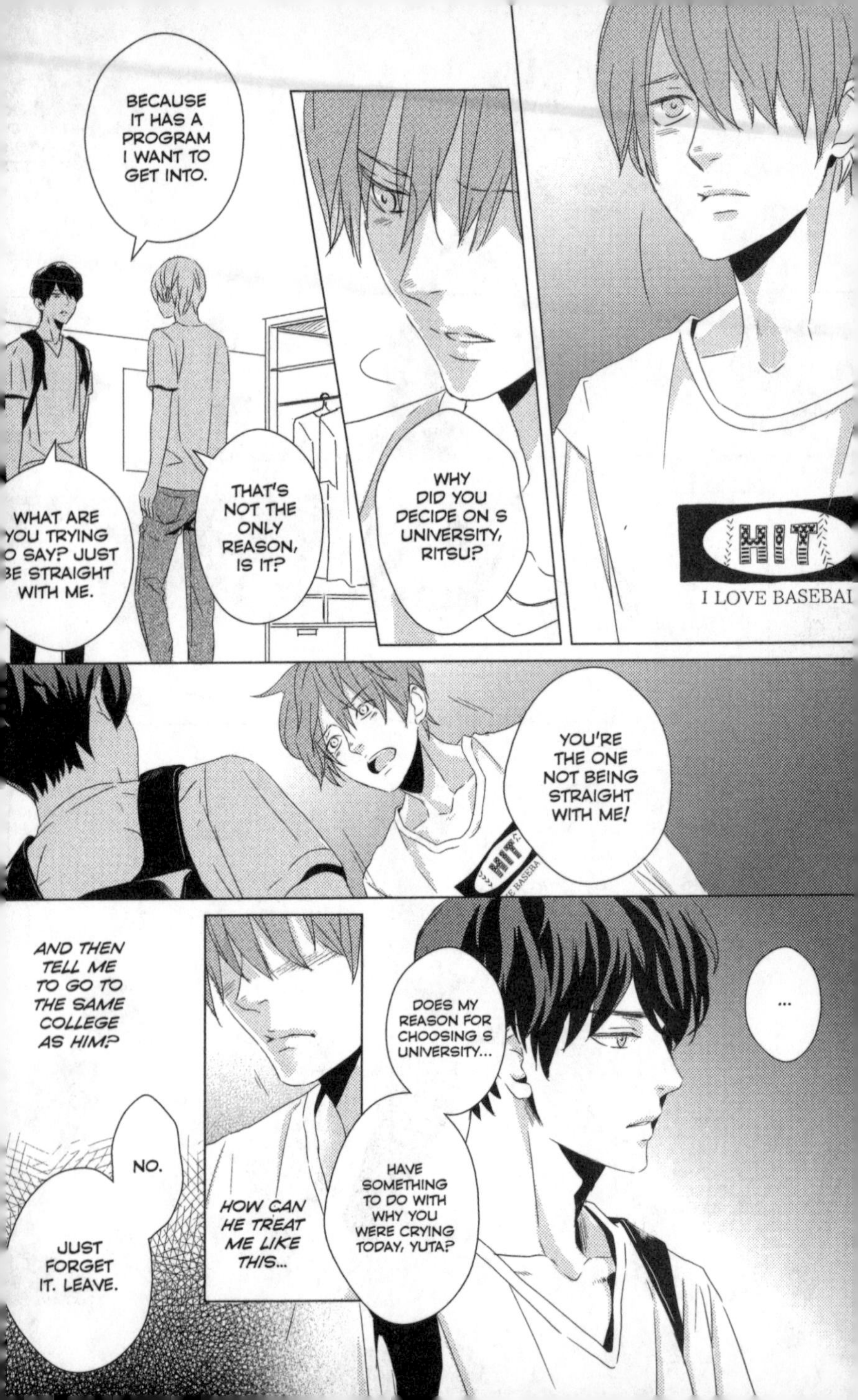
HIT
I LOVE BASEBAI
WHY DID YOU DECIDE ON S UNIVERSITY, RITSU?
BECAUSE IT HAS A PROGRAM I WANT TO GET INTO.
THAT'S NOT THE ONLY REASON, IS IT?
WHAT ARE YOU TRYING O SAY? JUST E STRAIGHT WITH ME.
YOU'RE THE ONE NOT BEING STRAIGHT WITH ME!
...
DOES MY REASON FOR CHOOSING S UNIVERSITY...
HAVE SOMETHING TO DO WITH WHY YOU WERE CRYING TODAY, YUTA?
HOW CAN HE TREAT ME LIKE THIS...
AND THEN TELL ME TO GO TO THE SAME COLLEGE AS HIM?
NO.
JUST FORGET IT. LEAVE.

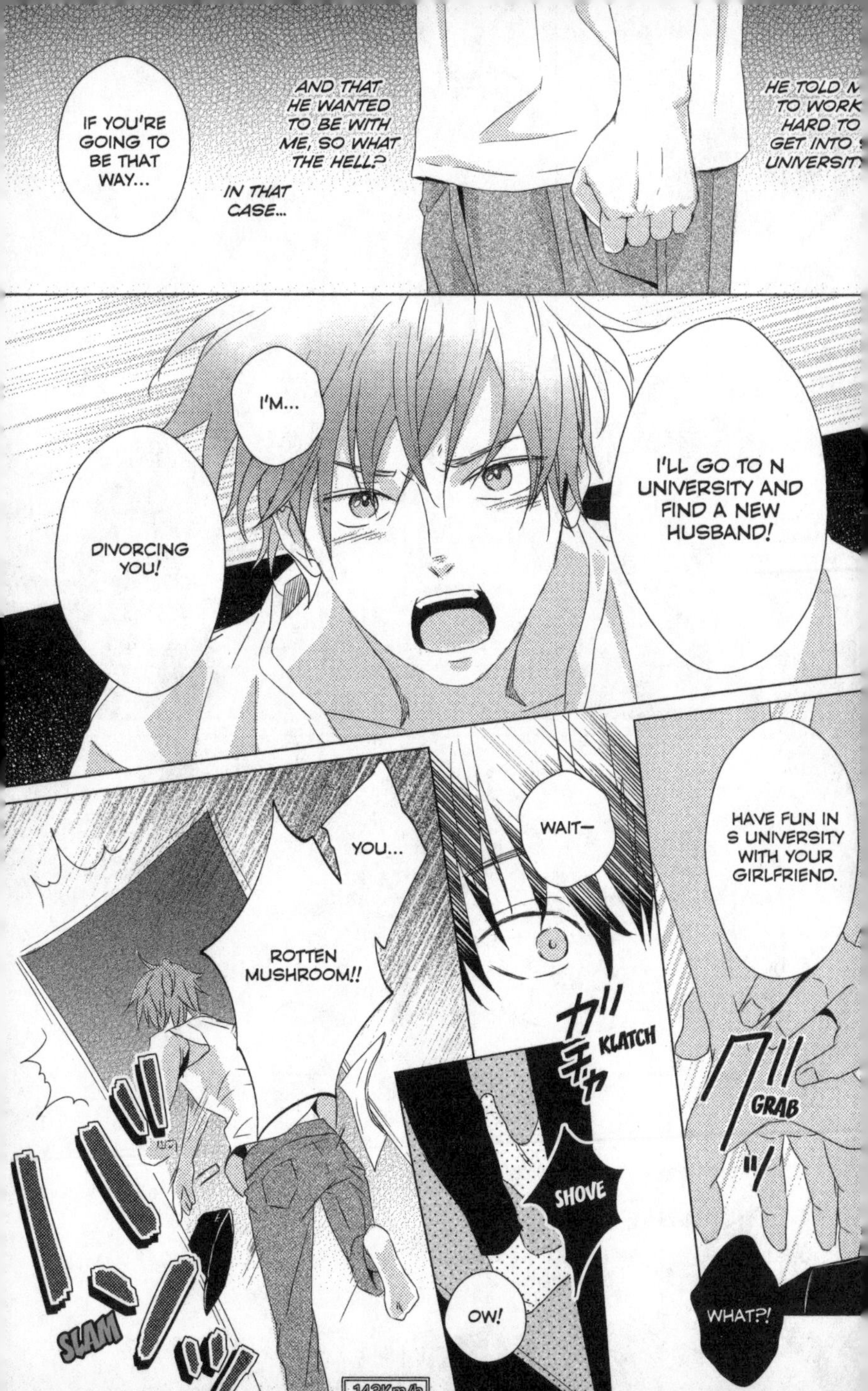
HE TOLD M
TO WORK HARD TO GET INTO
UNIVERSIT
AND THAT HE WANTED TO BE WITH ME, SO WHAT THE HELL?
IN THAT CASE...
IF YOU'RE GOING TO BE THAT WAY...
I'M...
DIVORCING YOU!
I'LL GO TO N UNIVERSITY AND FIND A NEW HUSBAND!
HAVE FUN IN S UNIVERSITY WITH YOUR GIRLFRIEND.
GRAB
WHAT?!
WAIT—
KLATCH
SHOVE
OW!
YOU...
ROTTEN MUSHROOM!!
SLAM

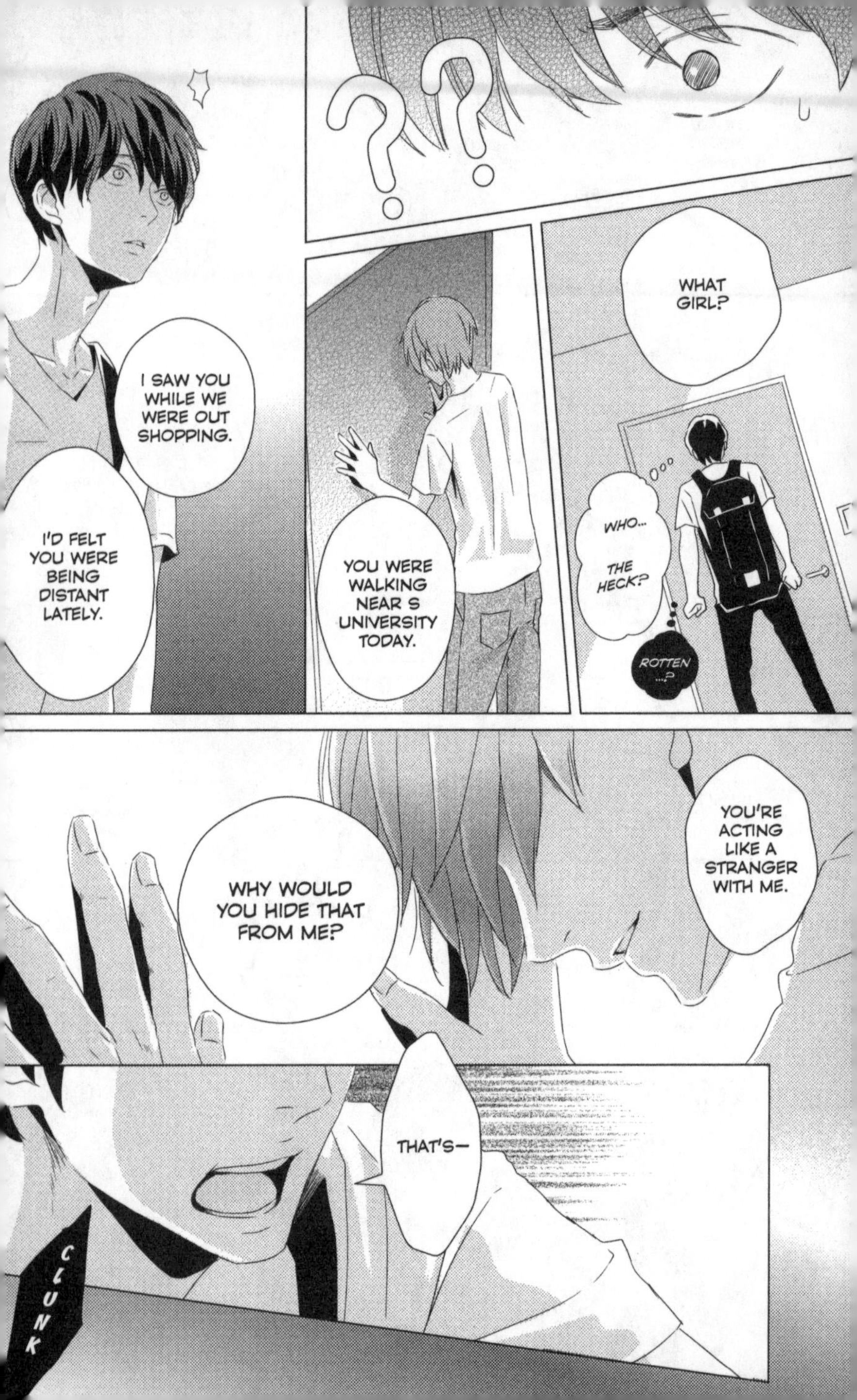
WHAT GIRL?
WHO... THE HECK?
ROTTEN ...?
YOU WERE WALKING NEAR S UNIVERSITY TODAY.
I SAW YOU WHILE WE WERE OUT SHOPPING.
I'D FELT YOU WERE BEING DISTANT LATELY.
YOU'RE ACTING LIKE A STRANGER WITH ME.
WHY WOULD YOU HIDE THAT FROM ME?
THAT'S—
CLUNK

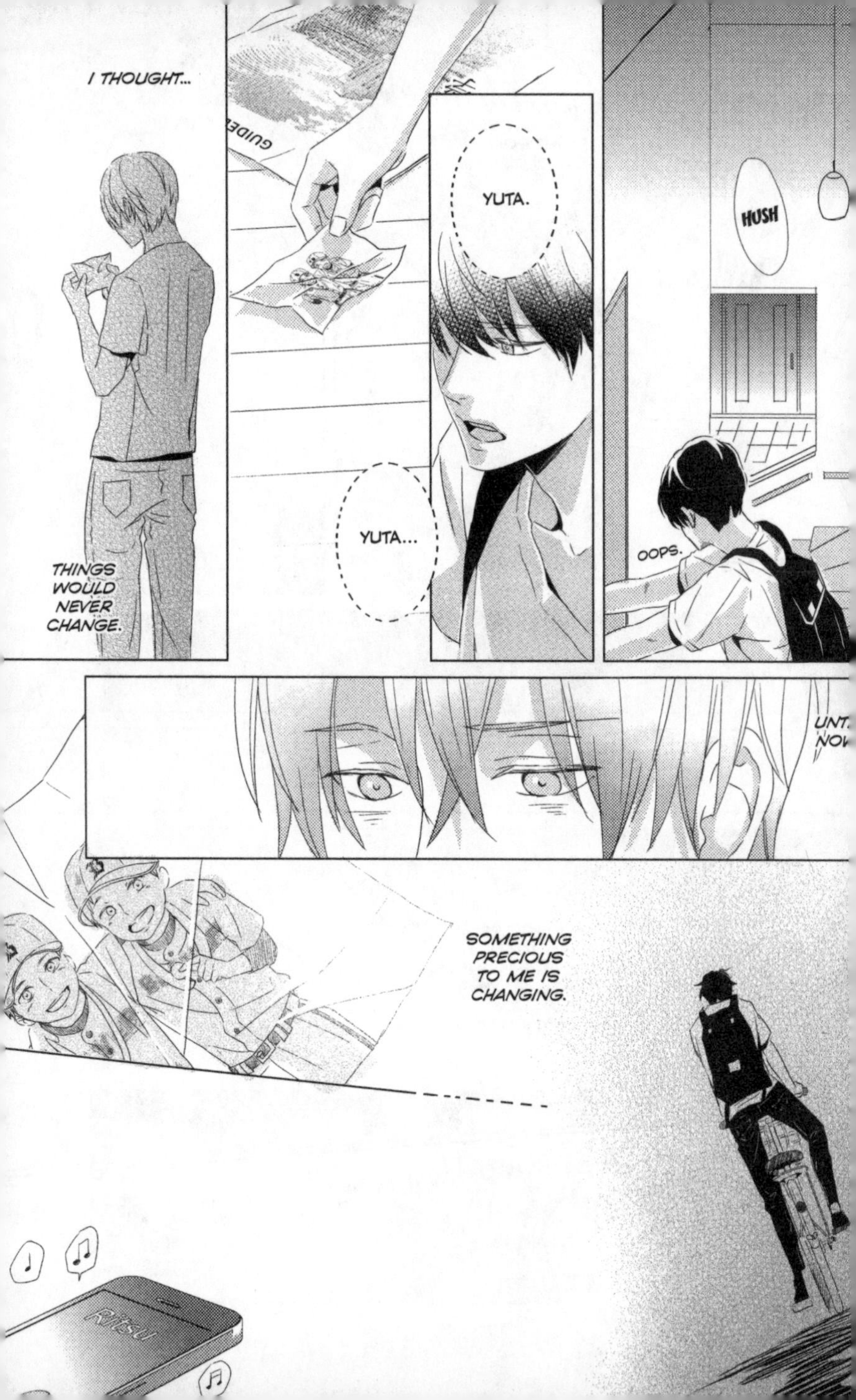
HUSH
OOPS.
YUTA.
YUTA...
GUIDE
I THOUGHT...
THINGS WOULD NEVER CHANGE.
SOMETHING PRECIOUS TO ME IS CHANGING.
RITSU

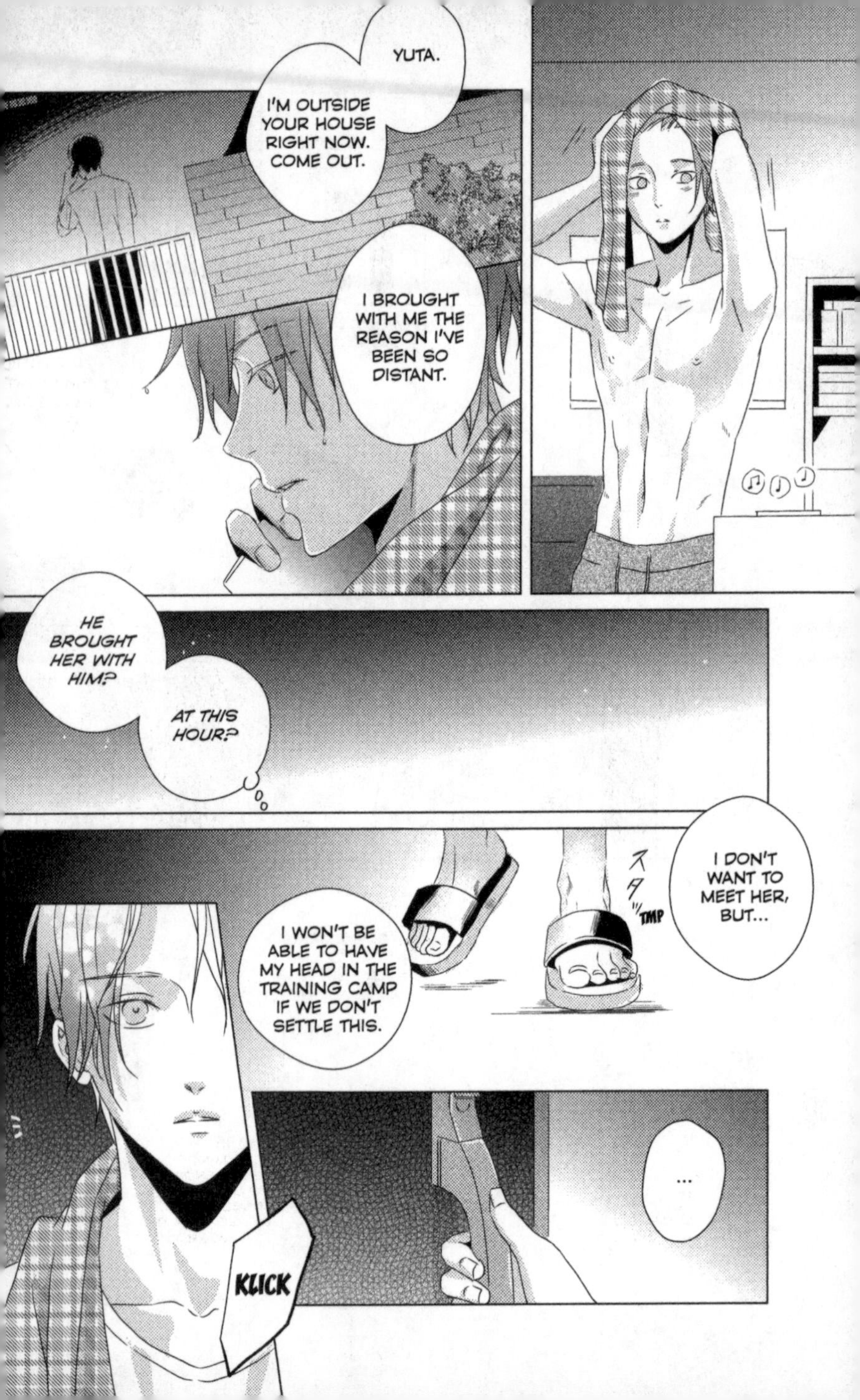
YUTA.
I'M OUTSIDE YOUR HOUSE RIGHT NOW. COME OUT.
I BROUGHT WITH ME THE REASON I'VE BEEN SO DISTANT.
HE BROUGHT HER WITH HIM?
AT THIS HOUR?
I DON'T WANT TO MEET HER, BUT...
スタ
TMP
I WON'T BE ABLE TO HAVE MY HEAD IN THE TRAINING CAMP IF WE DON'T SETTLE THIS.
...
KLICK

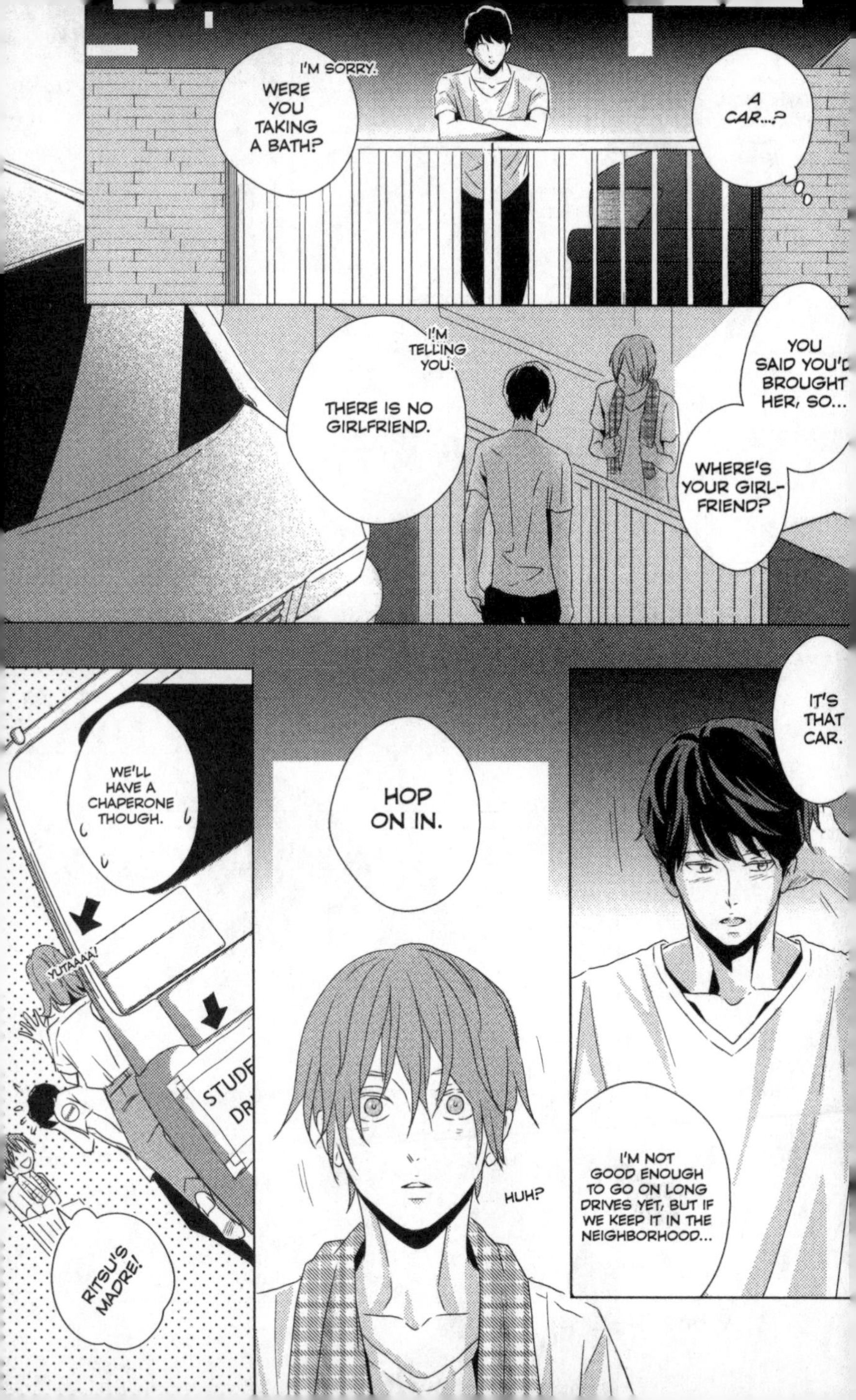
A CAR...?
I'M SORRY.
WERE YOU TAKING A BATH?
YOU SAID YOU'D BROUGHT HER, SO...
WHERE'S YOUR GIRLFRIEND?
I'M TELLING YOU.
THERE IS NO GIRLFRIEND.
IT'S THAT CAR.
I'M NOT GOOD ENOUGH TO GO ON LONG DRIVES YET, BUT IF WE KEEP IT IN THE NEIGHBORHOOD...
HOP ON IN.
HUH?
WE'LL HAVE A CHAPERONE THOUGH.
YUTAAAA!
RITSU'S MADRE!

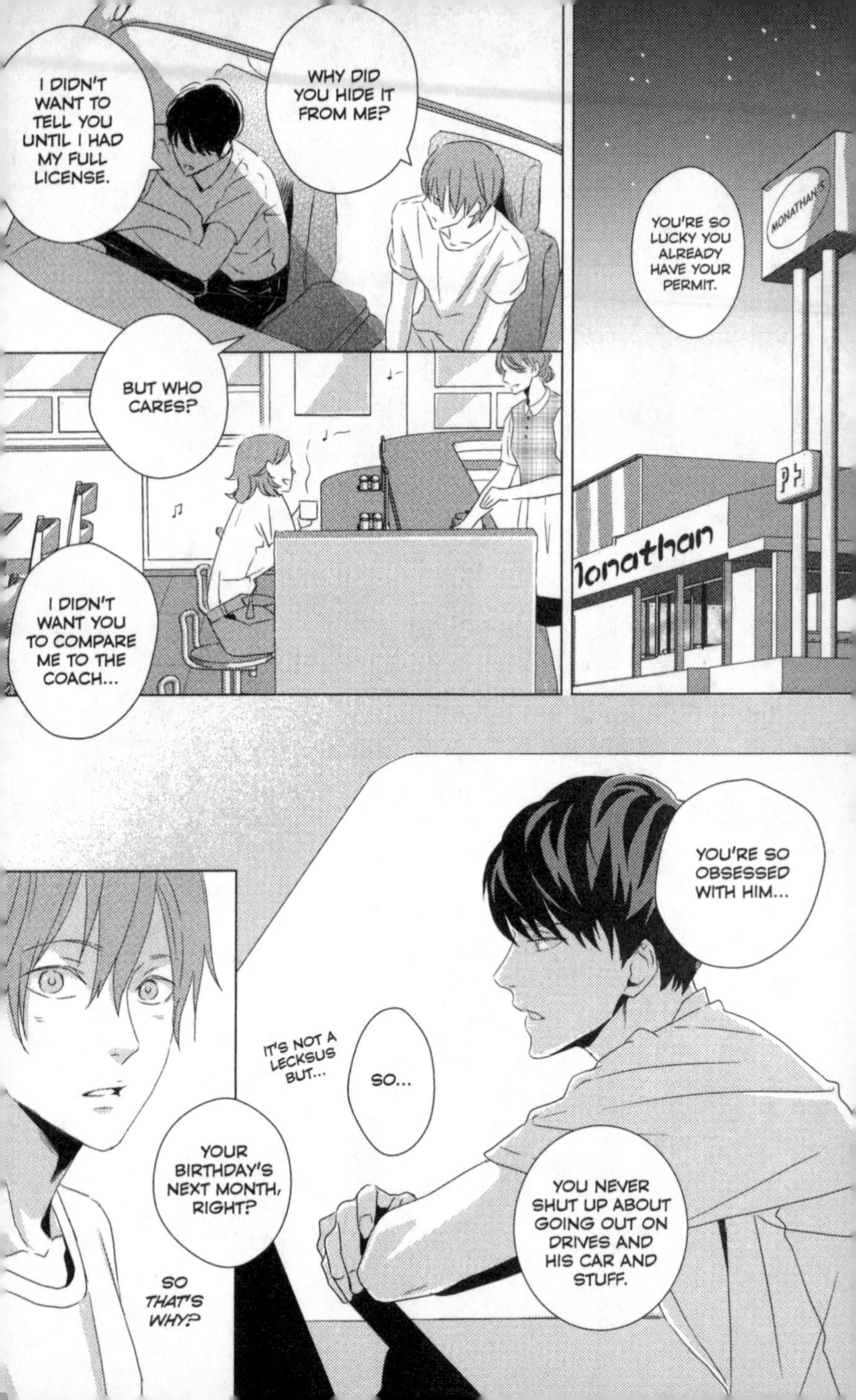
MONATHAN'S
YOU'RE SO LUCKY YOU ALREADY HAVE YOUR PERMIT.
WHY DID YOU HIDE IT FROM ME?
I DIDN'T WANT TO TELL YOU UNTIL I HAD MY FULL LICENSE.
BUT WHO CARES?
I DIDN'T WANT YOU TO COMPARE ME TO THE COACH...
YOU'RE SO OBSESSED WITH HIM...
YOU NEVER SHUT UP ABOUT GOING OUT ON DRIVES AND HIS CAR AND STUFF.
SO...
IT'S NOT A LECKSUS BUT...
YOUR BIRTHDAY'S NEXT MONTH, RIGHT?
SO *THAT'S* WHY?

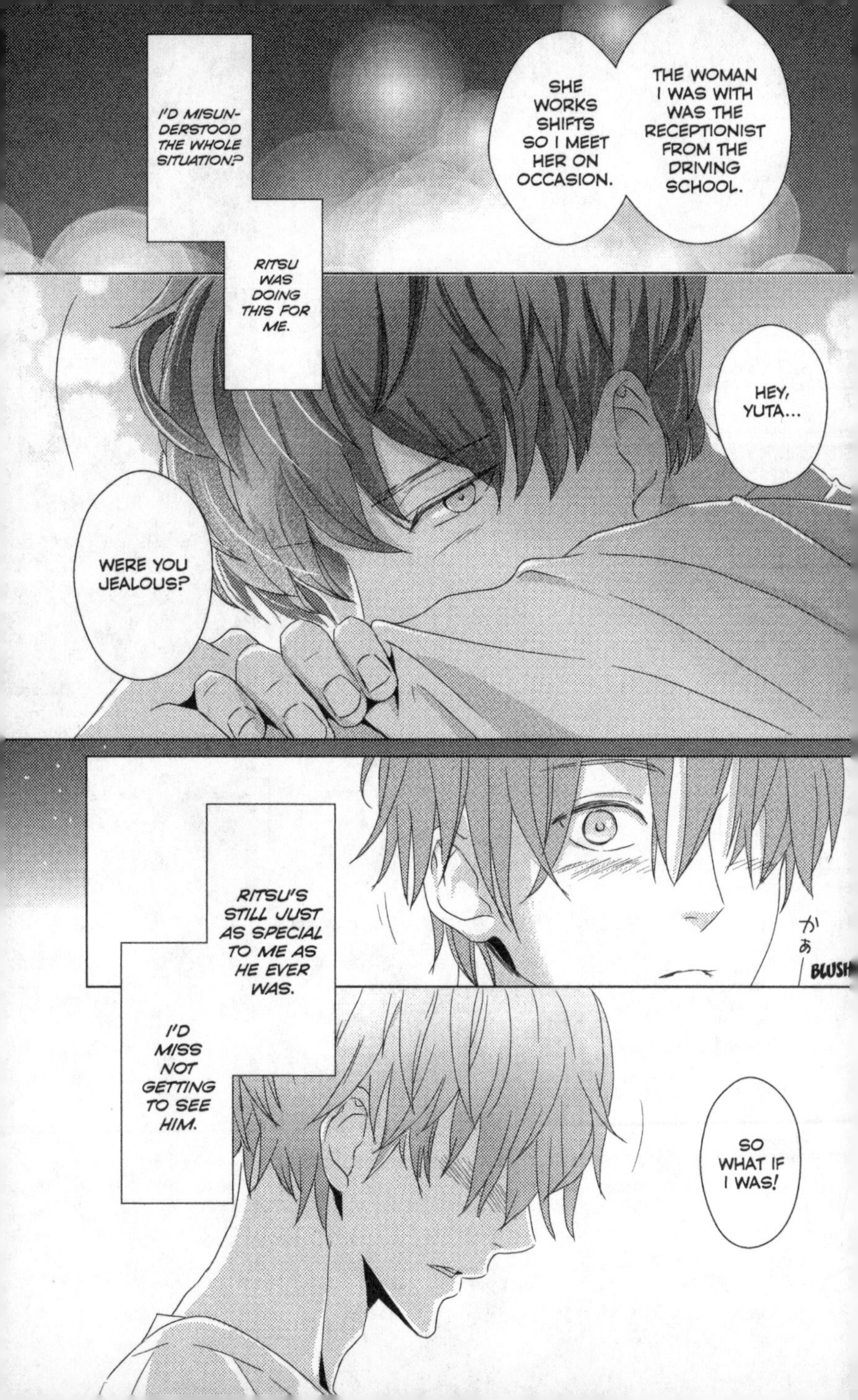
THE WOMAN I WAS WITH WAS THE RECEPTIONIST FROM THE DRIVING SCHOOL.
SHE WORKS SHIFTS SO I MEET HER ON OCCASION.
I'D MISUNDERSTOOD THE WHOLE SITUATION?
RITSU WAS DOING THIS FOR ME.
HEY, YUTA...
WERE YOU JEALOUS?
かぁ
BLUSH
RITSU'S STILL JUST AS SPECIAL TO ME AS HE EVER WAS.
I'D MISS NOT GETTING TO SEE HIM.
SO WHAT IF I WAS!

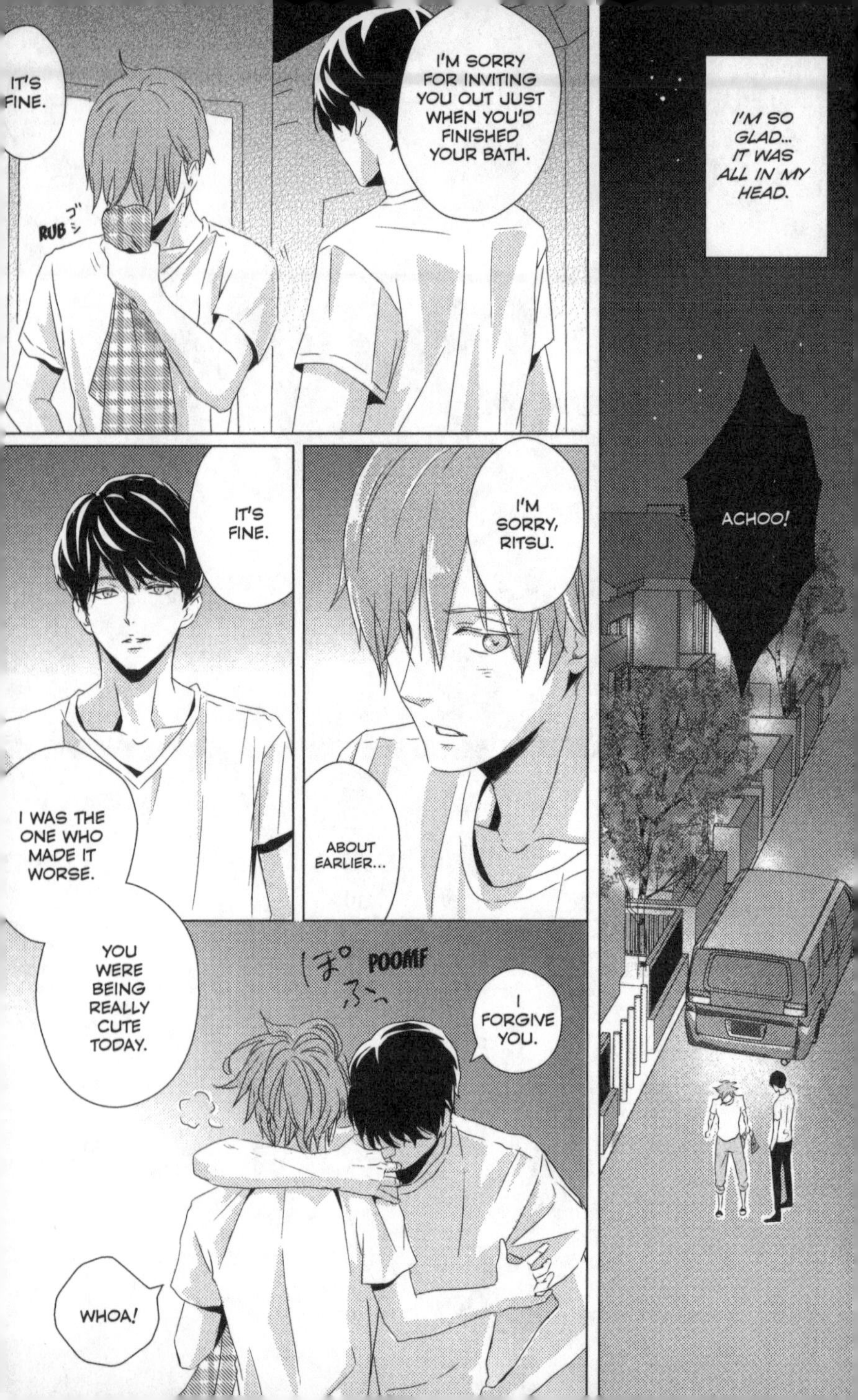
I'M SO GLAD... IT WAS ALL IN MY HEAD.
ACHOO!
I'M SORRY FOR INVITING YOU OUT JUST WHEN YOU'D FINISHED YOUR BATH.
IT'S FINE.
ゴシ RUB
I'M SORRY, RITSU.
ABOUT EARLIER...
IT'S FINE.
I WAS THE ONE WHO MADE IT WORSE.
YOU WERE BEING REALLY CUTE TODAY.
ぽふっ POOMF
I FORGIVE YOU.
WHOA!

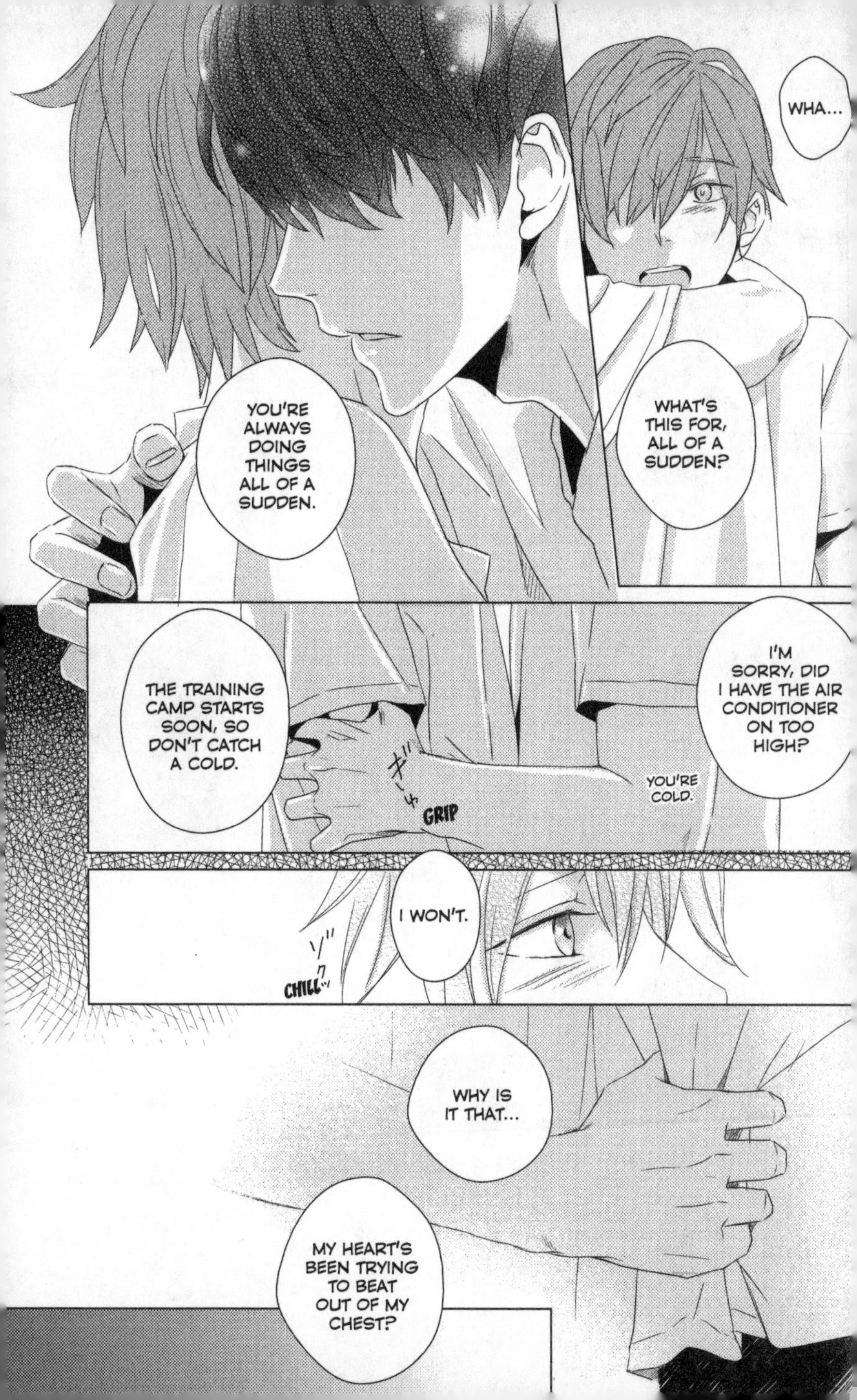
WHA...
WHAT'S THIS FOR, ALL OF A SUDDEN?
YOU'RE ALWAYS DOING THINGS ALL OF A SUDDEN.
I'M SORRY, DID I HAVE THE AIR CONDITIONER ON TOO HIGH?
YOU'RE COLD.
GRIP
THE TRAINING CAMP STARTS SOON, SO DON'T CATCH A COLD.
I WON'T.
CHILL
WHY IS IT THAT...
MY HEART'S BEEN TRYING TO BEAT OUT OF MY CHEST?

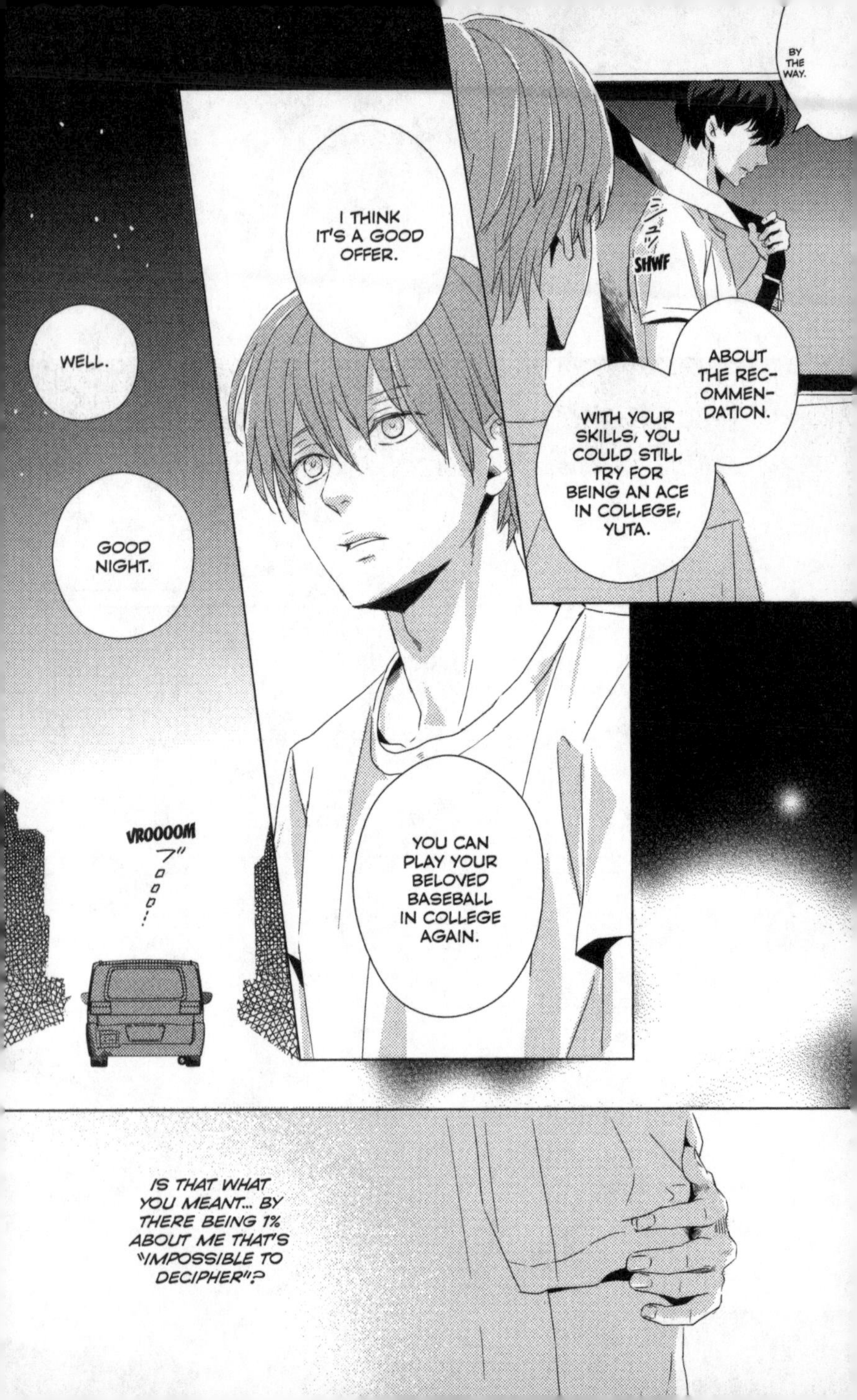
BY THE WAY.
ABOUT THE RECOMMENDATION.
WITH YOUR SKILLS, YOU COULD STILL TRY FOR BEING AN ACE IN COLLEGE, YUTA.
I THINK IT'S A GOOD OFFER.
YOU CAN PLAY YOUR BELOVED BASEBALL IN COLLEGE AGAIN.
WELL.
GOOD NIGHT.
VROOOOM
IS THAT WHAT YOU MEANT... BY THERE BEING 1% ABOUT ME THAT'S "IMPOSSIBLE TO DECIPHER"?

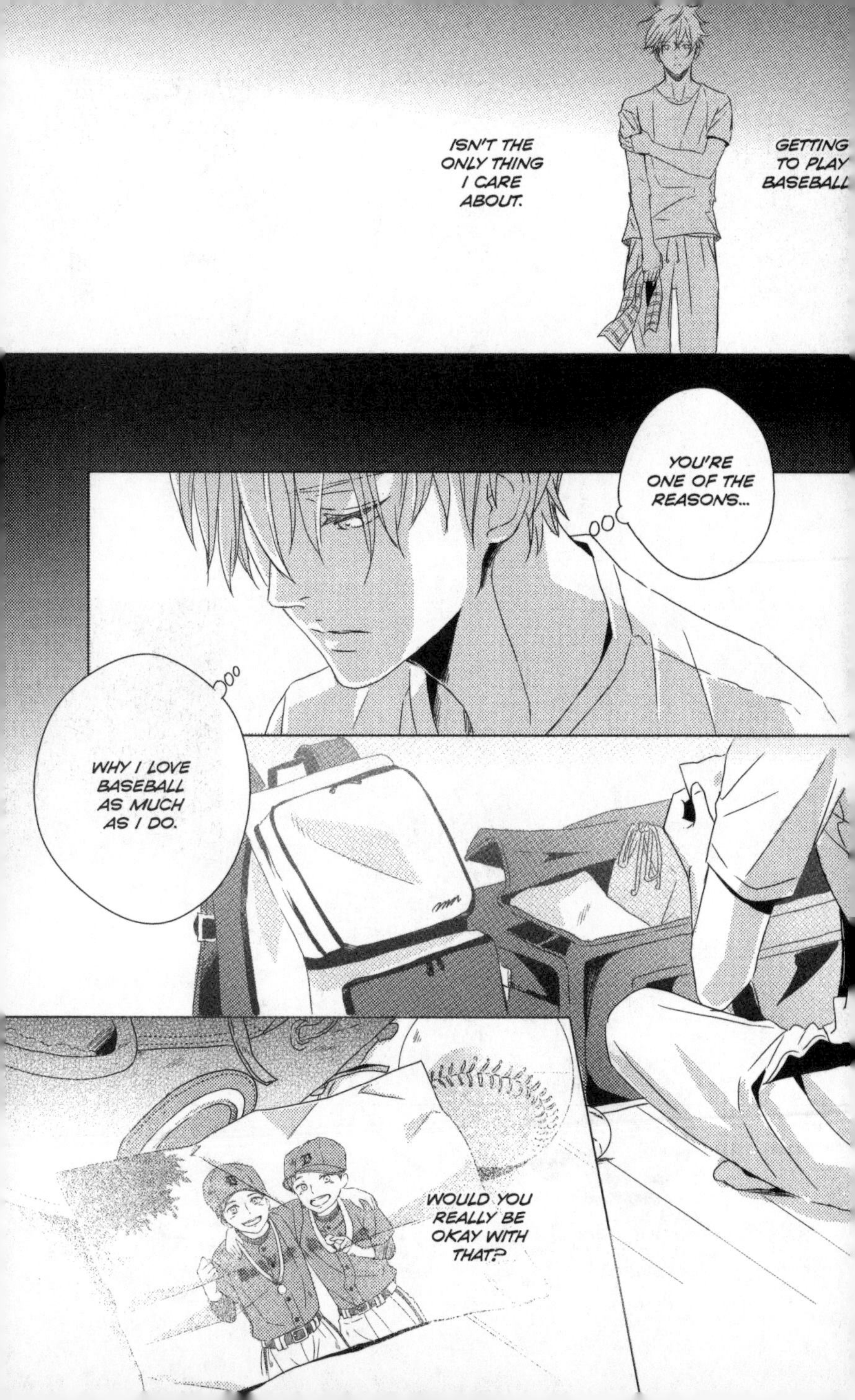
GETTING TO PLAY BASEBALL
ISN'T THE ONLY THING I CARE ABOUT.
YOU'RE ONE OF THE REASONS...
WHY I LOVE BASEBALL AS MUCH AS I DO.
WOULD YOU REALLY BE OKAY WITH THAT?

KINSHOU*

NAME: RITSU MASHINO

DATE OF BIRTH: APRIL 11, 2001

FUJIMI 1-

ER 10TH 1

OF

DRIVER'S LICENSE

240   ISSUED

番号  NUMBER:#30
二·小·原  MOTORCYCLES
他  VEHICLE/MOPE
OTHER
二種  SECOND KIND

TOKYO PUBLIC
SAFETY COMMISSION

*IN SHOGI, THE "GOLD GENERAL"

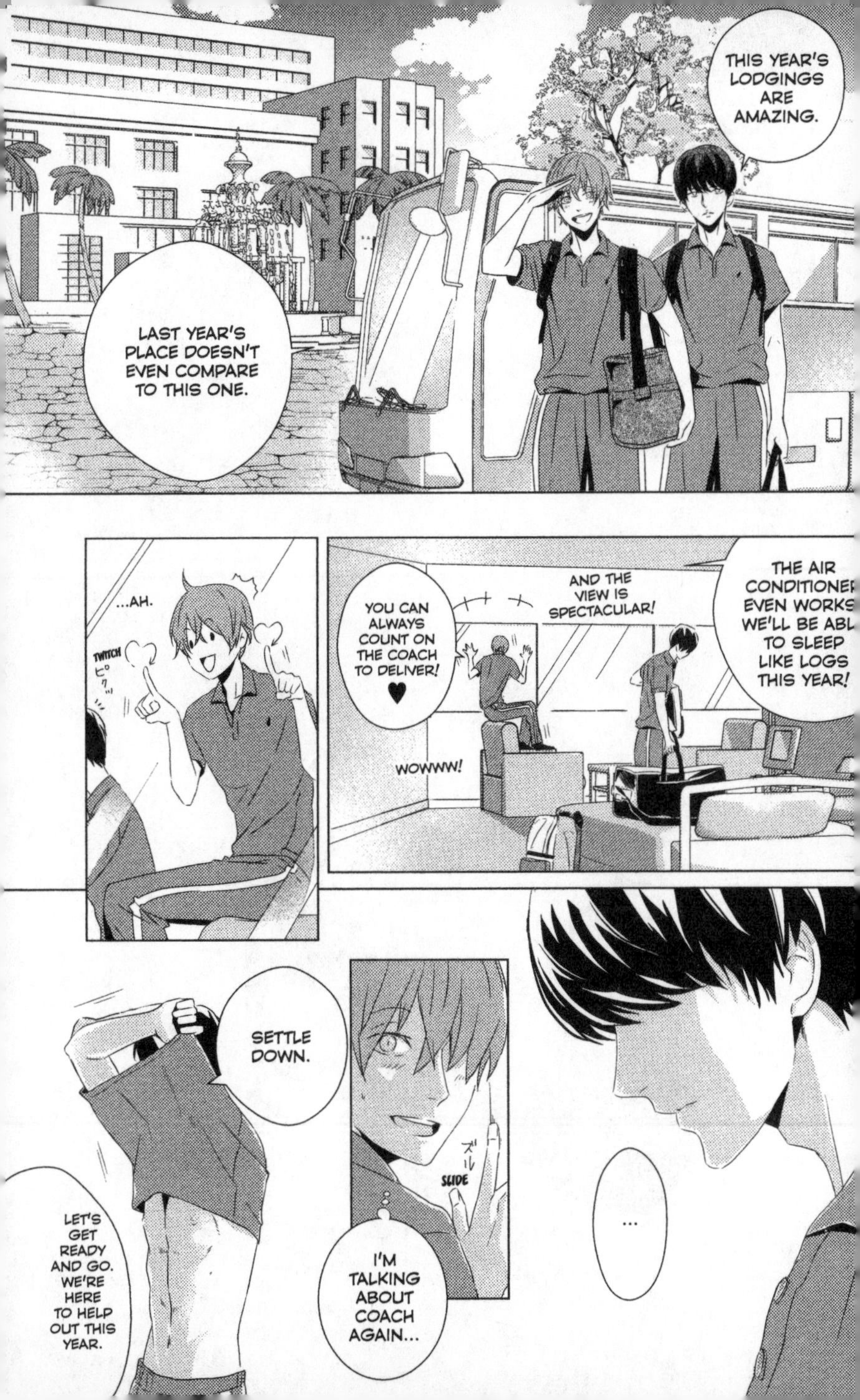
THIS YEAR'S LODGINGS ARE AMAZING.
LAST YEAR'S PLACE DOESN'T EVEN COMPARE TO THIS ONE.
THE AIR CONDITIONER EVEN WORKS WE'LL BE ABL TO SLEEP LIKE LOGS THIS YEAR!
AND THE VIEW IS SPECTACULAR!
YOU CAN ALWAYS COUNT ON THE COACH TO DELIVER! ♥
WOWWW!
...AH.
TWITCH
ピクッ
...
ズル
SLIDE
I'M TALKING ABOUT COACH AGAIN...
SETTLE DOWN.
LET'S GET READY AND GO. WE'RE HERE TO HELP OUT THIS YEAR.

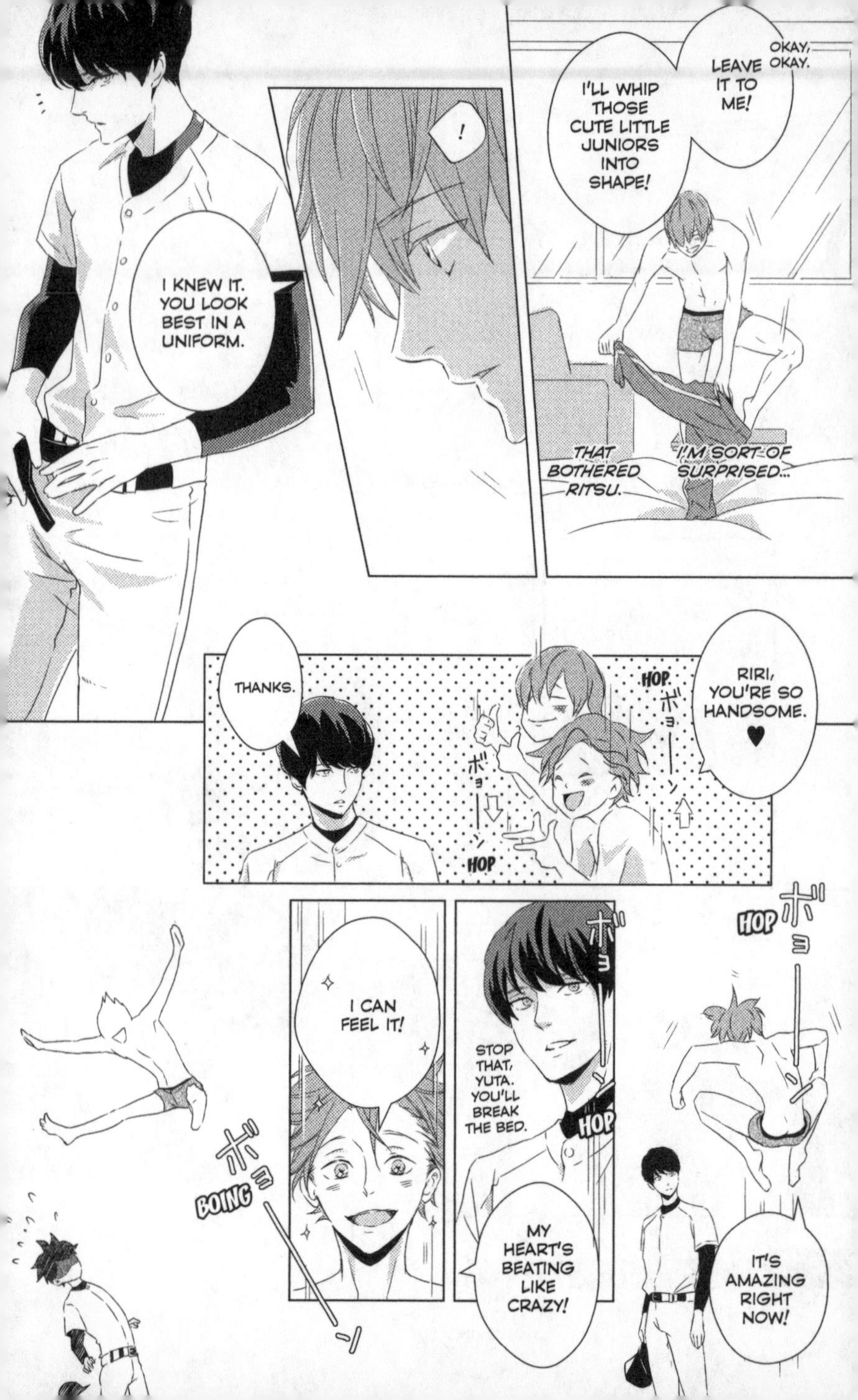
OKAY, OKAY. LEAVE IT TO ME!
I'LL WHIP THOSE CUTE LITTLE JUNIORS INTO SHAPE!
I'M SORT OF SURPRISED...
THAT BOTHERED RITSU.
!
I KNEW IT. YOU LOOK BEST IN A UNIFORM.
RIRI, YOU'RE SO HANDSOME. ♥
HOP
ボョーン
HOP
ボョン
THANKS.
HOP
ボョ
IT'S AMAZING RIGHT NOW!
ボョ
STOP THAT, YUTA. YOU'LL BREAK THE BED.
HOP
MY HEART'S BEATING LIKE CRAZY!
I CAN FEEL IT!
ボョ
BOING
ーン

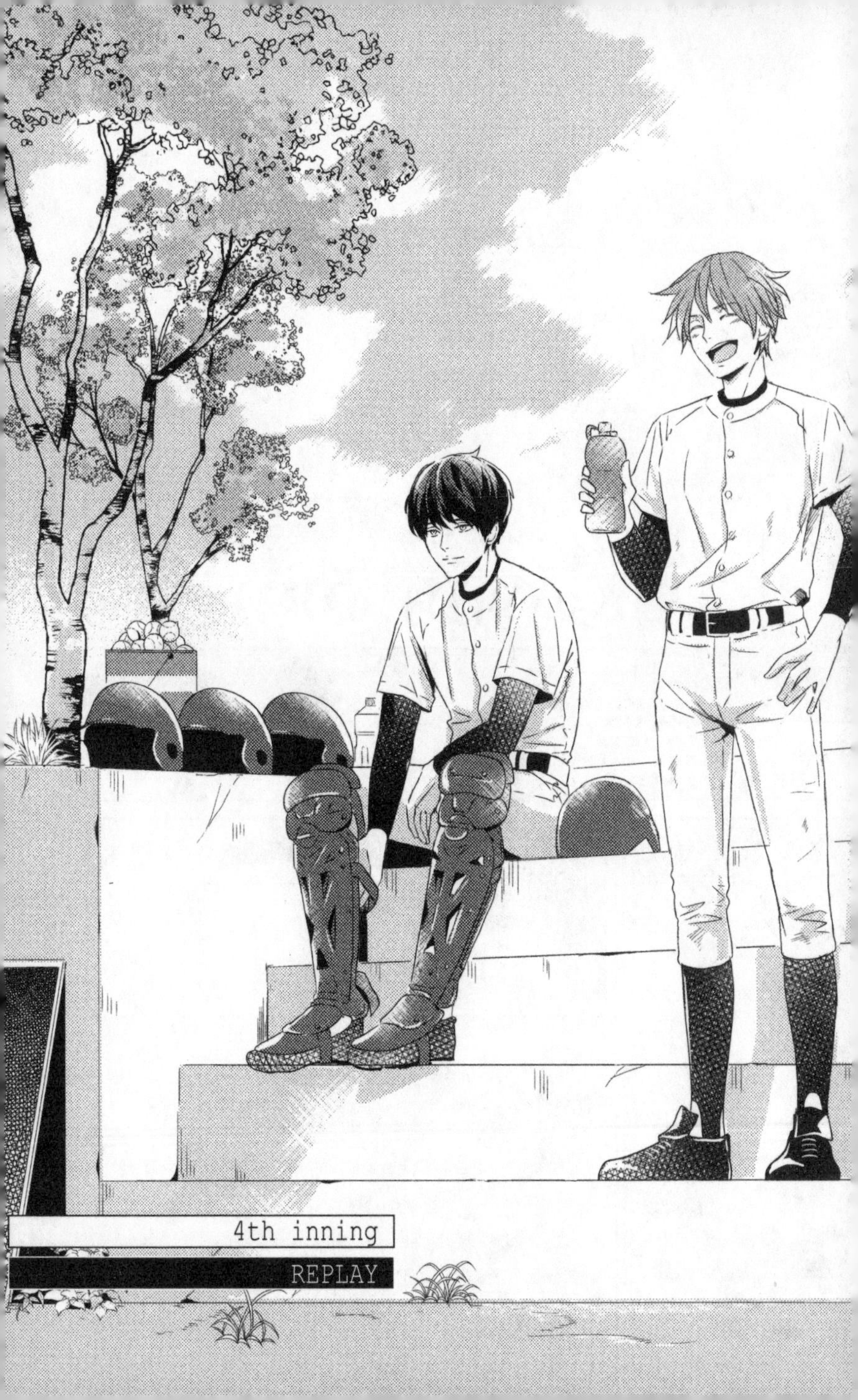
4th inning
REPLAY

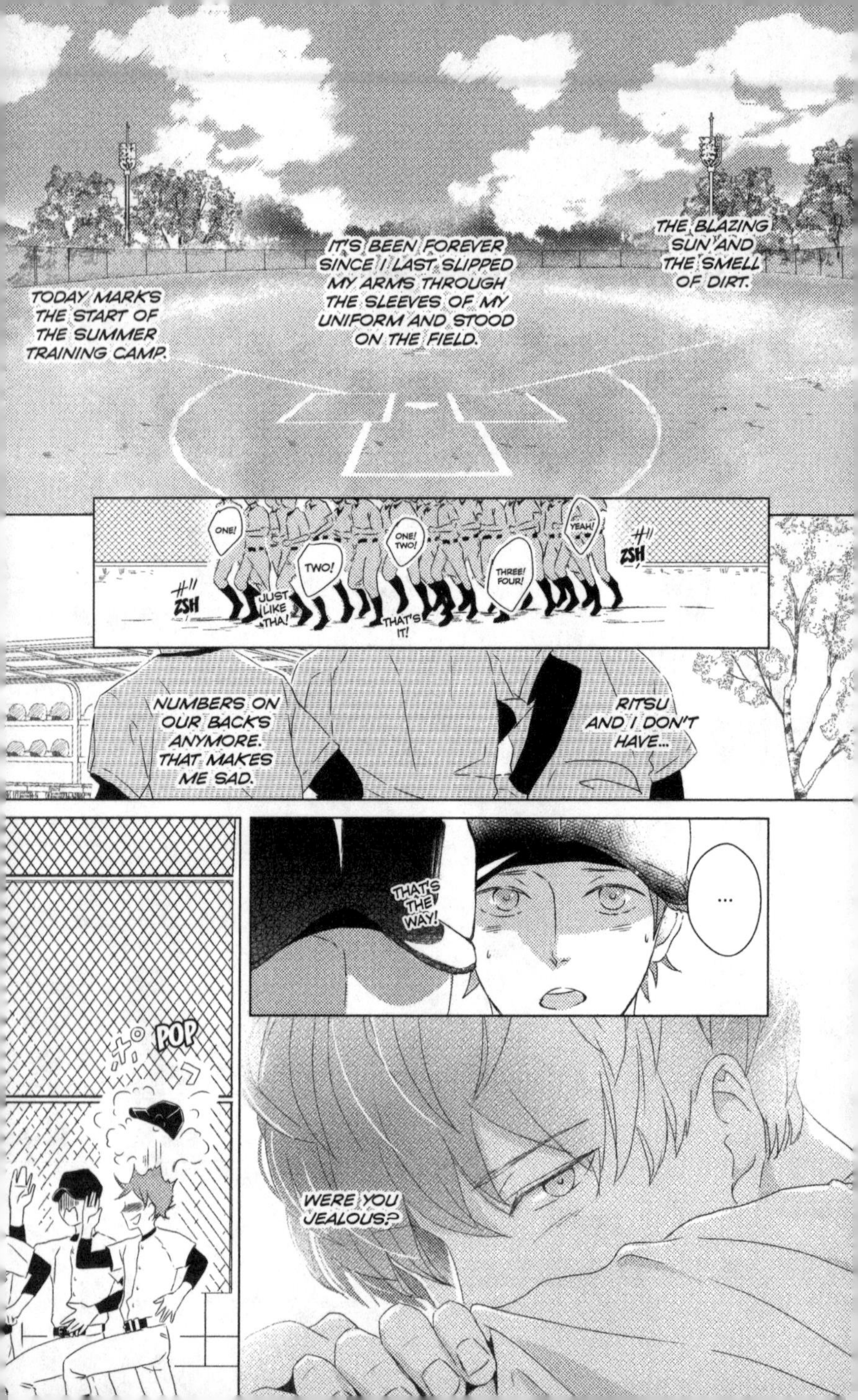
THE BLAZING SUN AND THE SMELL OF DIRT.
IT'S BEEN FOREVER SINCE I LAST SLIPPED MY ARMS THROUGH THE SLEEVES OF MY UNIFORM AND STOOD ON THE FIELD.
TODAY MARKS THE START OF THE SUMMER TRAINING CAMP.
ZSH
YEAH!
THREE! FOUR!
ONE! TWO!
THAT'S IT!
TWO!
JUST LIKE THA!
ONE!
ZSH
RITSU AND I DON'T HAVE...
NUMBERS ON OUR BACKS ANYMORE. THAT MAKES ME SAD.
...
THAT'S THE WAY!
WERE YOU JEALOUS?
POP

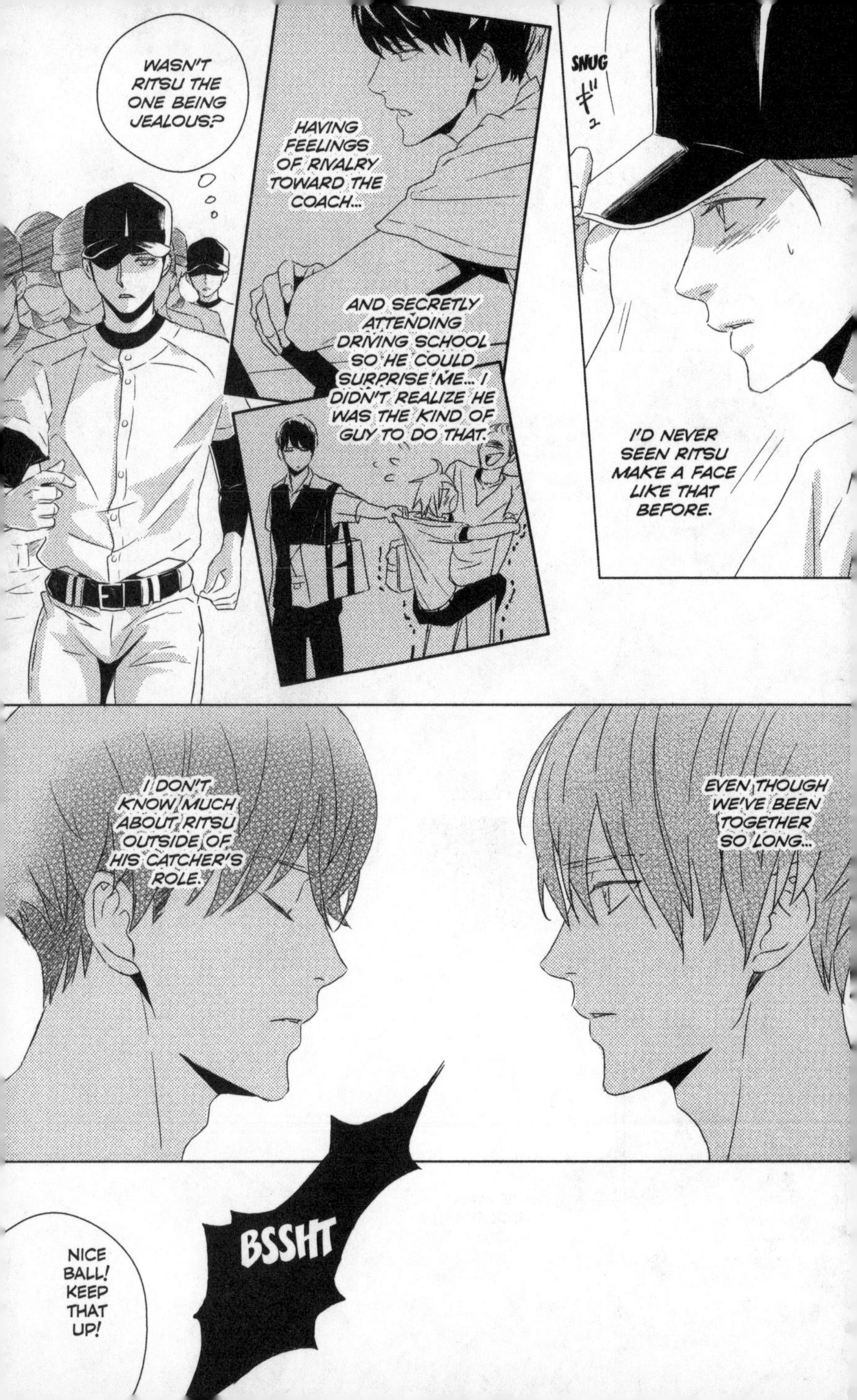
SNUG
I'D NEVER SEEN RITSU MAKE A FACE LIKE THAT BEFORE.
HAVING FEELINGS OF RIVALRY TOWARD THE COACH...
AND SECRETLY ATTENDING DRIVING SCHOOL SO HE COULD SURPRISE ME... I DIDN'T REALIZE HE WAS THE KIND OF GUY TO DO THAT.
WASN'T RITSU THE ONE BEING JEALOUS?
EVEN THOUGH WE'VE BEEN TOGETHER SO LONG...
I DON'T KNOW MUCH ABOUT RITSU OUTSIDE OF HIS CATCHER'S ROLE.
BSSHT
NICE BALL! KEEP THAT UP!

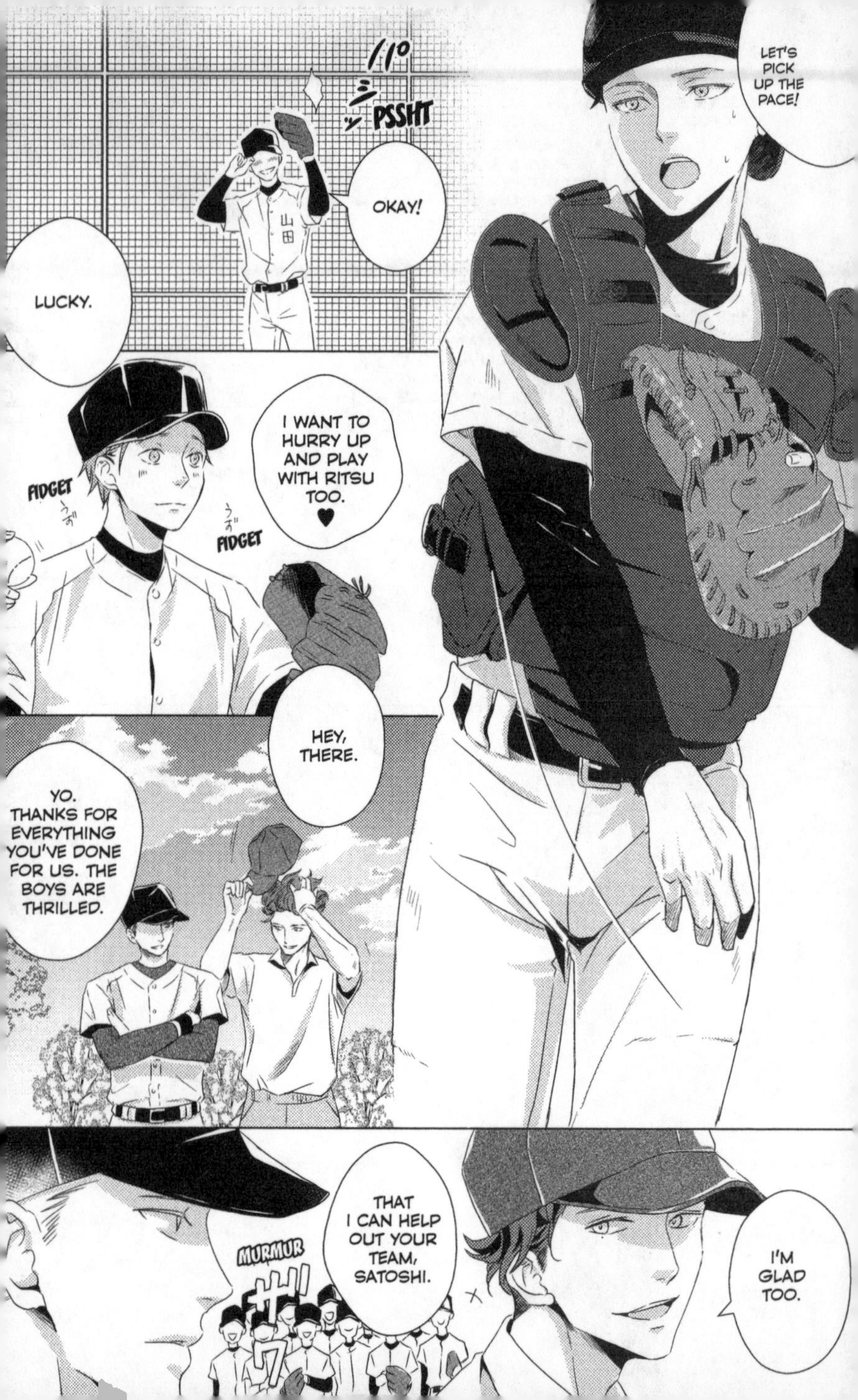
LET'S PICK UP THE PACE!
PSSHT
OKAY!
LUCKY.
I WANT TO HURRY UP AND PLAY WITH RITSU TOO. ♥
FIDGET
FIDGET
HEY, THERE.
YO. THANKS FOR EVERYTHING YOU'VE DONE FOR US. THE BOYS ARE THRILLED.
I'M GLAD TOO.
THAT I CAN HELP OUT YOUR TEAM, SATOSHI.
MURMUR

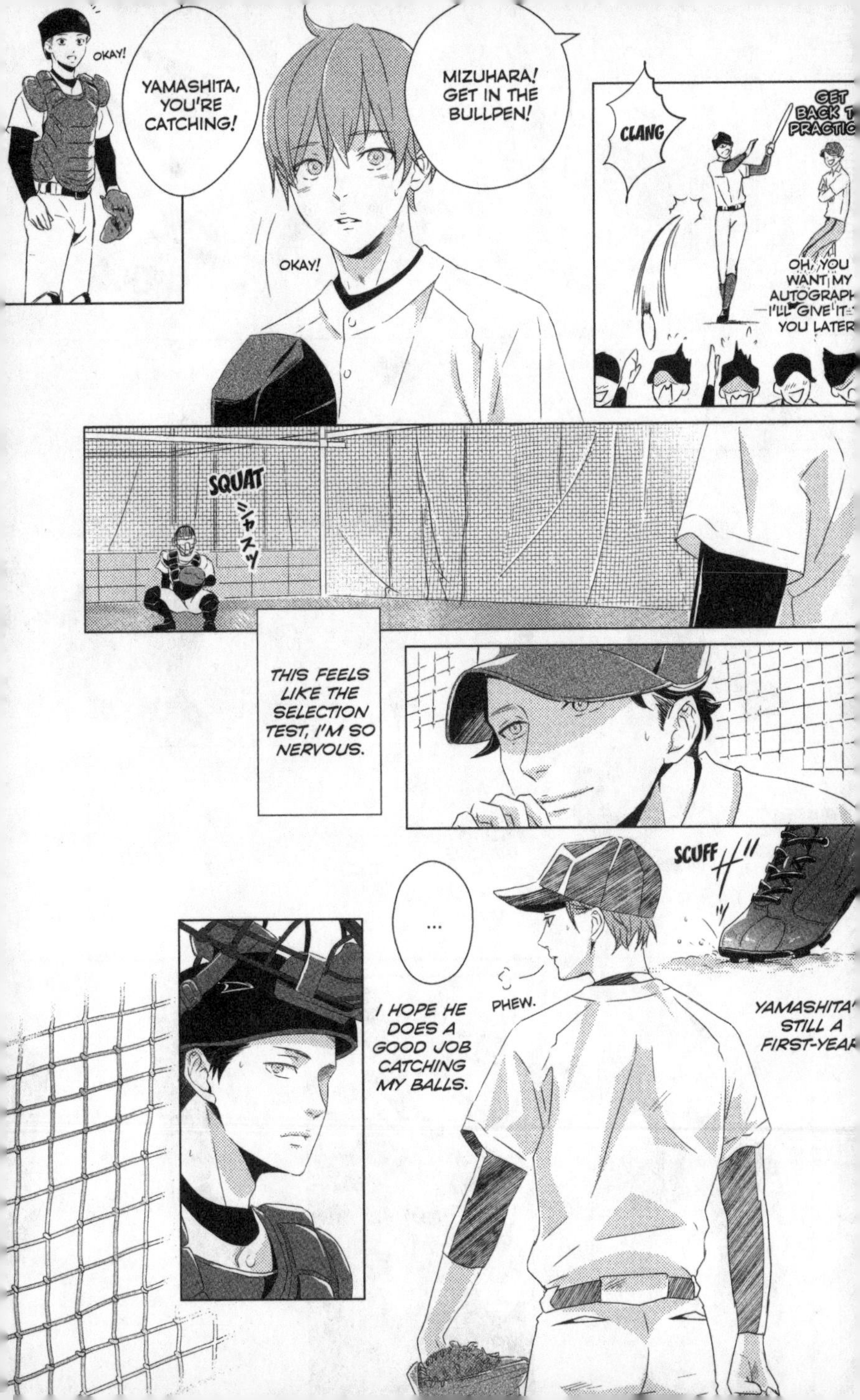
CLANG
GET BACK T PRACTIC
OH, YOU WANT MY AUTOGRAPH I'LL GIVE IT T YOU LATER
MIZUHARA! GET IN THE BULLPEN!
OKAY!
YAMASHITA, YOU'RE CATCHING!
OKAY!
SQUAT
シャスッ
THIS FEELS LIKE THE SELECTION TEST, I'M SO NERVOUS.
SCUFF
YAMASHITA' STILL A FIRST-YEAR
...
PHEW.
I HOPE HE DOES A GOOD JOB CATCHING MY BALLS.

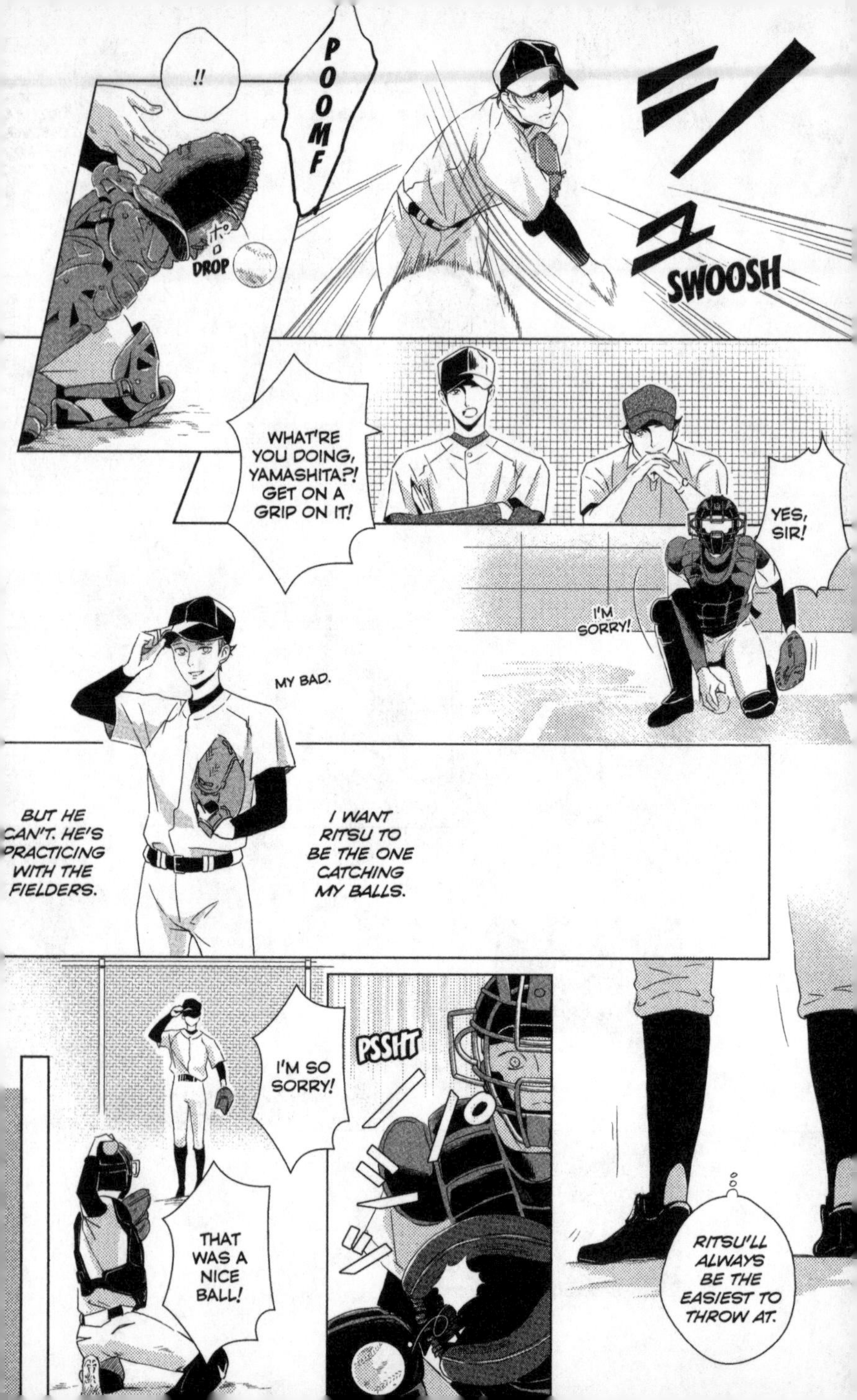
SWOOSH
POOMF
!!
DROP
WHAT'RE YOU DOING, YAMASHITA?! GET ON A GRIP ON IT!
YES, SIR!
I'M SORRY!
MY BAD.
I WANT RITSU TO BE THE ONE CATCHING MY BALLS.
BUT HE CAN'T. HE'S PRACTICING WITH THE FIELDERS.
RITSU'LL ALWAYS BE THE EASIEST TO THROW AT.
PSSHT
I'M SO SORRY!
THAT WAS A NICE BALL!

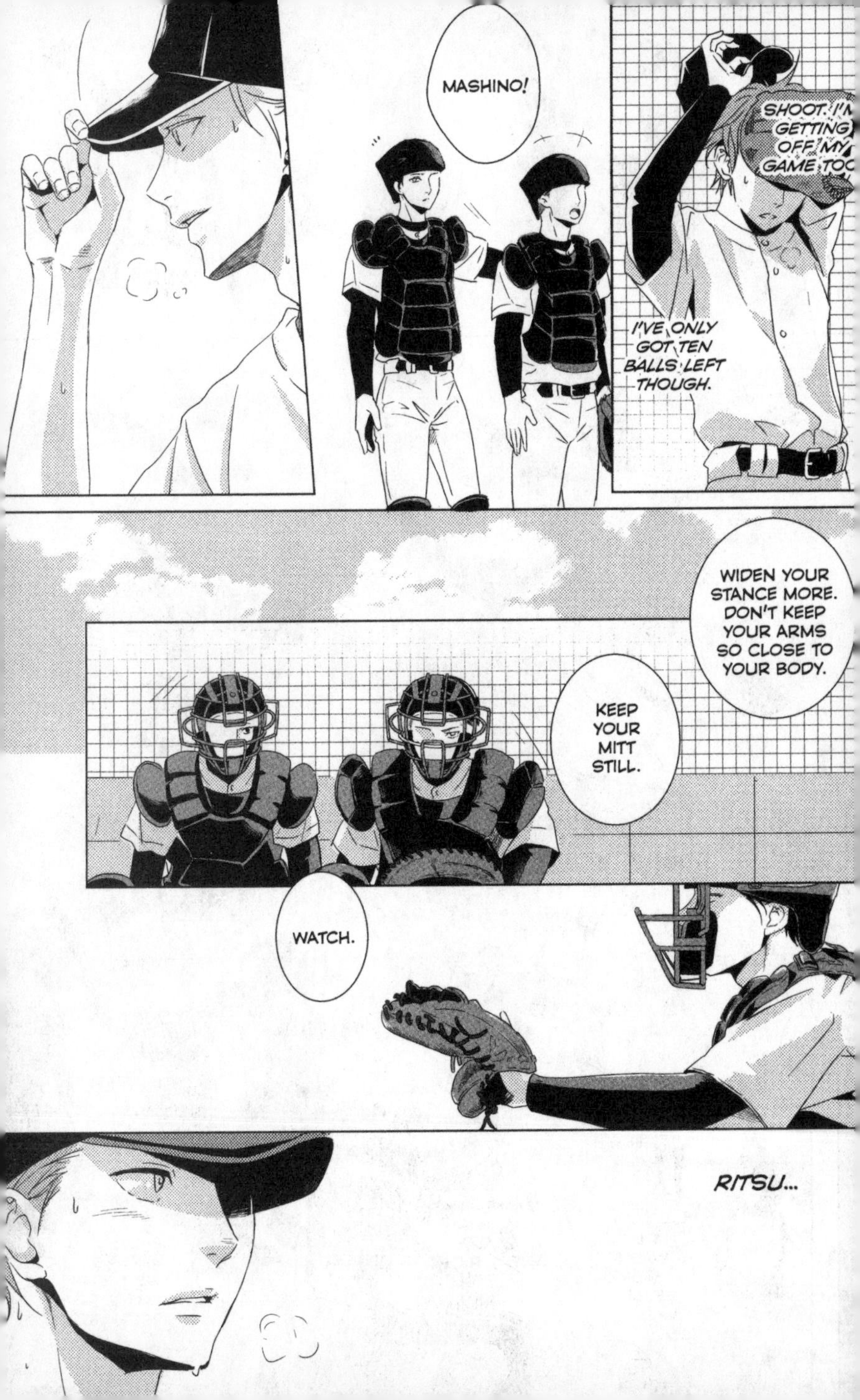
SHOOT. I'M GETTING OFF MY GAME TOO
I'VE ONLY GOT TEN BALLS LEFT THOUGH.
MASHINO!
WIDEN YOUR STANCE MORE. DON'T KEEP YOUR ARMS SO CLOSE TO YOUR BODY.
KEEP YOUR MITT STILL.
WATCH.
RITSU...

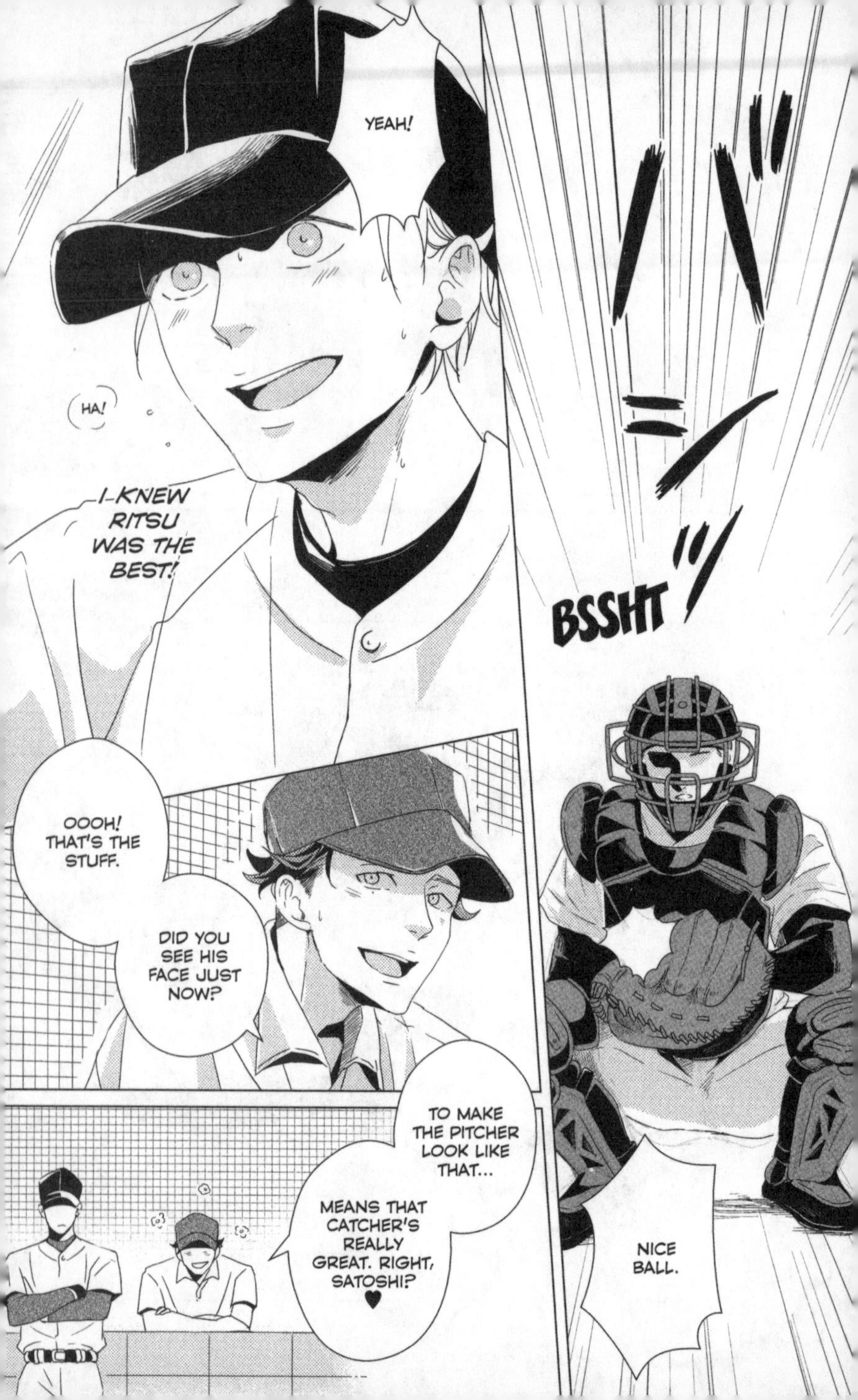

バシッ
BSSHT
NICE BALL.
YEAH!
HA!
I KNEW RITSU WAS THE BEST!
OOOH! THAT'S THE STUFF.
DID YOU SEE HIS FACE JUST NOW?
TO MAKE THE PITCHER LOOK LIKE THAT...
MEANS THAT CATCHER'S REALLY GREAT. RIGHT, SATOSHI? ♥

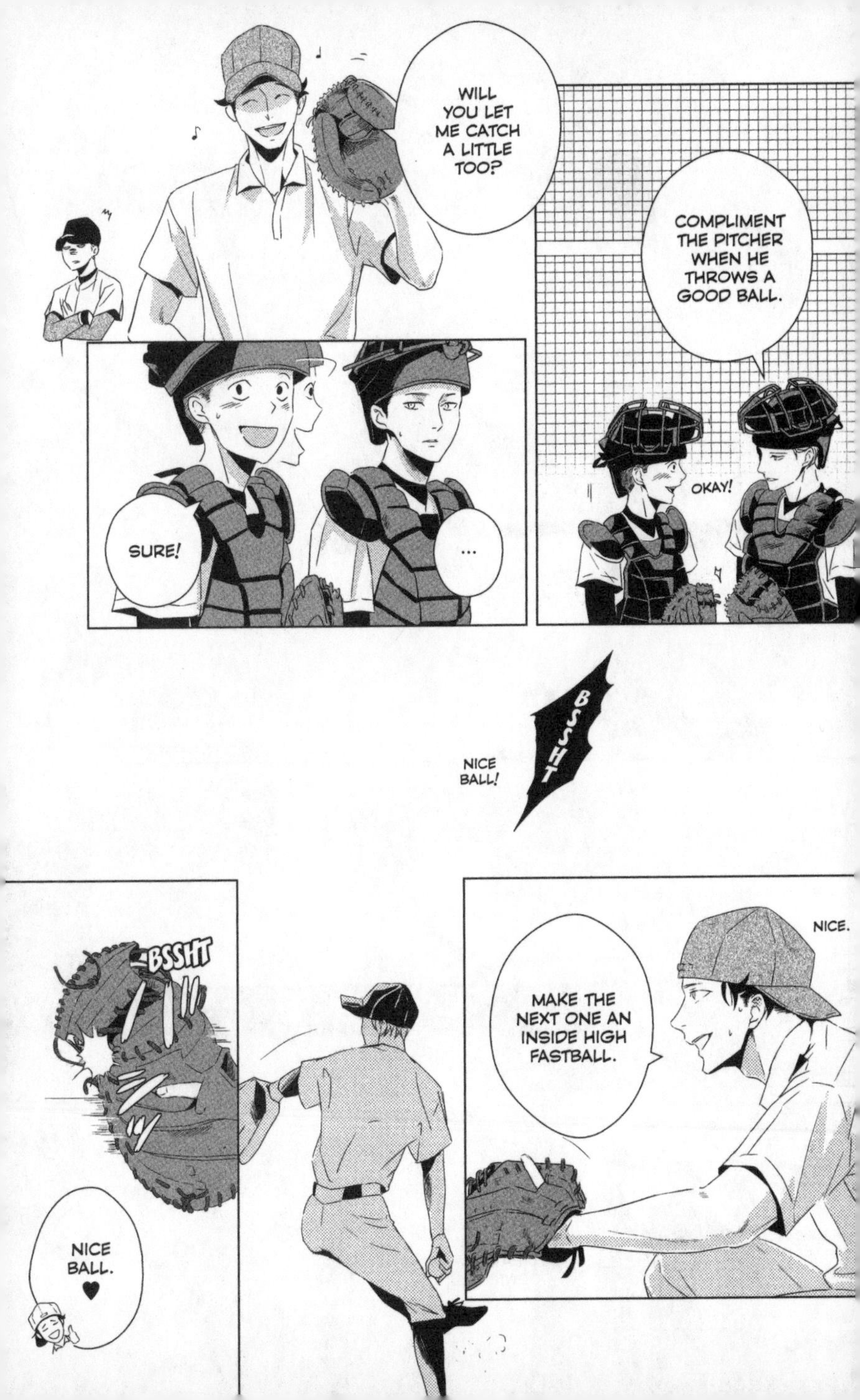
COMPLIMENT THE PITCHER WHEN HE THROWS A GOOD BALL.
OKAY!
WILL YOU LET ME CATCH A LITTLE TOO?
SURE!
...
BSSHT
NICE BALL!
NICE.
MAKE THE NEXT ONE AN INSIDE HIGH FASTBALL.
BSSHT
NICE BALL. ♥

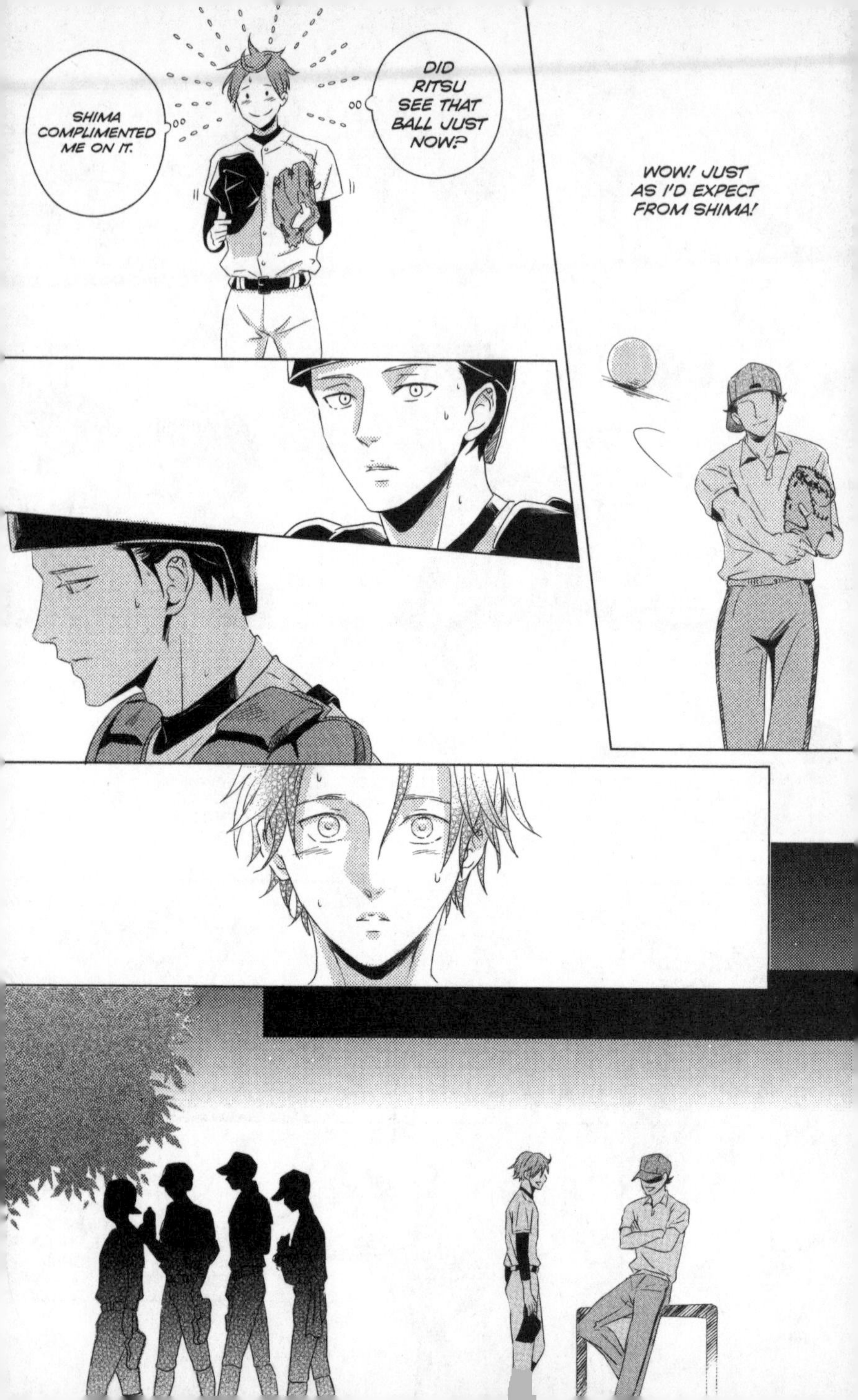
WOW! JUST AS I'D EXPECT FROM SHIMA!
DID RITSU SEE THAT BALL JUST NOW?
SHIMA COMPLIMENTED ME ON IT.

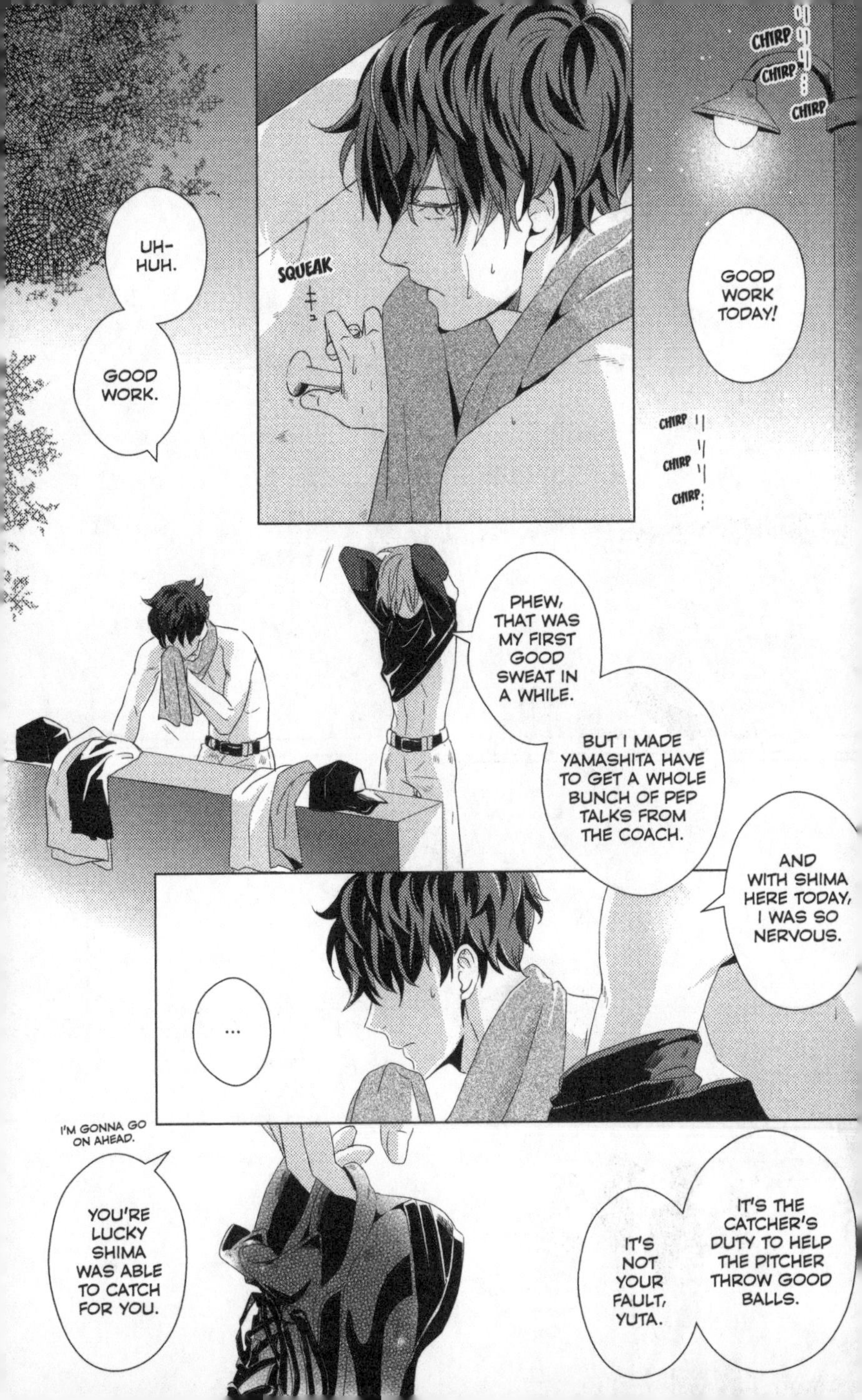
CHIRP
CHIRP
CHIRP
GOOD WORK TODAY!
CHIRP
CHIRP
CHIRP
SQUEAK
UH-HUH.
GOOD WORK.
PHEW, THAT WAS MY FIRST GOOD SWEAT IN A WHILE.
BUT I MADE YAMASHITA HAVE TO GET A WHOLE BUNCH OF PEP TALKS FROM THE COACH.
AND WITH SHIMA HERE TODAY, I WAS SO NERVOUS.
...
IT'S THE CATCHER'S DUTY TO HELP THE PITCHER THROW GOOD BALLS.
IT'S NOT YOUR FAULT, YUTA.
I'M GONNA GO ON AHEAD.
YOU'RE LUCKY SHIMA WAS ABLE TO CATCH FOR YOU.

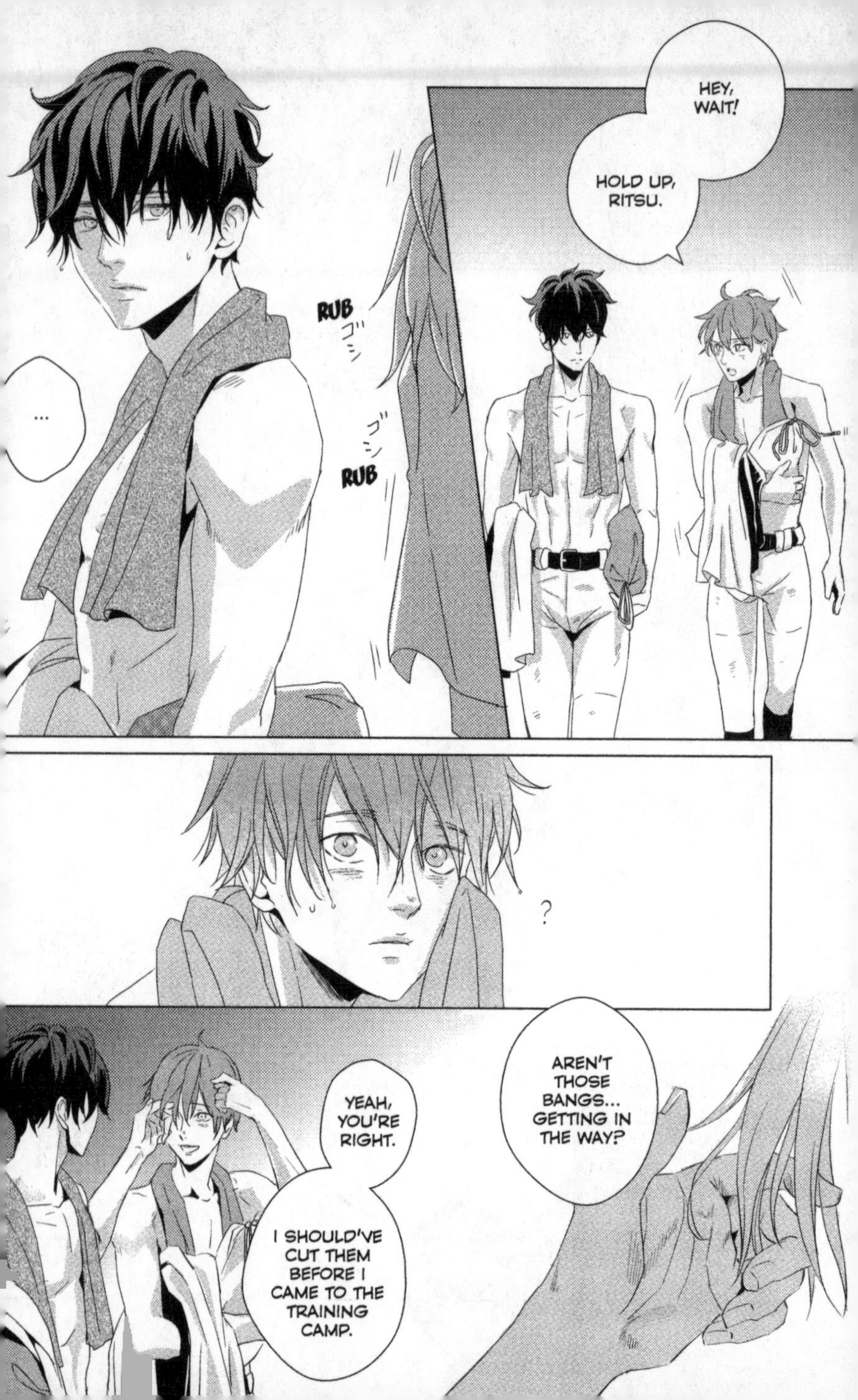
HEY, WAIT!
HOLD UP, RITSU.
RUB ゴシ
ゴシ RUB
...
?
AREN'T THOSE BANGS... GETTING IN THE WAY?
YEAH, YOU'RE RIGHT.
I SHOULD'VE CUT THEM BEFORE I CAME TO THE TRAINING CAMP.

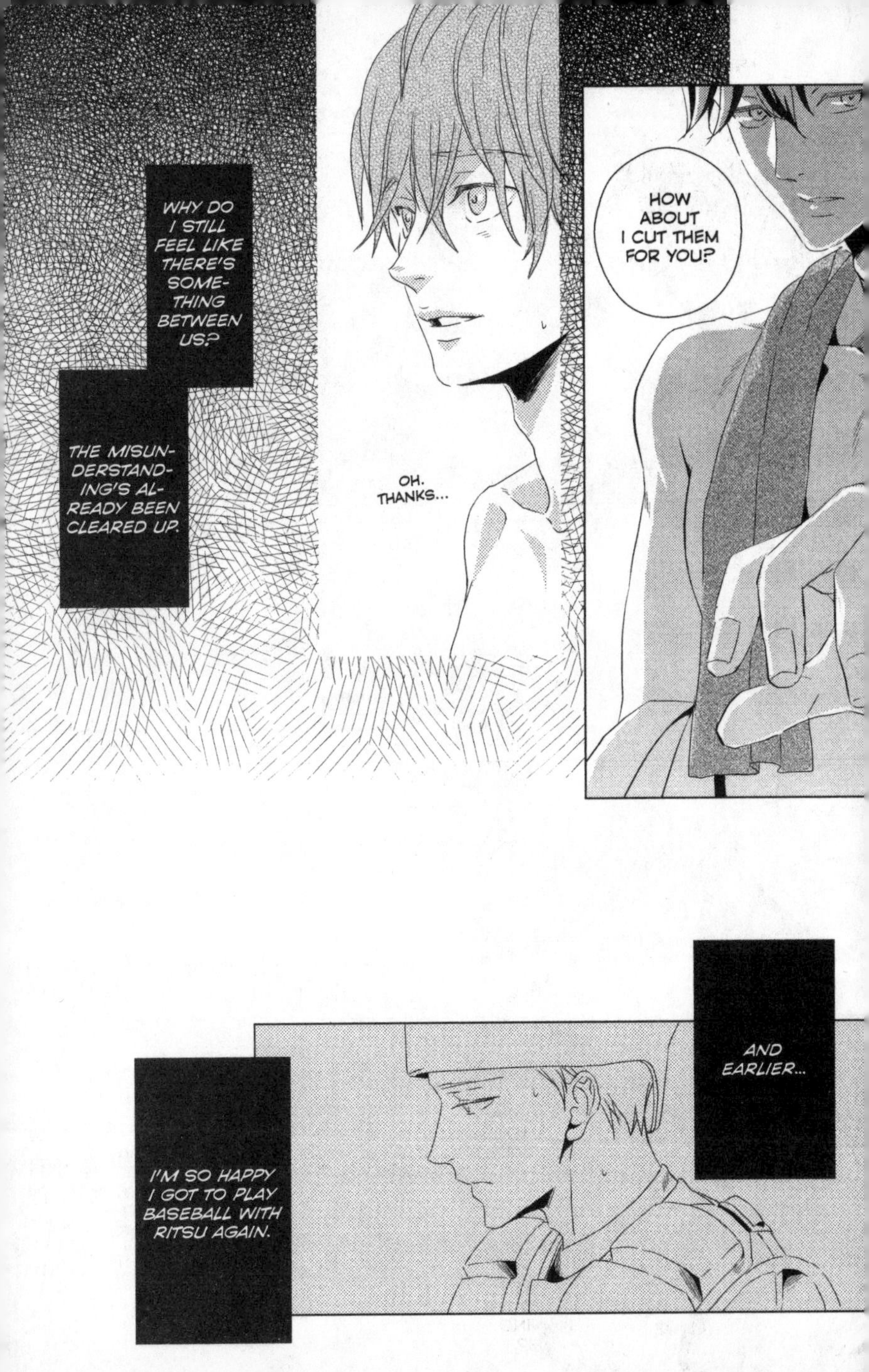
HOW ABOUT I CUT THEM FOR YOU?
OH. THANKS...
WHY DO I STILL FEEL LIKE THERE'S SOME-THING BETWEEN US?
THE MISUN-DERSTAND-ING'S AL-READY BEEN CLEARED UP.
AND EARLIER...
I'M SO HAPPY I GOT TO PLAY BASEBALL WITH RITSU AGAIN.

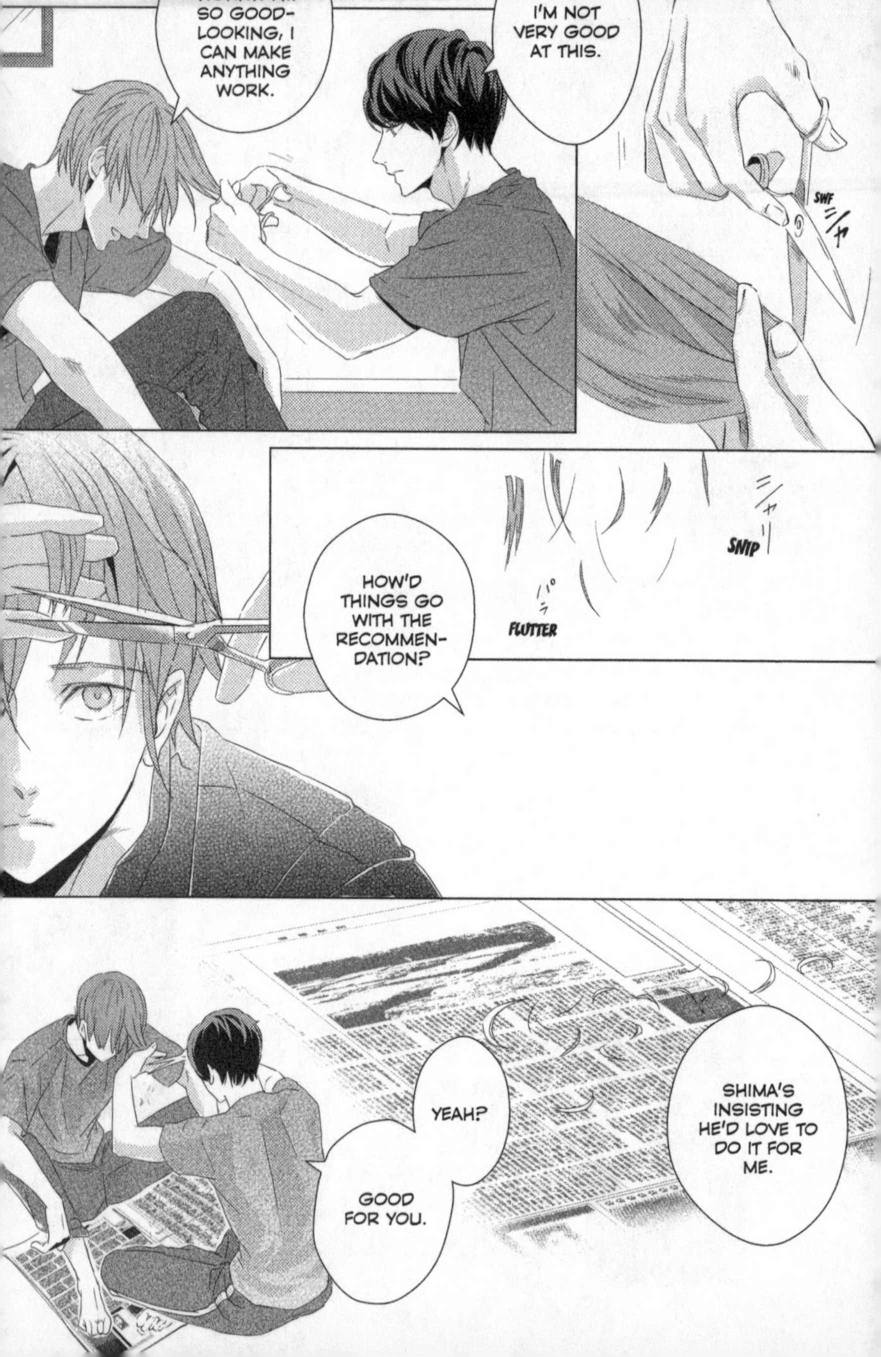
SWF
I'M NOT VERY GOOD AT THIS.
DON'T WORRY. I'M SO GOOD-LOOKING, I CAN MAKE ANYTHING WORK.
SNIP
FLUTTER
HOW'D THINGS GO WITH THE RECOMMEN-DATION?
SHIMA'S INSISTING HE'D LOVE TO DO IT FOR ME.
YEAH?
GOOD FOR YOU.

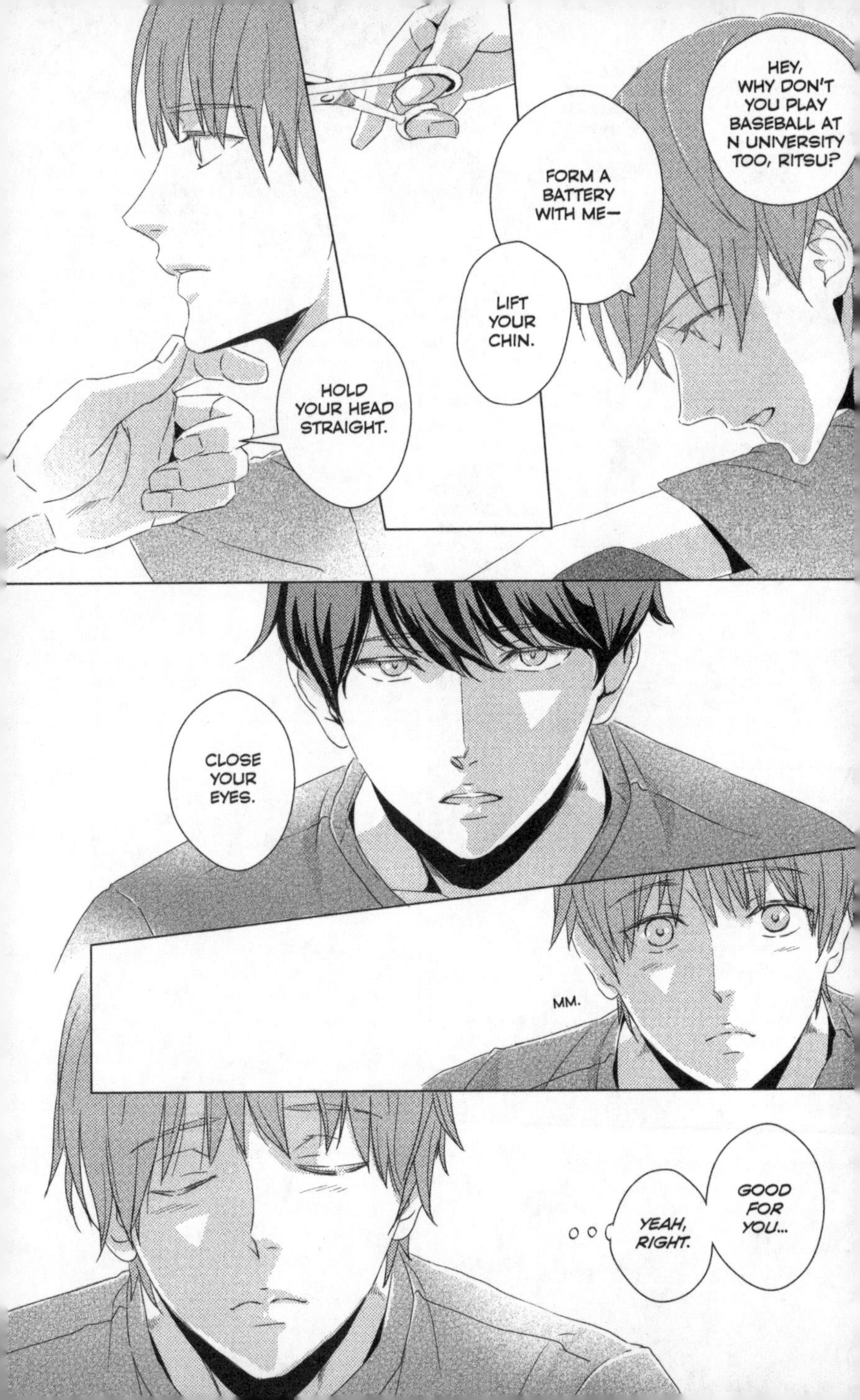
HEY, WHY DON'T YOU PLAY BASEBALL AT N UNIVERSITY TOO, RITSU?
FORM A BATTERY WITH ME—
LIFT YOUR CHIN.
HOLD YOUR HEAD STRAIGHT.
CLOSE YOUR EYES.
MM.
GOOD FOR YOU...
YEAH, RIGHT.

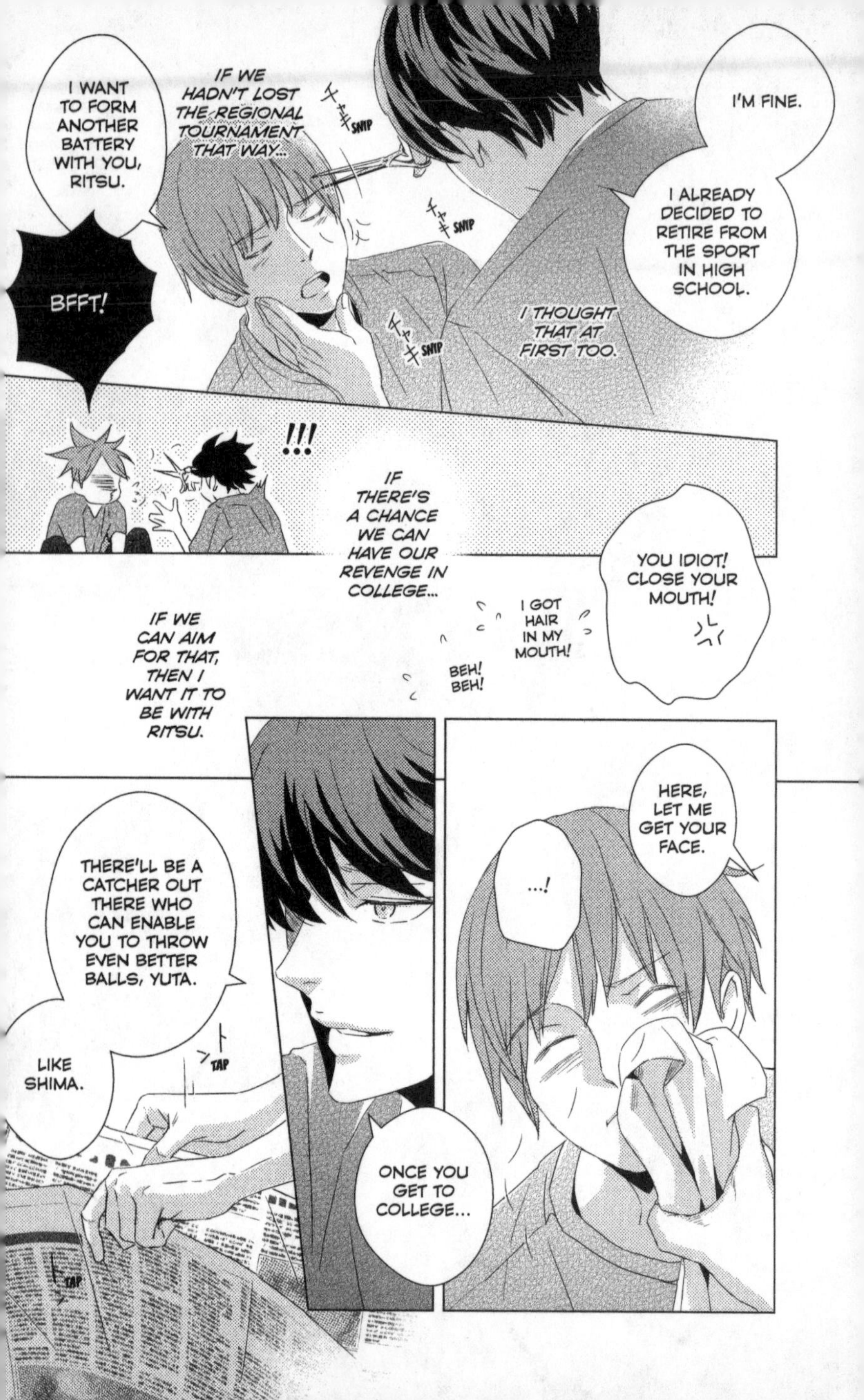
I'M FINE.
I ALREADY DECIDED TO RETIRE FROM THE SPORT IN HIGH SCHOOL.
I THOUGHT THAT AT FIRST TOO.
SNIP
SNIP
SNIP
IF WE HADN'T LOST THE REGIONAL TOURNAMENT THAT WAY...
I WANT TO FORM ANOTHER BATTERY WITH YOU, RITSU.
BFFT!
YOU IDIOT! CLOSE YOUR MOUTH!
I GOT HAIR IN MY MOUTH!
BEH! BEH!
IF THERE'S A CHANCE WE CAN HAVE OUR REVENGE IN COLLEGE...
!!!
IF WE CAN AIM FOR THAT, THEN I WANT IT TO BE WITH RITSU.
HERE, LET ME GET YOUR FACE.
...!
ONCE YOU GET TO COLLEGE...
THERE'LL BE A CATCHER OUT THERE WHO CAN ENABLE YOU TO THROW EVEN BETTER BALLS, YUTA.
TAP
LIKE SHIMA.
TAP

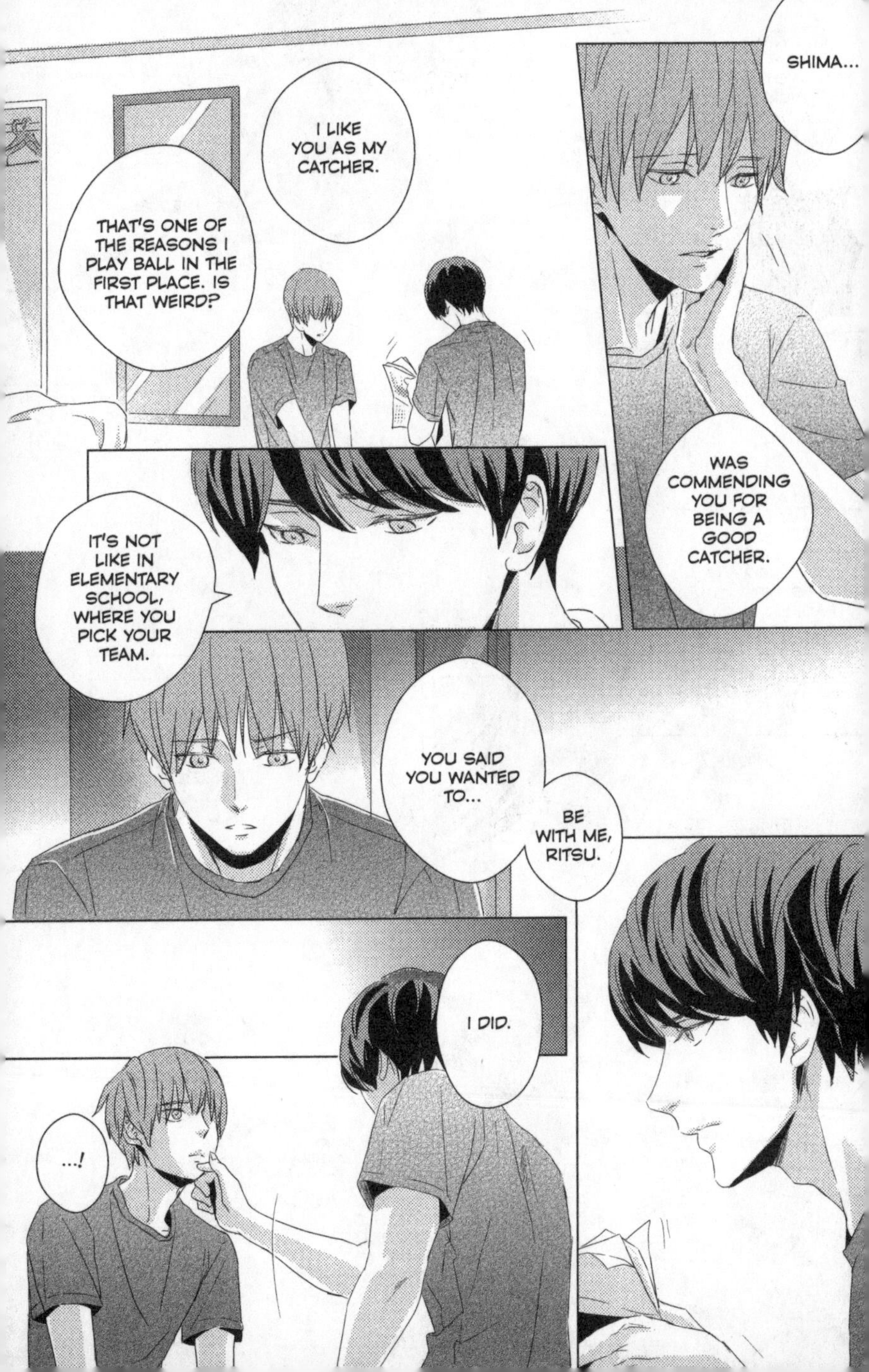
SHIMA...
WAS COMMENDING YOU FOR BEING A GOOD CATCHER.
I LIKE YOU AS MY CATCHER.
THAT'S ONE OF THE REASONS I PLAY BALL IN THE FIRST PLACE. IS THAT WEIRD?
IT'S NOT LIKE IN ELEMENTARY SCHOOL, WHERE YOU PICK YOUR TEAM.
YOU SAID YOU WANTED TO...
BE WITH ME, RITSU.
I DID.
...!

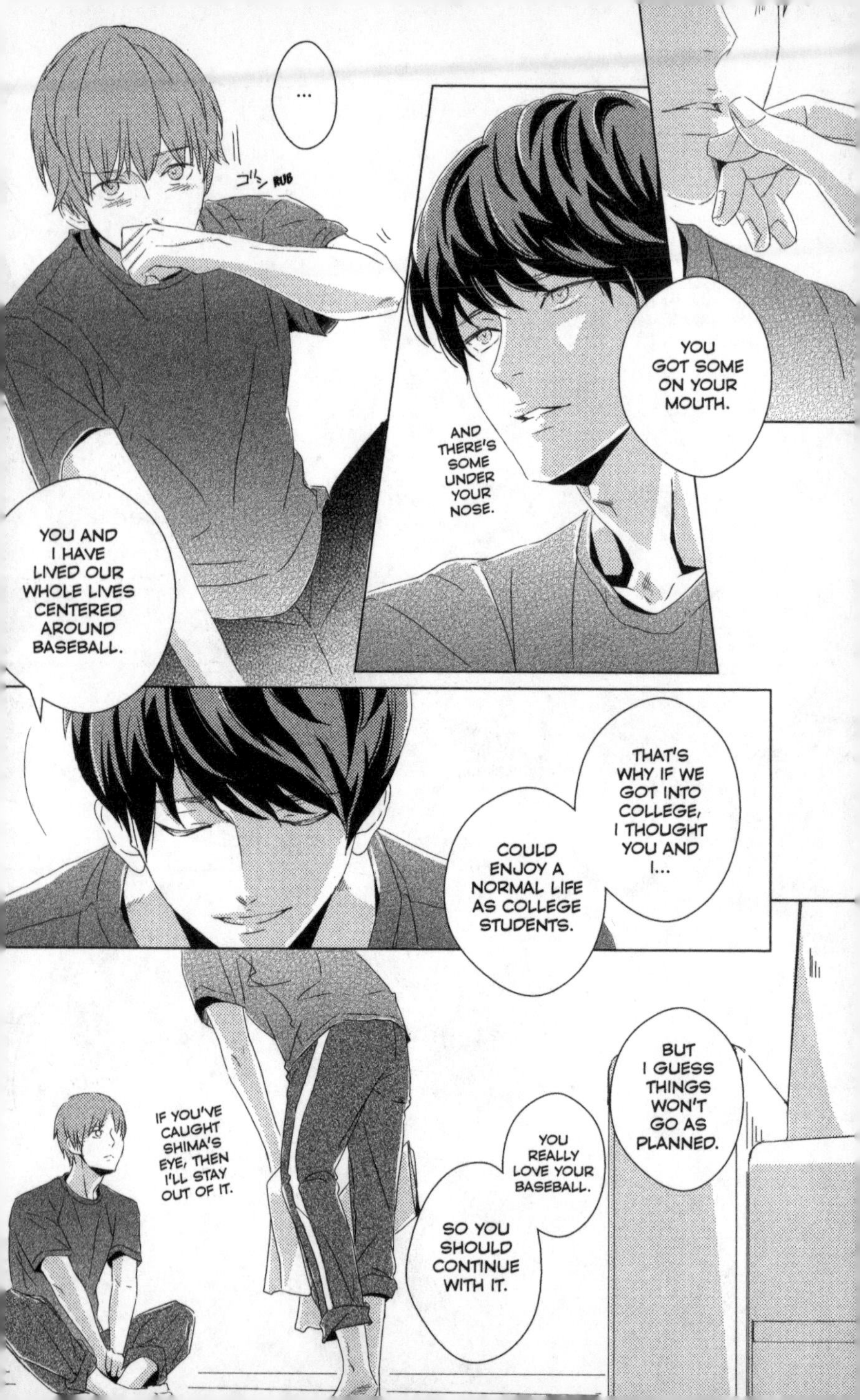
YOU GOT SOME ON YOUR MOUTH.
AND THERE'S SOME UNDER YOUR NOSE.
...
ゴシ RUB
YOU AND I HAVE LIVED OUR WHOLE LIVES CENTERED AROUND BASEBALL.
THAT'S WHY IF WE GOT INTO COLLEGE, I THOUGHT YOU AND I...
COULD ENJOY A NORMAL LIFE AS COLLEGE STUDENTS.
BUT I GUESS THINGS WON'T GO AS PLANNED.
YOU REALLY LOVE YOUR BASEBALL.
SO YOU SHOULD CONTINUE WITH IT.
IF YOU'VE CAUGHT SHIMA'S EYE, THEN I'LL STAY OUT OF IT.

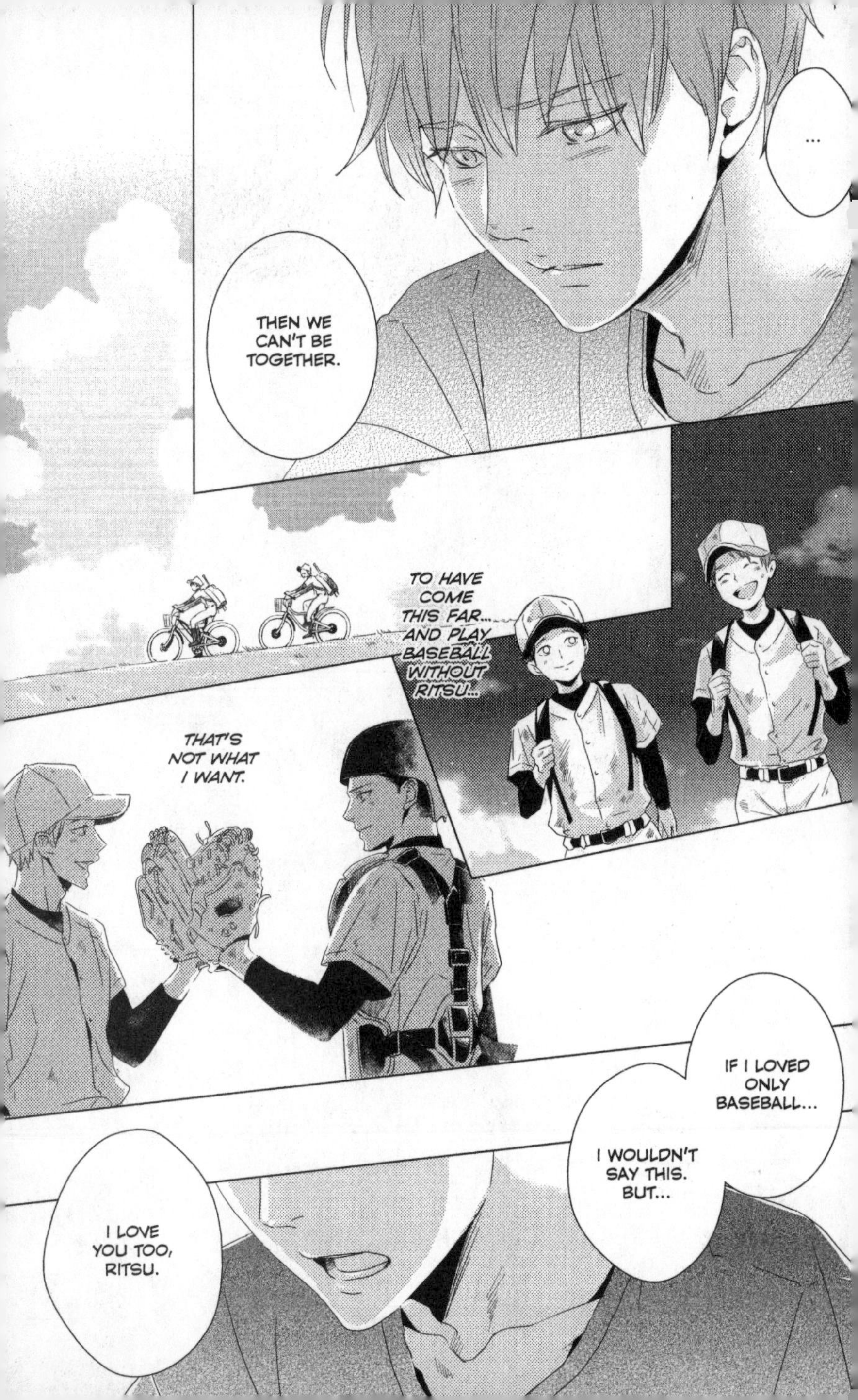
...
THEN WE CAN'T BE TOGETHER.
TO HAVE COME THIS FAR... AND PLAY BASEBALL WITHOUT RITSU...
THAT'S NOT WHAT I WANT.
IF I LOVED ONLY BASEBALL...
I WOULDN'T SAY THIS. BUT...
I LOVE YOU TOO, RITSU.

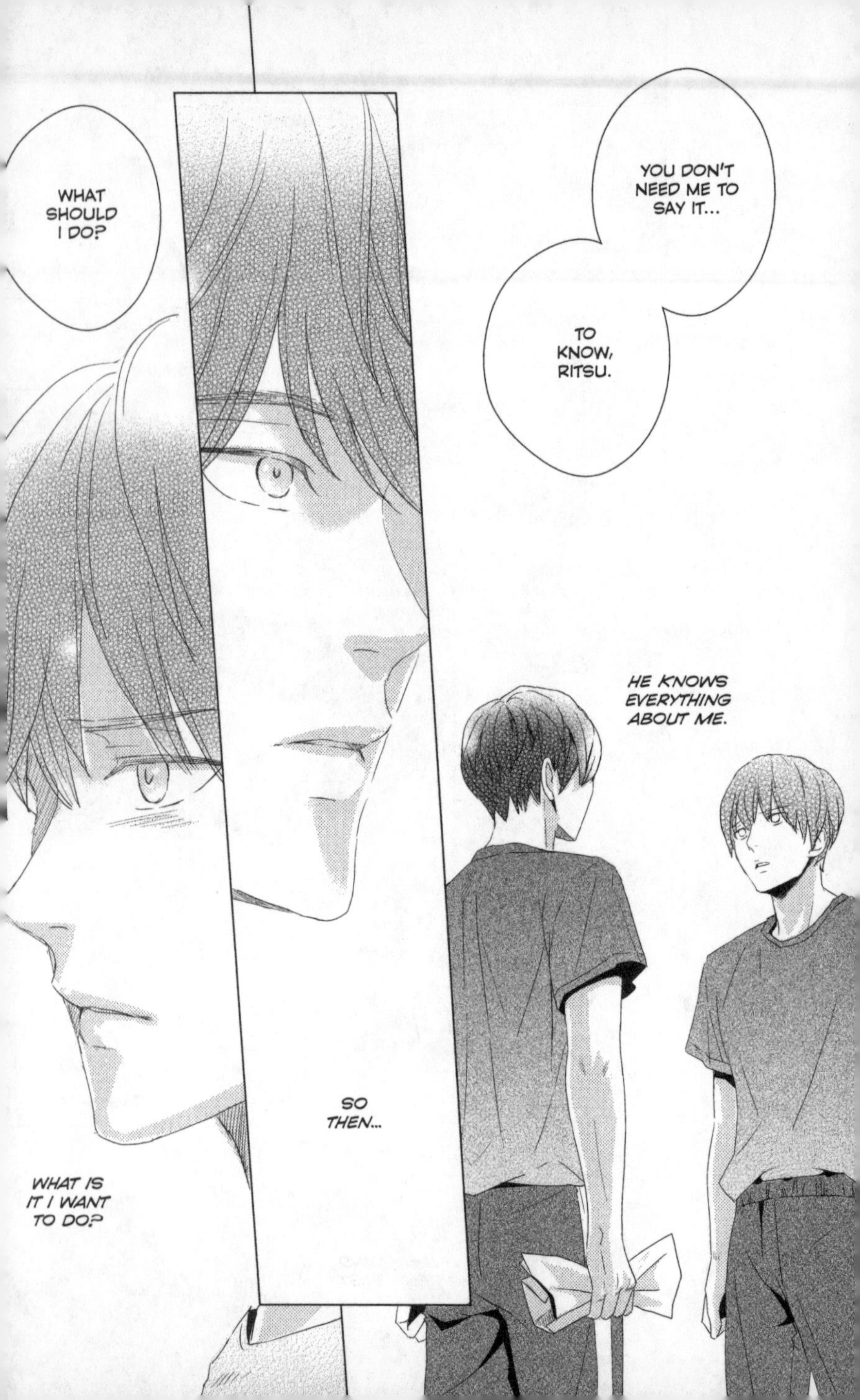
YOU DON'T NEED ME TO SAY IT...
TO KNOW, RITSU.
WHAT SHOULD I DO?
HE KNOWS EVERYTHING ABOUT ME.
SO THEN...
WHAT IS IT I WANT TO DO?

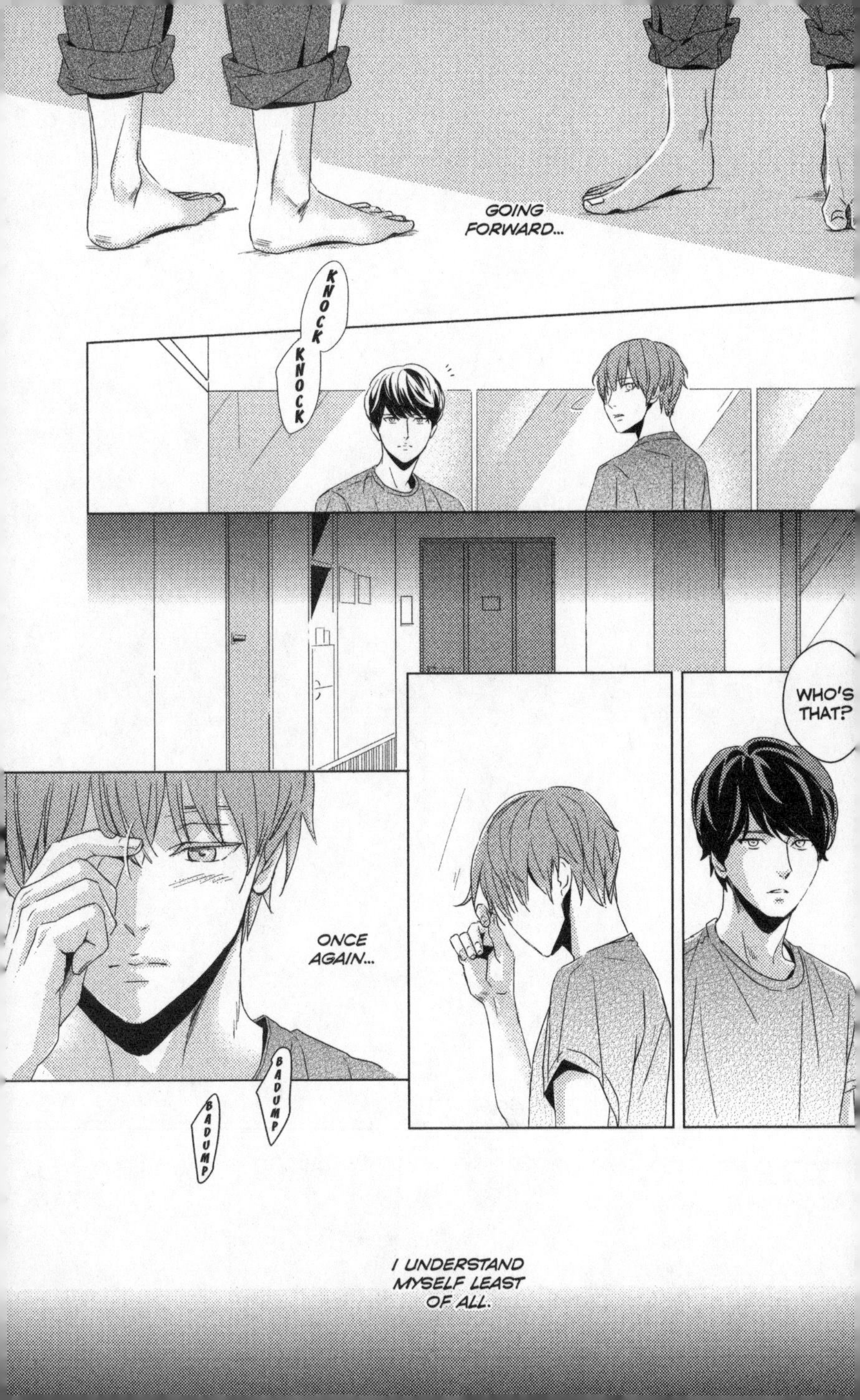
GOING FORWARD...
KNOCK KNOCK
WHO'S THAT?
ONCE AGAIN...
BADUMP
BADUMP
I UNDERSTAND MYSELF LEAST OF ALL.

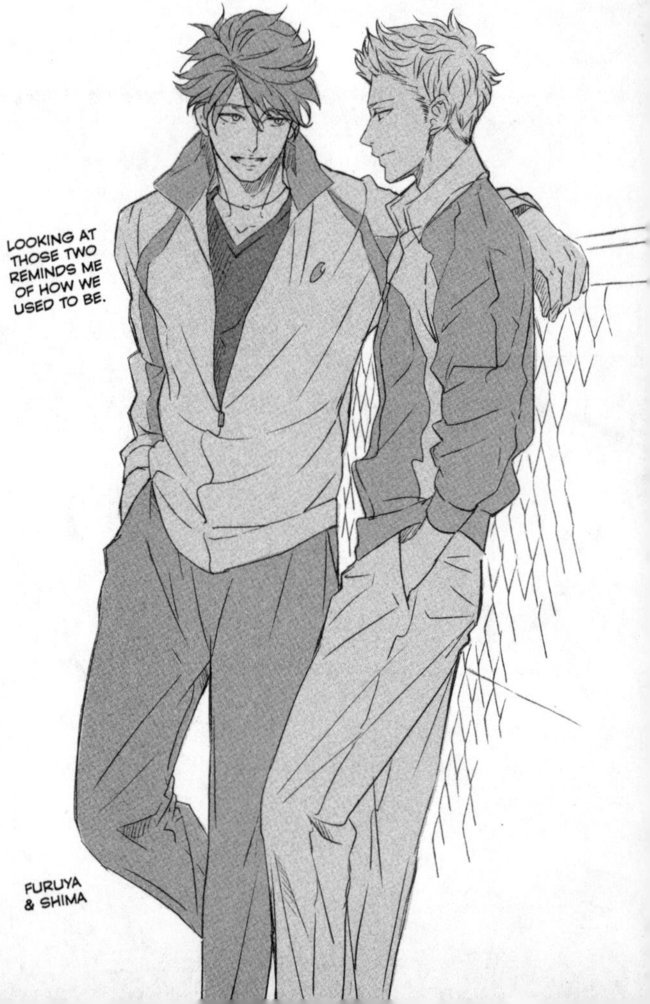
LOOKING AT THOSE TWO REMINDS ME OF HOW WE USED TO BE.
FURUYA & SHIMA

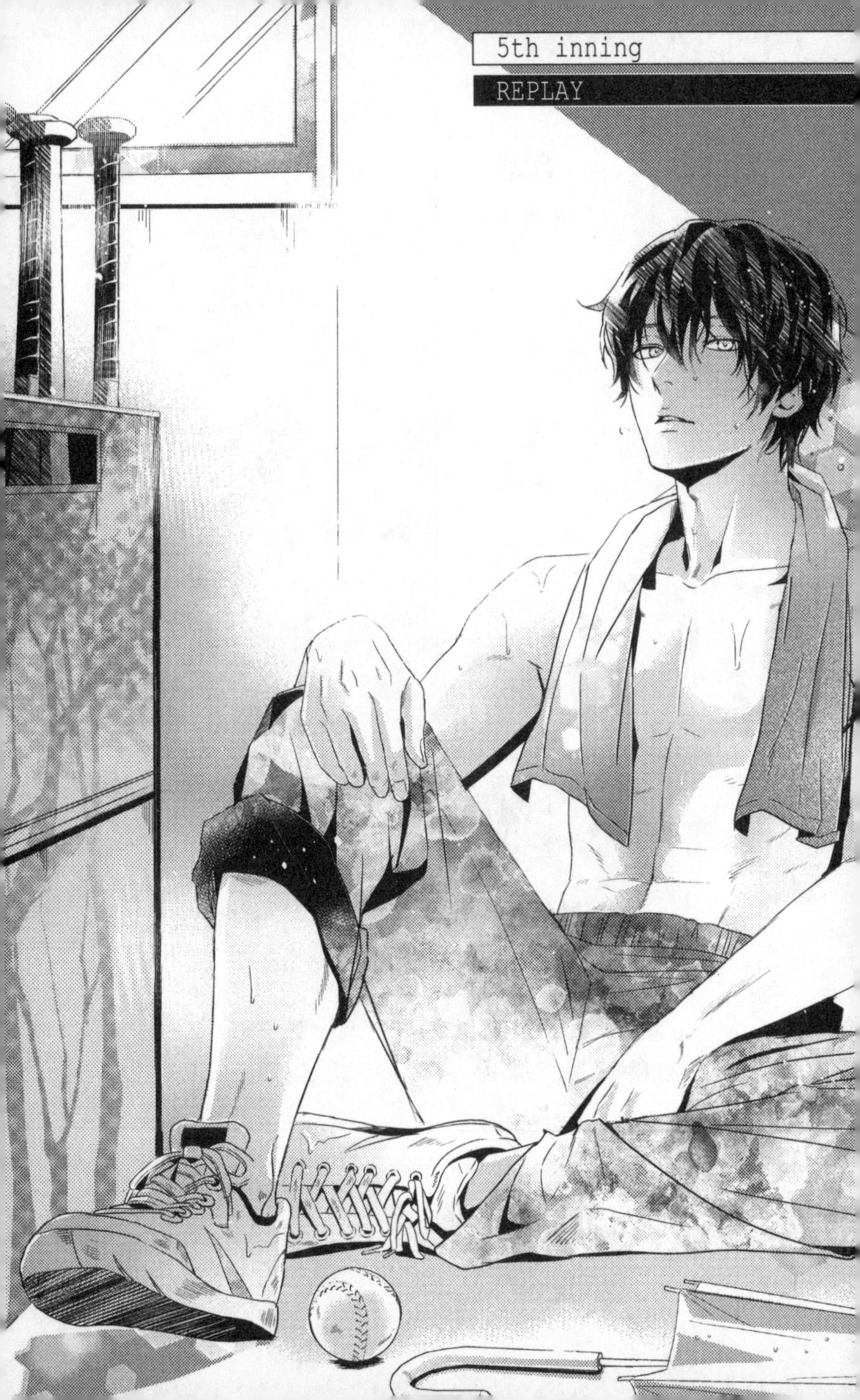
5th inning
REPLAY

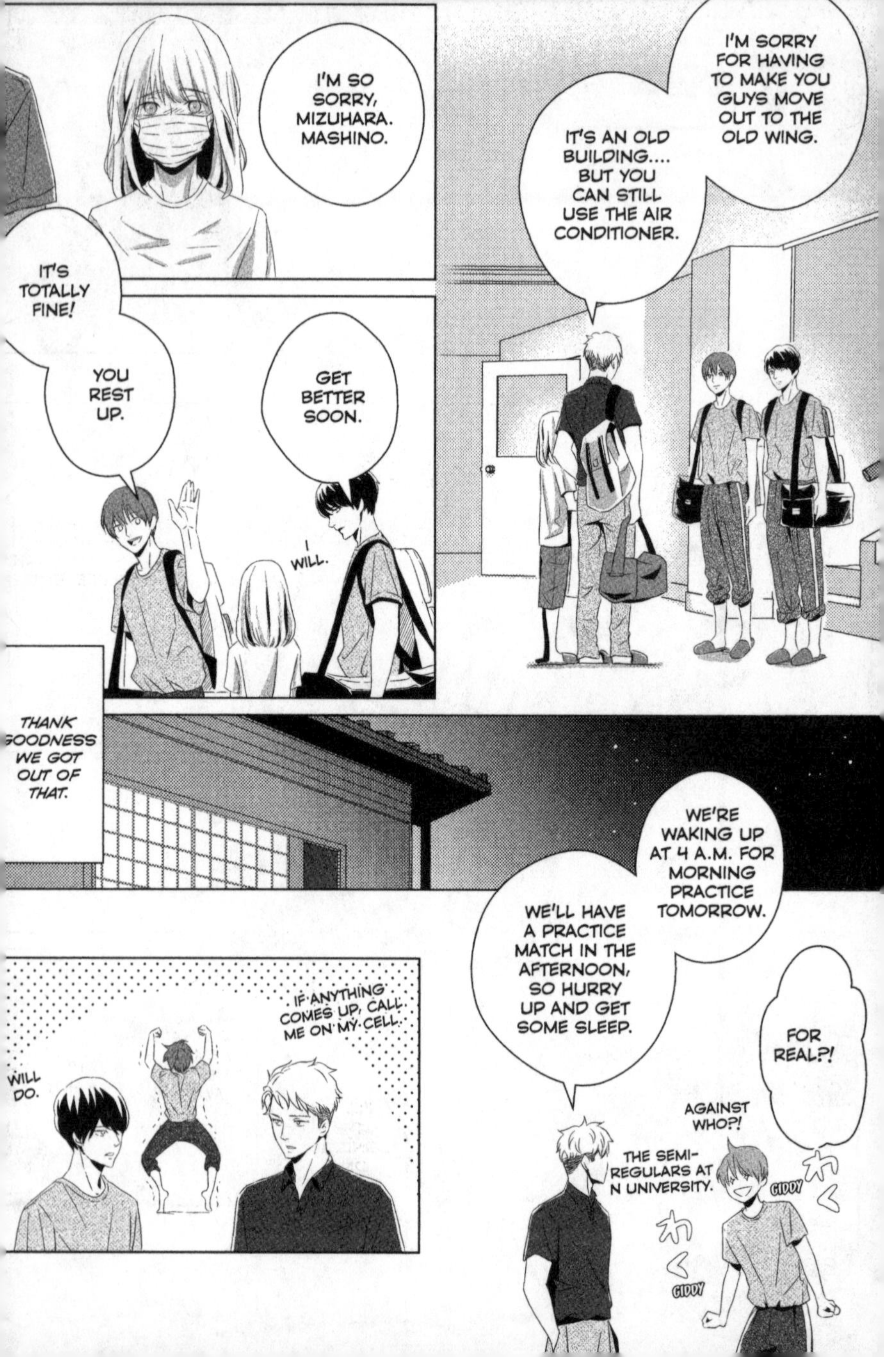
I'M SORRY FOR HAVING TO MAKE YOU GUYS MOVE OUT TO THE OLD WING.
IT'S AN OLD BUILDING.... BUT YOU CAN STILL USE THE AIR CONDITIONER.
I'M SO SORRY, MIZUHARA. MASHINO.
IT'S TOTALLY FINE!
YOU REST UP.
GET BETTER SOON.
I WILL.
THANK GOODNESS WE GOT OUT OF THAT.
WE'RE WAKING UP AT 4 A.M. FOR MORNING PRACTICE TOMORROW.
WE'LL HAVE A PRACTICE MATCH IN THE AFTERNOON, SO HURRY UP AND GET SOME SLEEP.
FOR REAL?!
AGAINST WHO?!
わく GIDDY
THE SEMI-REGULARS AT N UNIVERSITY.
わく GIDDY
IF ANYTHING COMES UP, CALL ME ON MY CELL.
WILL DO.

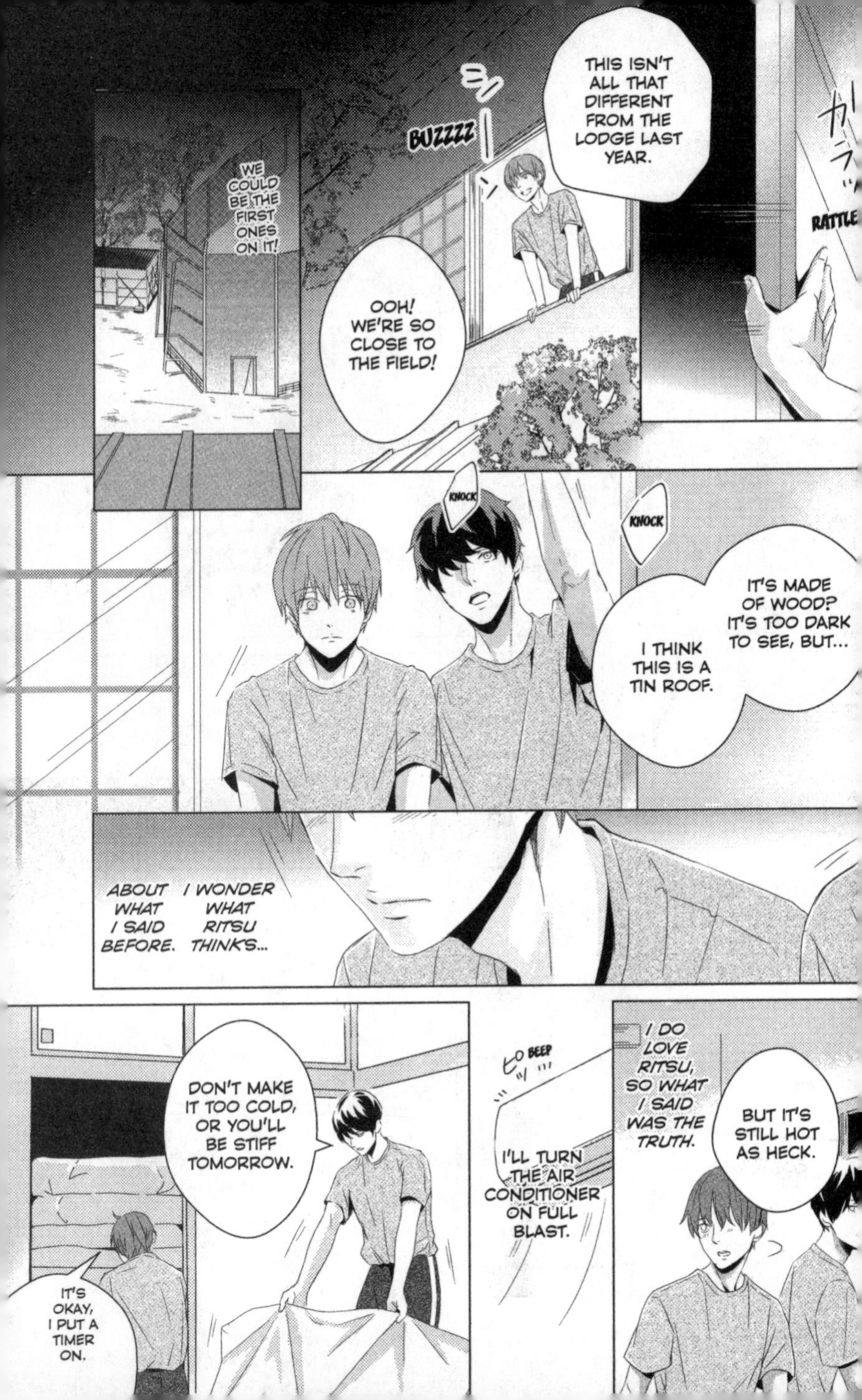
ガラッ
RATTLE
THIS ISN'T ALL THAT DIFFERENT FROM THE LODGE LAST YEAR.
BUZZZZ
OOH! WE'RE SO CLOSE TO THE FIELD!
WE COULD BE THE FIRST ONES ON IT!
KNOCK
KNOCK
IT'S MADE OF WOOD? IT'S TOO DARK TO SEE, BUT...
I THINK THIS IS A TIN ROOF.
I WONDER WHAT RITSU THINKS...
ABOUT WHAT I SAID BEFORE.
I DO LOVE RITSU, SO WHAT I SAID WAS THE TRUTH.
BUT IT'S STILL HOT AS HECK.
BEEP
I'LL TURN THE AIR CONDITIONER ON FULL BLAST.
DON'T MAKE IT TOO COLD, OR YOU'LL BE STIFF TOMORROW.
IT'S OKAY, I PUT A TIMER ON.

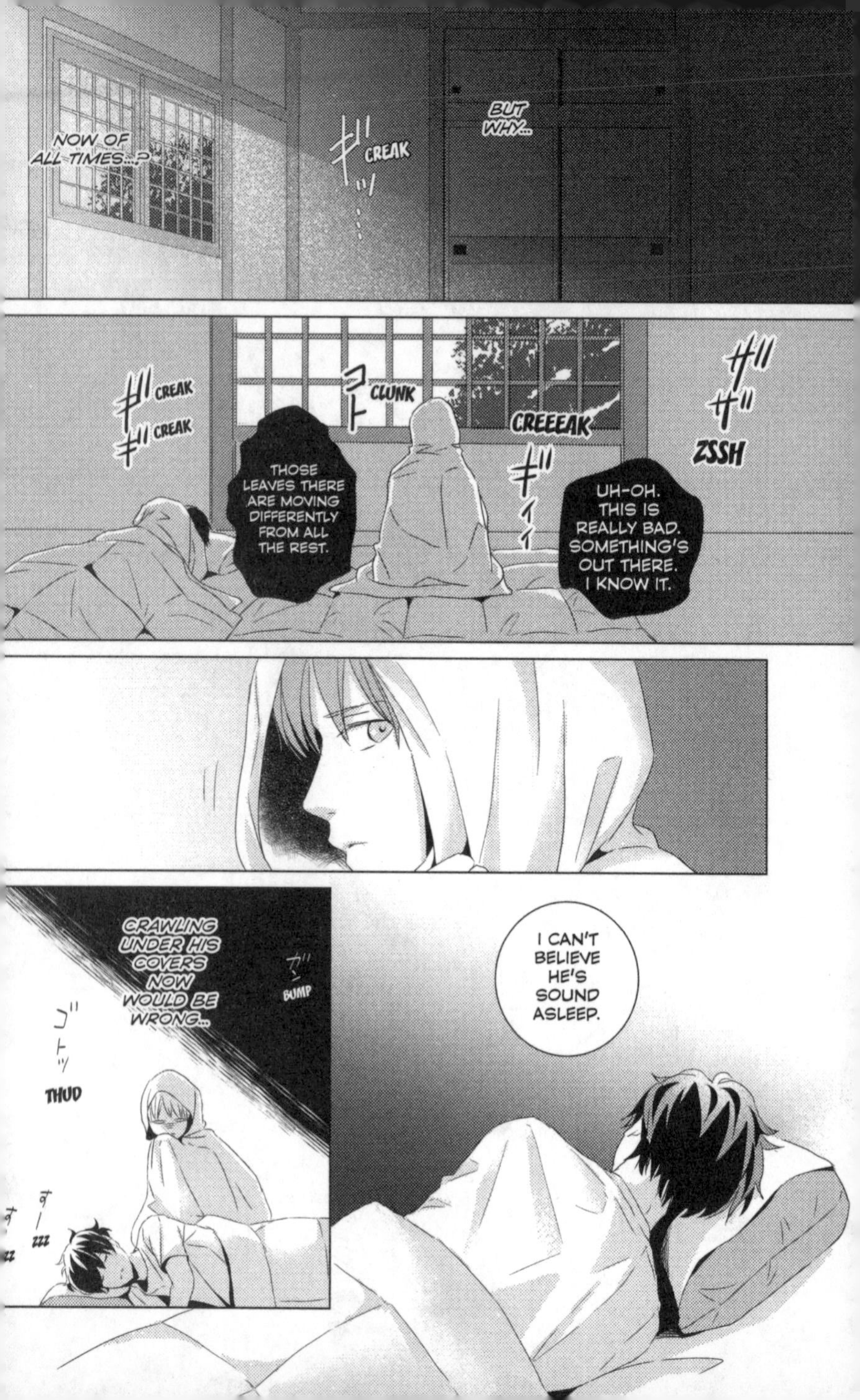
BUT WHY...
CREAK
NOW OF ALL TIMES...?
ZSSH
UH-OH. THIS IS REALLY BAD. SOMETHING'S OUT THERE. I KNOW IT.
CREEEAK
CLUNK
THOSE LEAVES THERE ARE MOVING DIFFERENTLY FROM ALL THE REST.
CREAK
CREAK
I CAN'T BELIEVE HE'S SOUND ASLEEP.
CRAWLING UNDER HIS COVERS NOW WOULD BE WRONG...
BUMP
THUD
ZZZ
ZZ

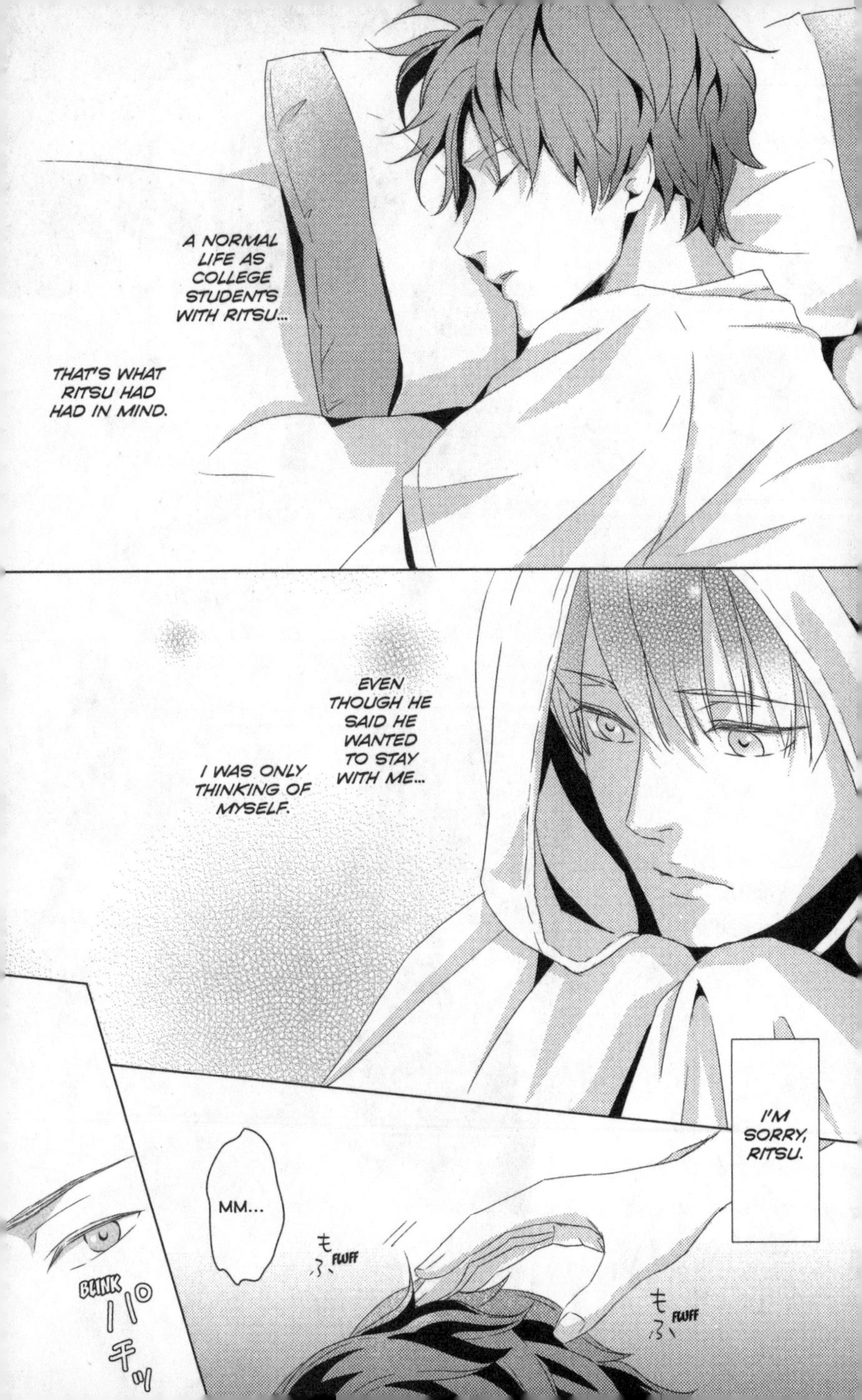
A NORMAL LIFE AS COLLEGE STUDENTS WITH RITSU...
THAT'S WHAT RITSU HAD HAD IN MIND.
EVEN THOUGH HE SAID HE WANTED TO STAY WITH ME...
I WAS ONLY THINKING OF MYSELF.
I'M SORRY, RITSU.
もふ FLUFF
もふ FLUFF
MM...
パチッ BLINK

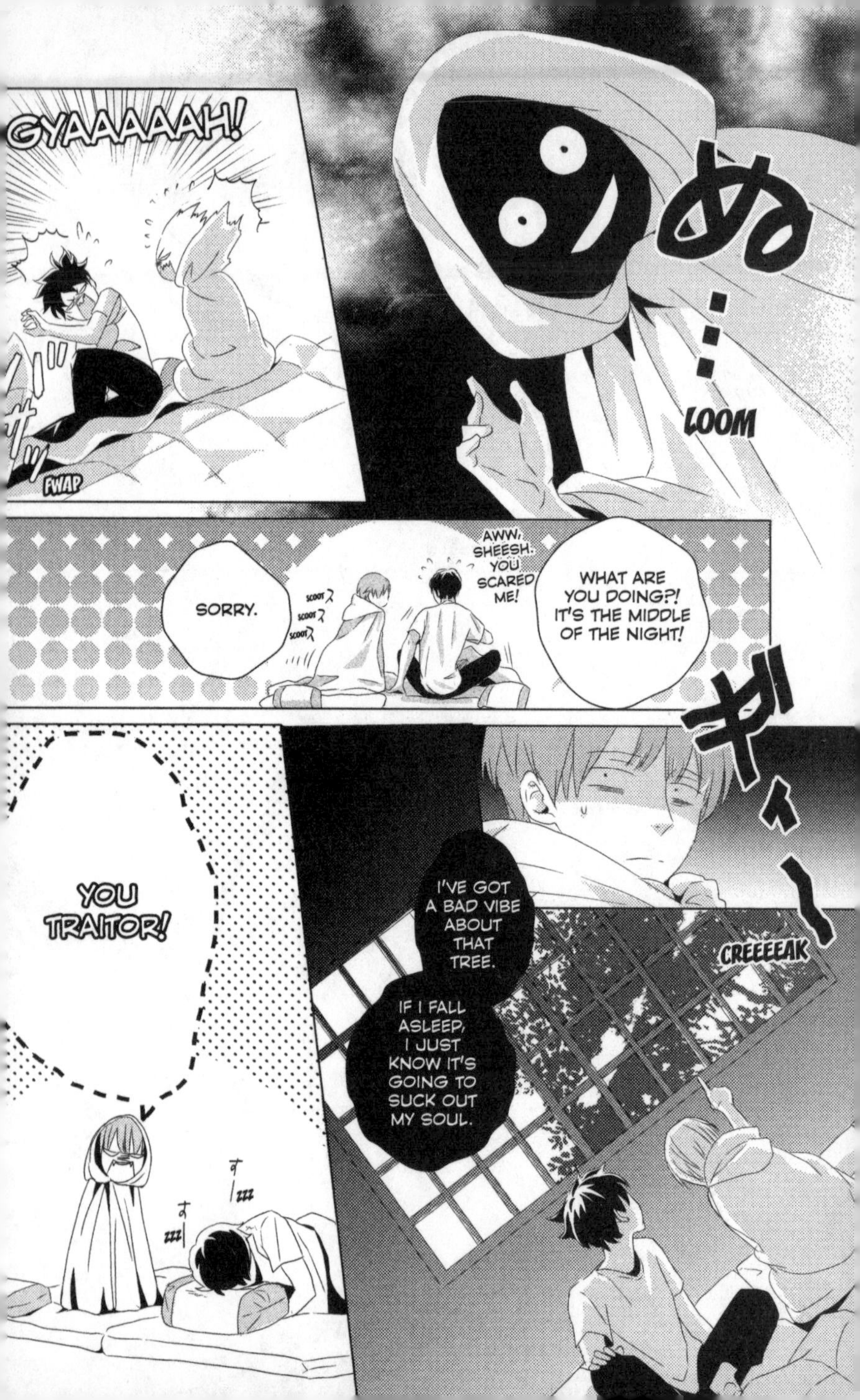
LOOM
GYAAAAAH!
FWAP
WHAT ARE YOU DOING?! IT'S THE MIDDLE OF THE NIGHT!
AWW, SHEESH. YOU SCARED ME!
SCOOT
SCOOT
SCOOT
SORRY.
CREEEEAK
I'VE GOT A BAD VIBE ABOUT THAT TREE.
IF I FALL ASLEEP, I JUST KNOW IT'S GOING TO SUCK OUT MY SOUL.
YOU TRAITOR!
ZZZ
ZZZ

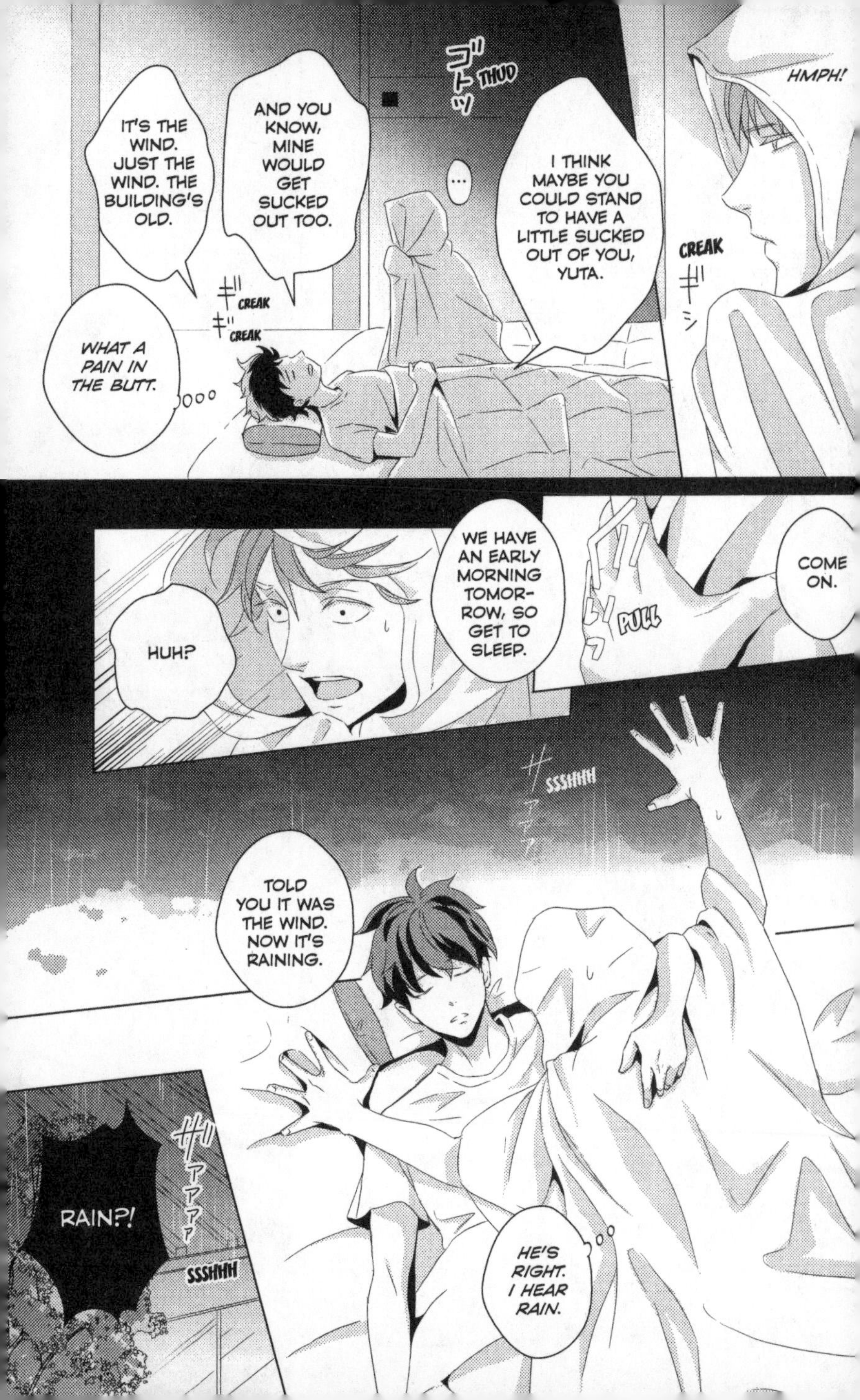
HMPH!
THUD
I THINK MAYBE YOU COULD STAND TO HAVE A LITTLE SUCKED OUT OF YOU, YUTA.
CREAK
...
AND YOU KNOW, MINE WOULD GET SUCKED OUT TOO.
IT'S THE WIND. JUST THE WIND. THE BUILDING'S OLD.
CREAK
CREAK
WHAT A PAIN IN THE BUTT.
COME ON.
PULL
WE HAVE AN EARLY MORNING TOMOR-ROW, SO GET TO SLEEP.
HUH?
SSSHHH
TOLD YOU IT WAS THE WIND. NOW IT'S RAINING.
HE'S RIGHT. I HEAR RAIN.
SSSHHH
RAIN?!

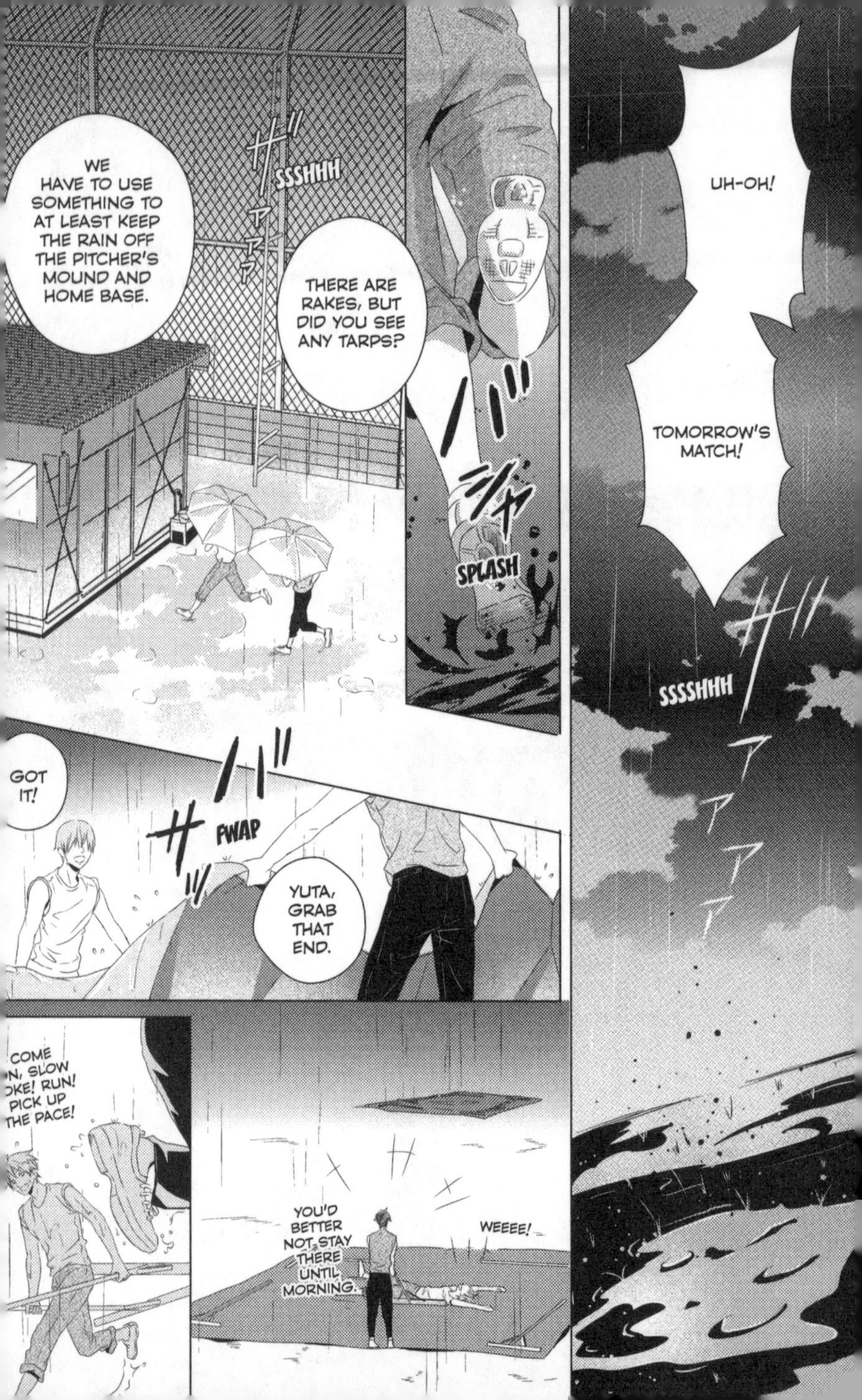
UH-OH!
TOMORROW'S MATCH!
SSSSHHH
SPLASH
SSSHHH
WE HAVE TO USE SOMETHING TO AT LEAST KEEP THE RAIN OFF THE PITCHER'S MOUND AND HOME BASE.
THERE ARE RAKES, BUT DID YOU SEE ANY TARPS?
YUTA, GRAB THAT END.
FWAP
GOT IT!
WEEEE!
YOU'D BETTER NOT STAY THERE UNTIL MORNING.
COME N, SLOW OKE! RUN! PICK UP THE PACE!

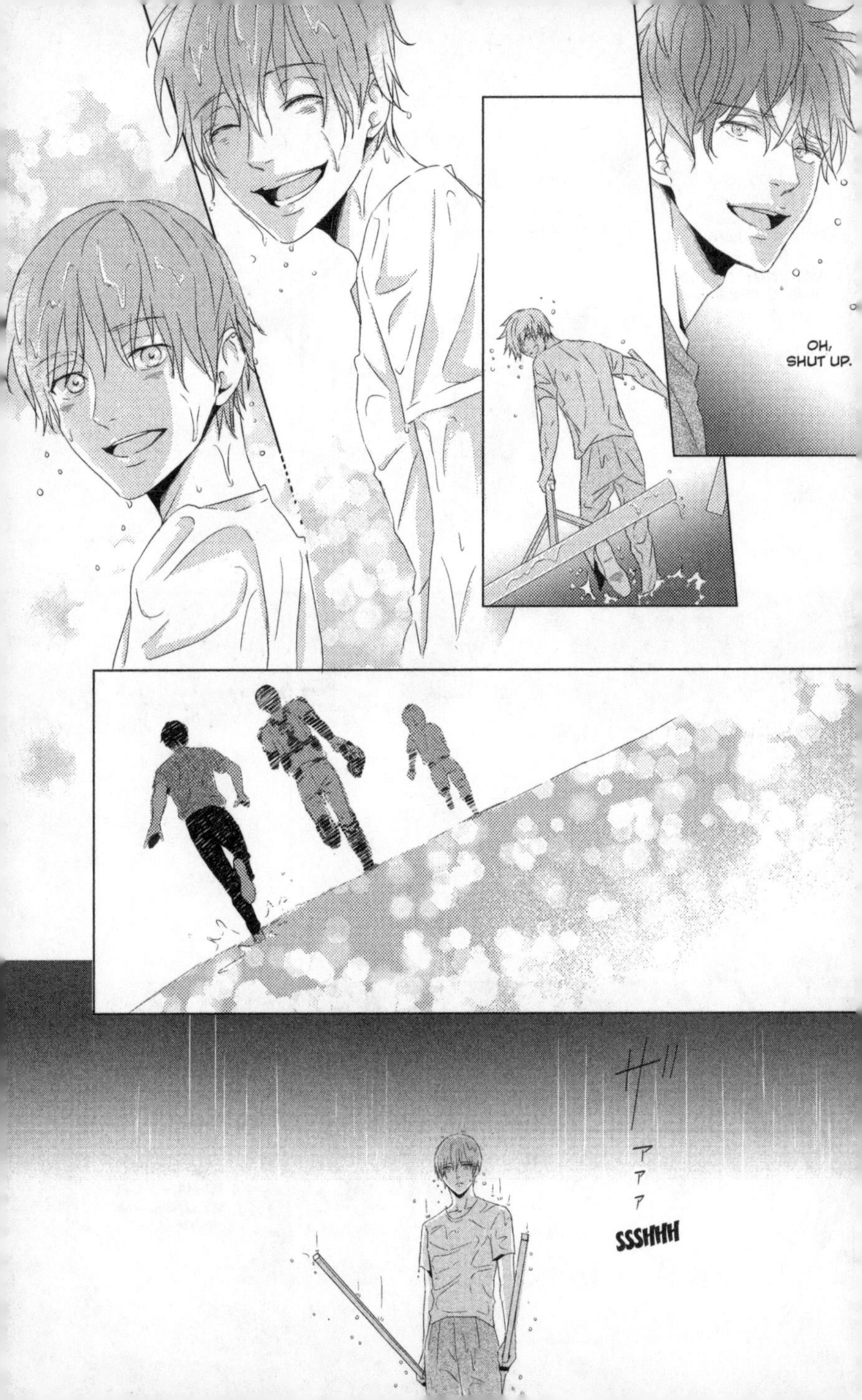
OH, SHUT UP.
ザァァ
SSSHHH

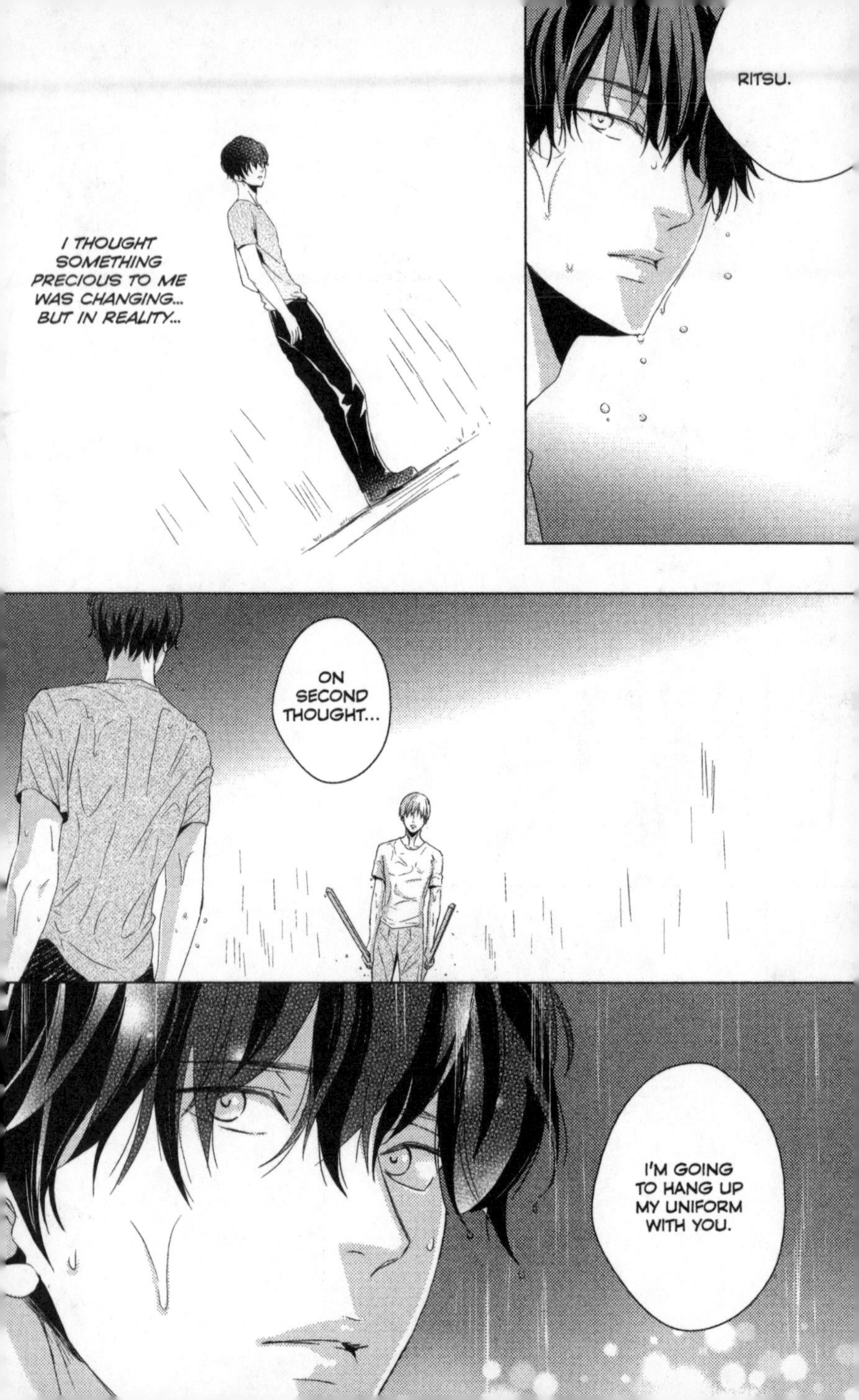
RITSU.
I THOUGHT SOMETHING PRECIOUS TO ME WAS CHANGING... BUT IN REALITY...
ON SECOND THOUGHT...
I'M GOING TO HANG UP MY UNIFORM WITH YOU.

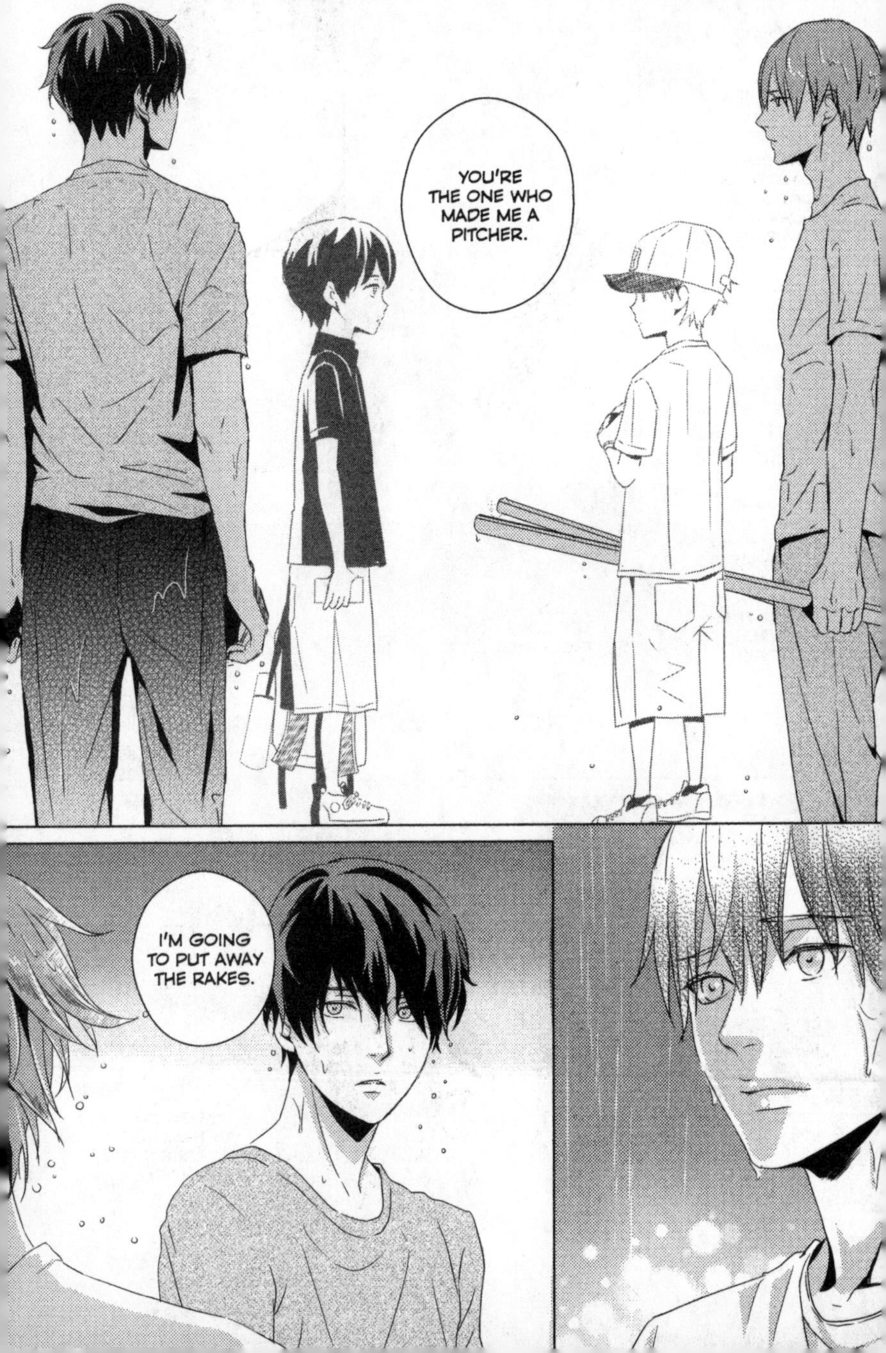
YOU'RE THE ONE WHO MADE ME A PITCHER.
I'M GOING TO PUT AWAY THE RAKES.

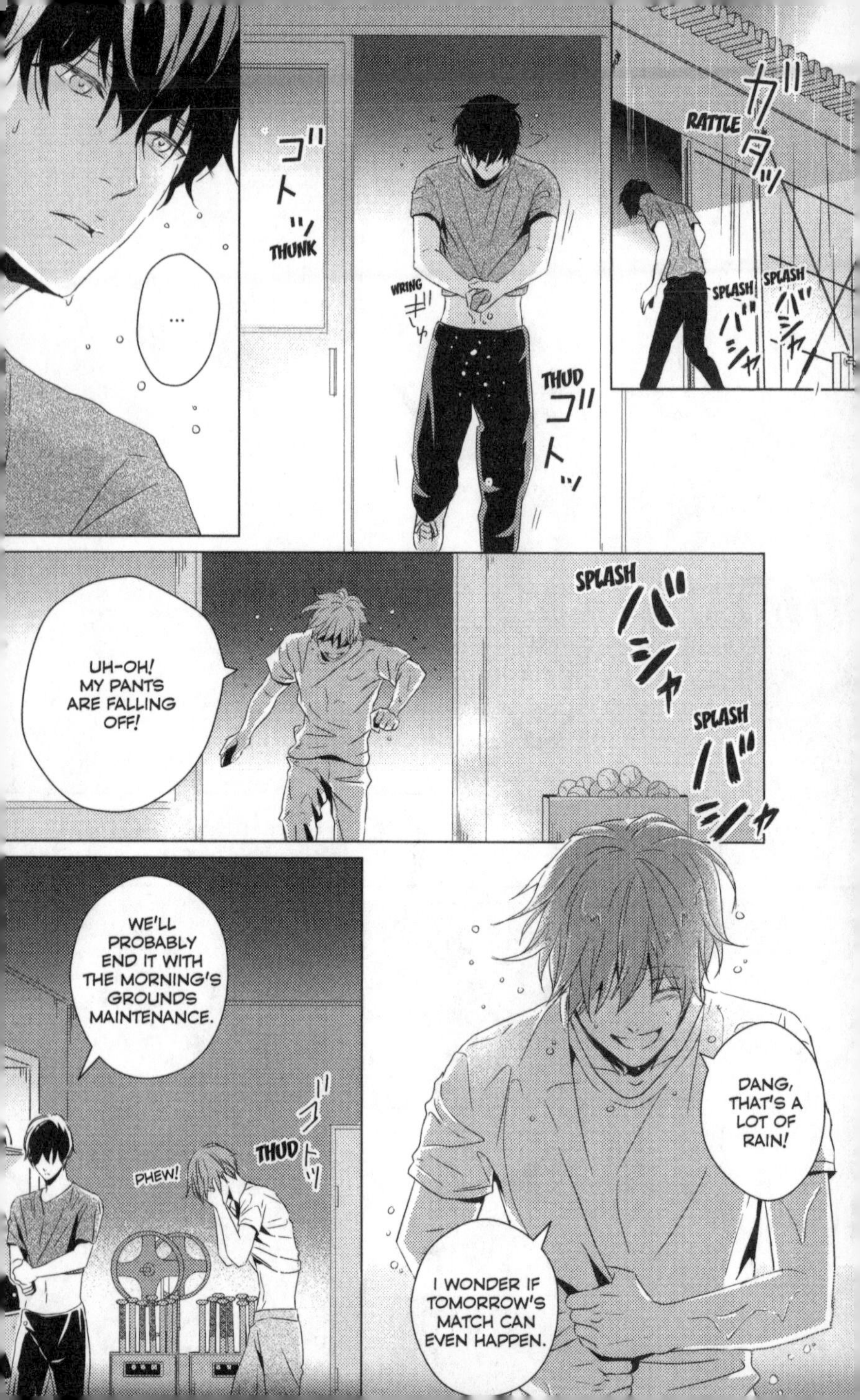
RATTLE
ガタッ
SPLASH
バシャ
SPLASH
バシャ
ゴトッ
THUNK
WRING
ぎゅ
THUD
ゴトッ
...
SPLASH
バシャ
SPLASH
バシャ
UH-OH! MY PANTS ARE FALLING OFF!
DANG, THAT'S A LOT OF RAIN!
I WONDER IF TOMORROW'S MATCH CAN EVEN HAPPEN.
WE'LL PROBABLY END IT WITH THE MORNING'S GROUNDS MAINTENANCE.
THUD
ゴトッ
PHEW!

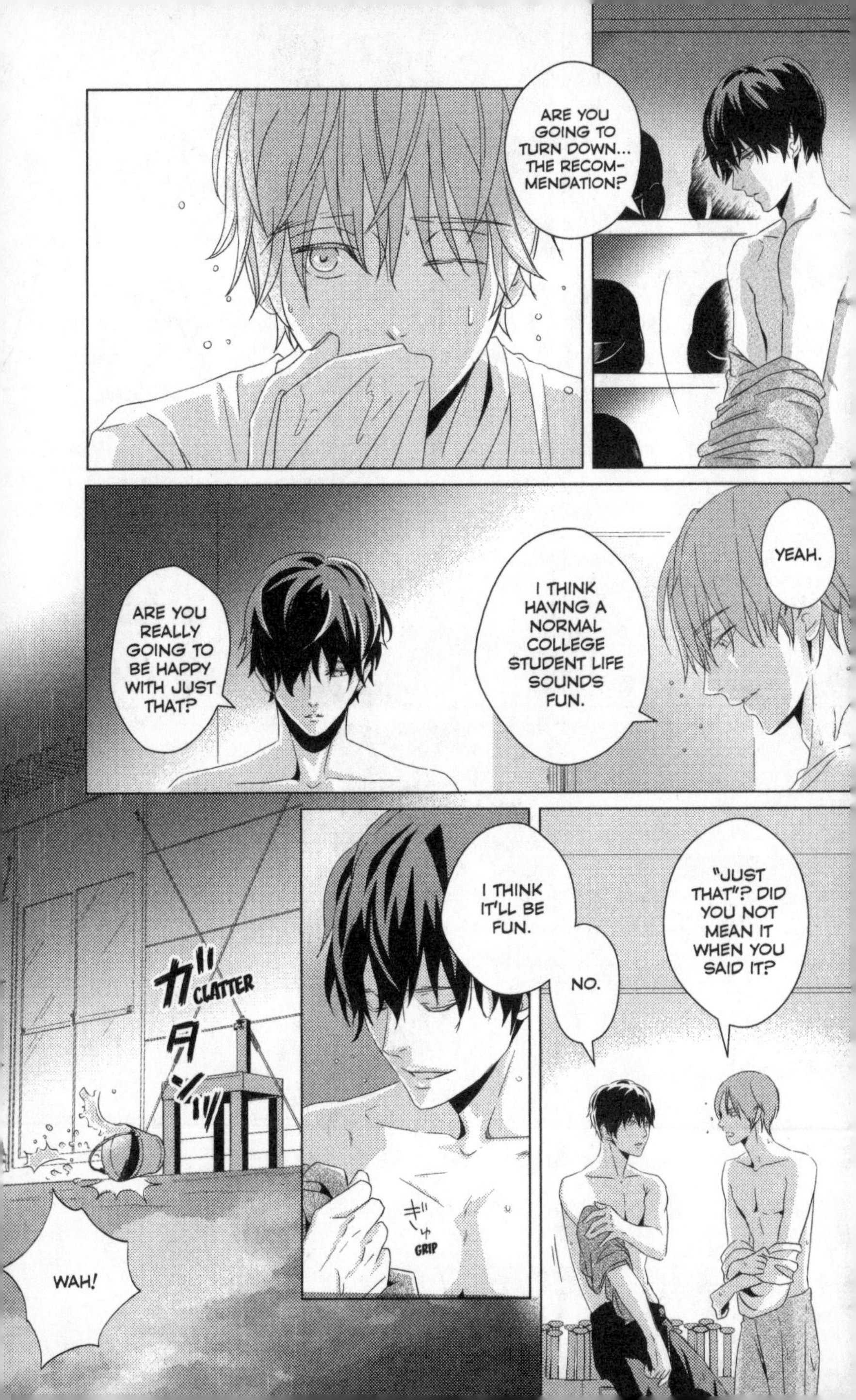
ARE YOU GOING TO TURN DOWN... THE RECOMMENDATION?
YEAH.
I THINK HAVING A NORMAL COLLEGE STUDENT LIFE SOUNDS FUN.
ARE YOU REALLY GOING TO BE HAPPY WITH JUST THAT?
"JUST THAT"? DID YOU NOT MEAN IT WHEN YOU SAID IT?
NO.
I THINK IT'LL BE FUN.
ぎゅ
GRIP
ガッ
CLATTER
タンッ
WAH!

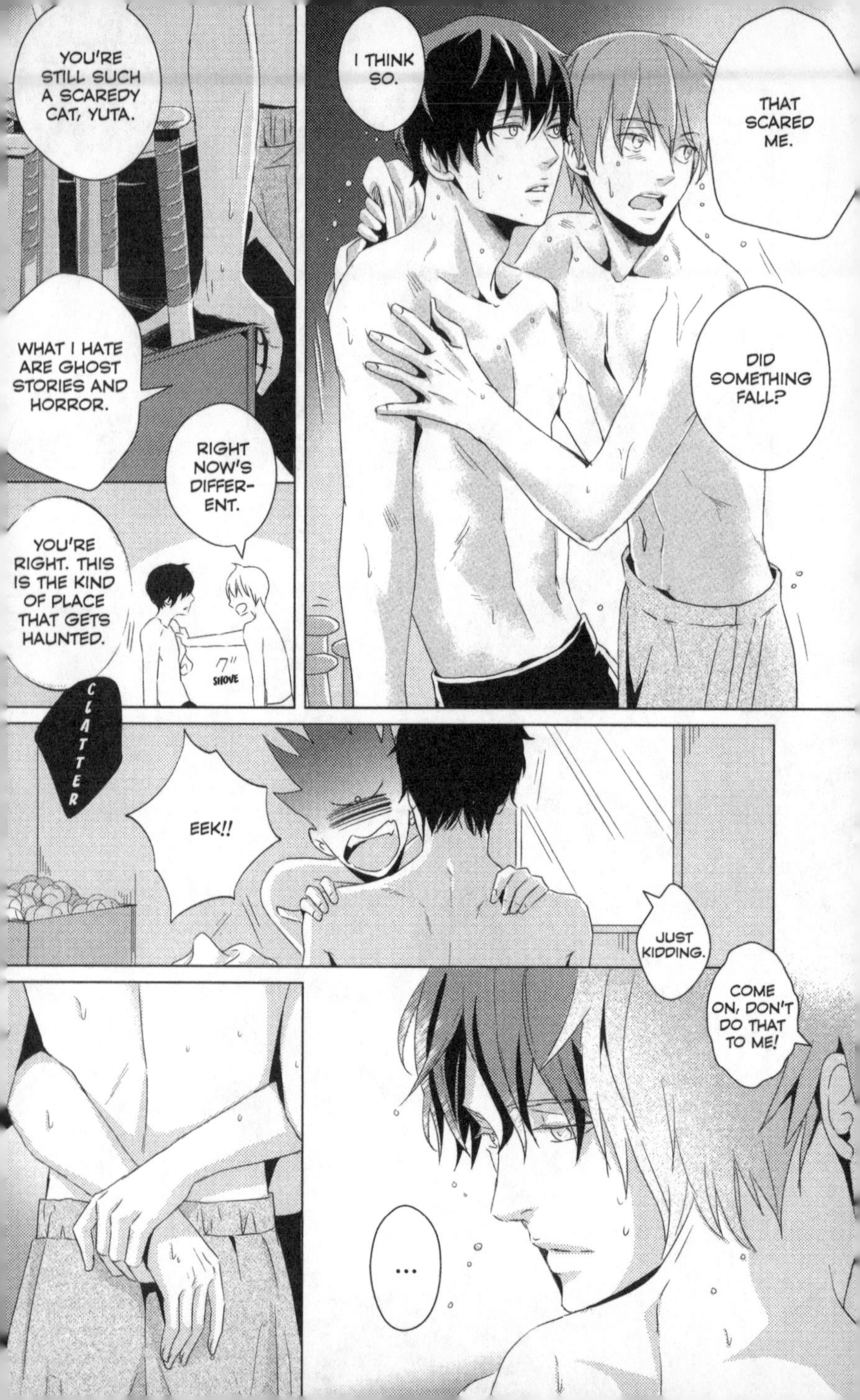
THAT SCARED ME.
DID SOMETHING FALL?
I THINK SO.
YOU'RE STILL SUCH A SCAREDY CAT, YUTA.
WHAT I HATE ARE GHOST STORIES AND HORROR.
RIGHT NOW'S DIFFER-ENT.
YOU'RE RIGHT. THIS IS THE KIND OF PLACE THAT GETS HAUNTED.
SHOVE
CLATTER
EEK!!
JUST KIDDING.
COME ON, DON'T DO THAT TO ME!
...

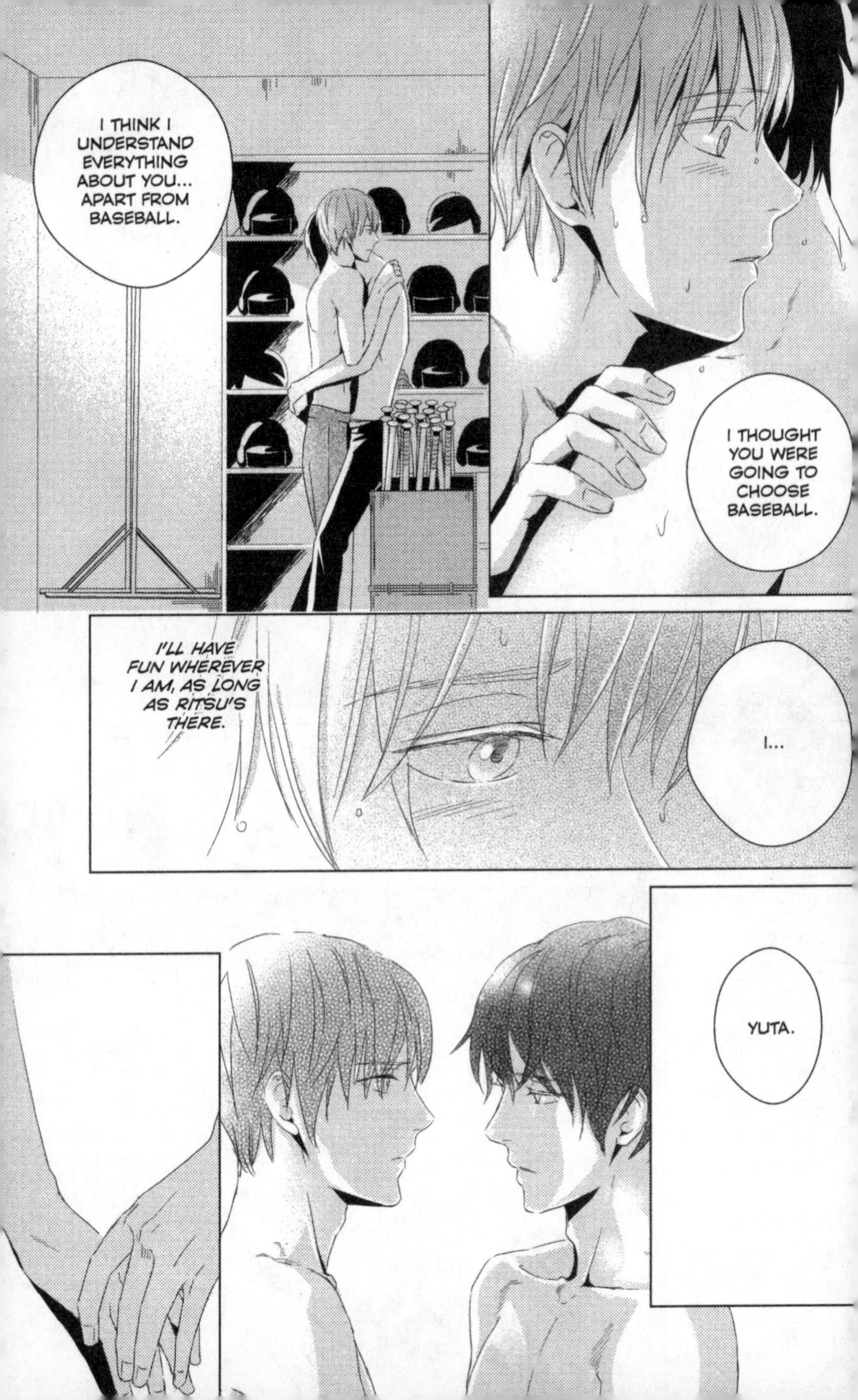
I THOUGHT YOU WERE GOING TO CHOOSE BASEBALL.
I THINK I UNDERSTAND EVERYTHING ABOUT YOU... APART FROM BASEBALL.
I...
I'LL HAVE FUN WHEREVER I AM, AS LONG AS RITSU'S THERE.
YUTA.

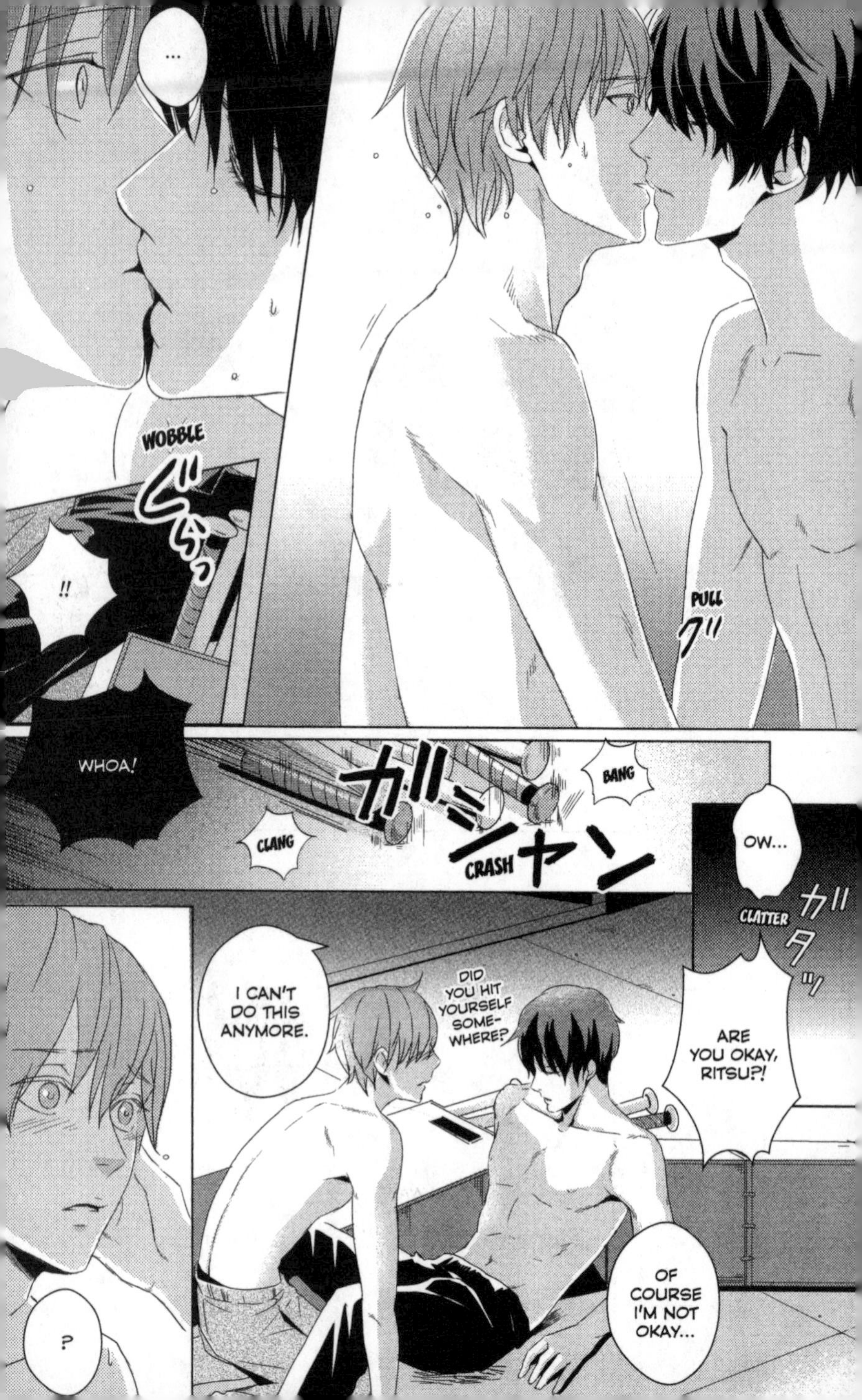
PULL
グ
...
WOBBLE
ぐらっ
!!
WHOA!
BANG
ガシャン
CRASH
CLANG
OW...
CLATTER
ガタッ
ARE YOU OKAY, RITSU?!
OF COURSE I'M NOT OKAY...
DID YOU HIT YOURSELF SOME-WHERE?
I CAN'T DO THIS ANYMORE.
?

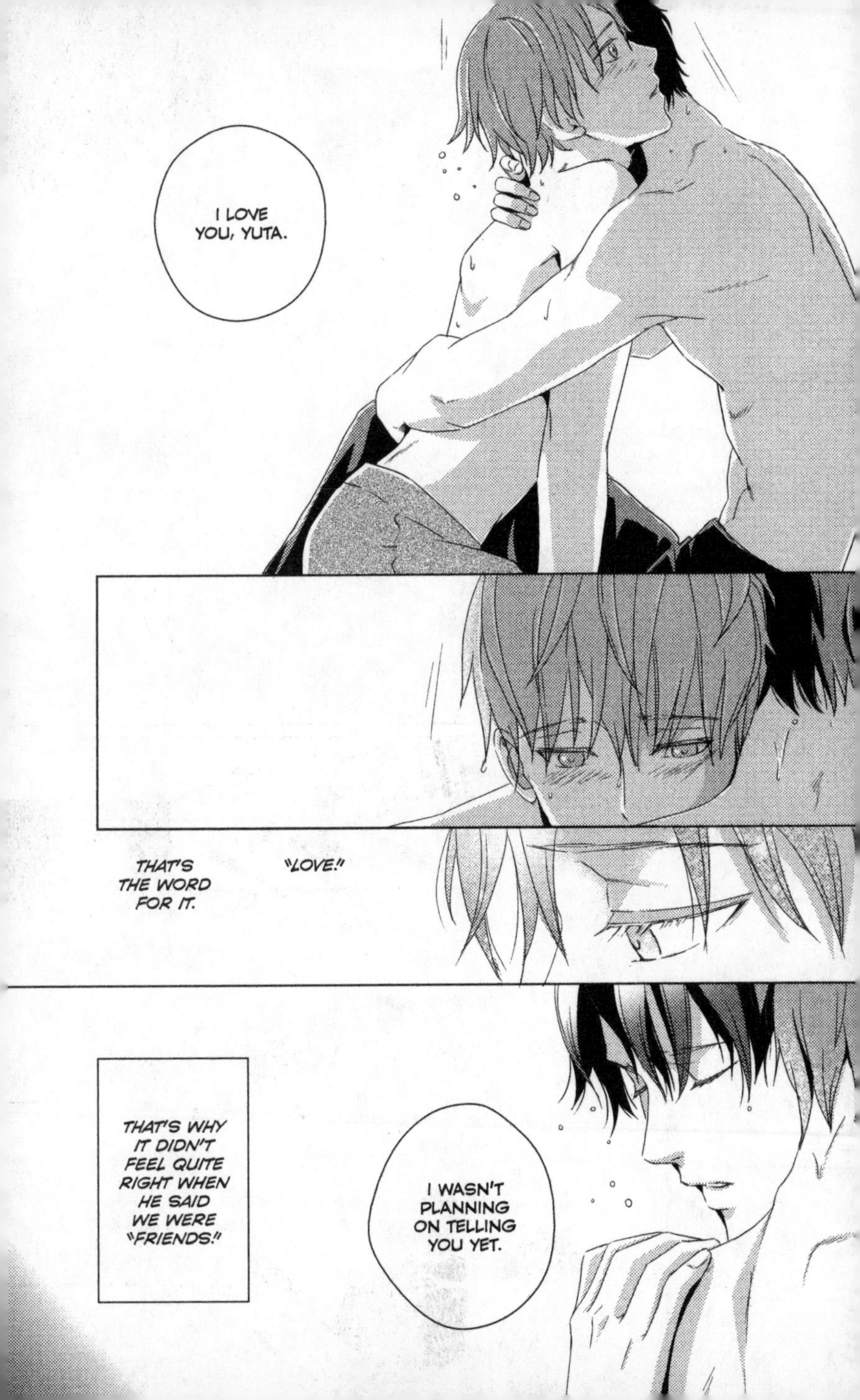
I LOVE YOU, YUTA.
"LOVE."
THAT'S THE WORD FOR IT.
I WASN'T PLANNING ON TELLING YOU YET.
THAT'S WHY IT DIDN'T FEEL QUITE RIGHT WHEN HE SAID WE WERE "FRIENDS."

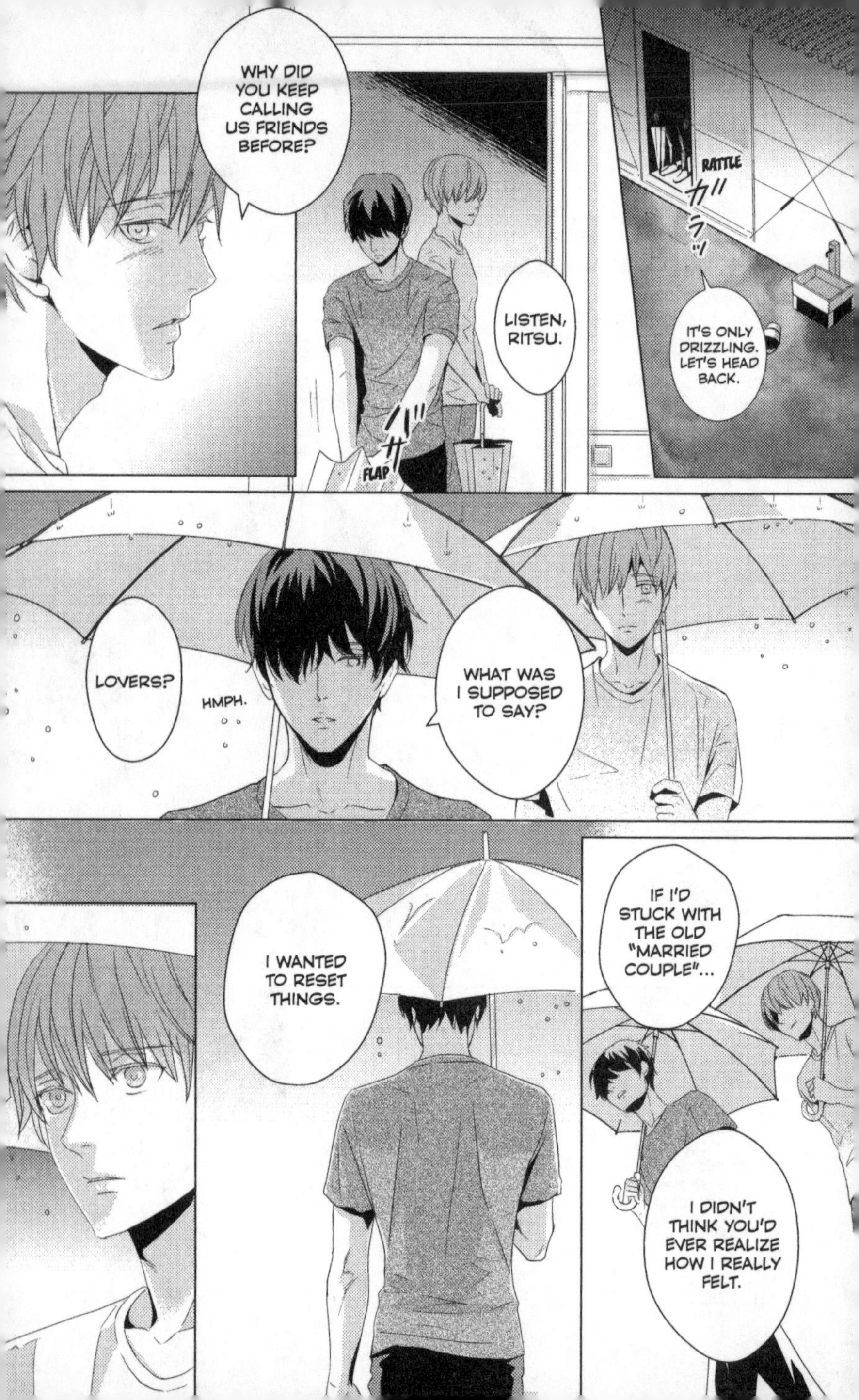
RATTLE
ガラッ
IT'S ONLY DRIZZLING. LET'S HEAD BACK.
LISTEN, RITSU.
FLAP
WHY DID YOU KEEP CALLING US FRIENDS BEFORE?
WHAT WAS I SUPPOSED TO SAY?
HMPH.
LOVERS?
IF I'D STUCK WITH THE OLD "MARRIED COUPLE"...
I DIDN'T THINK YOU'D EVER REALIZE HOW I REALLY FELT.
I WANTED TO RESET THINGS.

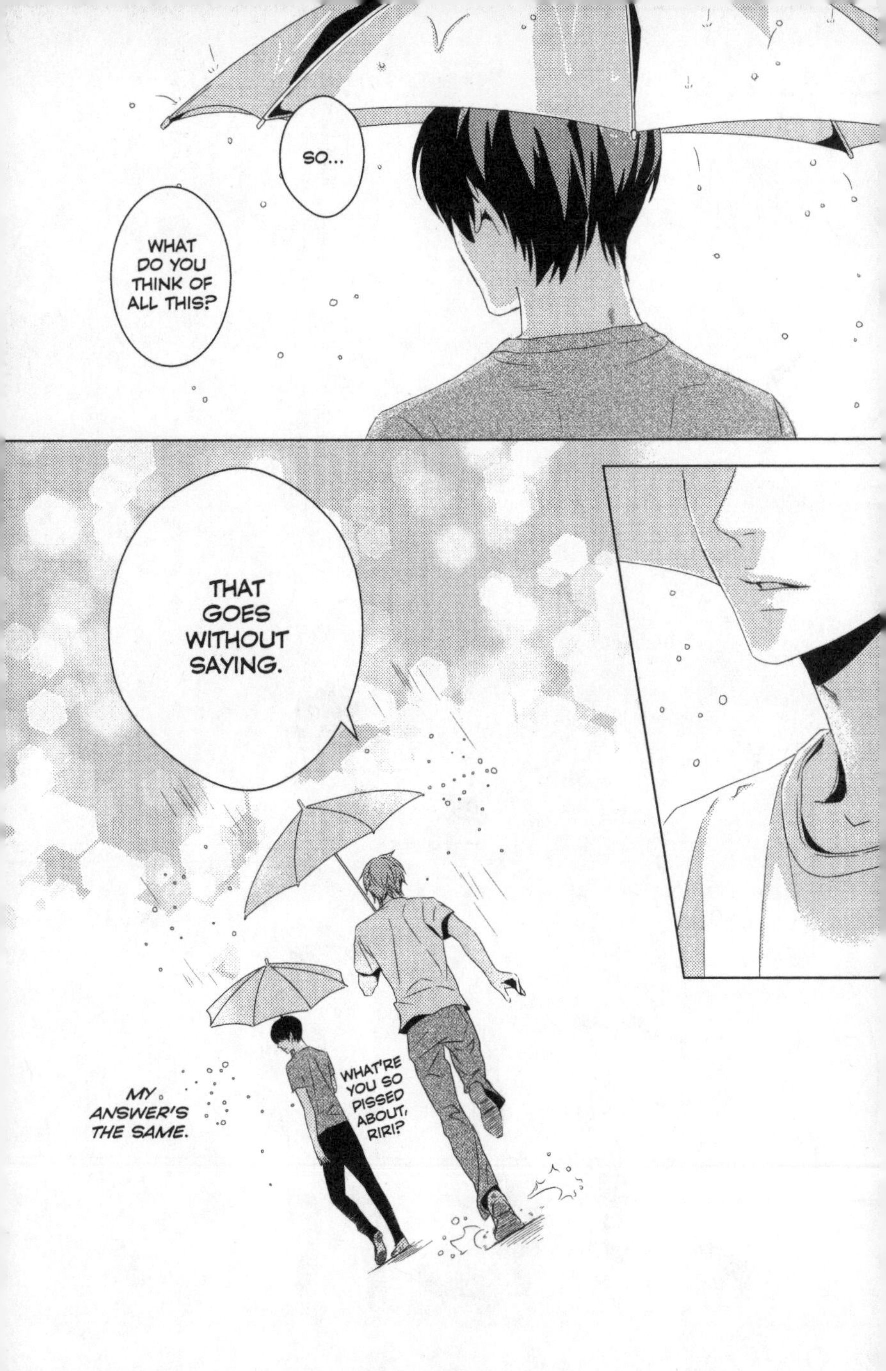
SO...
WHAT DO YOU THINK OF ALL THIS?
THAT GOES WITHOUT SAYING.
WHAT'RE YOU SO PISSED ABOUT, RIRI?
MY ANSWER'S THE SAME.

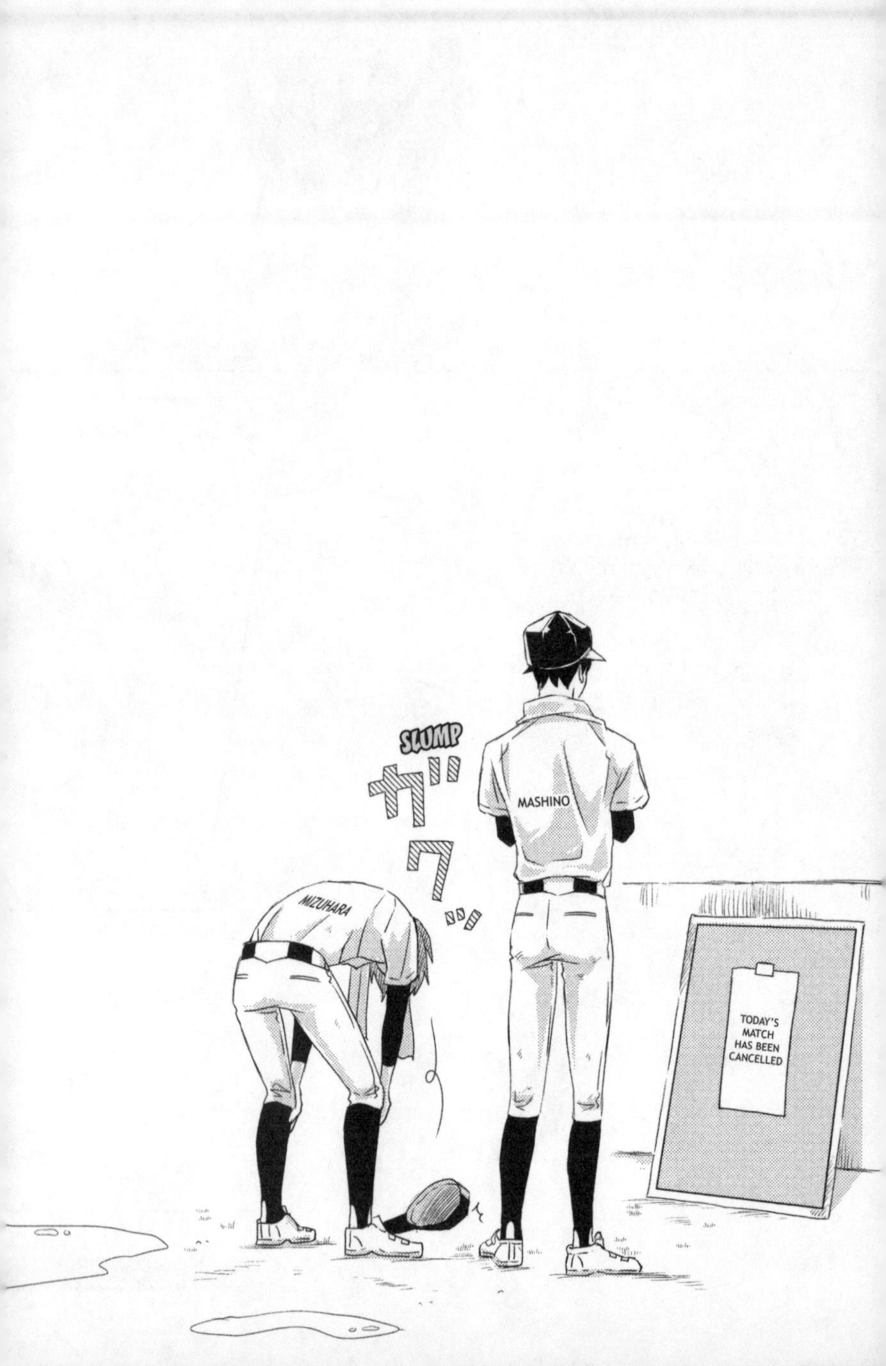
SLUMP
ガック…!!
MASHINO
MIZUHARA
TODAY'S MATCH HAS BEEN CANCELLED

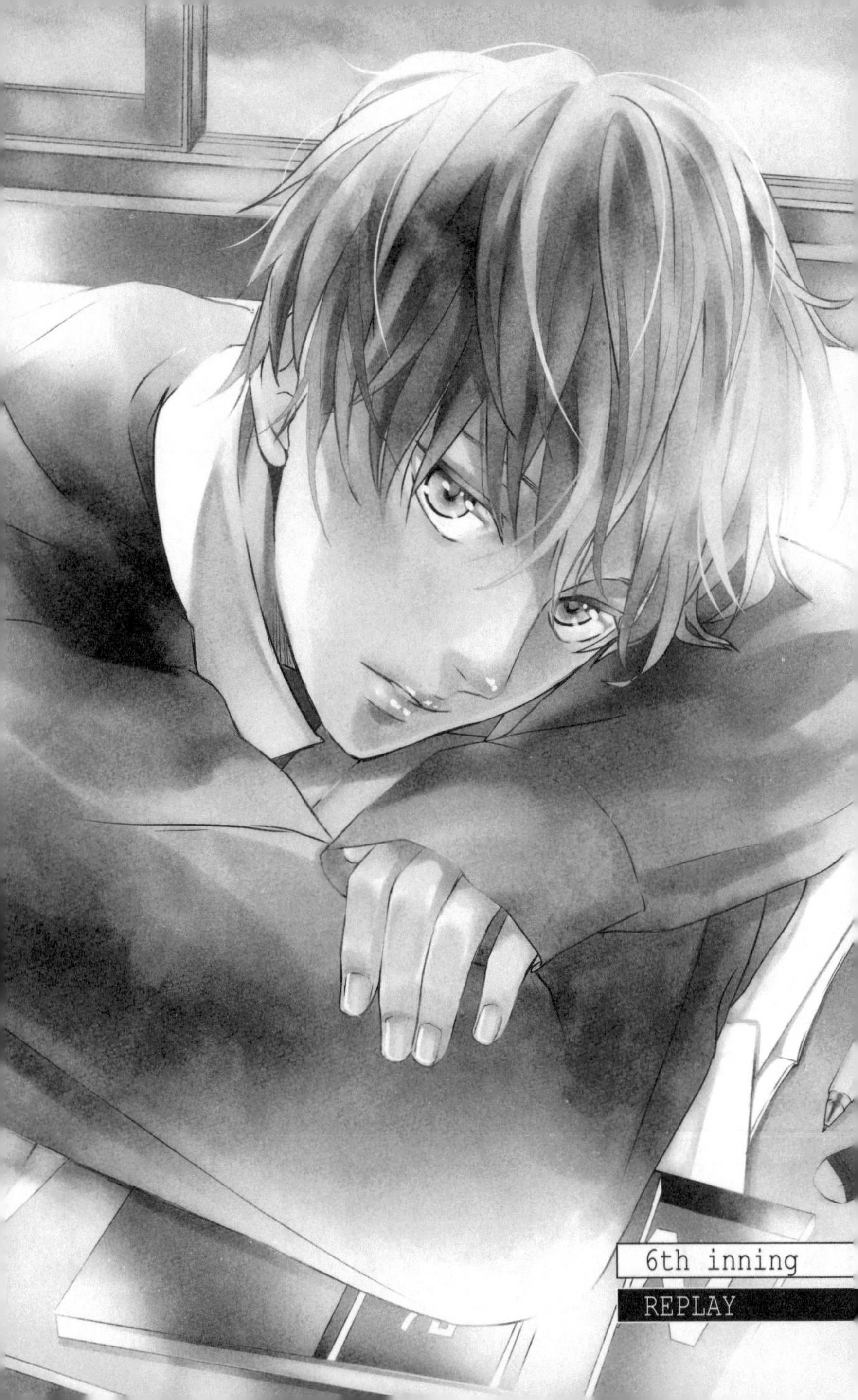
6th inning
REPLAY

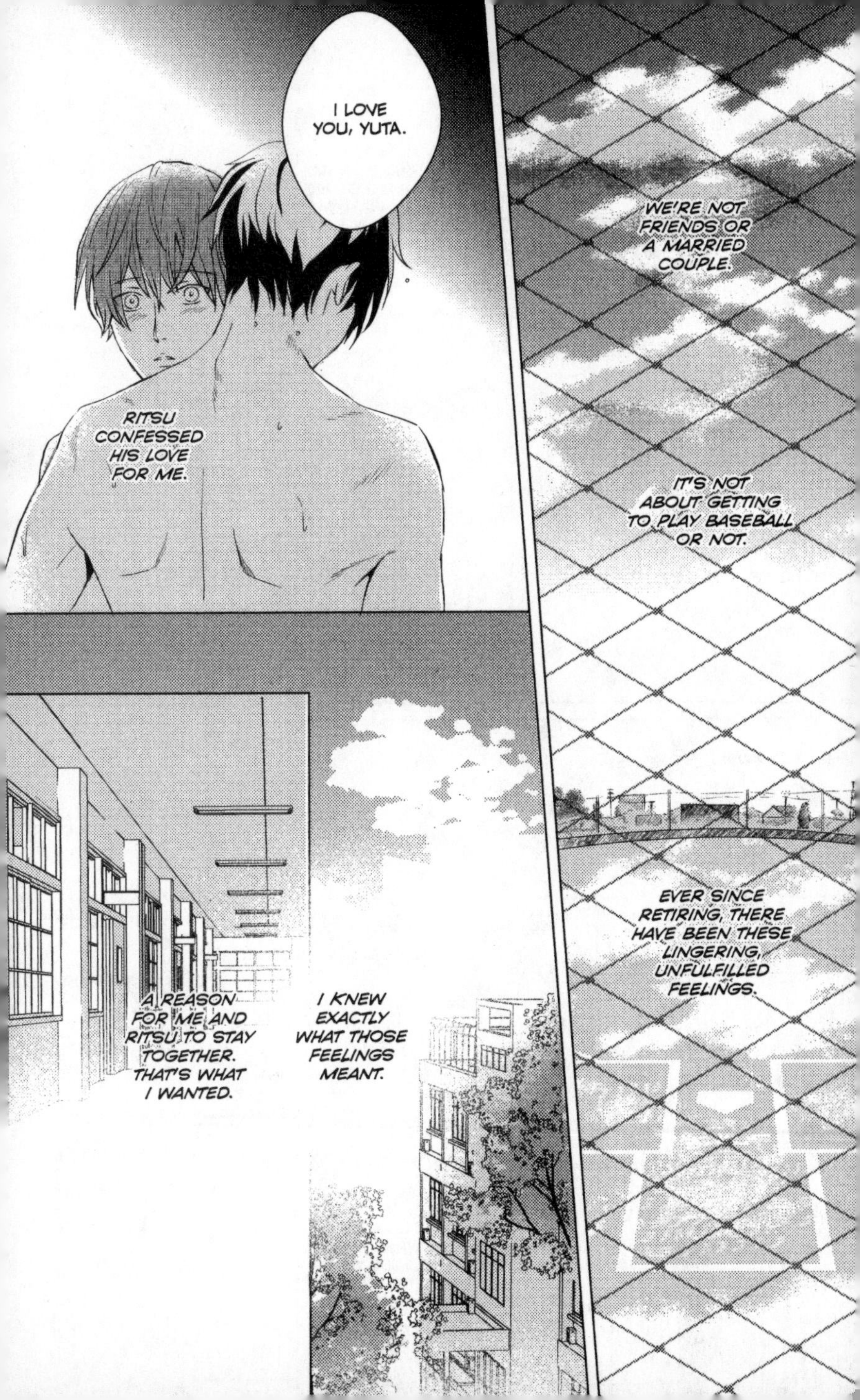
WE'RE NOT FRIENDS OR A MARRIED COUPLE.
IT'S NOT ABOUT GETTING TO PLAY BASEBALL OR NOT.
EVER SINCE RETIRING, THERE HAVE BEEN THESE LINGERING, UNFULFILLED FEELINGS.
I LOVE YOU, YUTA.
RITSU CONFESSED HIS LOVE FOR ME.
I KNEW EXACTLY WHAT THOSE FEELINGS MEANT.
A REASON FOR ME AND RITSU TO STAY TOGETHER. THAT'S WHAT I WANTED.

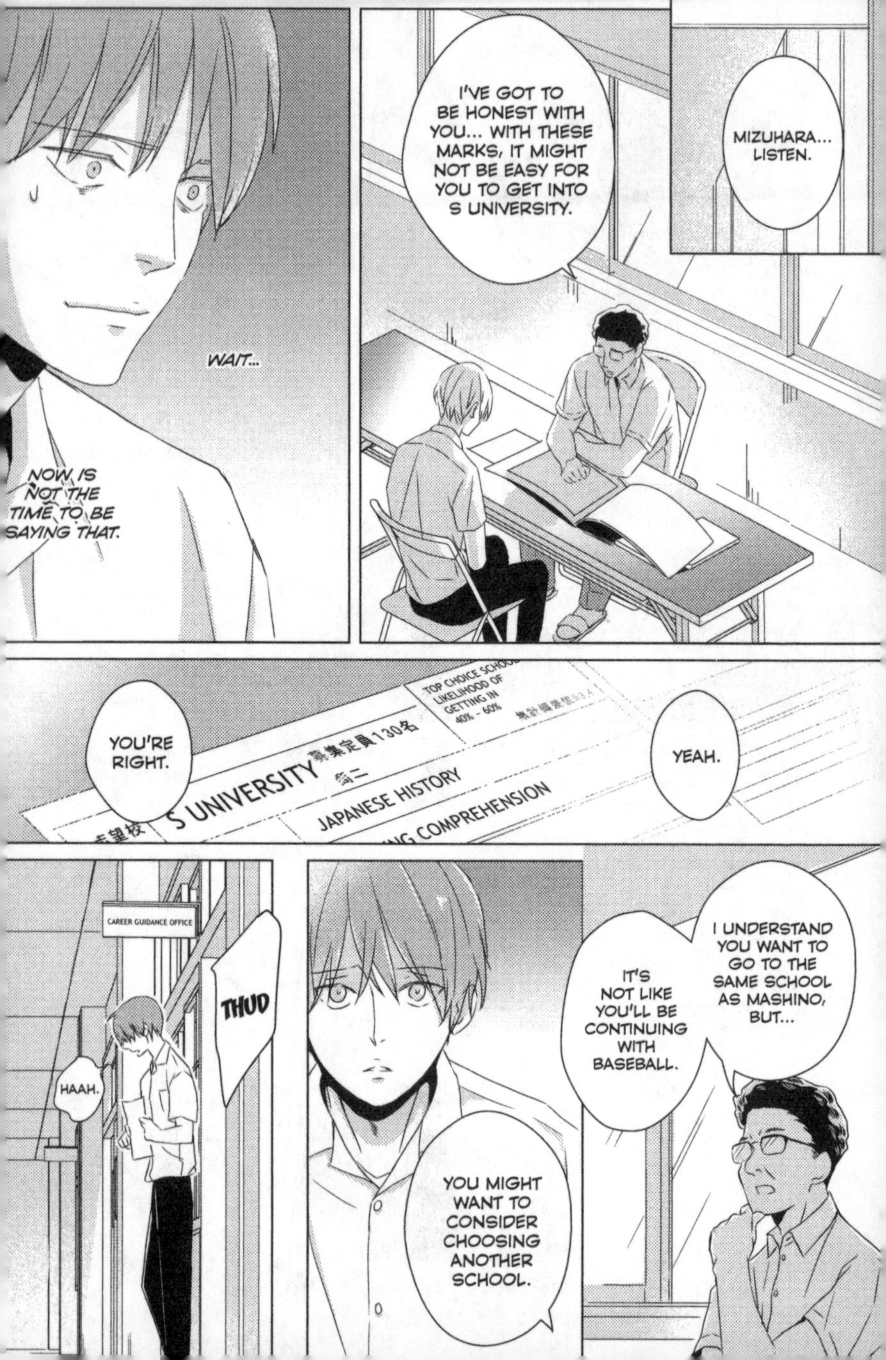
MIZUHARA... LISTEN.
I'VE GOT TO BE HONEST WITH YOU... WITH THESE MARKS, IT MIGHT NOT BE EASY FOR YOU TO GET INTO S UNIVERSITY.
WAIT...
NOW IS NOT THE TIME TO BE SAYING THAT.
YEAH.
TOP CHOICE SCHOOL LIKELIHOOD OF GETTING IN 40% - 60%
S UNIVERSITY
JAPANESE HISTORY
COMPREHENSION
YOU'RE RIGHT.
I UNDERSTAND YOU WANT TO GO TO THE SAME SCHOOL AS MASHINO, BUT...
IT'S NOT LIKE YOU'LL BE CONTINUING WITH BASEBALL.
YOU MIGHT WANT TO CONSIDER CHOOSING ANOTHER SCHOOL.
CAREER GUIDANCE OFFICE
THUD
HAAH.

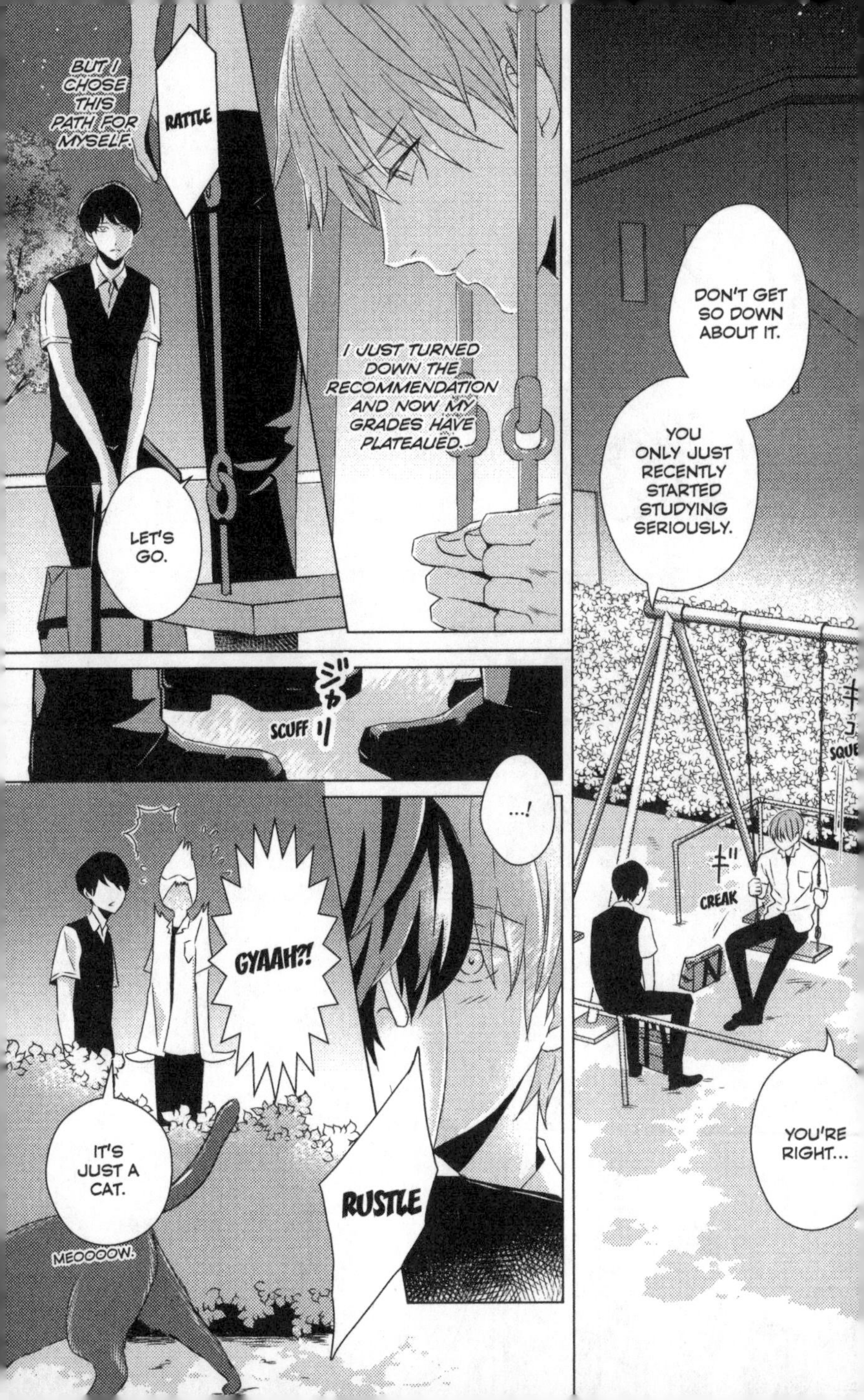

DON'T GET SO DOWN ABOUT IT.
YOU ONLY JUST RECENTLY STARTED STUDYING SERIOUSLY.
ギ
CREAK
YOU'RE RIGHT...
I JUST TURNED DOWN THE RECOMMENDATION AND NOW MY GRADES HAVE PLATEAUED.
BUT I CHOSE THIS PATH FOR MYSELF.
RATTLE
LET'S GO.
ジャリ
SCUFF
...!
RUSTLE
GYAAH?!
IT'S JUST A CAT.
MEOOOOW.

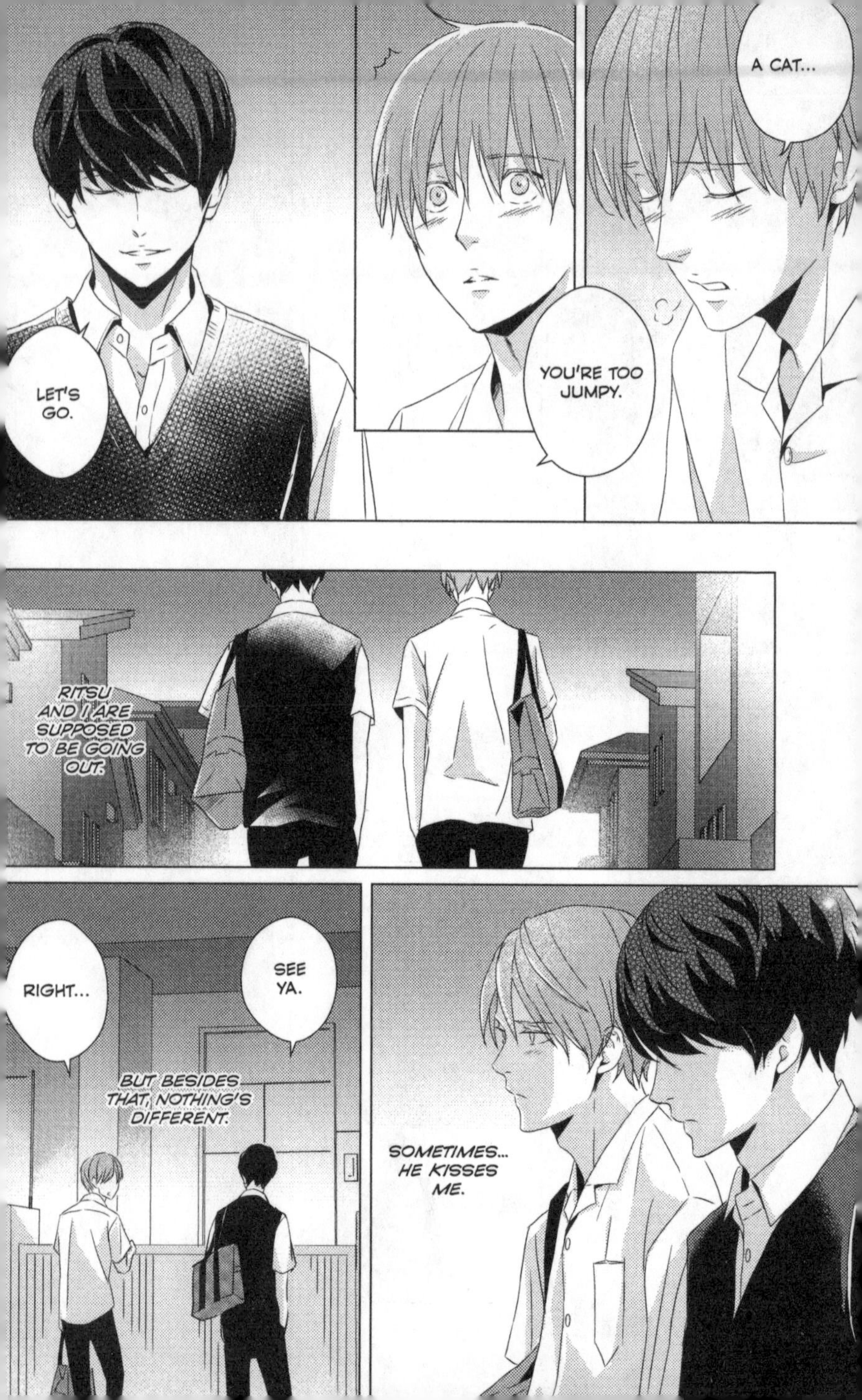
A CAT...
YOU'RE TOO JUMPY.
LET'S GO.
RITSU AND I ARE SUPPOSED TO BE GOING OUT.
SOMETIMES... HE KISSES ME.
SEE YA.
RIGHT...
BUT BESIDES THAT, NOTHING'S DIFFERENT.

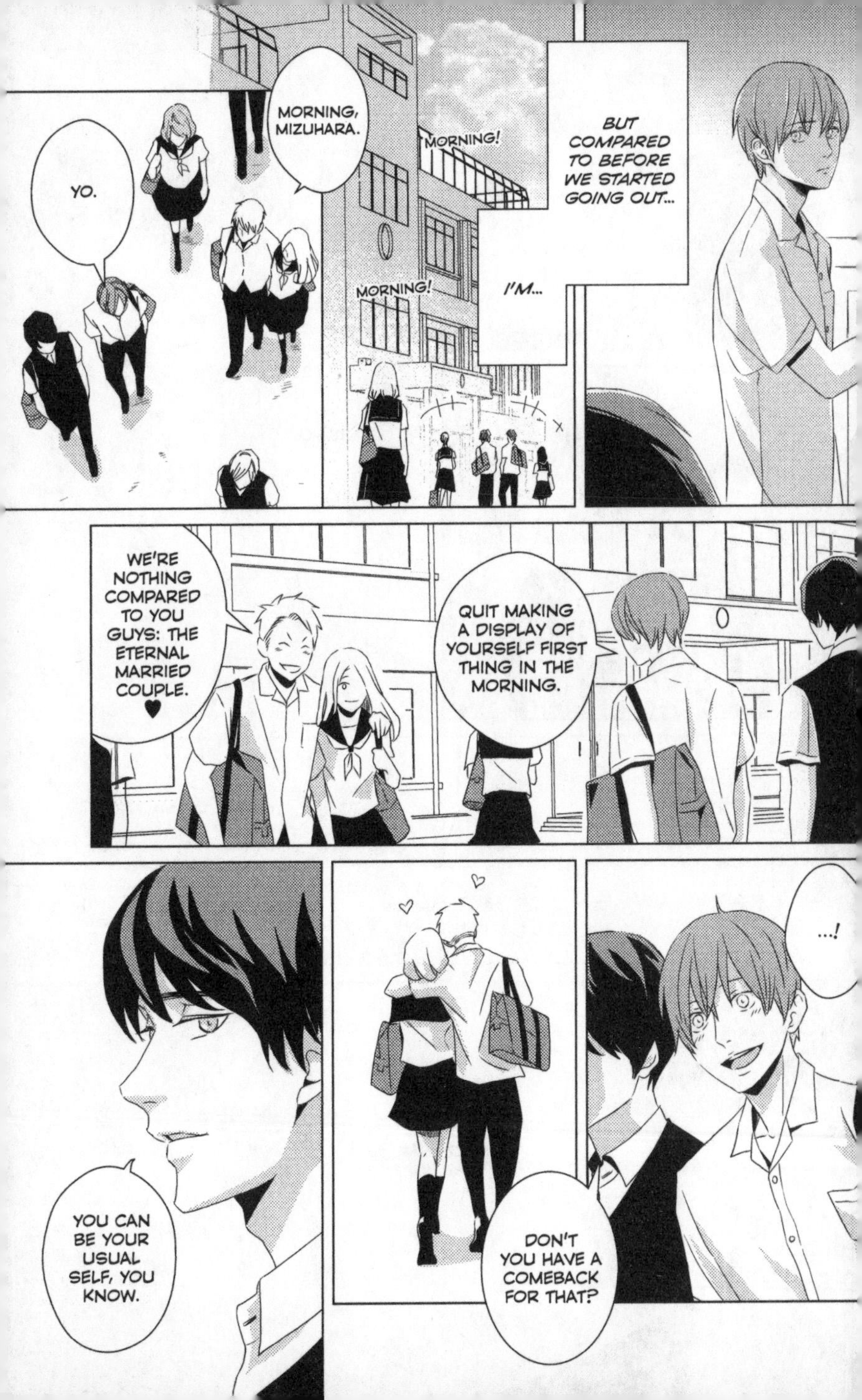
BUT COMPARED TO BEFORE WE STARTED GOING OUT...
I'M...
MORNING, MIZUHARA.
MORNING!
MORNING!
YO.
QUIT MAKING A DISPLAY OF YOURSELF FIRST THING IN THE MORNING.
WE'RE NOTHING COMPARED TO YOU GUYS: THE ETERNAL MARRIED COUPLE. ♥
...!
DON'T YOU HAVE A COMEBACK FOR THAT?
YOU CAN BE YOUR USUAL SELF, YOU KNOW.

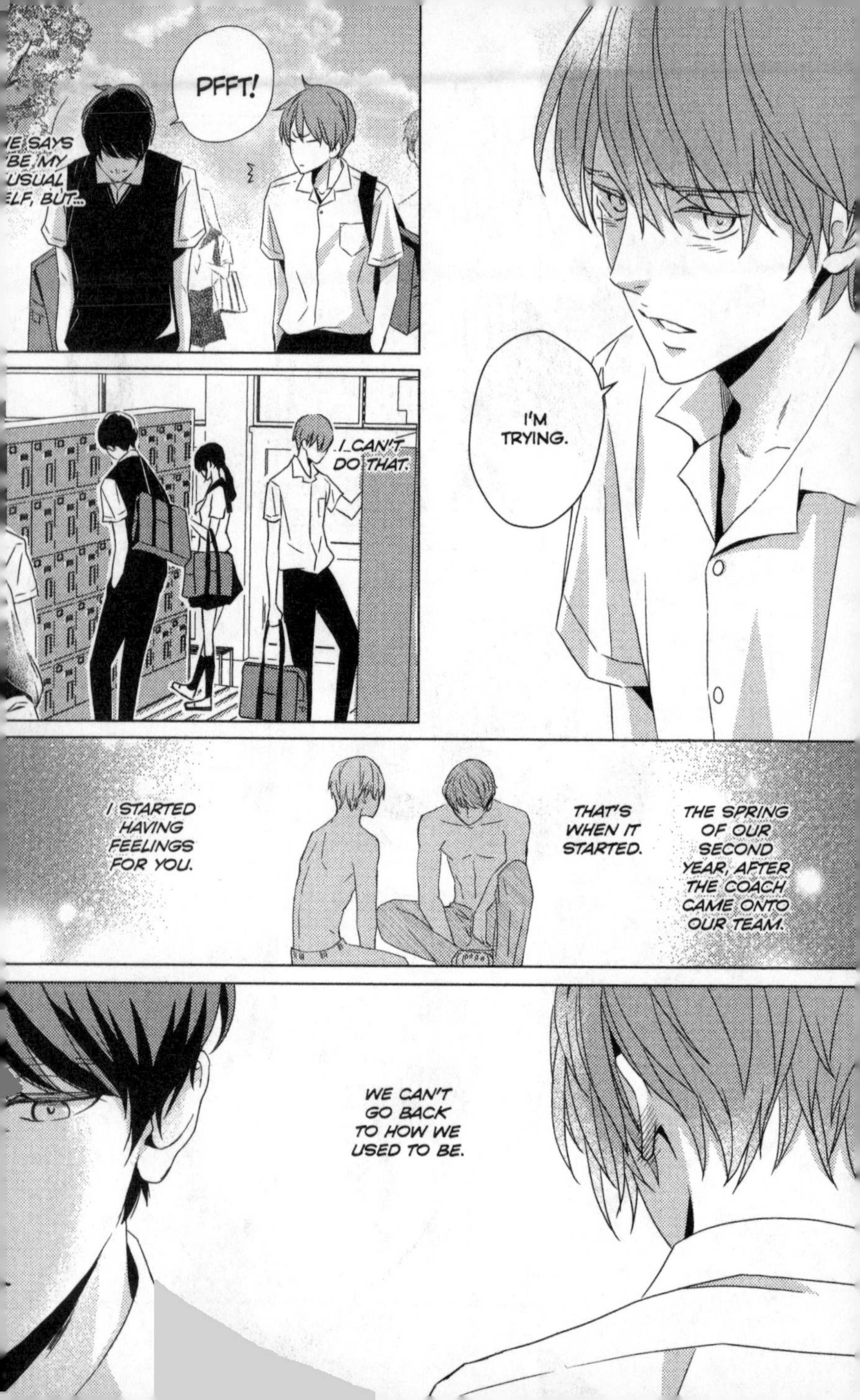
I'M TRYING.
PFFT!
E SAYS BE MY USUAL ELF, BUT...
I CAN'T DO THAT.
THE SPRING OF OUR SECOND YEAR, AFTER THE COACH CAME ONTO OUR TEAM.
THAT'S WHEN IT STARTED.
I STARTED HAVING FEELINGS FOR YOU.
WE CAN'T GO BACK TO HOW WE USED TO BE.

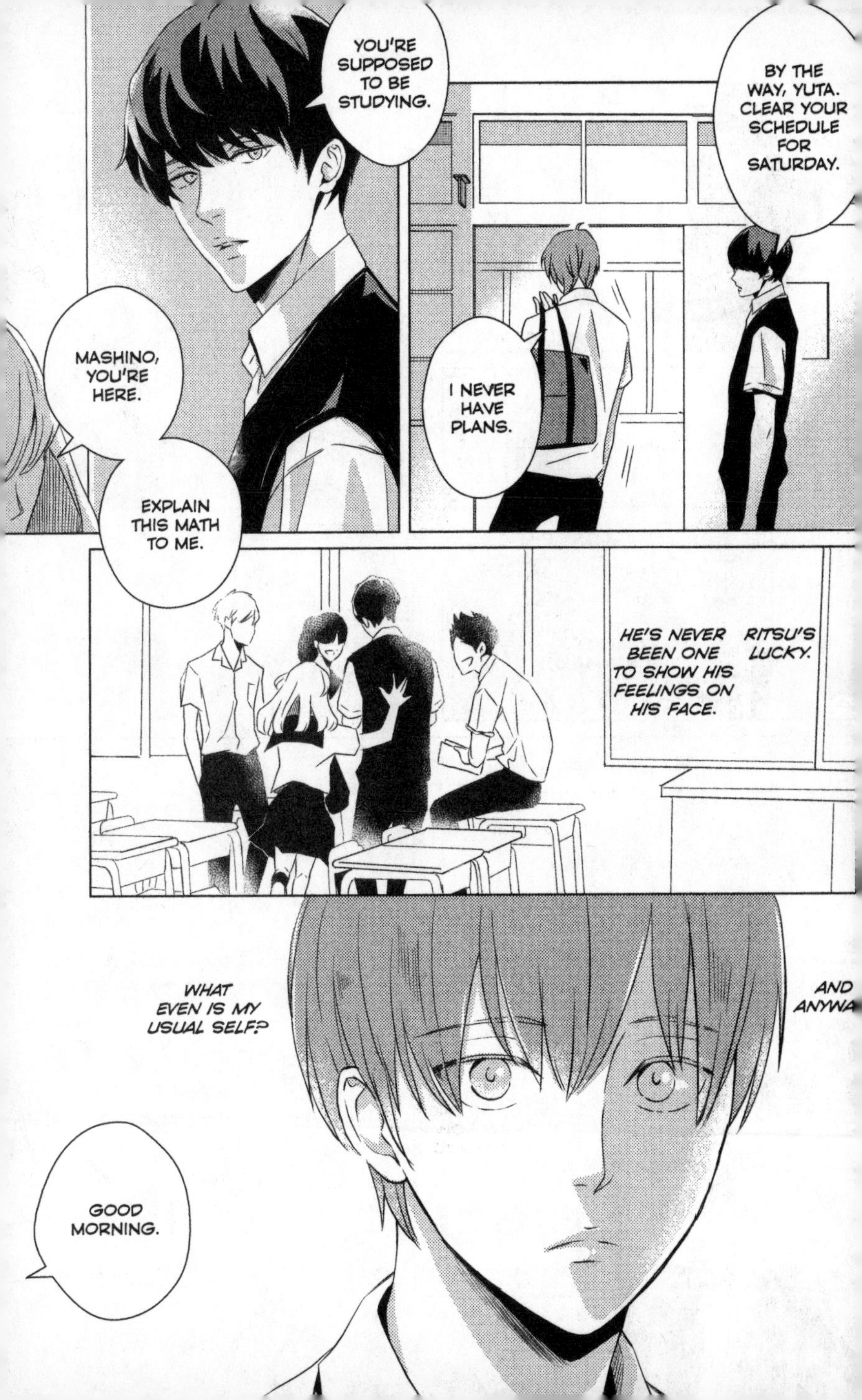
BY THE WAY, YUTA. CLEAR YOUR SCHEDULE FOR SATURDAY.
I NEVER HAVE PLANS.
MASHINO, YOU'RE HERE.
EXPLAIN THIS MATH TO ME.
YOU'RE SUPPOSED TO BE STUDYING.
RITSU'S LUCKY.
HE'S NEVER BEEN ONE TO SHOW HIS FEELINGS ON HIS FACE.
AND ANYWA
WHAT EVEN IS MY USUAL SELF?
GOOD MORNING.

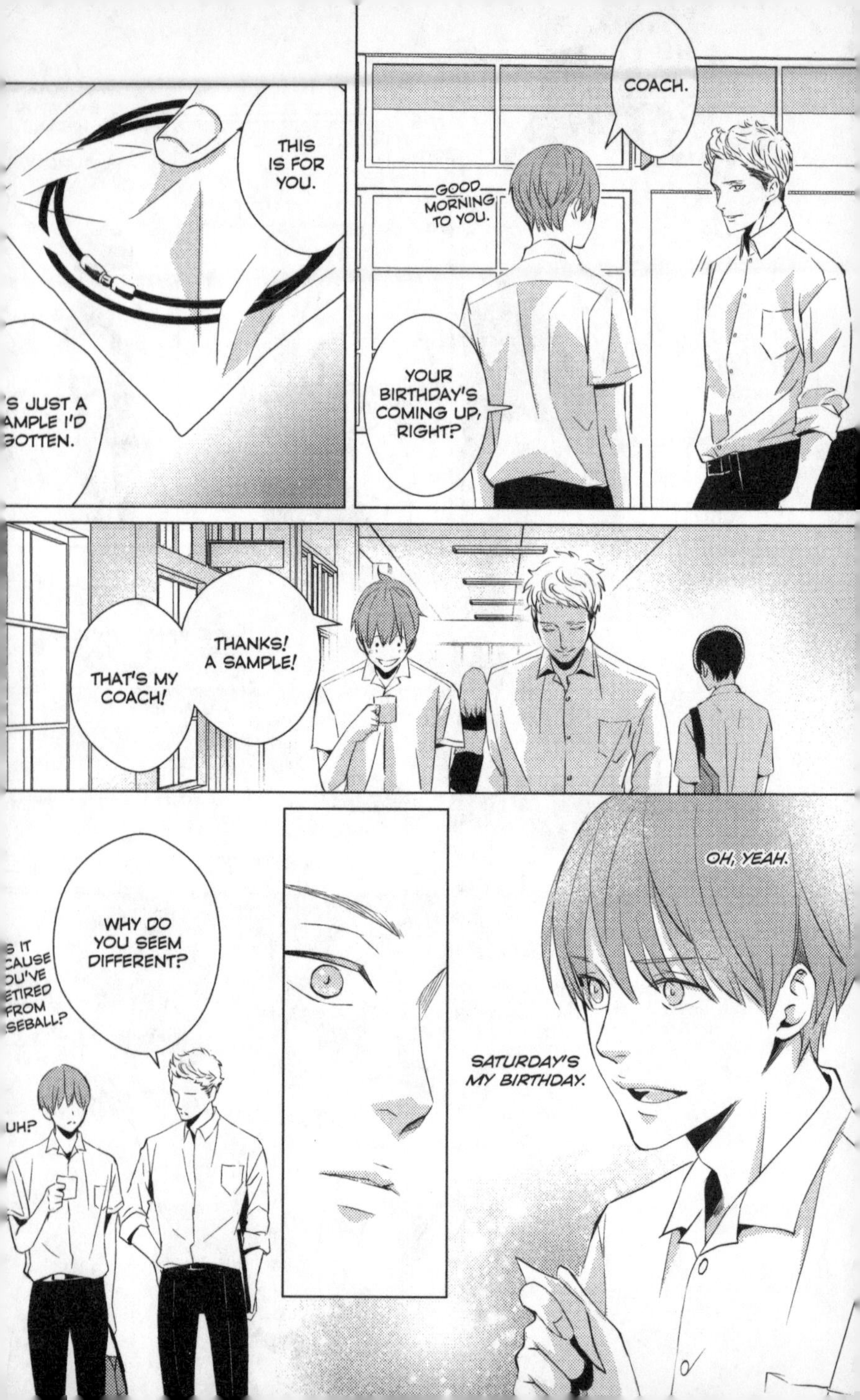
COACH.
GOOD MORNING TO YOU.
YOUR BIRTHDAY'S COMING UP, RIGHT?
THIS IS FOR YOU.
'S JUST A AMPLE I'D GOTTEN.
THANKS! A SAMPLE!
THAT'S MY COACH!
OH, YEAH.
SATURDAY'S MY BIRTHDAY.
WHY DO YOU SEEM DIFFERENT?
S IT CAUSE OU'VE ETIRED FROM SEBALL?
UH?

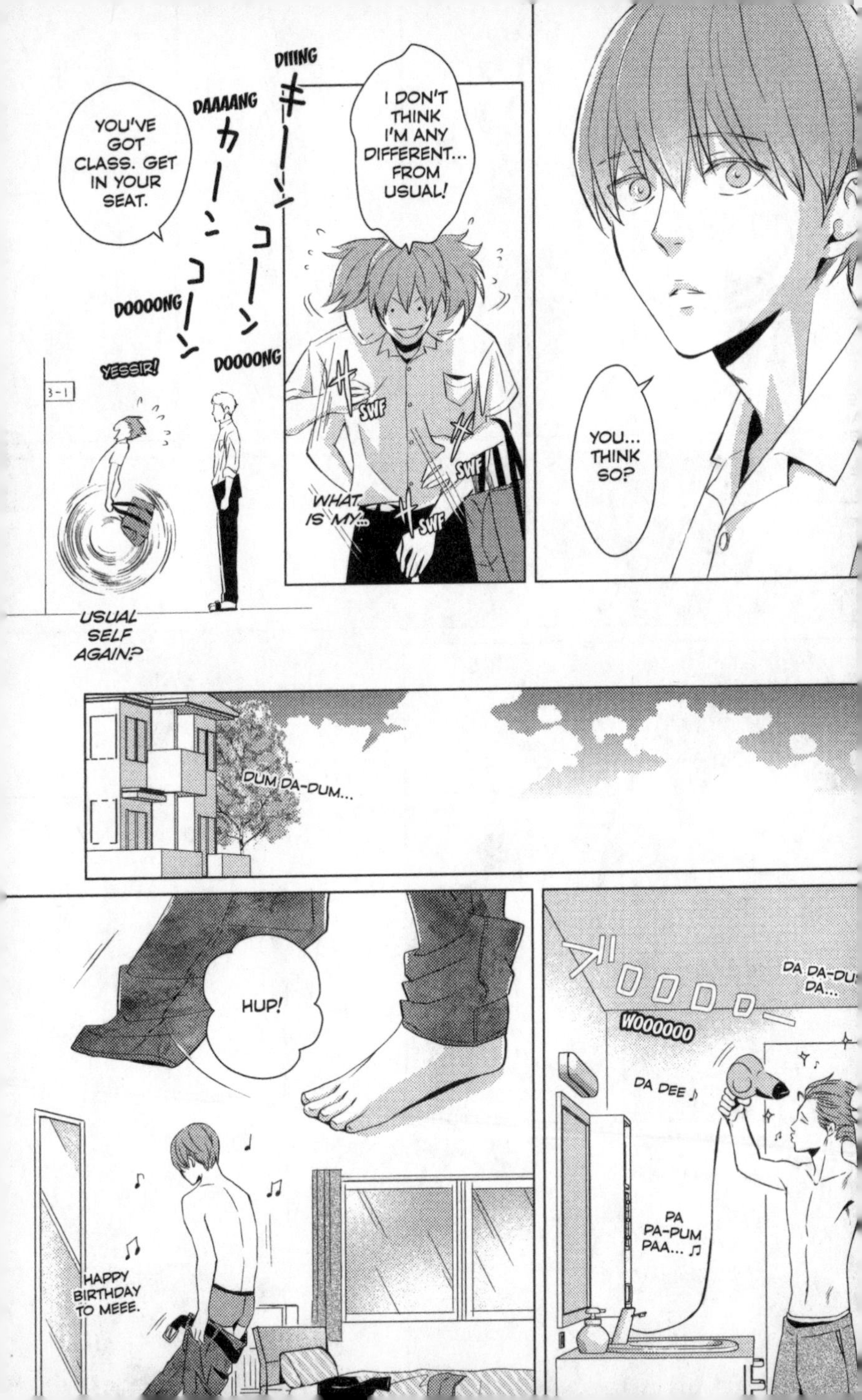
YOU... THINK SO?
DIIING
I DON'T THINK I'M ANY DIFFERENT... FROM USUAL!
SWF
SWF
SWF
WHAT IS MY...
DAAAANG
YOU'VE GOT CLASS. GET IN YOUR SEAT.
DOOOONG
DOOOONG
YESSIR!
3-1
USUAL SELF AGAIN?
DUM DA-DUM...
WOOOOOO
DA DA-DU DA...
DA DEE ♪
PA PA-PUM PAA... ♫
HUP!
HAPPY BIRTHDAY TO MEEE.

...

FWAP

WHY'RE YOU DRESSED LIKE THAT?

THIS WAS THE MOST "USUAL ME" I COULD THINK OF.

VRRRRRROOM

HM?

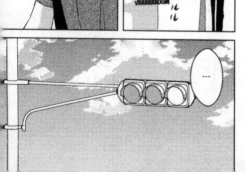

...

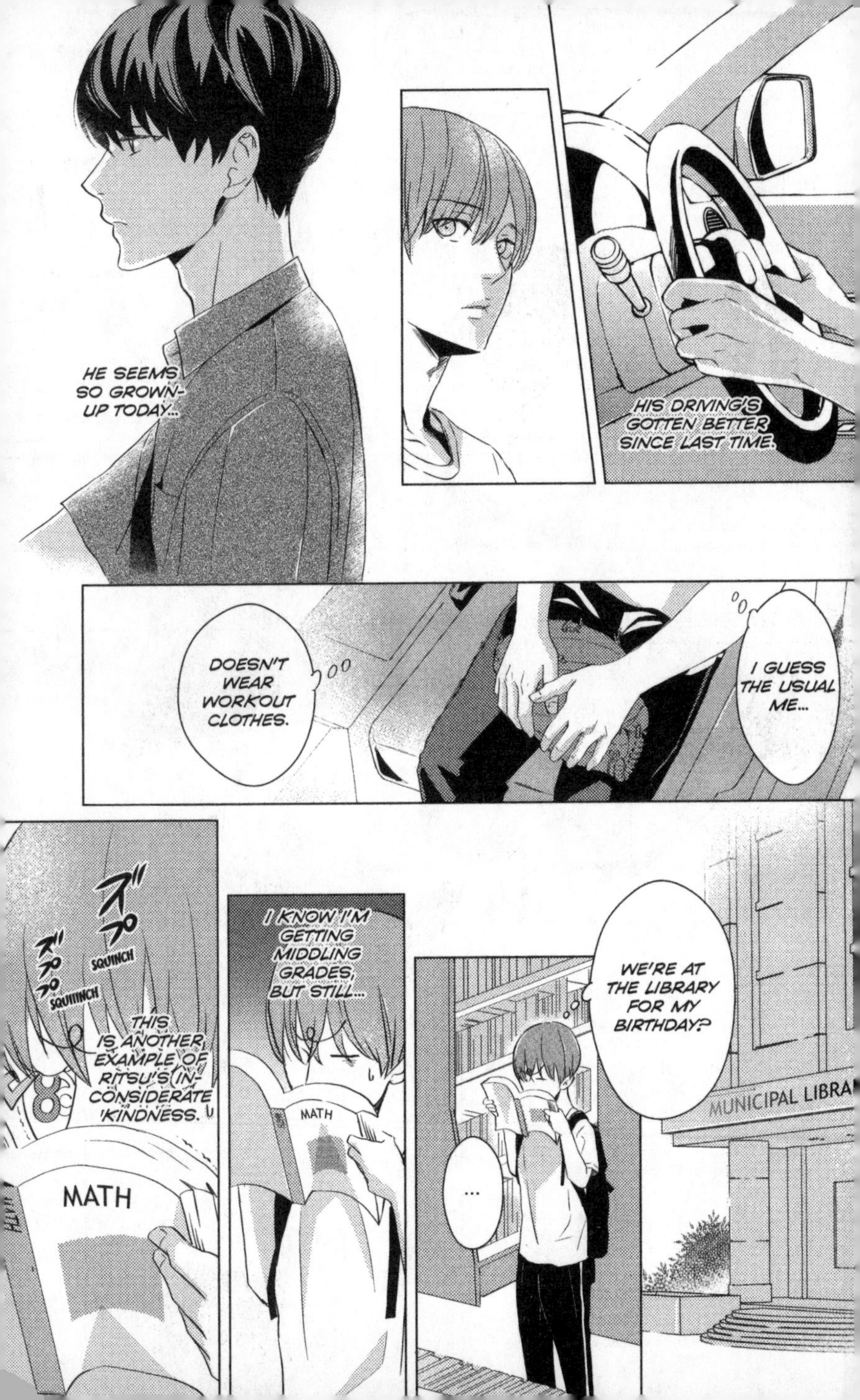
HIS DRIVING'S GOTTEN BETTER SINCE LAST TIME.
HE SEEMS SO GROWN-UP TODAY...
I GUESS THE USUAL ME...
DOESN'T WEAR WORKOUT CLOTHES.
MUNICIPAL LIBRA
WE'RE AT THE LIBRARY FOR MY BIRTHDAY?
...
I KNOW I'M GETTING MIDDLING GRADES, BUT STILL...
MATH
ズプ
SQUINCH
ズププ
SQUIIINCH
THIS IS ANOTHER EXAMPLE OF RITSU'S IN-CONSIDERATE KINDNESS.
MATH

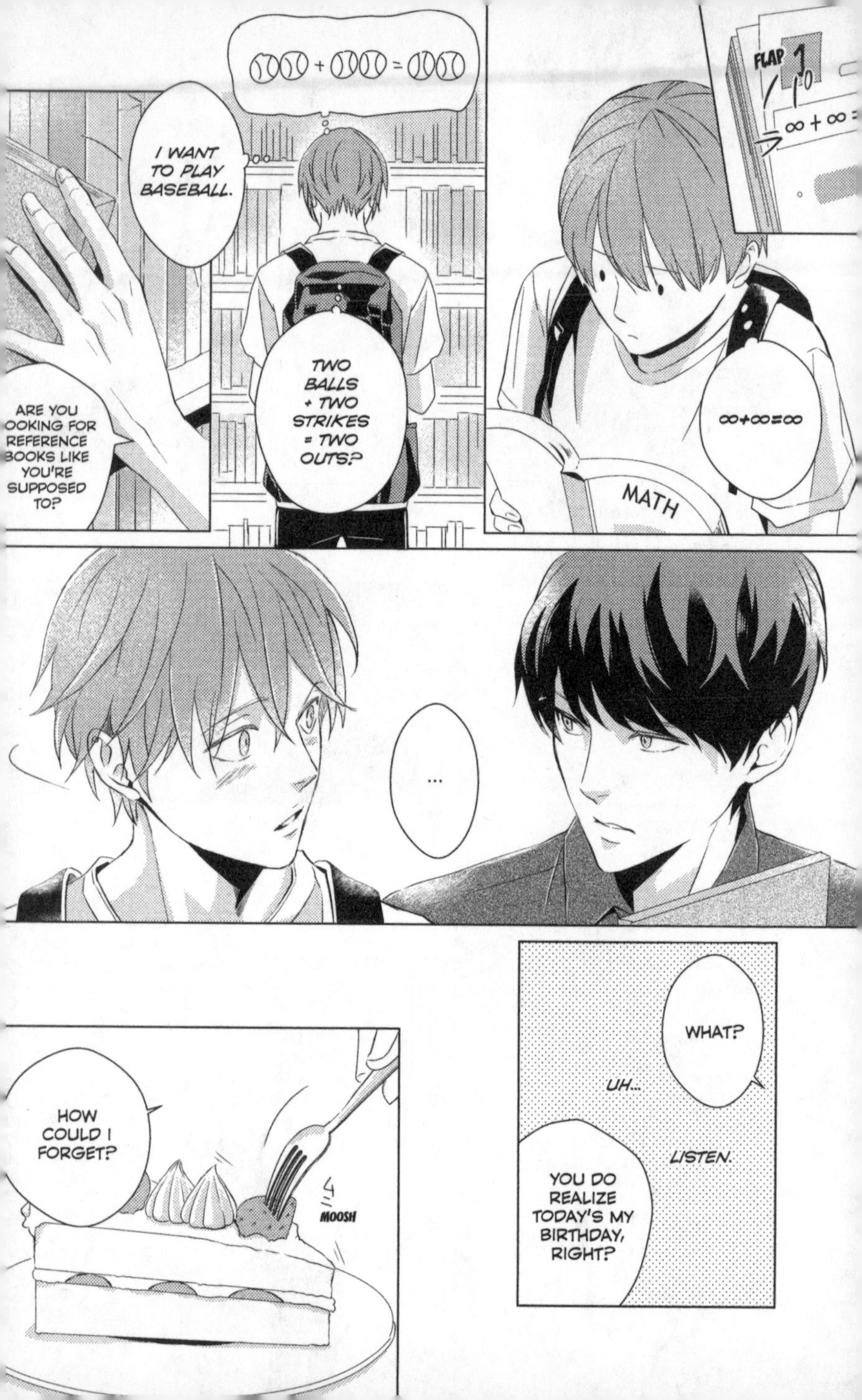

FLAP
∞+∞=∞
MATH
TWO BALLS + TWO STRIKES = TWO OUTS?
I WANT TO PLAY BASEBALL.
ARE YOU OOKING FOR REFERENCE BOOKS LIKE YOU'RE SUPPOSED TO?
...
WHAT?
UH...
LISTEN.
YOU DO REALIZE TODAY'S MY BIRTHDAY, RIGHT?
HOW COULD I FORGET?
MOOSH

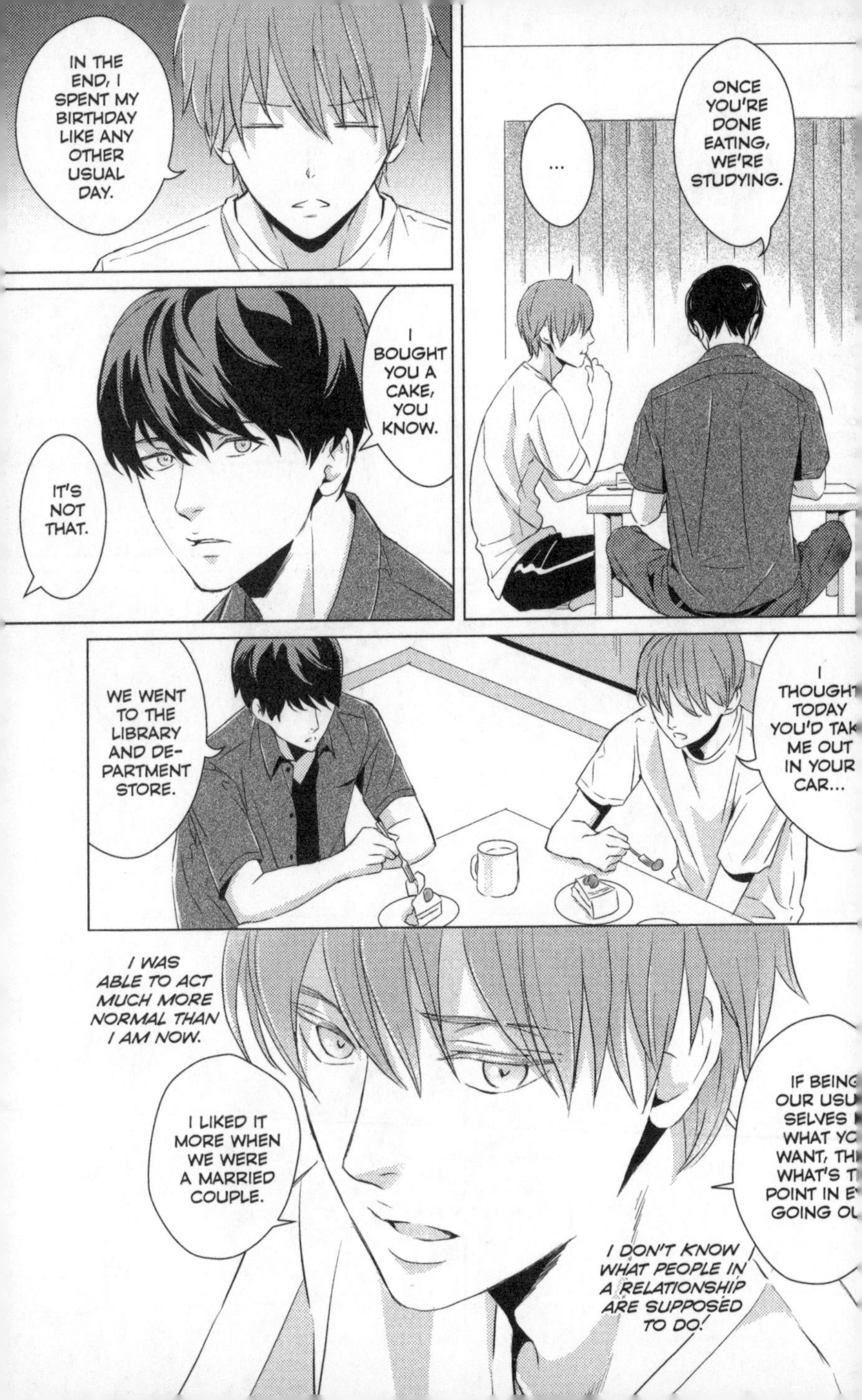
ONCE YOU'RE DONE EATING, WE'RE STUDYING.
...
IN THE END, I SPENT MY BIRTHDAY LIKE ANY OTHER USUAL DAY.
I BOUGHT YOU A CAKE, YOU KNOW.
IT'S NOT THAT.
I THOUGHT TODAY YOU'D TAK ME OUT IN YOUR CAR...
WE WENT TO THE LIBRARY AND DE- PARTMENT STORE.
IF BEING OUR USU SELVES I WHAT YO WANT, TH WHAT'S T POINT IN E GOING OU
I WAS ABLE TO ACT MUCH MORE NORMAL THAN I AM NOW.
I LIKED IT MORE WHEN WE WERE A MARRIED COUPLE.
I DON'T KNOW WHAT PEOPLE IN A RELATIONSHIP ARE SUPPOSED TO DO!

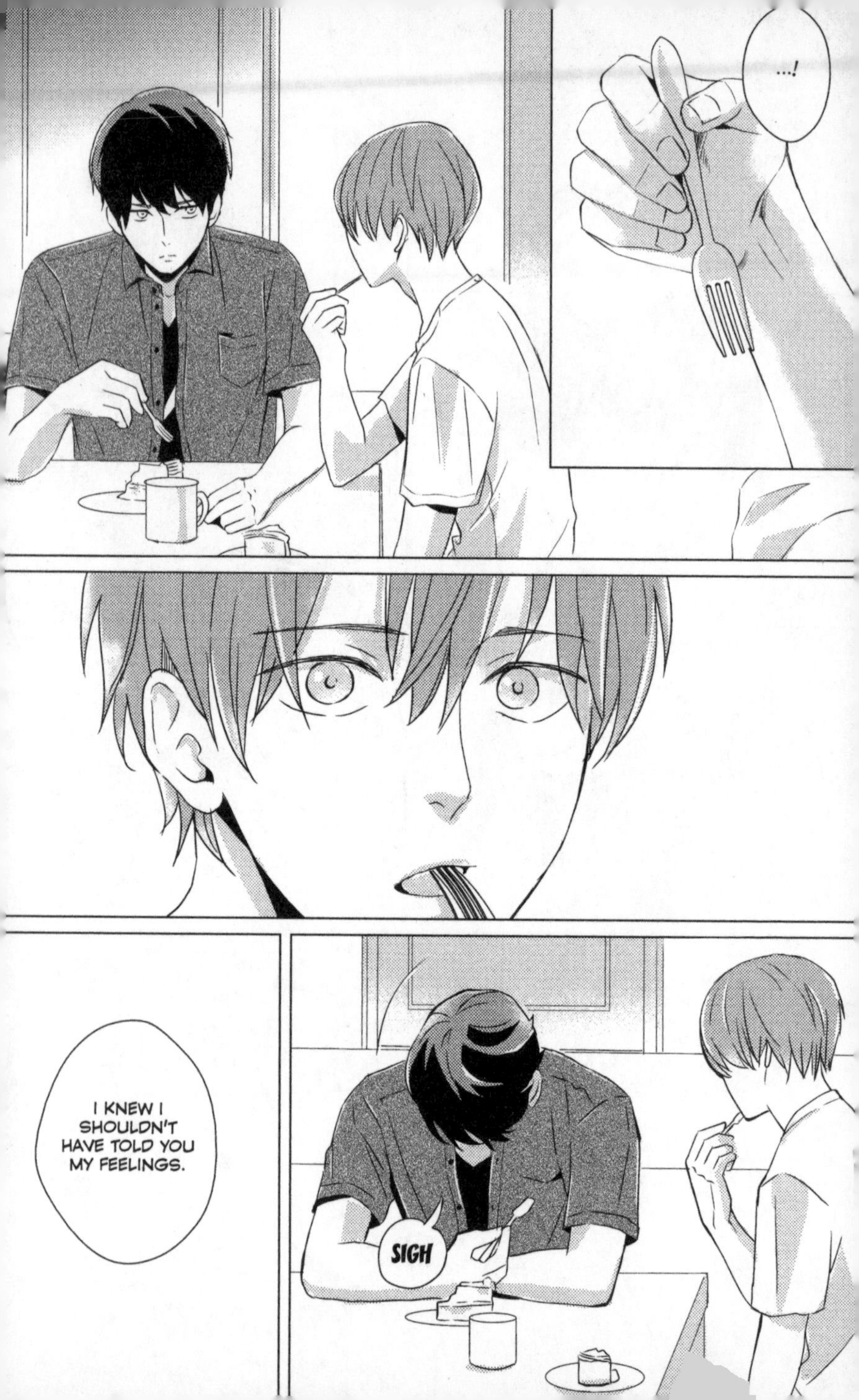
...!
SIGH
I KNEW I SHOULDN'T HAVE TOLD YOU MY FEELINGS.

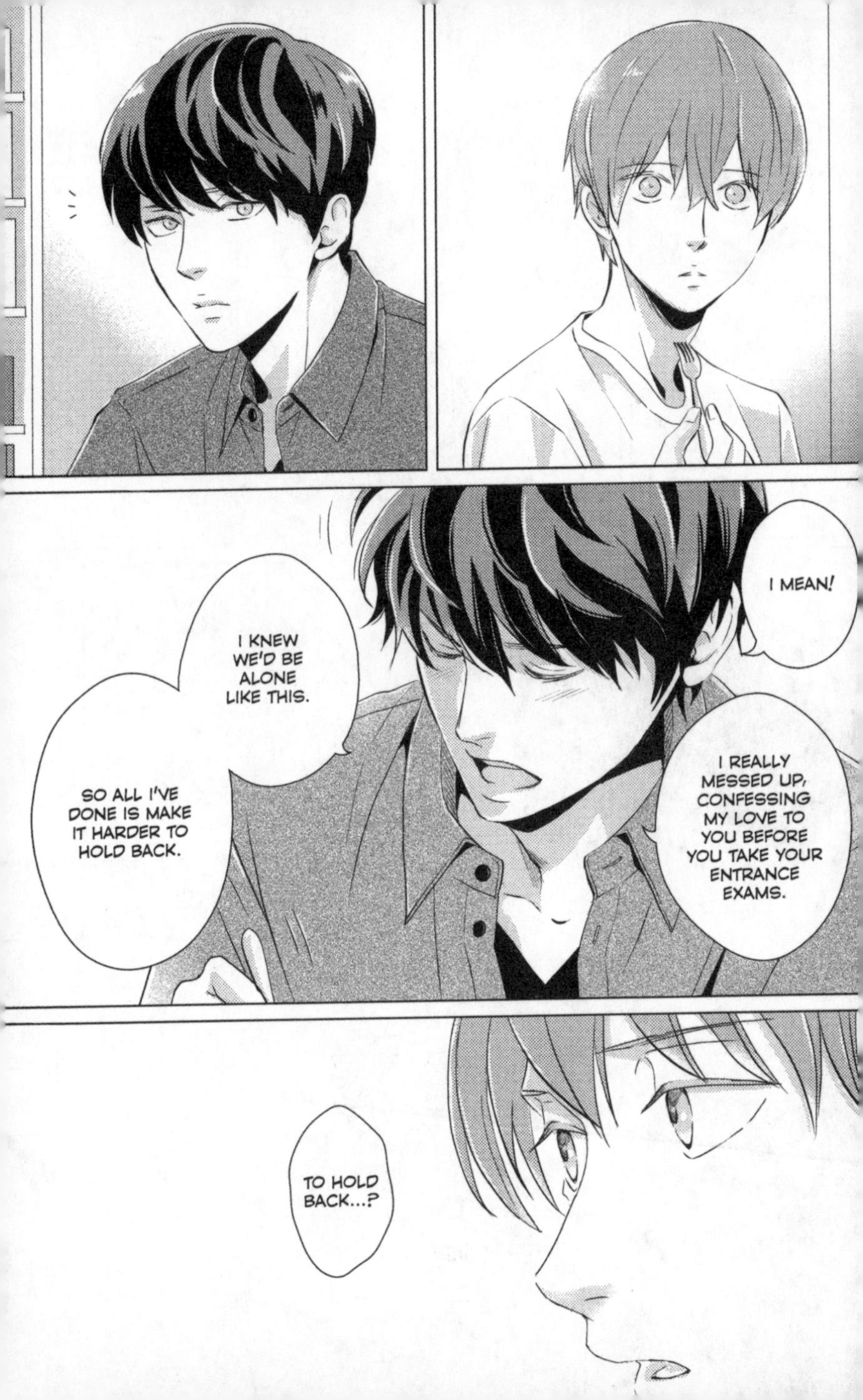
I MEAN!
I REALLY MESSED UP, CONFESSING MY LOVE TO YOU BEFORE YOU TAKE YOUR ENTRANCE EXAMS.
I KNEW WE'D BE ALONE LIKE THIS.
SO ALL I'VE DONE IS MAKE IT HARDER TO HOLD BACK.
TO HOLD BACK...?

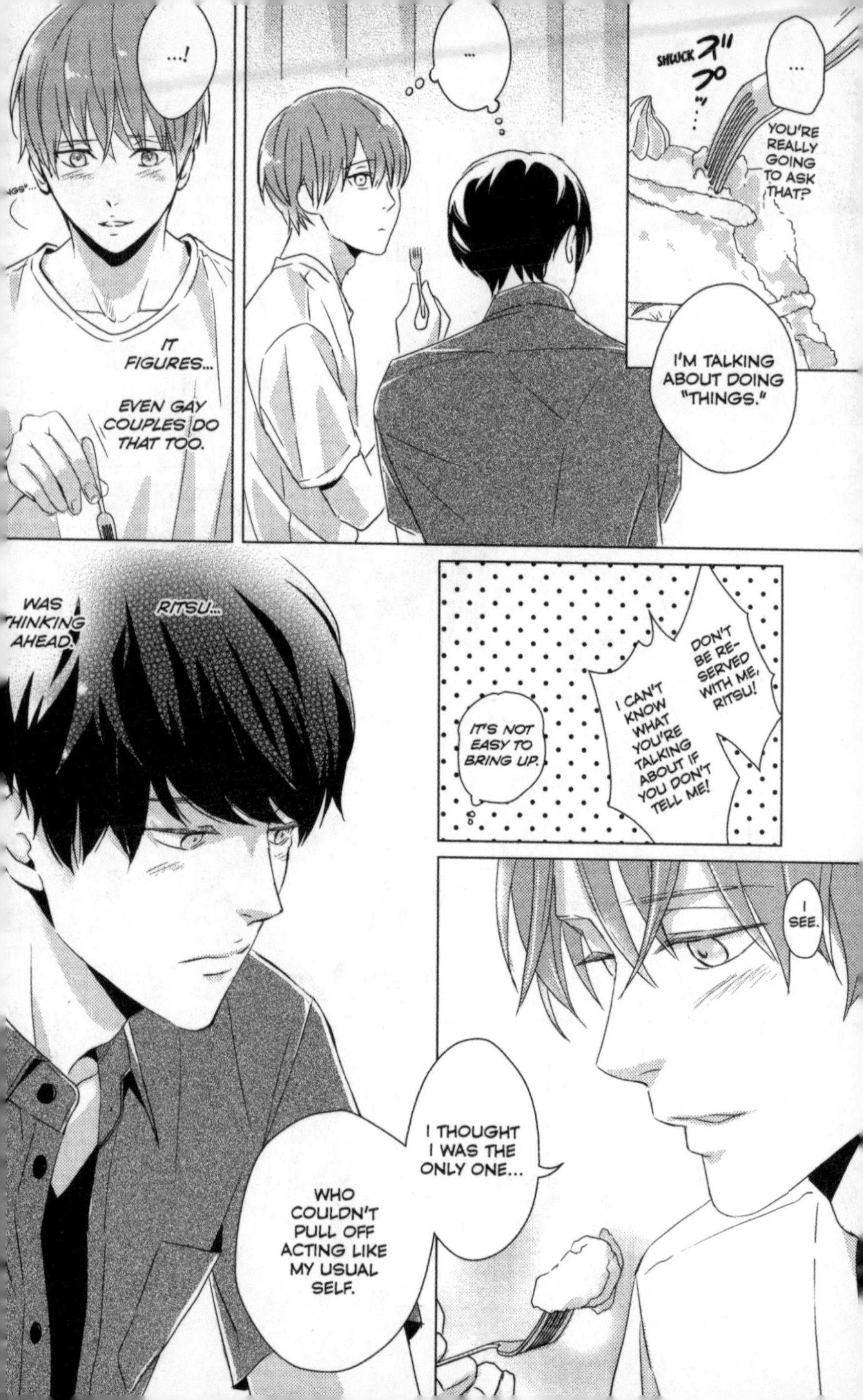
...
SHUCK
YOU'RE REALLY GOING TO ASK THAT?
I'M TALKING ABOUT DOING "THINGS."
...
...!
IT FIGURES...
EVEN GAY COUPLES DO THAT TOO.
DON'T BE RE-SERVED WITH ME, RITSU!
I CAN'T KNOW WHAT YOU'RE TALKING ABOUT IF YOU DON'T TELL ME!
IT'S NOT EASY TO BRING UP.
I SEE.
I THOUGHT I WAS THE ONLY ONE...
WHO COULDN'T PULL OFF ACTING LIKE MY USUAL SELF.
RITSU...
WAS THINKING AHEAD.

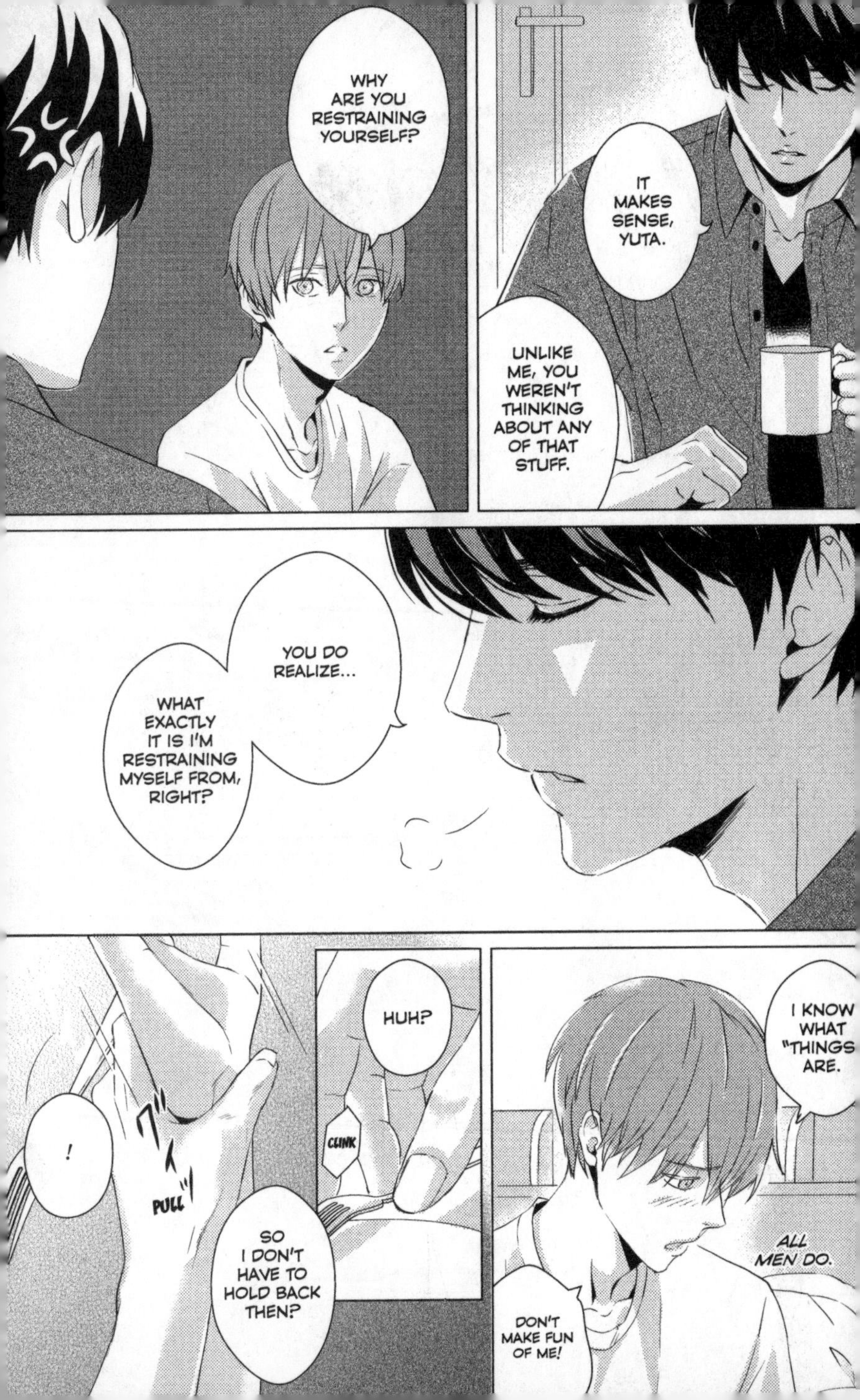
IT MAKES SENSE, YUTA.
UNLIKE ME, YOU WEREN'T THINKING ABOUT ANY OF THAT STUFF.
WHY ARE YOU RESTRAINING YOURSELF?
YOU DO REALIZE...
WHAT EXACTLY IT IS I'M RESTRAINING MYSELF FROM, RIGHT?
I KNOW WHAT "THINGS ARE.
ALL MEN DO.
DON'T MAKE FUN OF ME!
HUH?
CLINK
SO I DON'T HAVE TO HOLD BACK THEN?
!
PULL

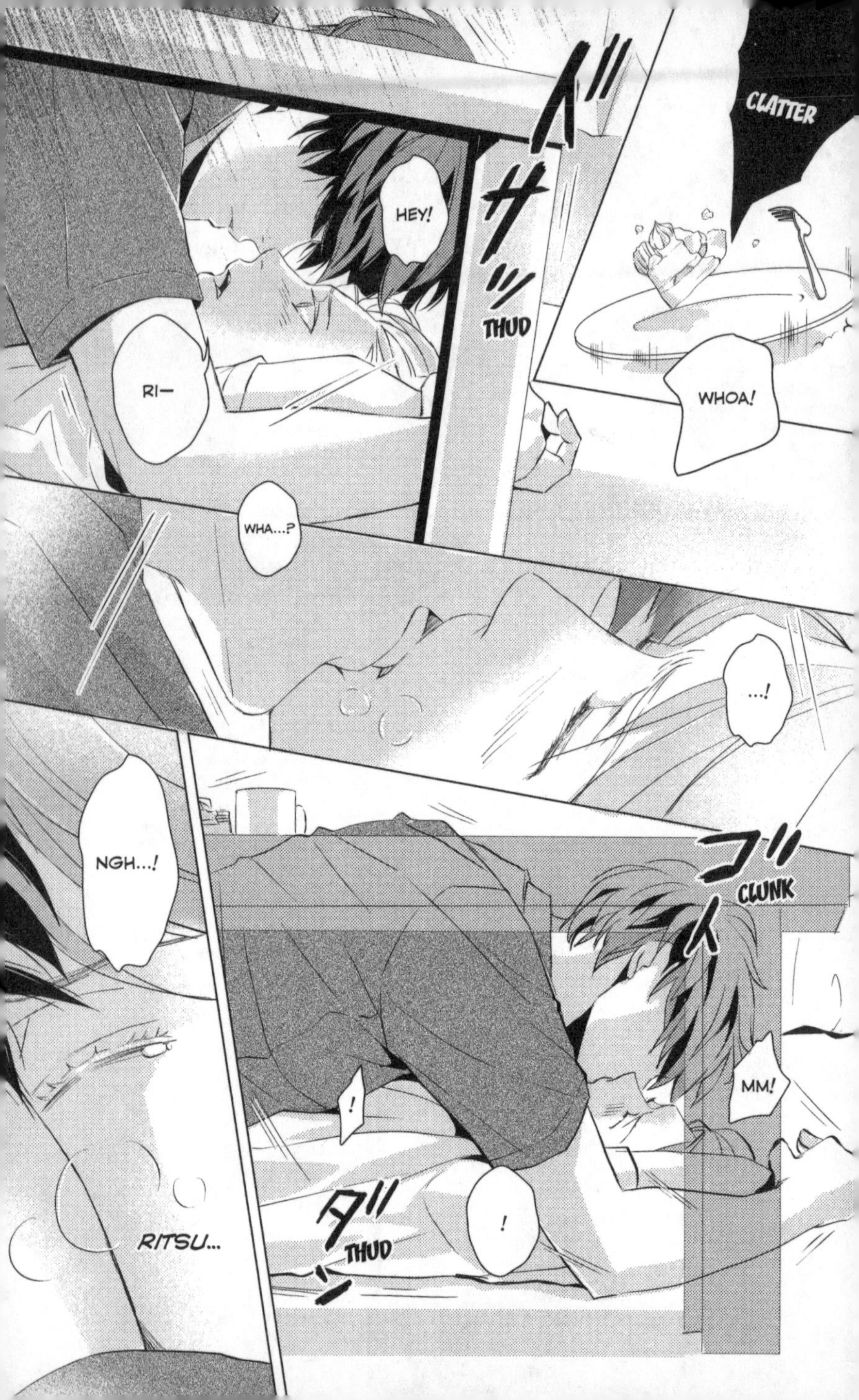
CLATTER
WHOA!
THUD
HEY!
RI—
WHA...?
...!
CLUNK
MM!
!
!
THUD
NGH...!
RITSU...

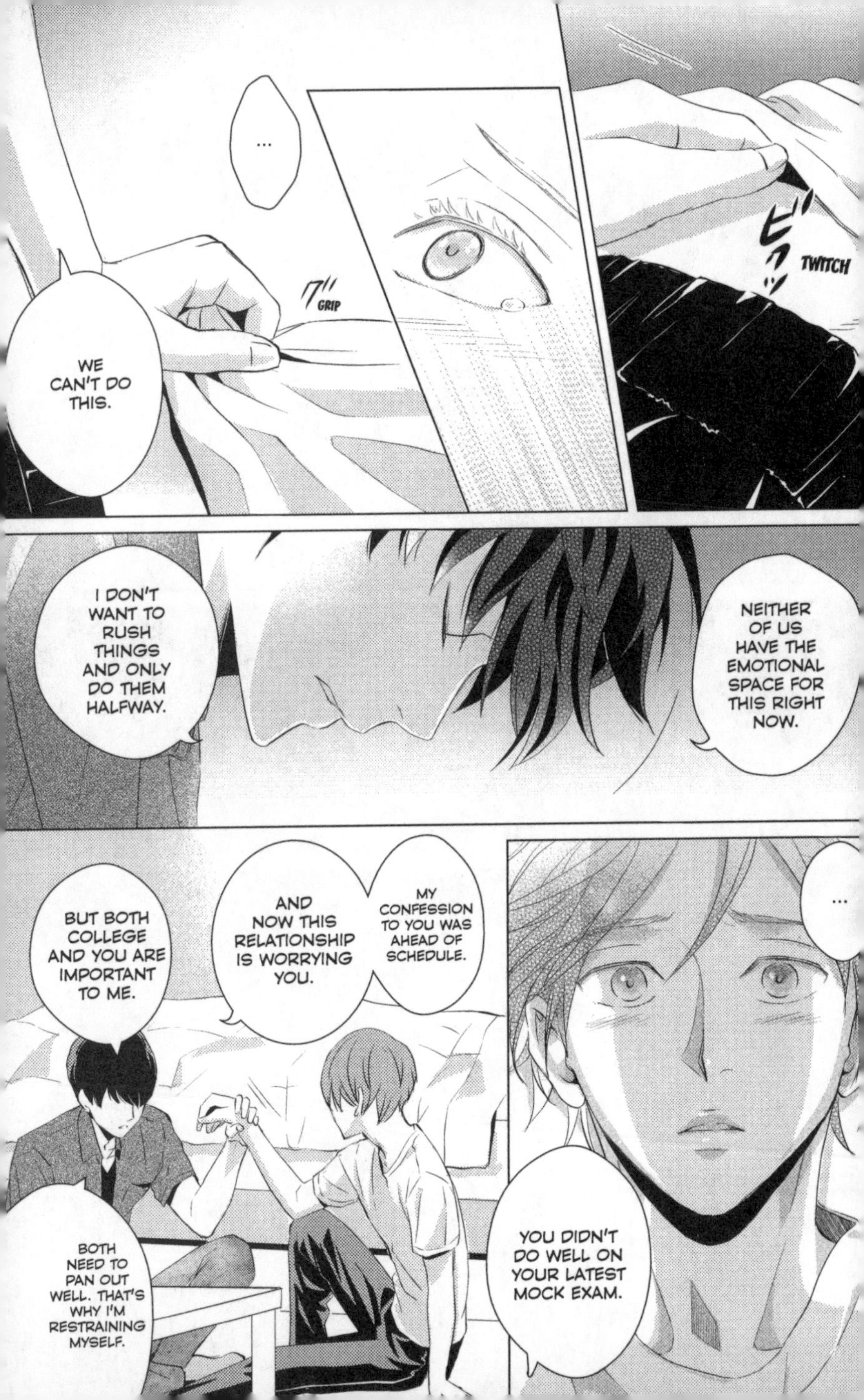
ビクッ
TWITCH
...
グッ
GRIP
WE CAN'T DO THIS.
NEITHER OF US HAVE THE EMOTIONAL SPACE FOR THIS RIGHT NOW.
I DON'T WANT TO RUSH THINGS AND ONLY DO THEM HALFWAY.
...
YOU DIDN'T DO WELL ON YOUR LATEST MOCK EXAM.
MY CONFESSION TO YOU WAS AHEAD OF SCHEDULE.
AND NOW THIS RELATIONSHIP IS WORRYING YOU.
BUT BOTH COLLEGE AND YOU ARE IMPORTANT TO ME.
BOTH NEED TO PAN OUT WELL. THAT'S WHY I'M RESTRAINING MYSELF.

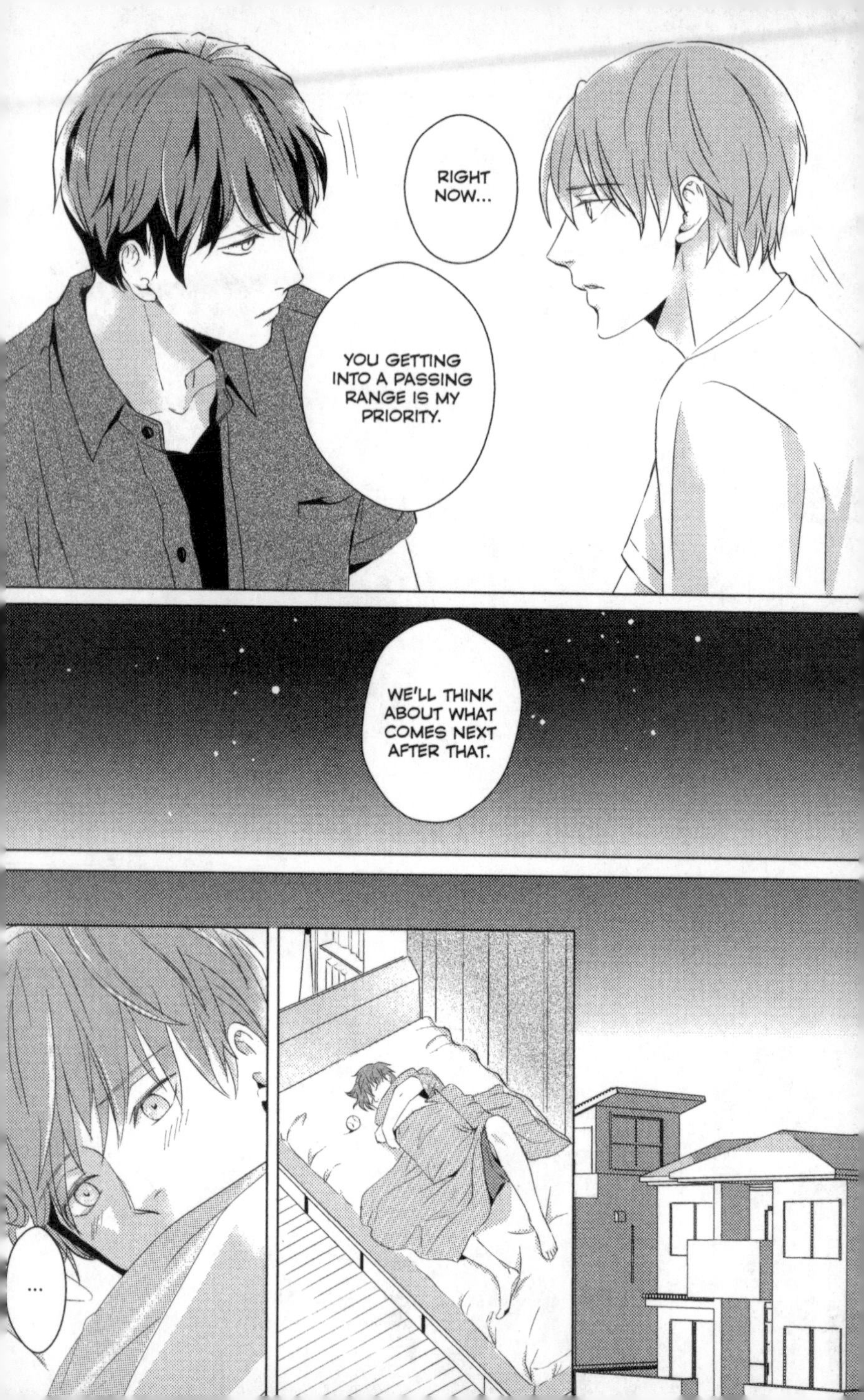
RIGHT NOW...
YOU GETTING INTO A PASSING RANGE IS MY PRIORITY.
WE'LL THINK ABOUT WHAT COMES NEXT AFTER THAT.
...

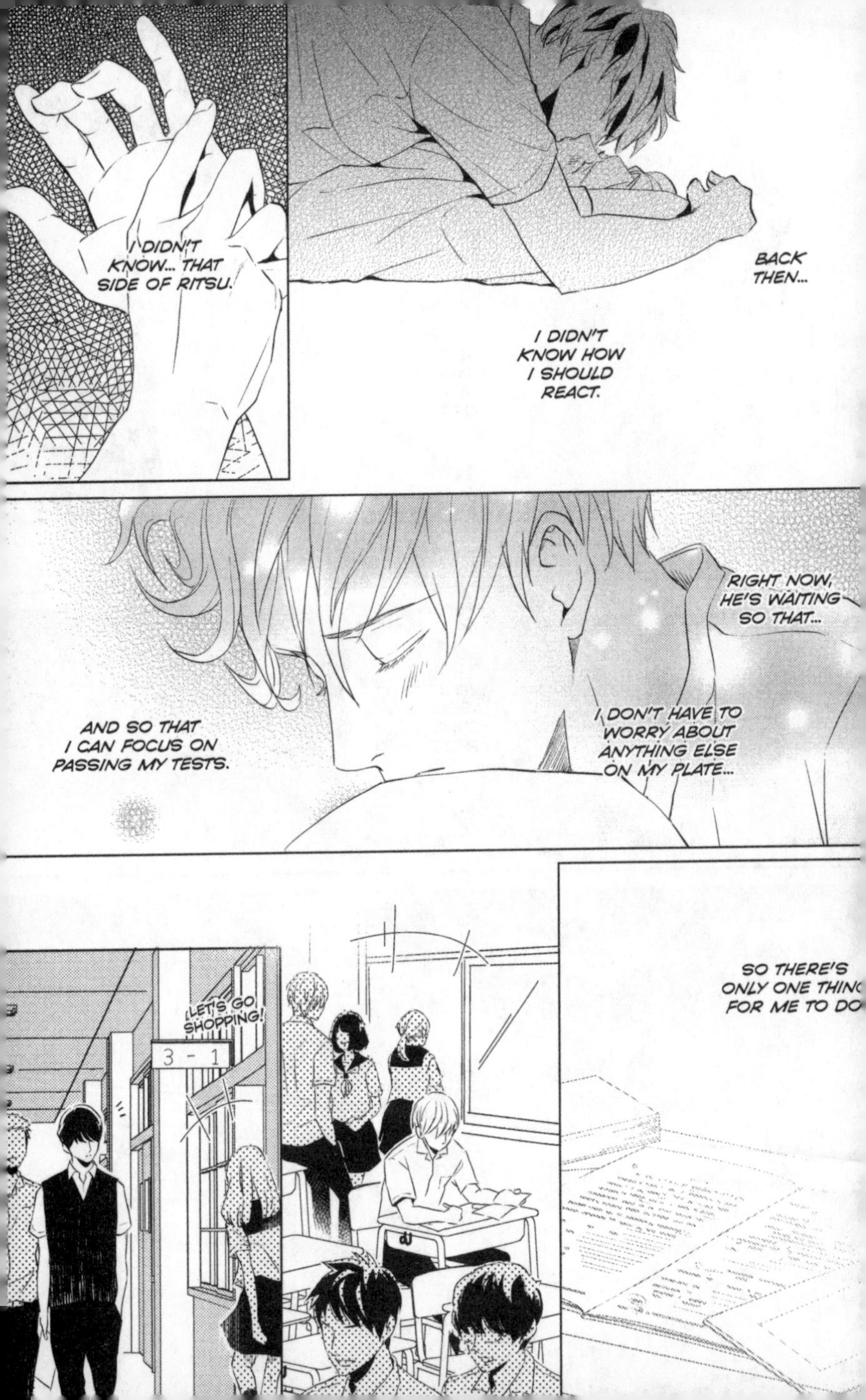
BACK THEN...
I DIDN'T KNOW HOW I SHOULD REACT.
I DIDN'T KNOW... THAT SIDE OF RITSU.
RIGHT NOW, HE'S WAITING SO THAT...
I DON'T HAVE TO WORRY ABOUT ANYTHING ELSE ON MY PLATE...
AND SO THAT I CAN FOCUS ON PASSING MY TESTS.
SO THERE'S ONLY ONE THIN FOR ME TO DO
LET'S GO SHOPPING!
3 - 1

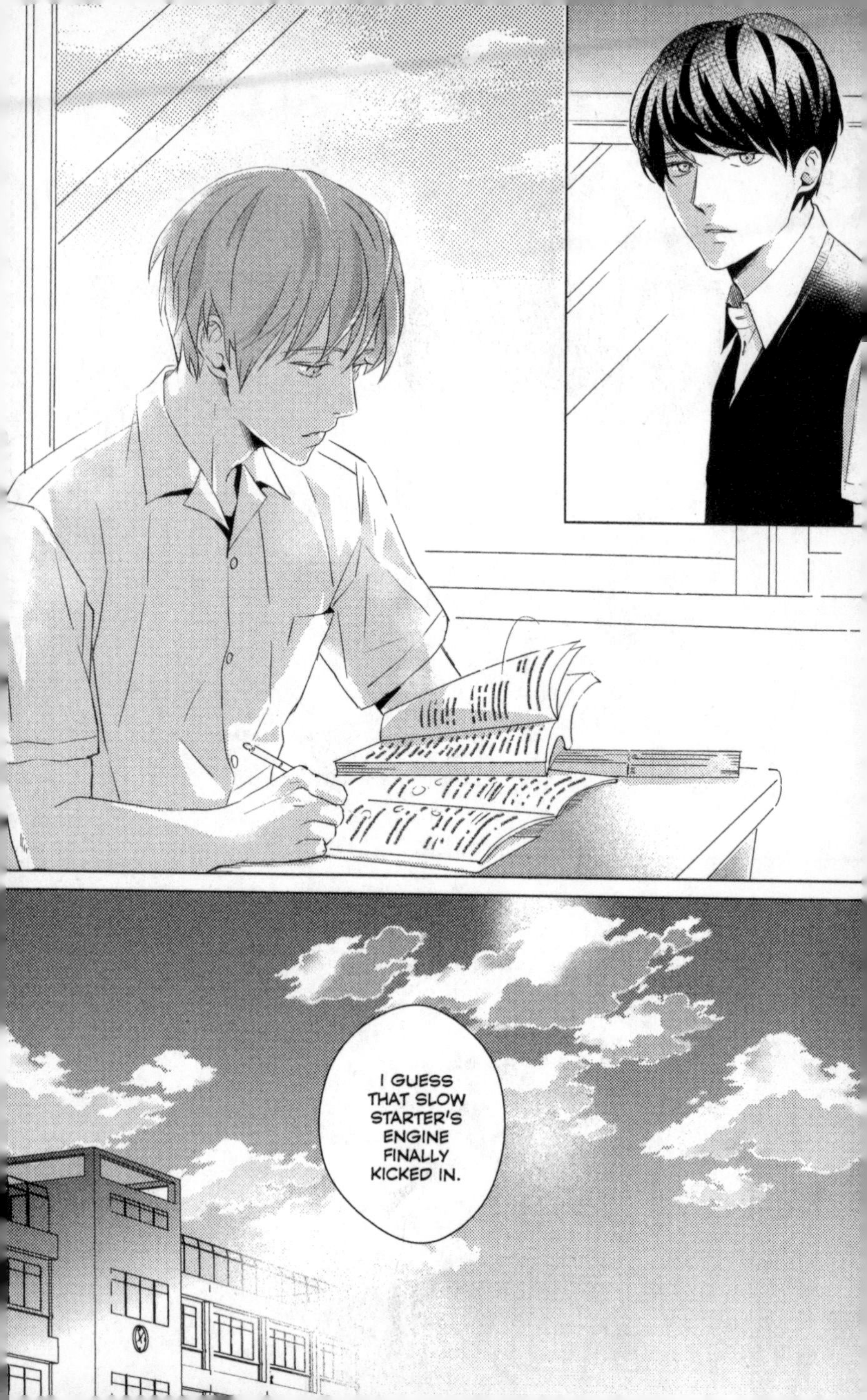
I GUESS THAT SLOW STARTER'S ENGINE FINALLY KICKED IN.

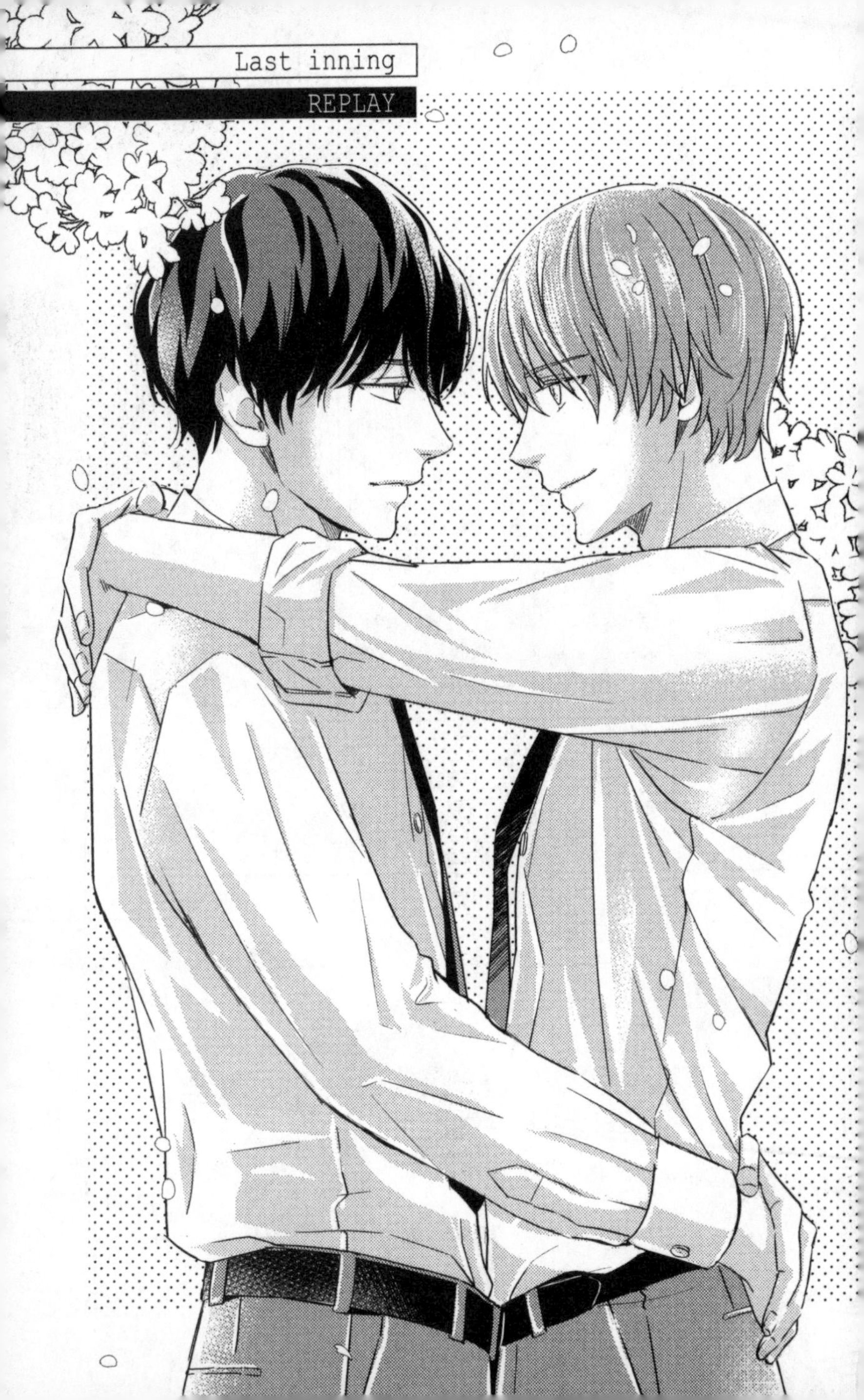
Last inning
REPLAY

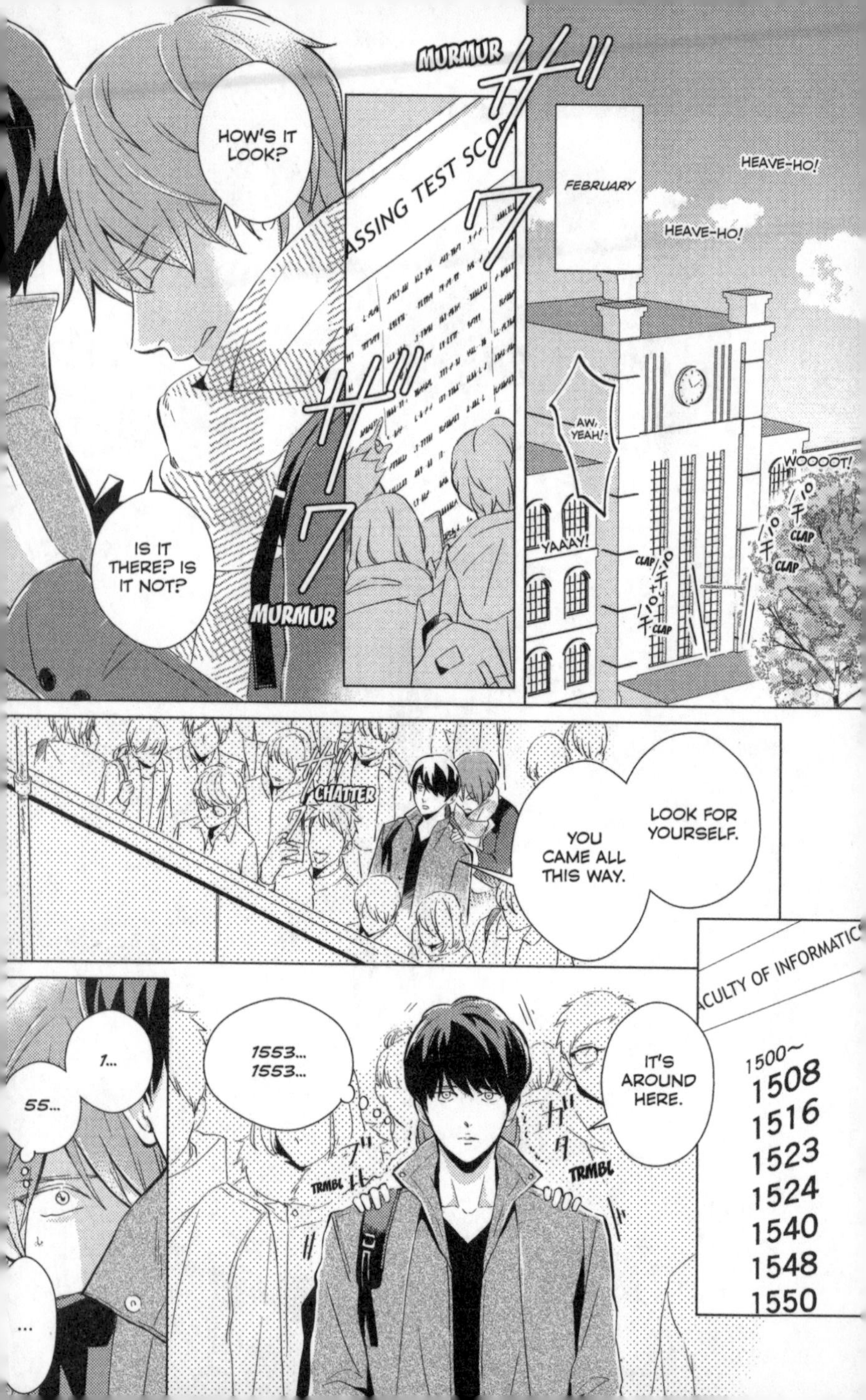
FEBRUARY
HEAVE-HO!
HEAVE-HO!
AW, YEAH!
WOOOOT!
CLAP
CLAP
YAAAY!
CLAP
CLAP
MURMUR
ASSING TEST SCO
HOW'S IT LOOK?
IS IT THERE? IS IT NOT?
MURMUR
CHATTER
YOU CAME ALL THIS WAY. LOOK FOR YOURSELF.
ACULTY OF INFORMATIC
1500~
1508
1516
1523
1524
1540
1548
1550
IT'S AROUND HERE.
TRMBL
1553... 1553...
TRMBL
1...
55...
...

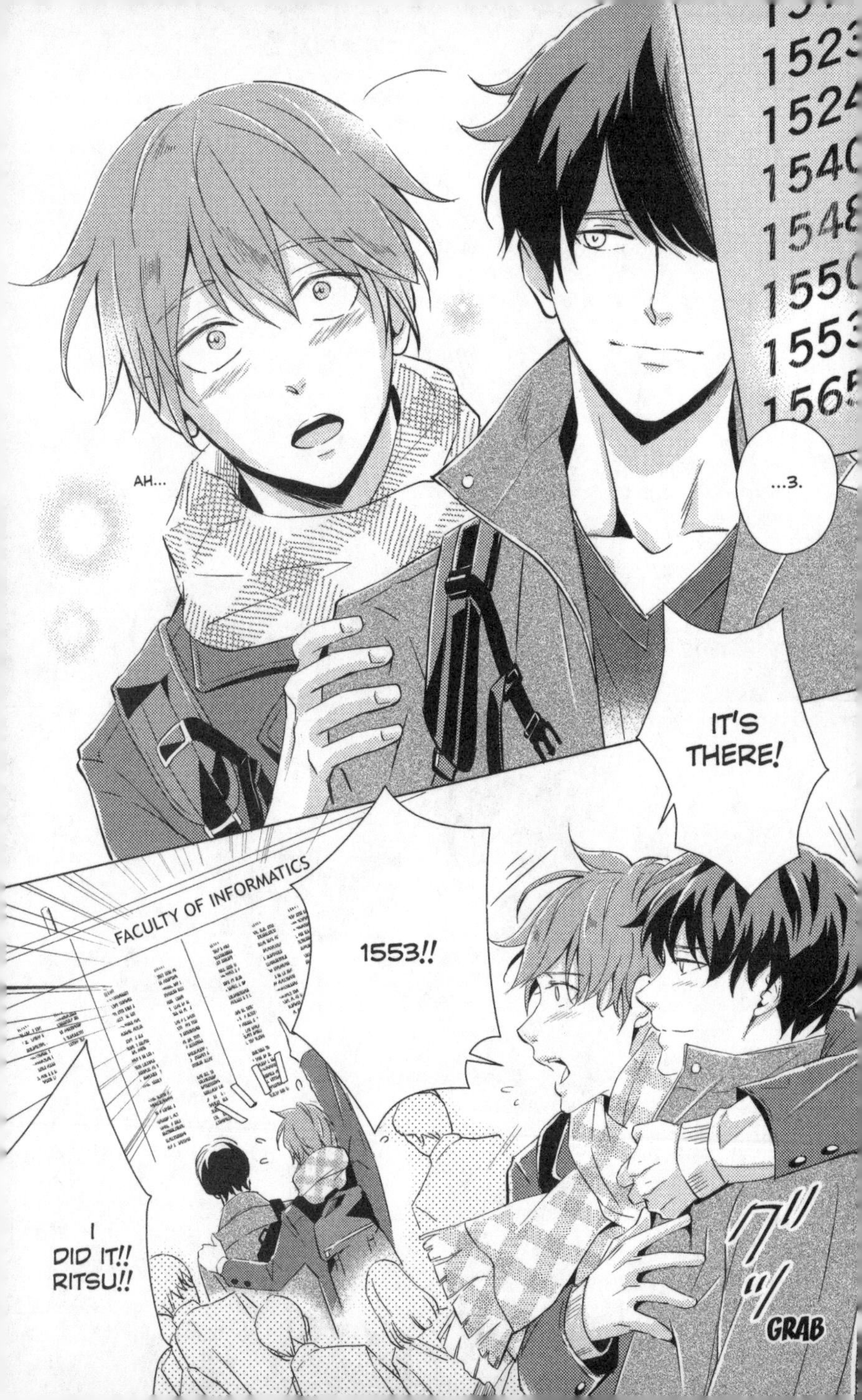
1523
1524
1548
1553
...3.
AH...
IT'S THERE!
1553!!
FACULTY OF INFORMATICS
GRAB
I DID IT!! RITSU!!

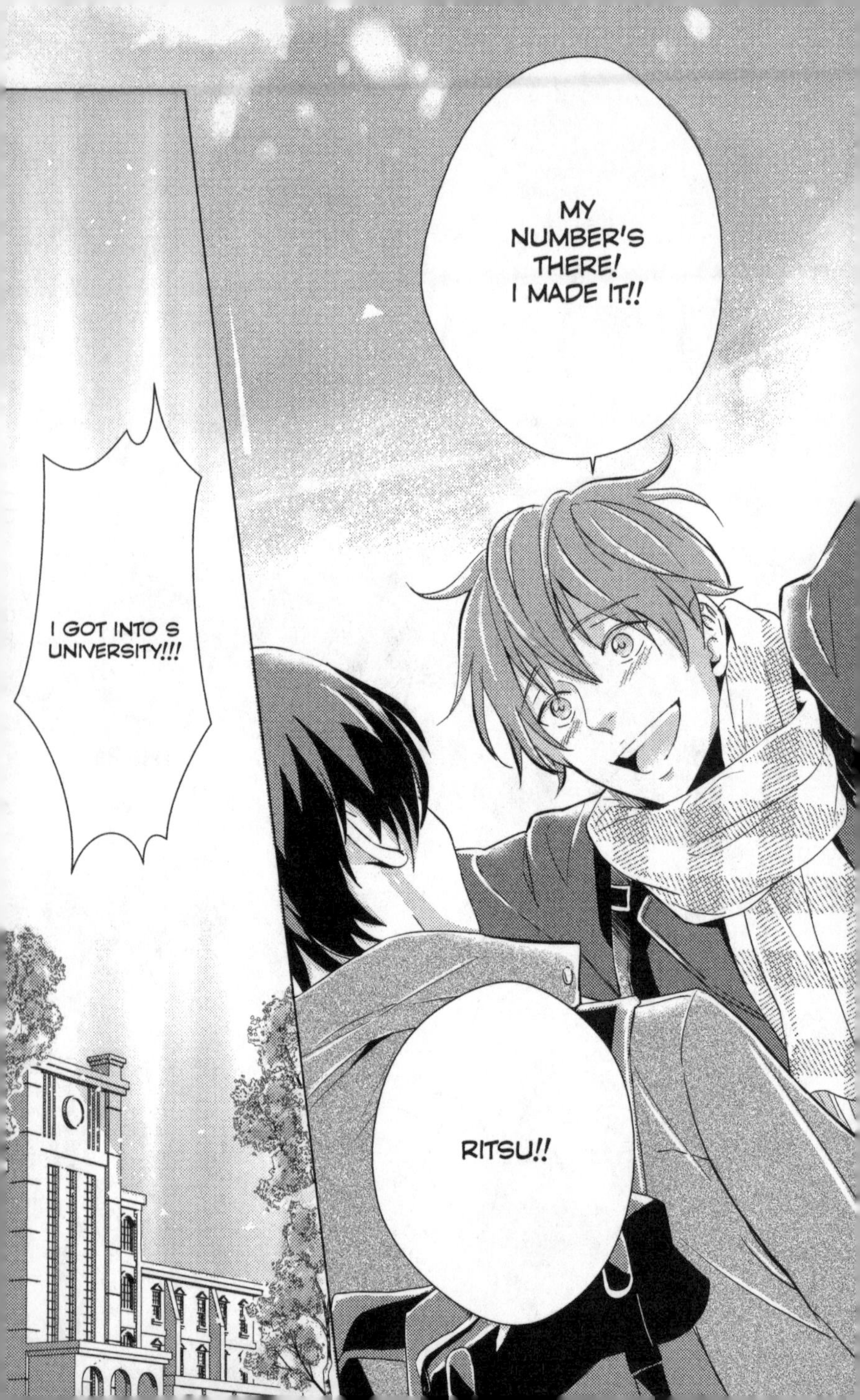
MY NUMBER'S THERE! I MADE IT!!
RITSU!!
I GOT INTO S UNIVERSITY!!!

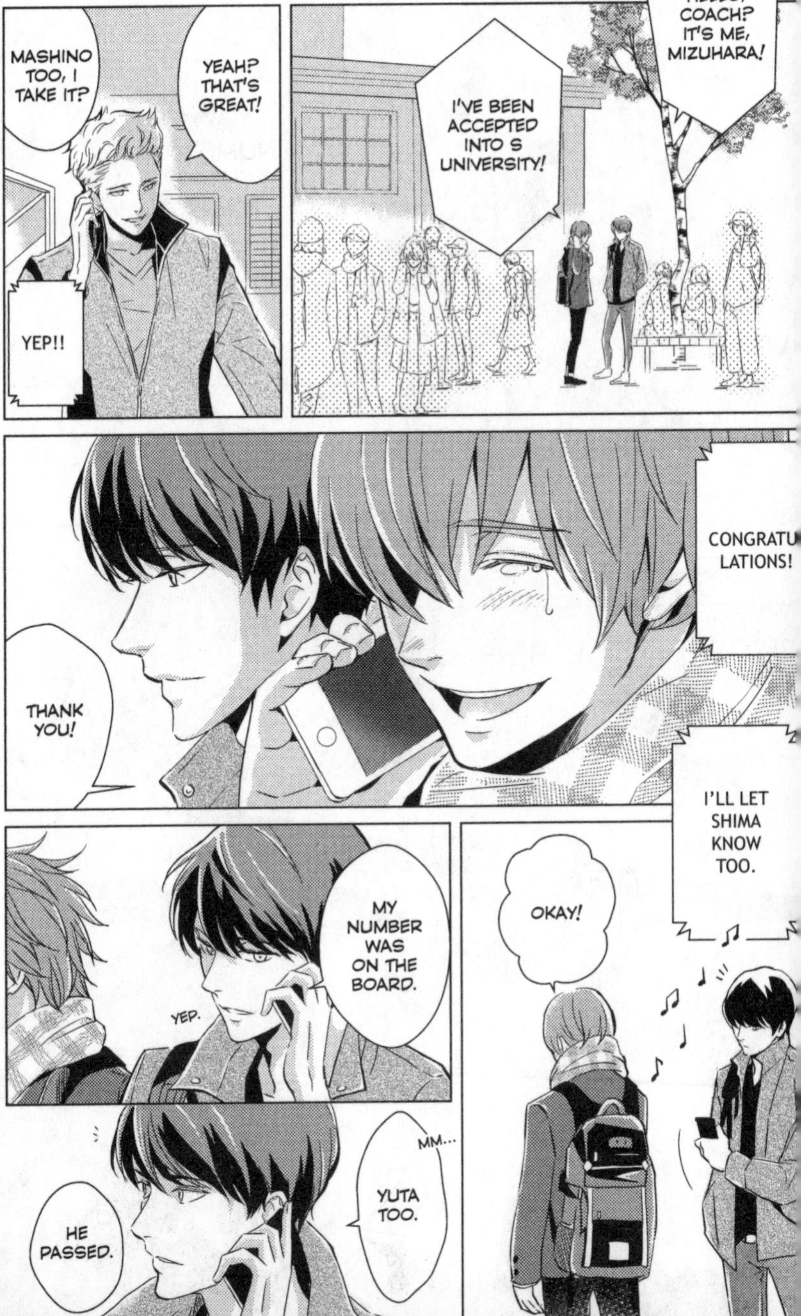
HELLO, COACH? IT'S ME, MIZUHARA!
I'VE BEEN ACCEPTED INTO S UNIVERSITY!
YEAH? THAT'S GREAT!
MASHINO TOO, I TAKE IT?
YEP!!
CONGRATULATIONS!
THANK YOU!
I'LL LET SHIMA KNOW TOO.
OKAY!
MY NUMBER WAS ON THE BOARD.
YEP.
MM...
YUTA TOO.
HE PASSED.

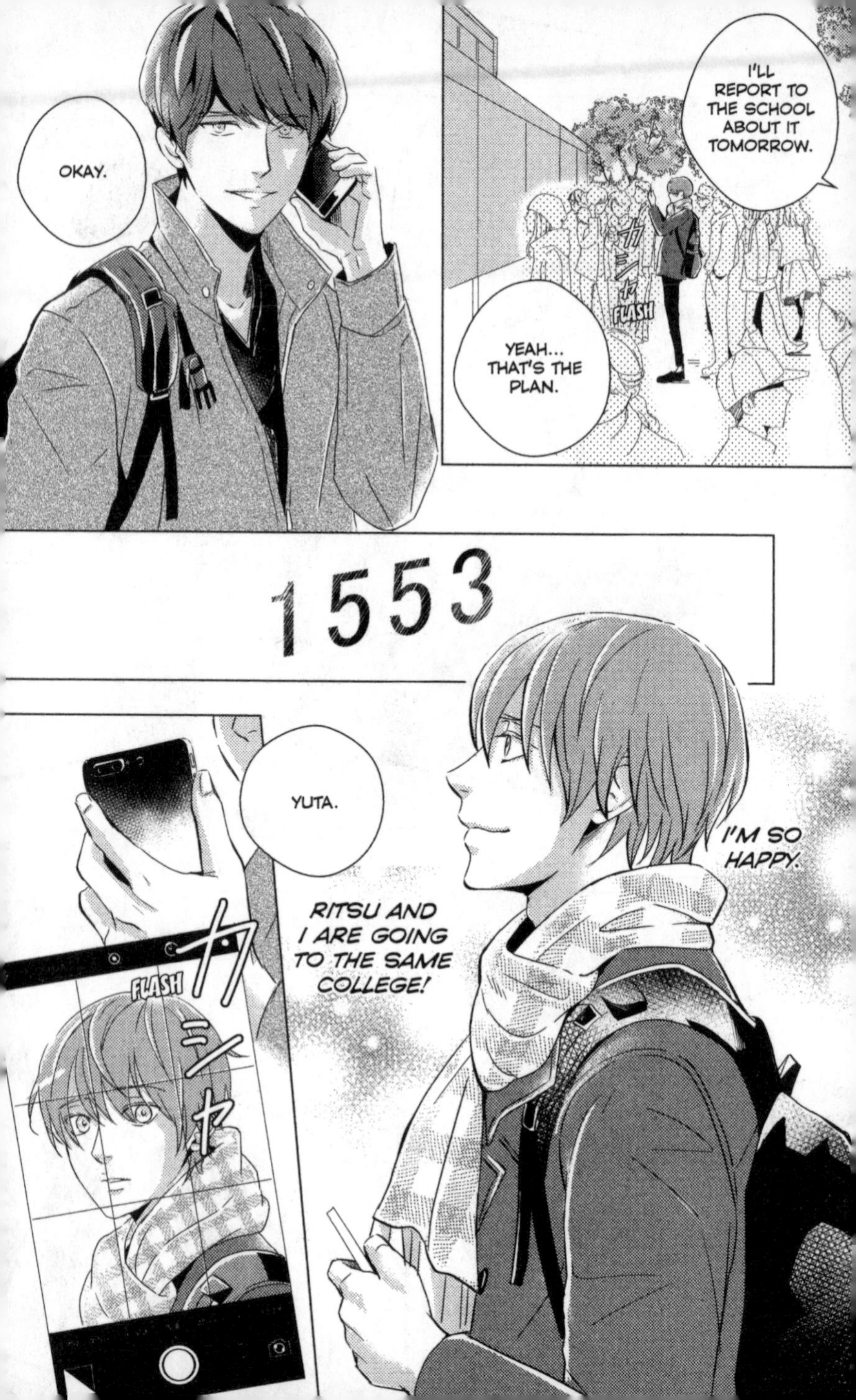
I'LL REPORT TO THE SCHOOL ABOUT IT TOMORROW.
YEAH... THAT'S THE PLAN.
FLASH
OKAY.
1553
I'M SO HAPPY.
RITSU AND I ARE GOING TO THE SAME COLLEGE!
YUTA.
FLASH

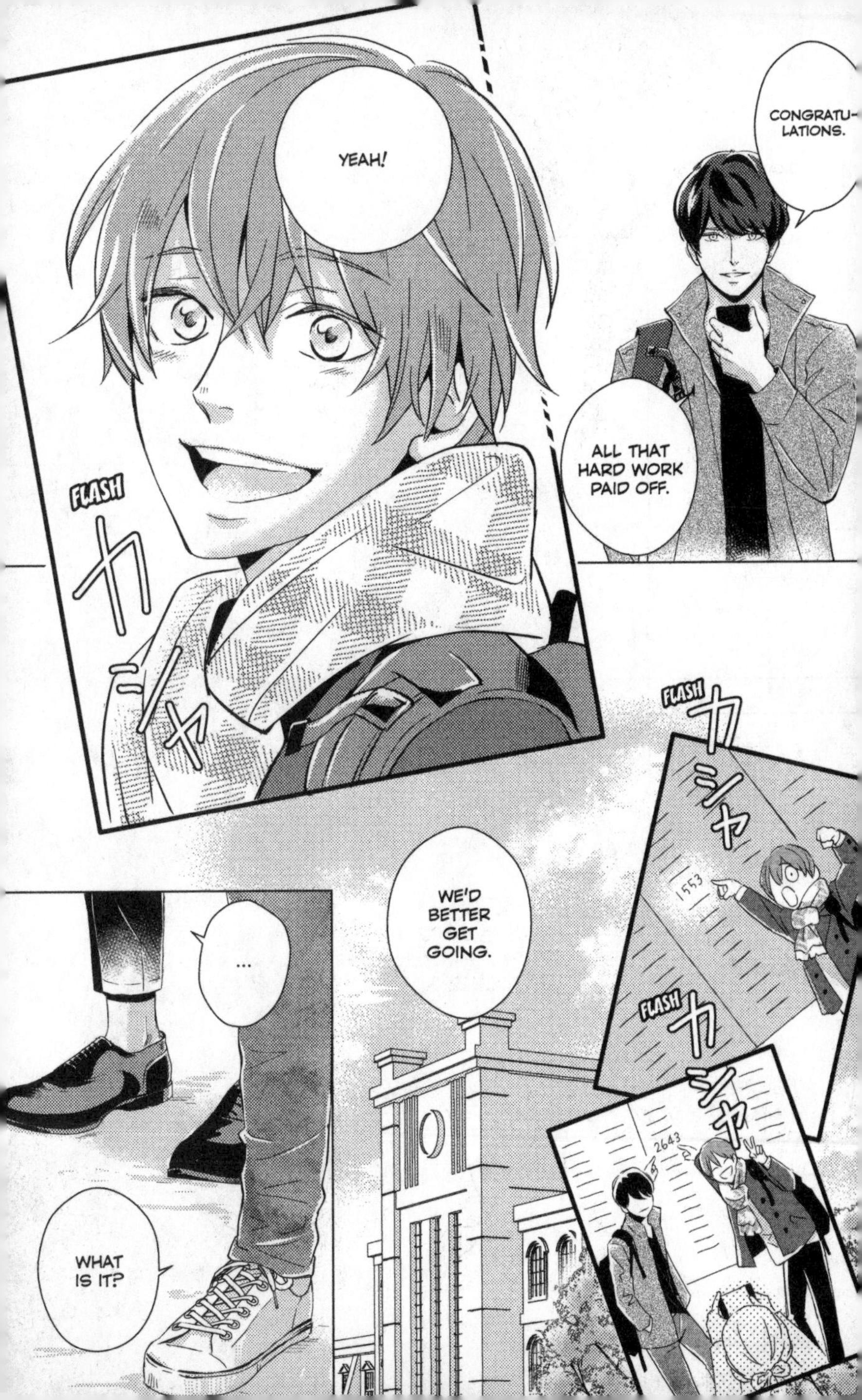
CONGRATU-LATIONS.
ALL THAT HARD WORK PAID OFF.
YEAH!
FLASH
カシャ
FLASH
カシャ
1553
FLASH
カシャ
2643
WE'D BETTER GET GOING.
...
WHAT IS IT?

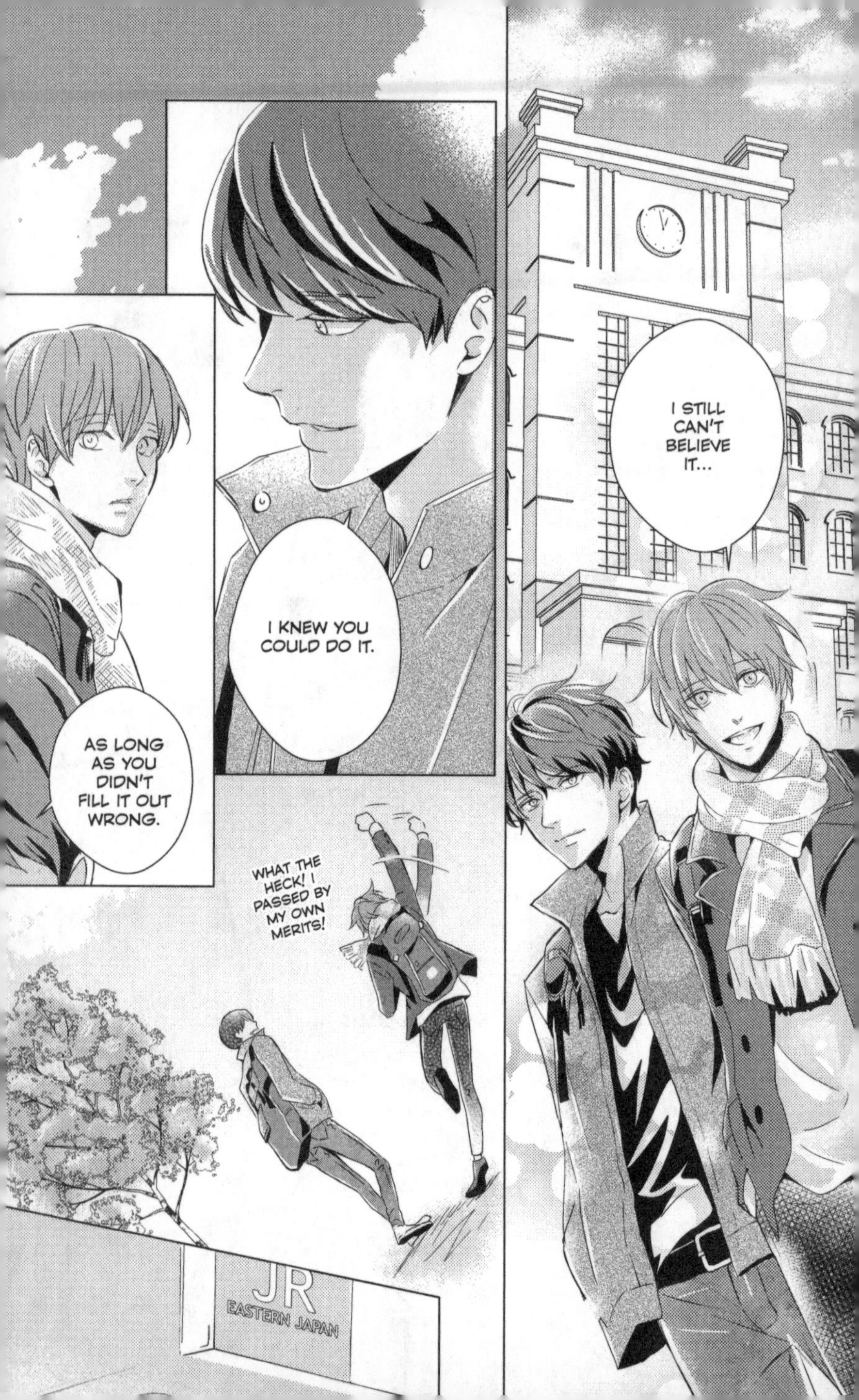
I STILL CAN'T BELIEVE IT...
I KNEW YOU COULD DO IT.
AS LONG AS YOU DIDN'T FILL IT OUT WRONG.
WHAT THE HECK! I PASSED BY MY OWN MERITS!
JR
EASTERN JAPAN

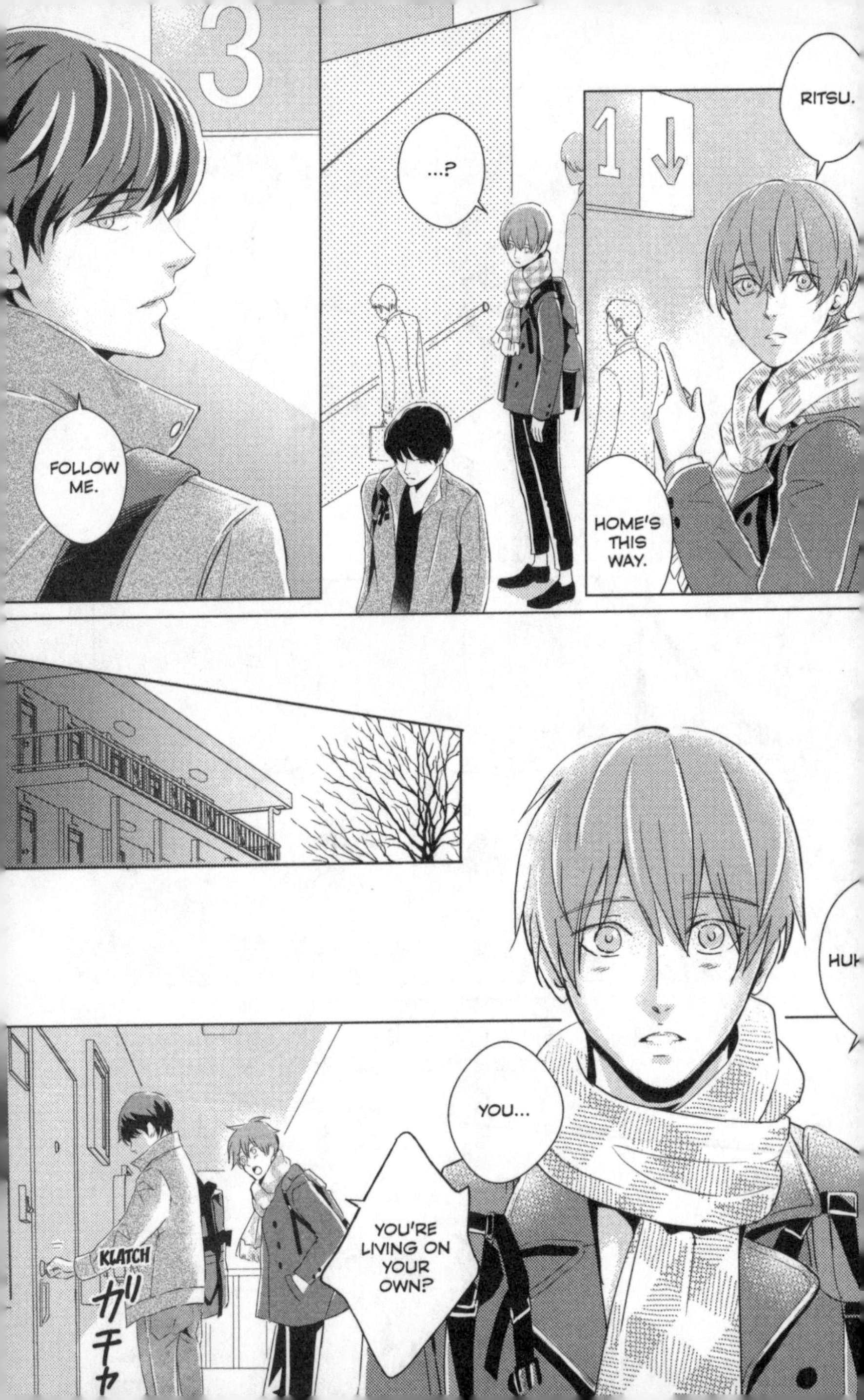
RITSU.
HOME'S THIS WAY.
...?
FOLLOW ME.
HU
YOU...
YOU'RE LIVING ON YOUR OWN?
KLATCH
ガチャ

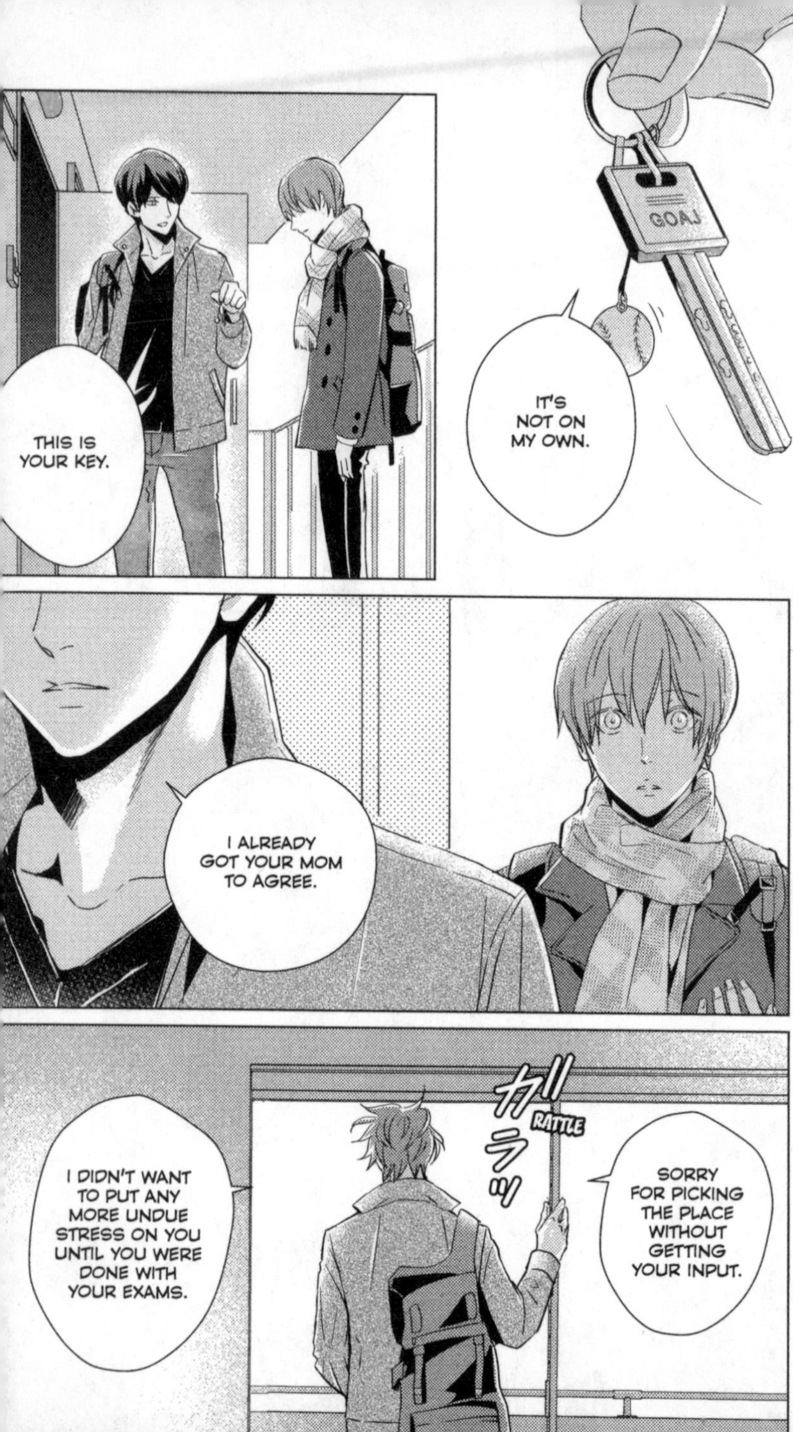
IT'S NOT ON MY OWN.
THIS IS YOUR KEY.
I ALREADY GOT YOUR MOM TO AGREE.
SORRY FOR PICKING THE PLACE WITHOUT GETTING YOUR INPUT.
RATTLE
I DIDN'T WANT TO PUT ANY MORE UNDUE STRESS ON YOU UNTIL YOU WERE DONE WITH YOUR EXAMS.

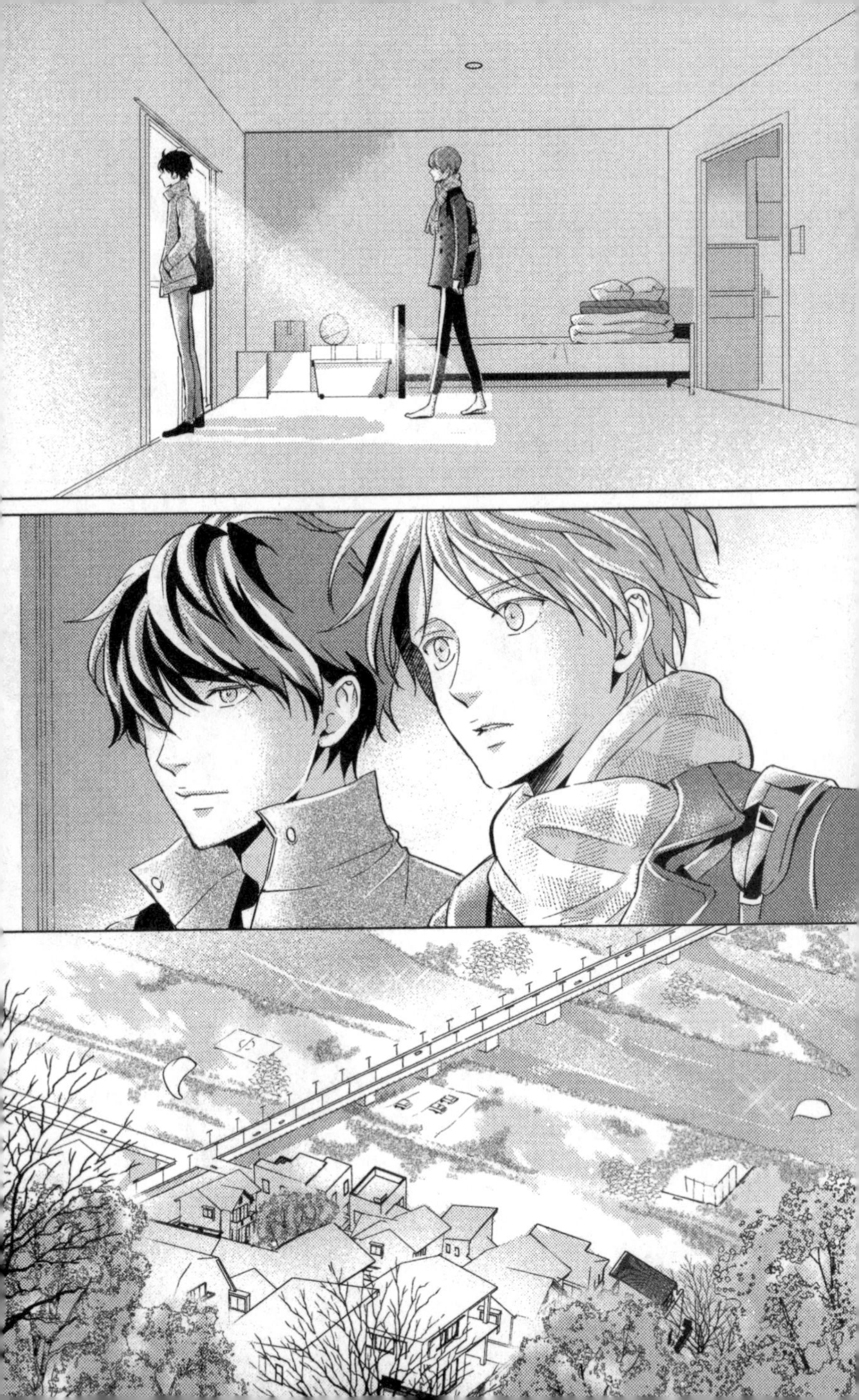

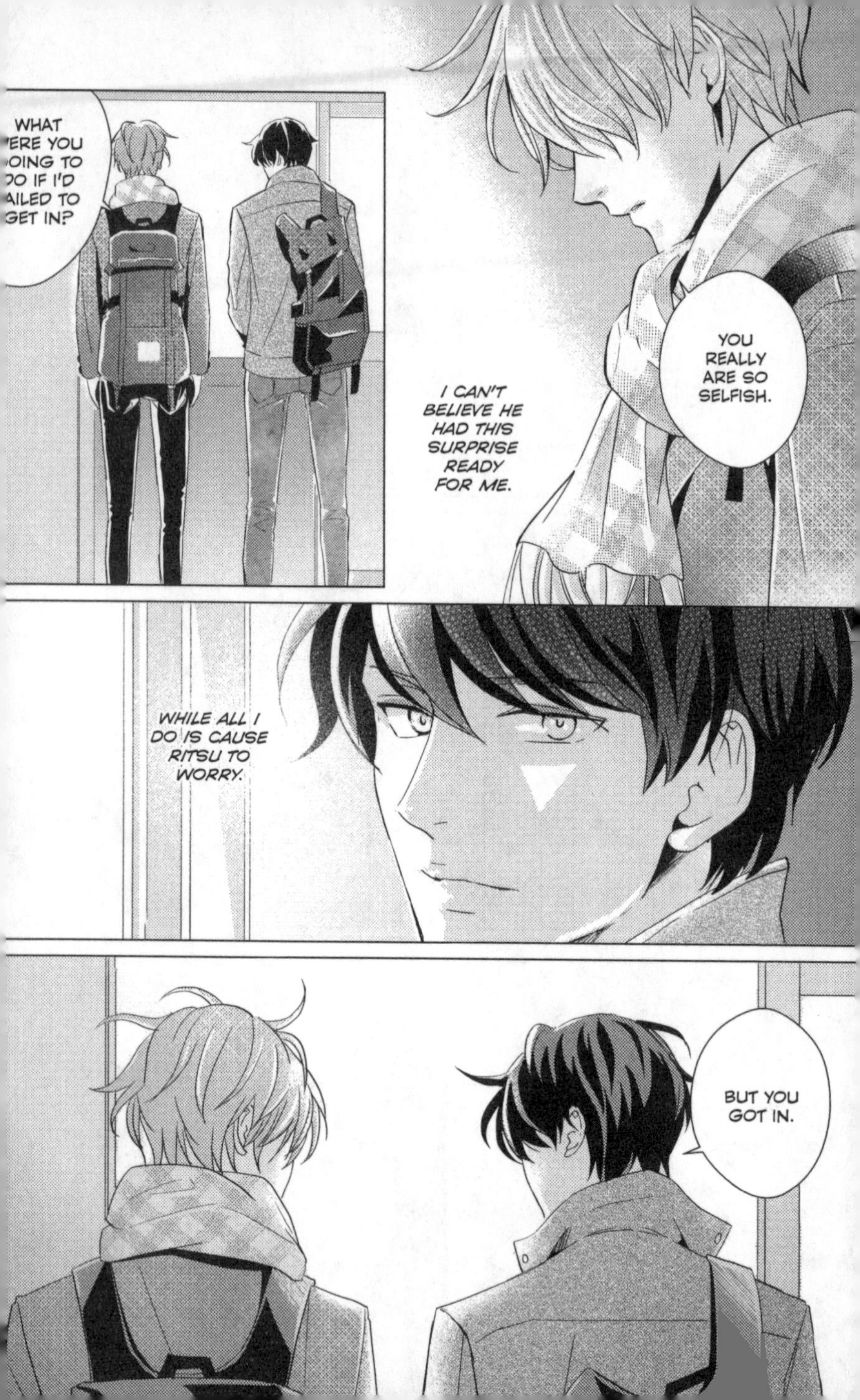
YOU REALLY ARE SO SELFISH.
I CAN'T BELIEVE HE HAD THIS SURPRISE READY FOR ME.
WHAT ERE YOU OING TO O IF I'D AILED TO GET IN?
WHILE ALL I DO IS CAUSE RITSU TO WORRY.
BUT YOU GOT IN.

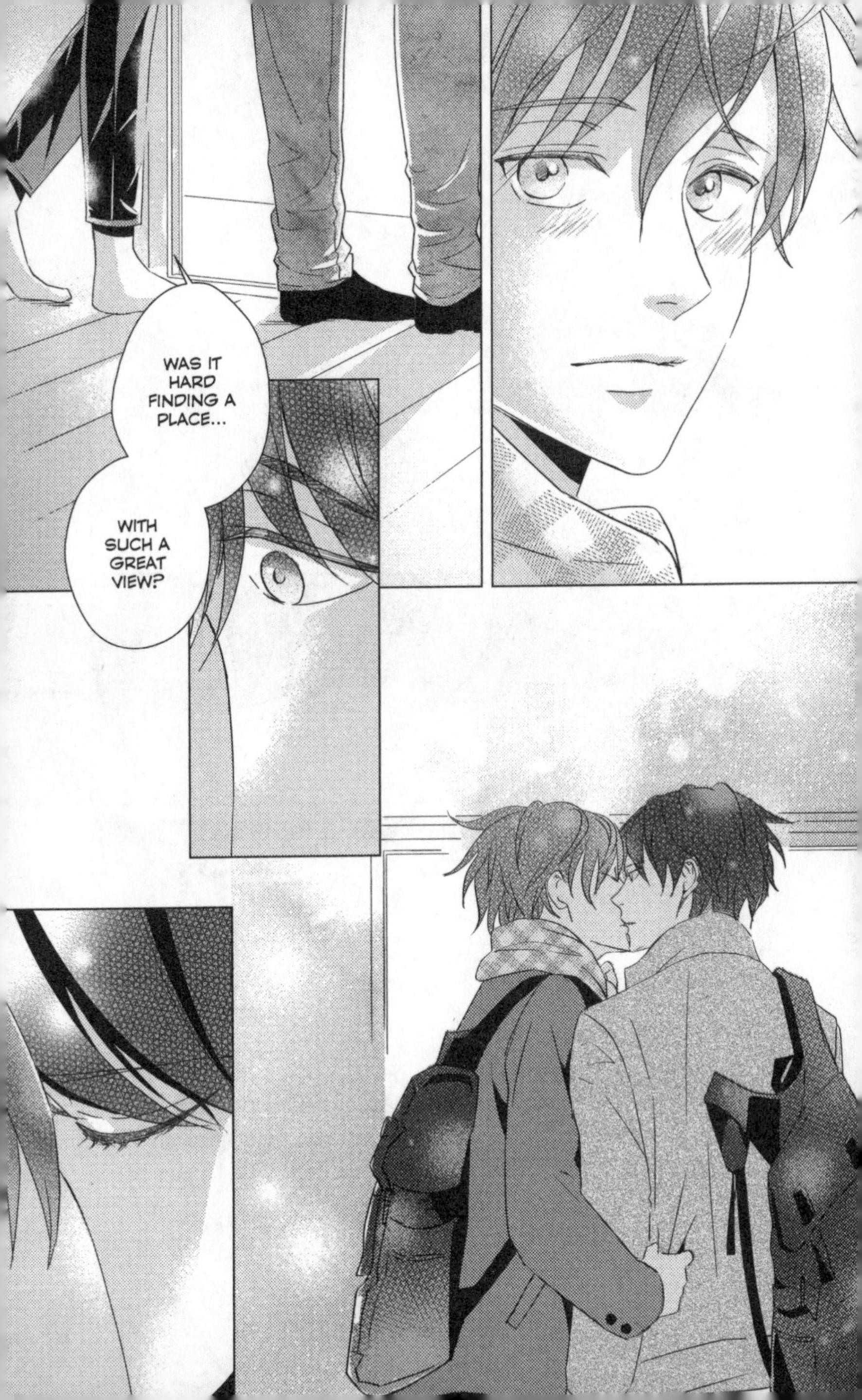
WAS IT HARD FINDING A PLACE...
WITH SUCH A GREAT VIEW?

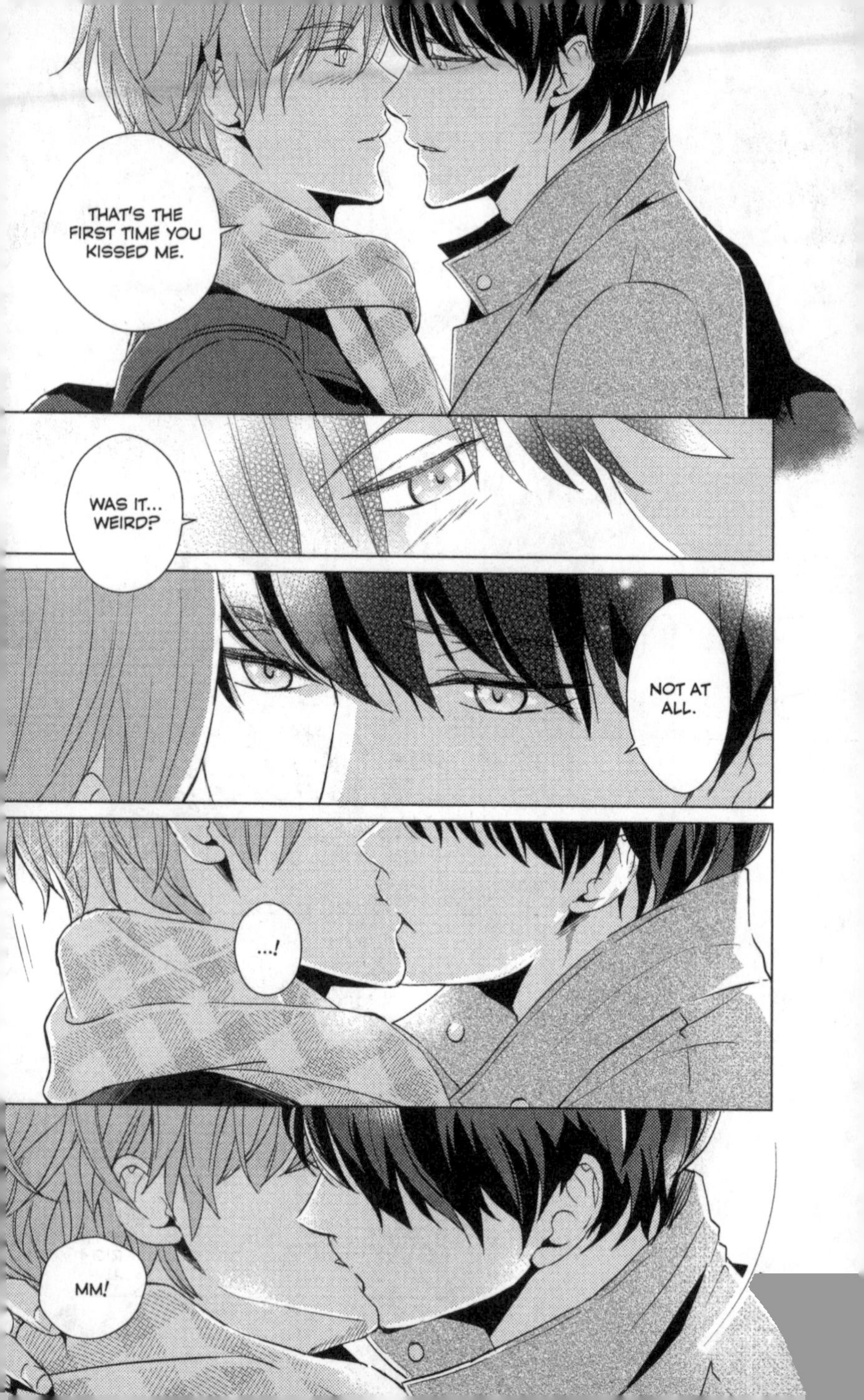
THAT'S THE FIRST TIME YOU KISSED ME.
WAS IT... WEIRD?
NOT AT ALL.
...!
MM!

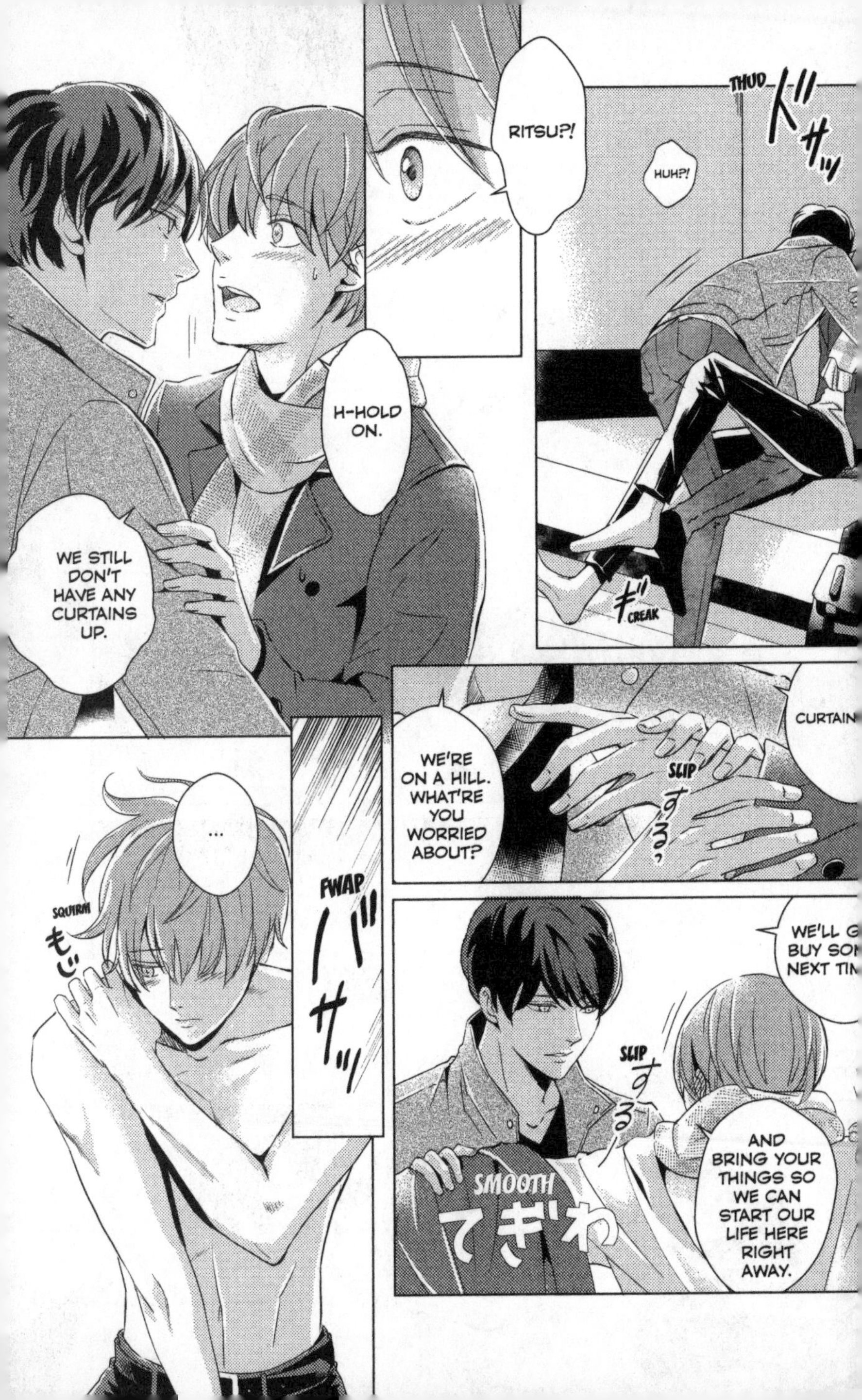
THUD ドサッ
HUH?!
ギ CREAK
RITSU?!
H-HOLD ON.
WE STILL DON'T HAVE ANY CURTAINS UP.
CURTAIN
WE'RE ON A HILL. WHAT'RE YOU WORRIED ABOUT?
SLIP する
WE'LL G BUY SO NEXT TI
SLIP する
SMOOTH てきわ
AND BRING YOUR THINGS SO WE CAN START OUR LIFE HERE RIGHT AWAY.
FWAP バサッ
...
SQUIRM もじ

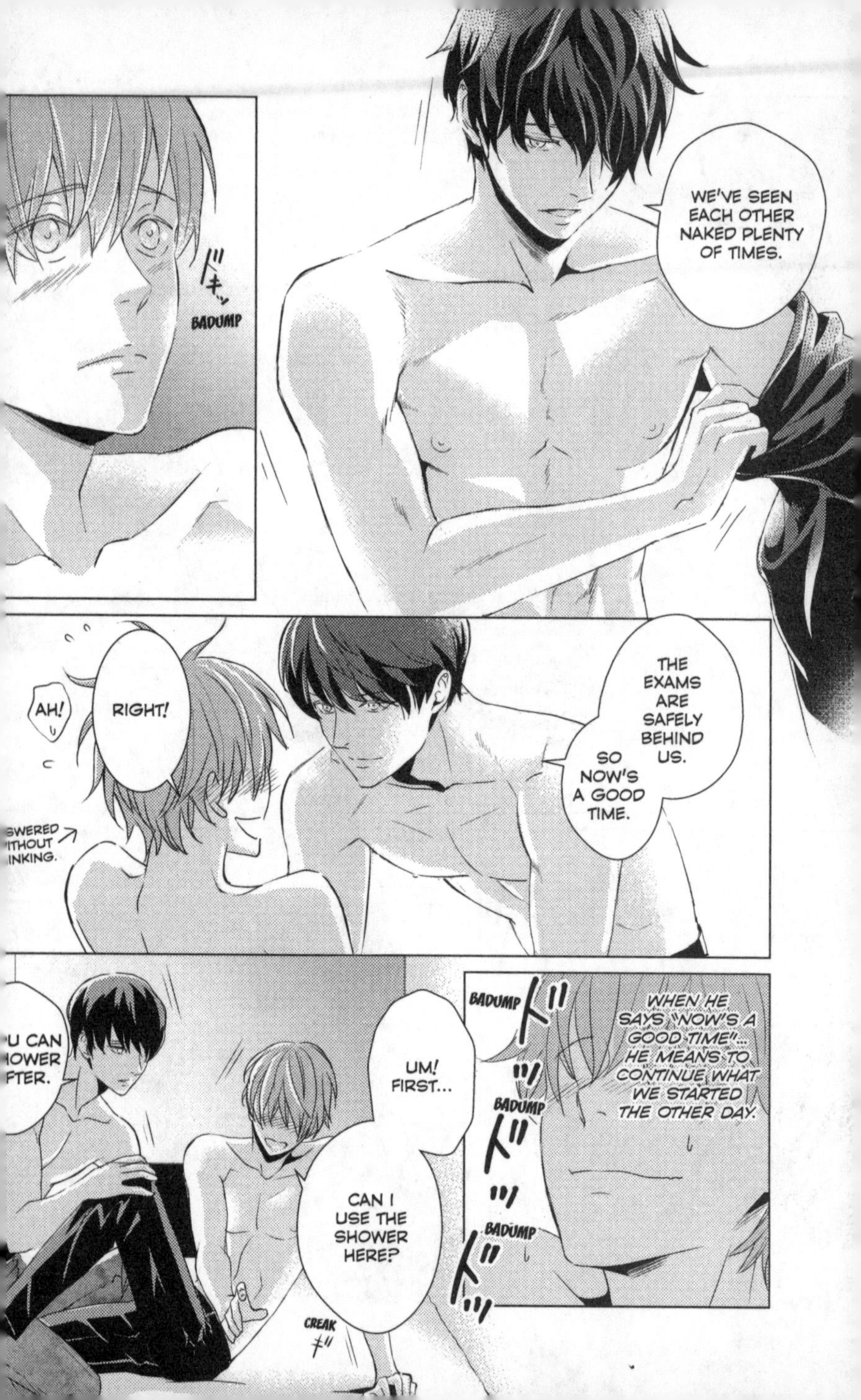
WE'VE SEEN EACH OTHER NAKED PLENTY OF TIMES.
ドキッ
BADUMP
THE EXAMS ARE SAFELY BEHIND US.
SO NOW'S A GOOD TIME.
RIGHT!
AH!
SWERED ITHOUT INKING.
BADUMP ドッ
BADUMP ドッ
BADUMP ドッ
WHEN HE SAYS "NOW'S A GOOD TIME"... HE MEANS TO CONTINUE WHAT WE STARTED THE OTHER DAY.
UM! FIRST...
CAN I USE THE SHOWER HERE?
U CAN HOWER FTER.
CREAK ギッ

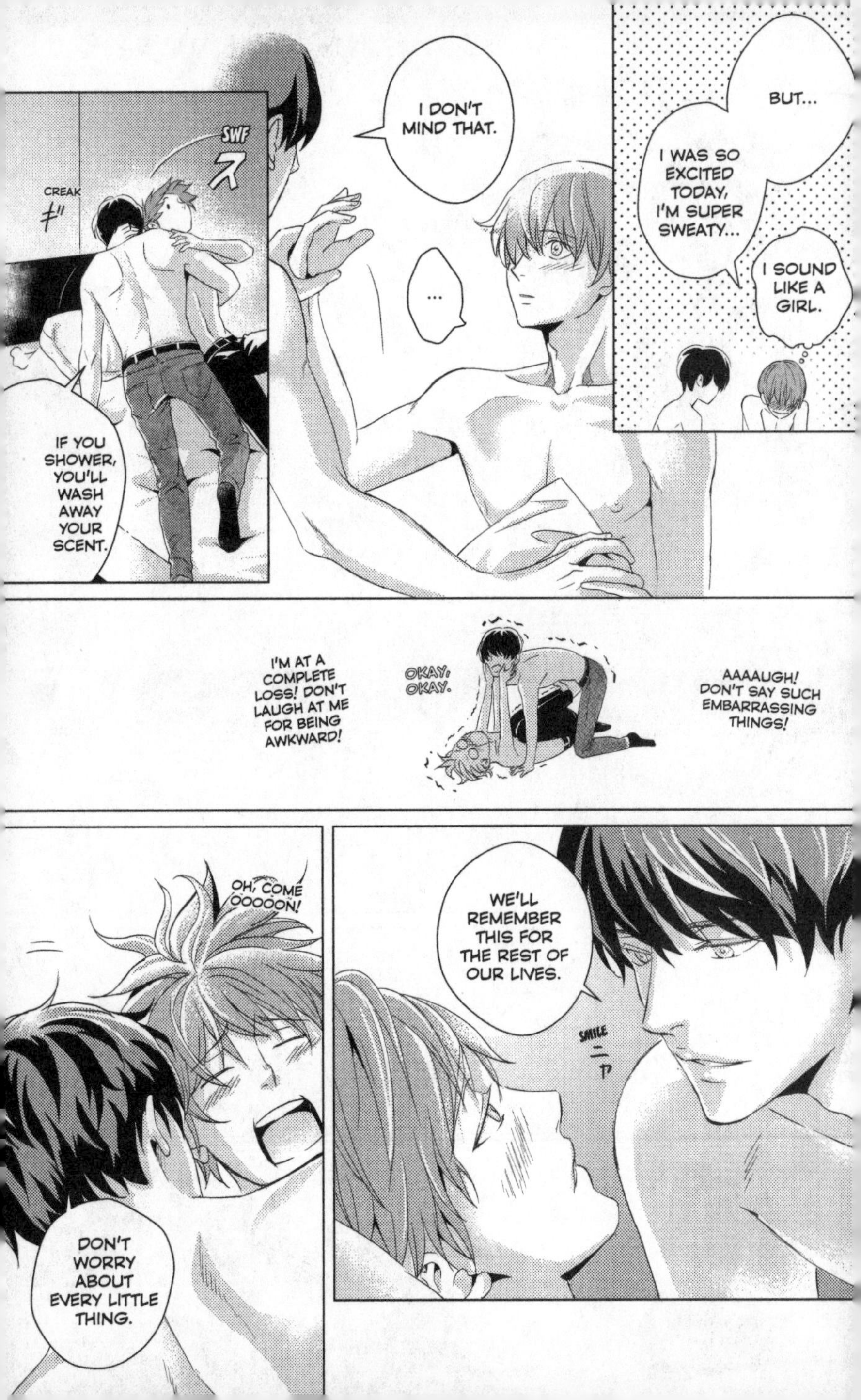
BUT...
I WAS SO EXCITED TODAY, I'M SUPER SWEATY...
I SOUND LIKE A GIRL.
I DON'T MIND THAT.
...
SWF
CREAK
IF YOU SHOWER, YOU'LL WASH AWAY YOUR SCENT.
AAAAUGH! DON'T SAY SUCH EMBARRASSING THINGS!
OKAY, OKAY.
I'M AT A COMPLETE LOSS! DON'T LAUGH AT ME FOR BEING AWKWARD!
WE'LL REMEMBER THIS FOR THE REST OF OUR LIVES.
SMILE
OH, COME OOOOON!
DON'T WORRY ABOUT EVERY LITTLE THING.

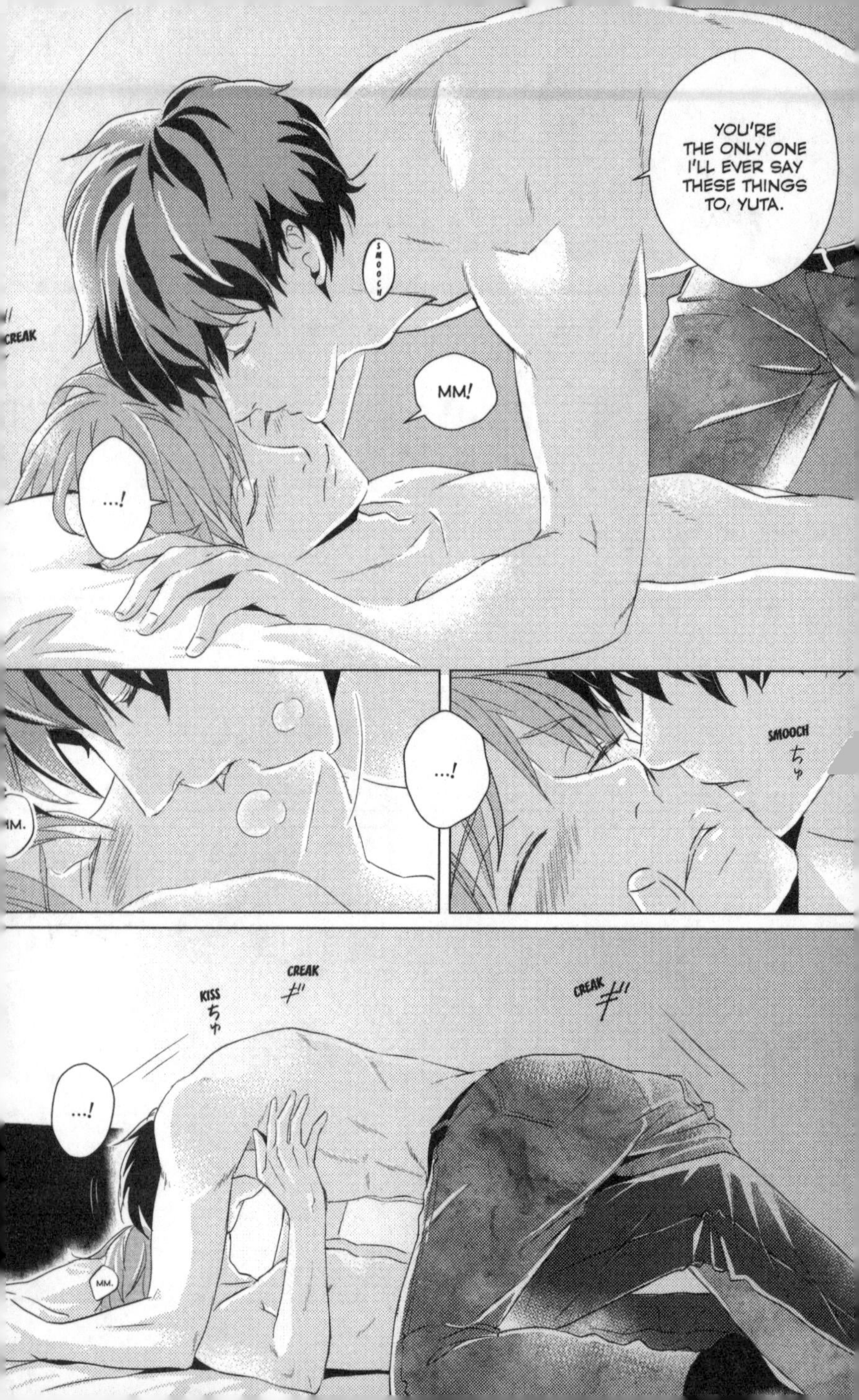
YOU'RE THE ONLY ONE I'LL EVER SAY THESE THINGS TO, YUTA.
SMOOCH
MM!
CREAK
...!
SMOOCH ちゅ
...!
CREAK ギ
CREAK ギ
KISS ちゅ
...!
MM.

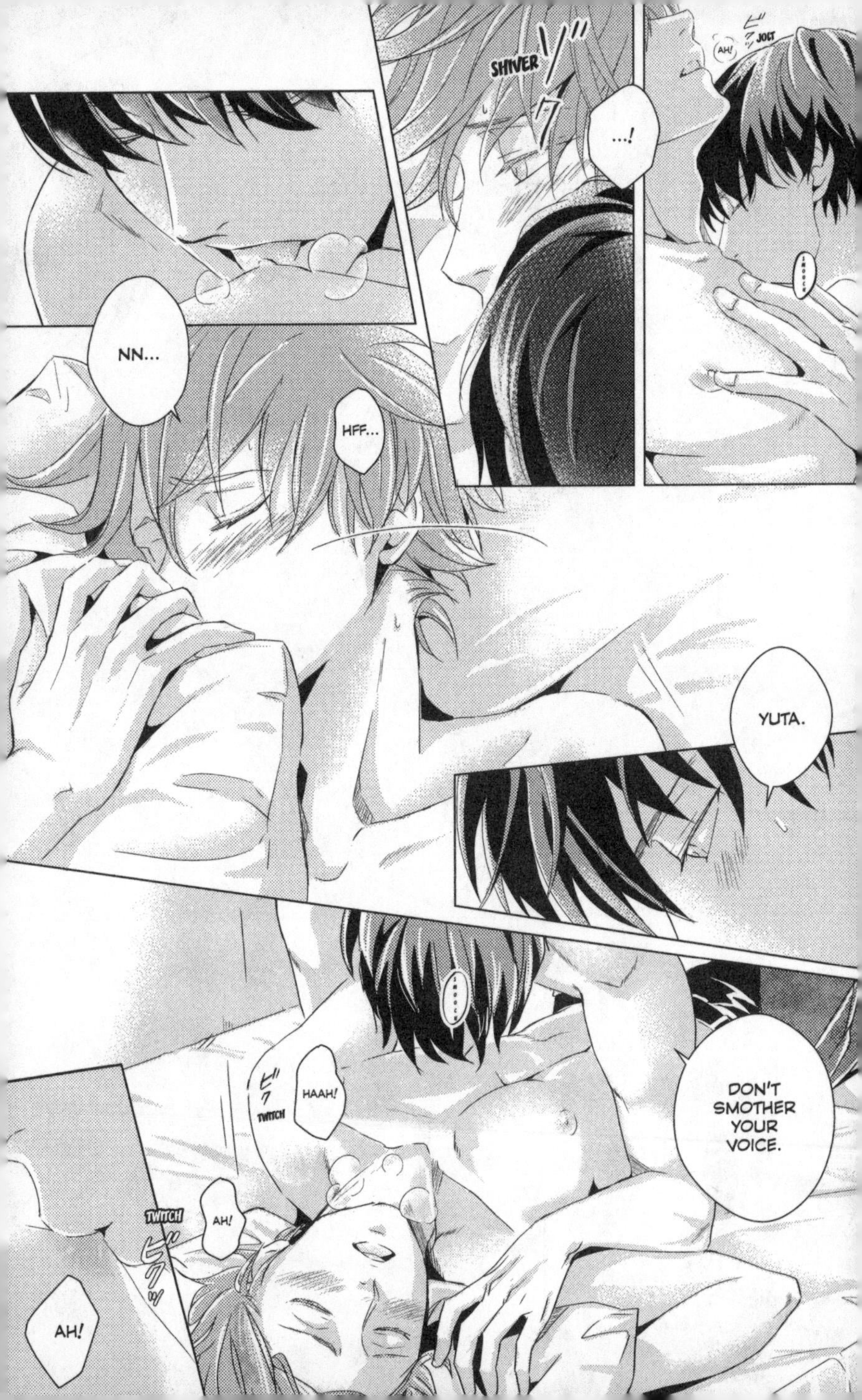
AH!
JOLT
SMOOCH
SHIVER
...!
NN...
HFF...
YUTA.
DON'T SMOTHER YOUR VOICE.
SMOOCH
HAAH!
TWITCH
AH!
TWITCH
AH!

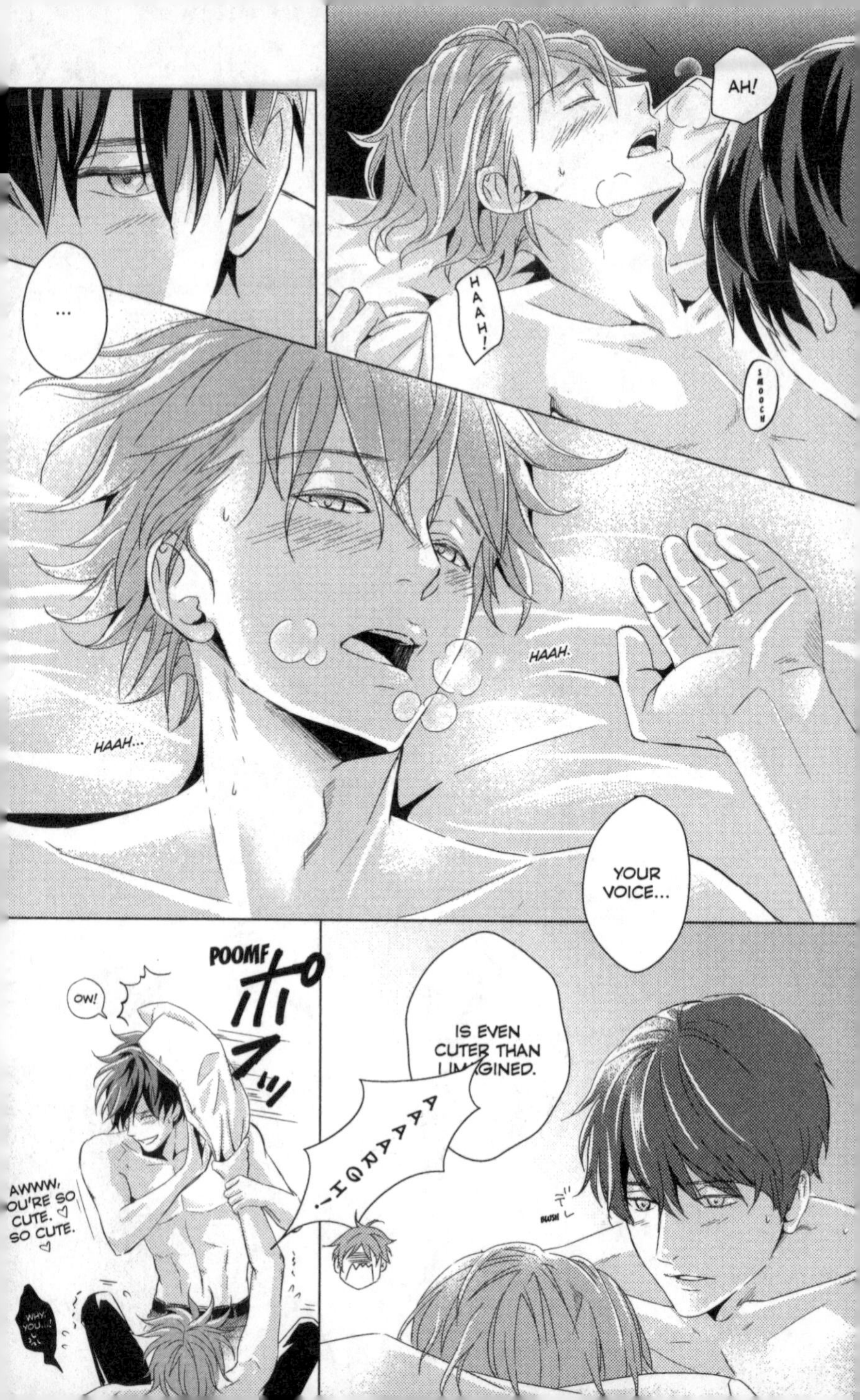
AH!
HAAH!
SMOOCH
...
HAAH.
HAAH...
YOUR VOICE...
IS EVEN CUTER THAN I IMAGINED.
BLUSH
AAAARGH!
POOMF
ポフッ
OW!
AWWW, OU'RE SO CUTE. ♡ SO CUTE. ♡
WHY, YOU...!!

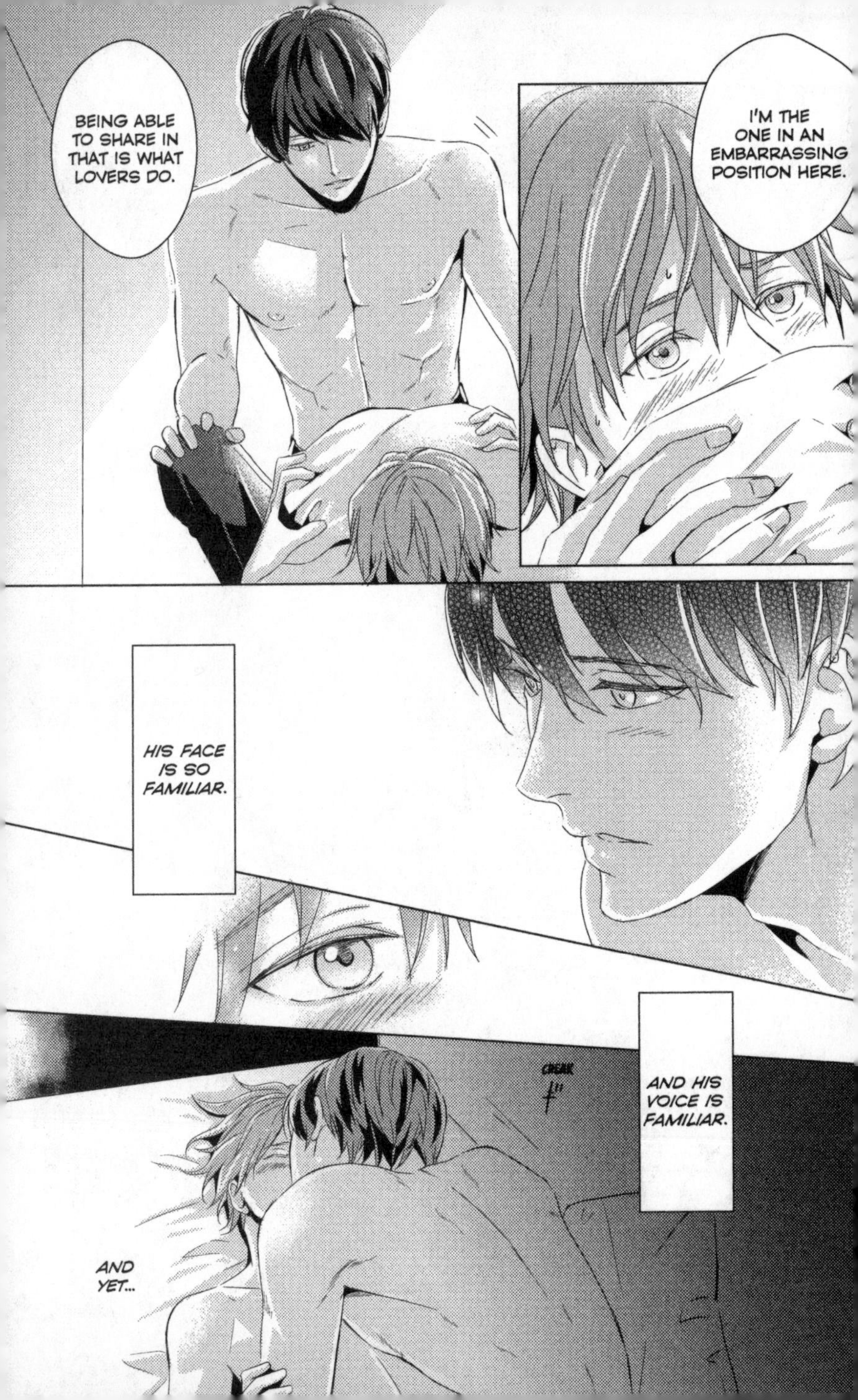
I'M THE ONE IN AN EMBARRASSING POSITION HERE.
BEING ABLE TO SHARE IN THAT IS WHAT LOVERS DO.
HIS FACE IS SO FAMILIAR.
AND HIS VOICE IS FAMILIAR.
CREAK
AND YET...

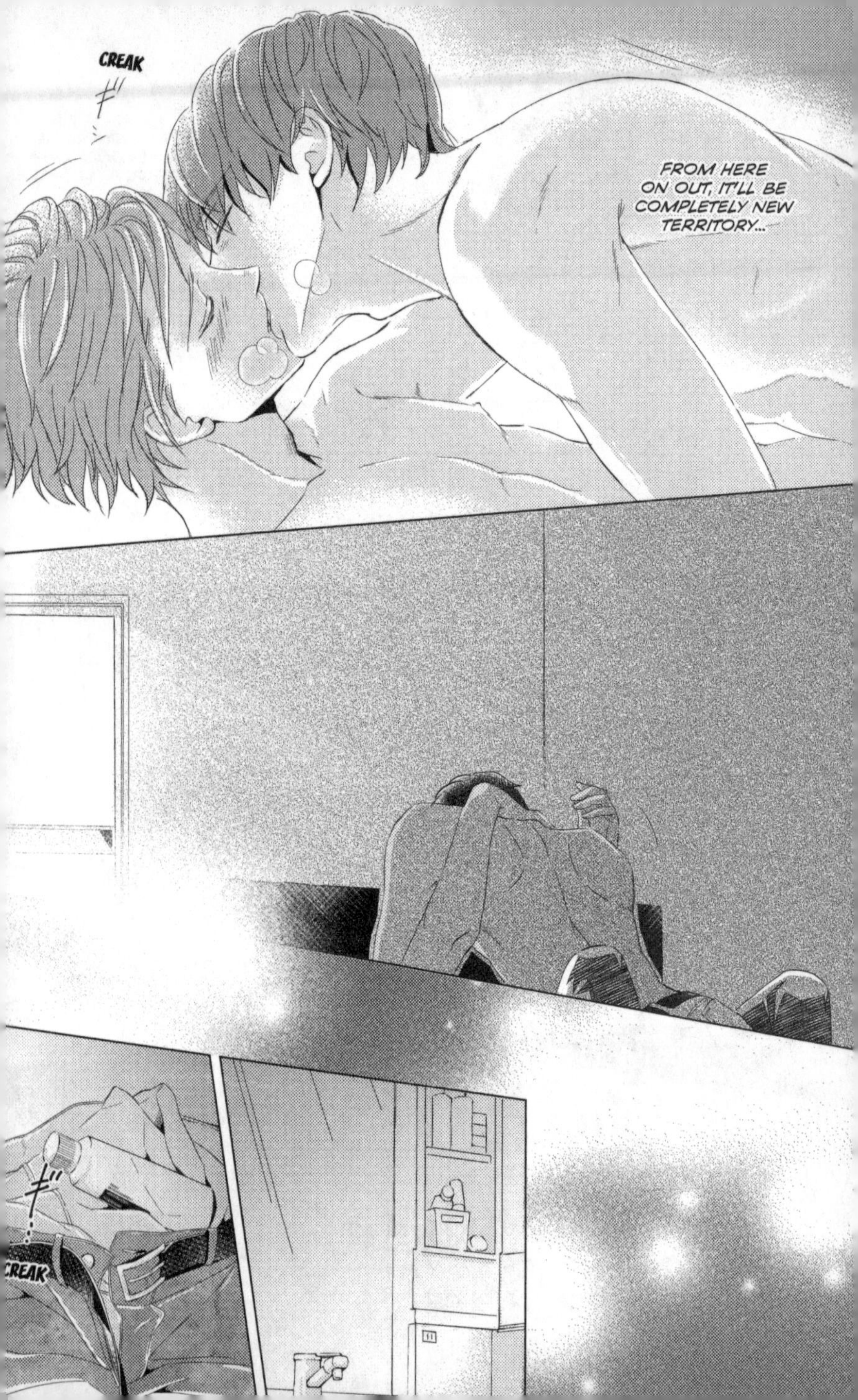
FROM HERE ON OUT, IT'LL BE COMPLETELY NEW TERRITORY...
CREAK
CREAK

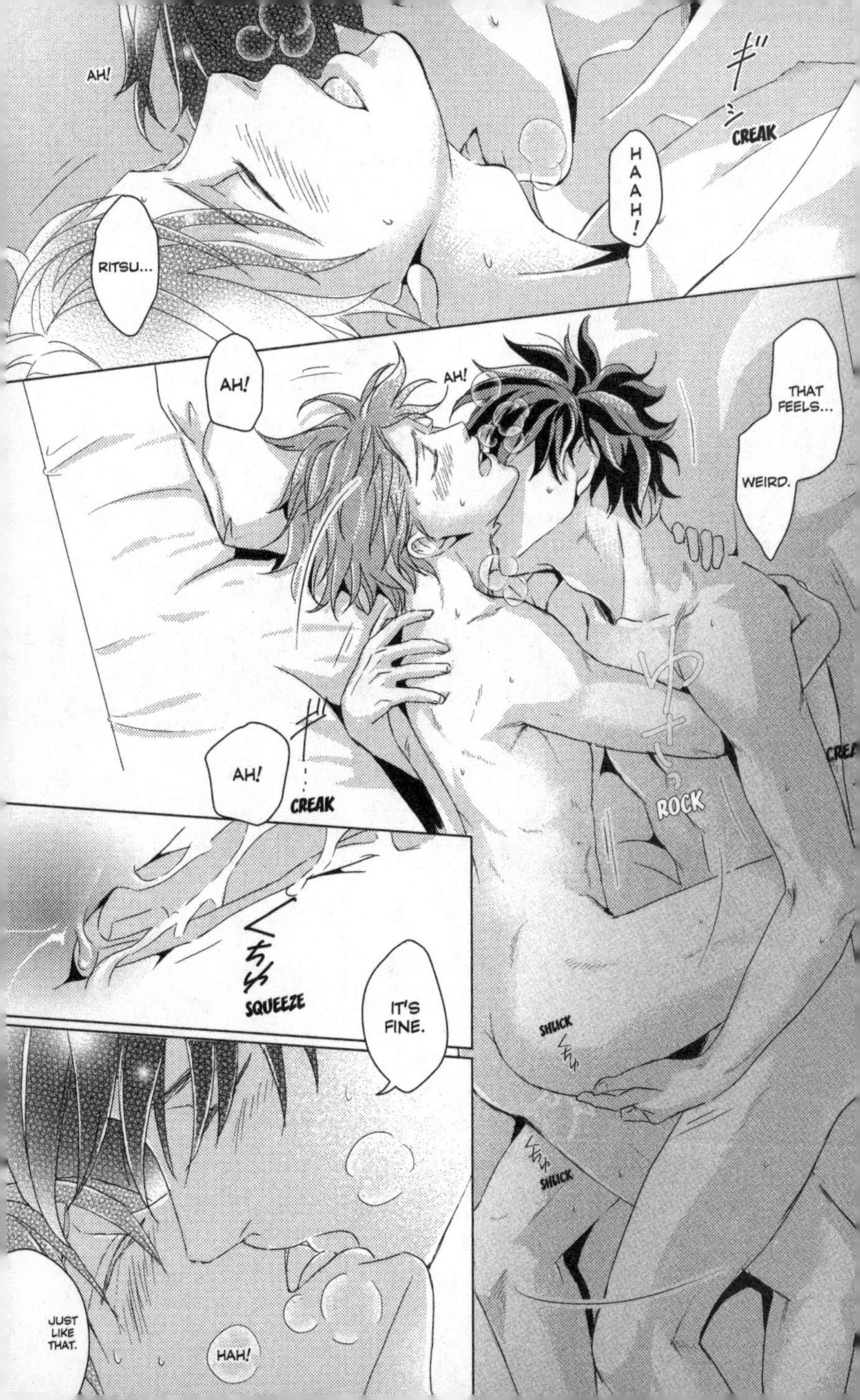
ギシ
CREAK
HAAAH!
AH!
RITSU...
THAT FEELS...
WEIRD.
ゆさっ
ROCK
CREA
AH!
AH!
ギシ
CREAK
AH!
SHLICK
くちゅ
くちゅ
SHLICK
IT'S FINE.
くちゅ
SQUEEZE
HAH!
JUST LIKE THAT.

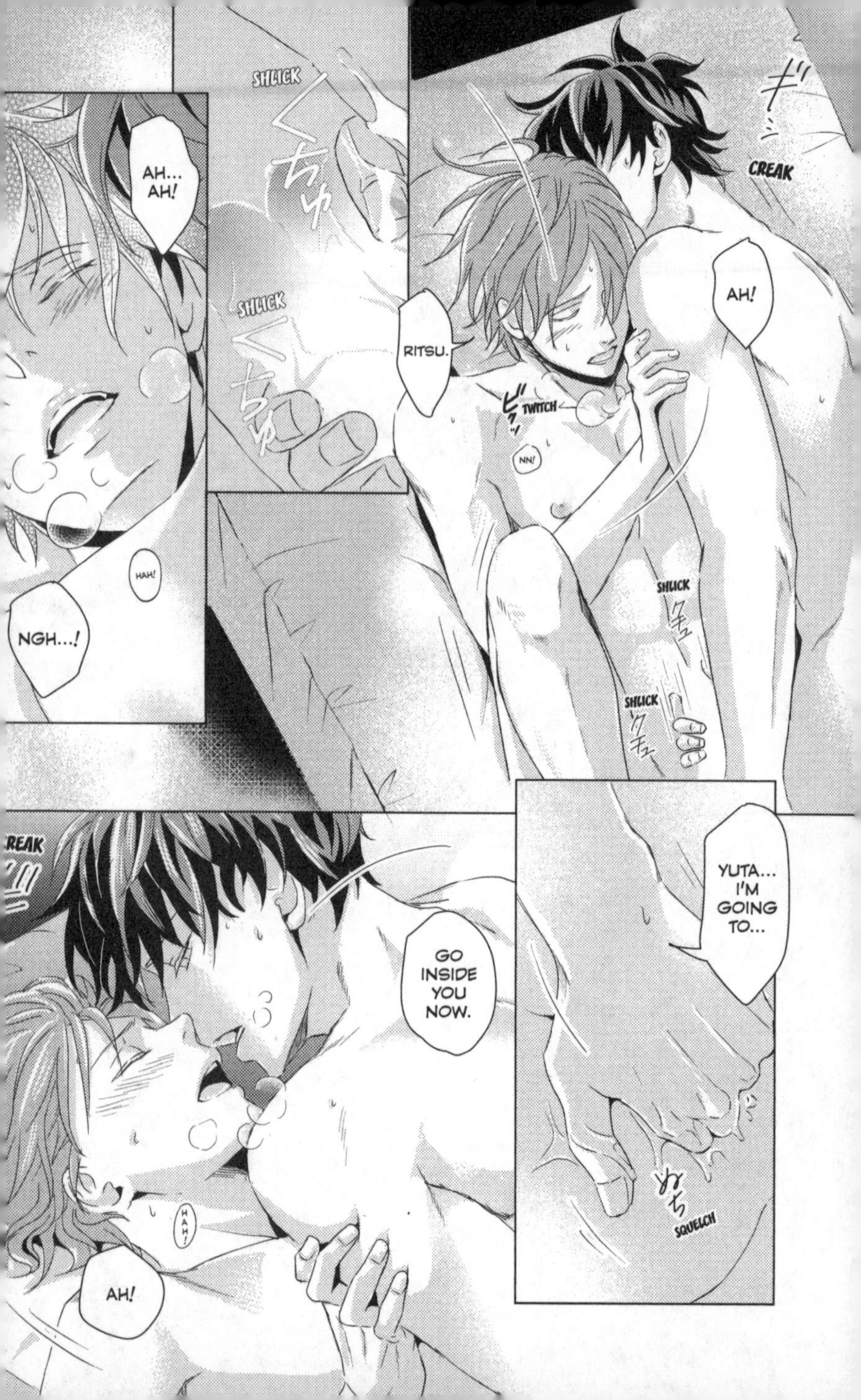
ギシ
CREAK
AH!
RITSU.
ビクッ
TWITCH
NN!
SHLICK
クチュ
SHLICK
クチュ
SHLICK
くちゅ
SHLICK
くちゅ
AH... AH!
HAH!
NGH...!
YUTA... I'M GOING TO...
ぬち
SQUELCH
REAK
GO INSIDE YOU NOW.
HAH!
AH!

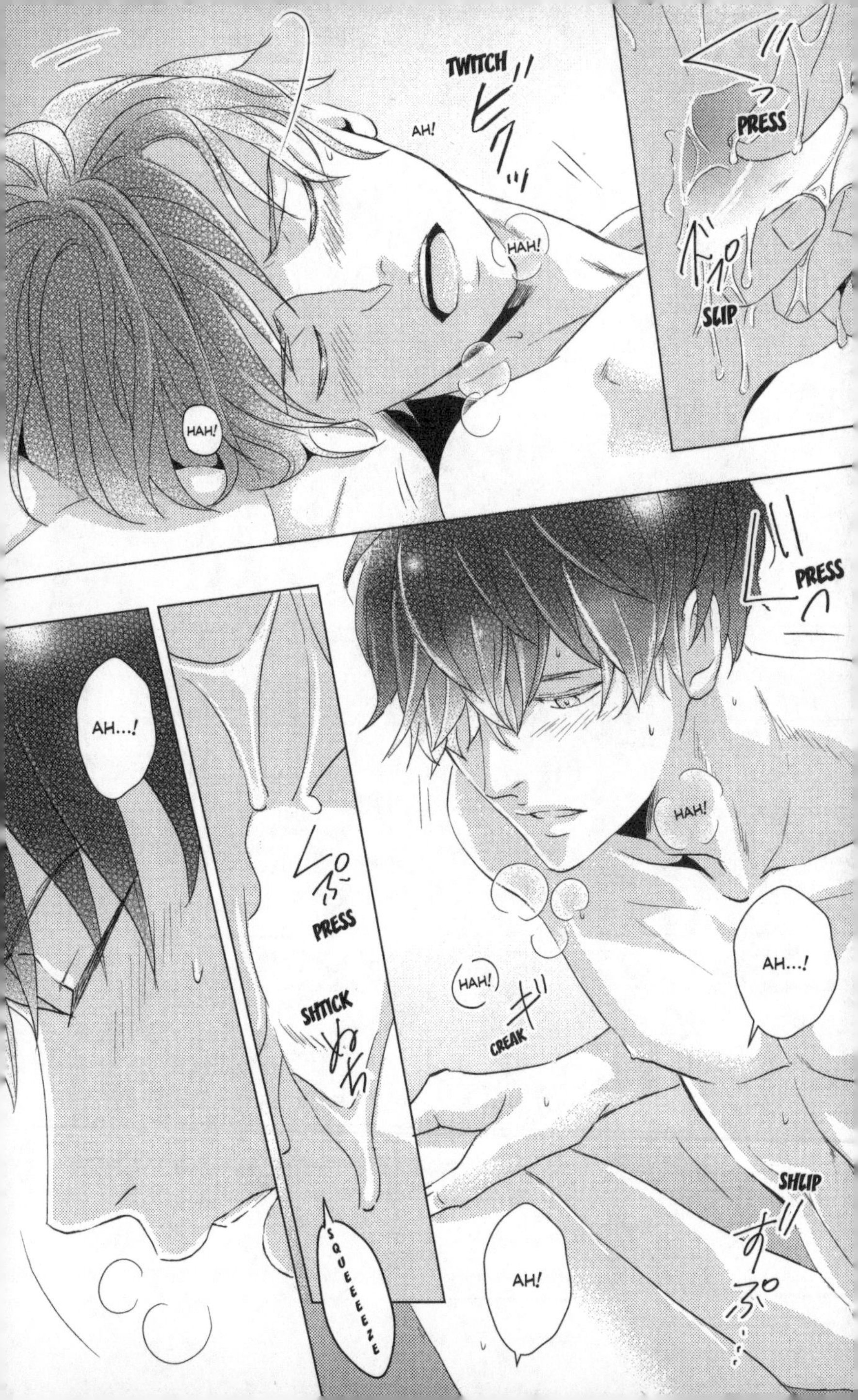
PRESS
SLIP
TWITCH
AH!
HAH!
HAH!
PRESS
HAH!
AH...!
HAH!
CREAK
SHLIP
AH!
PRESS
SHTICK
SQUEEEEEZE
AH...!

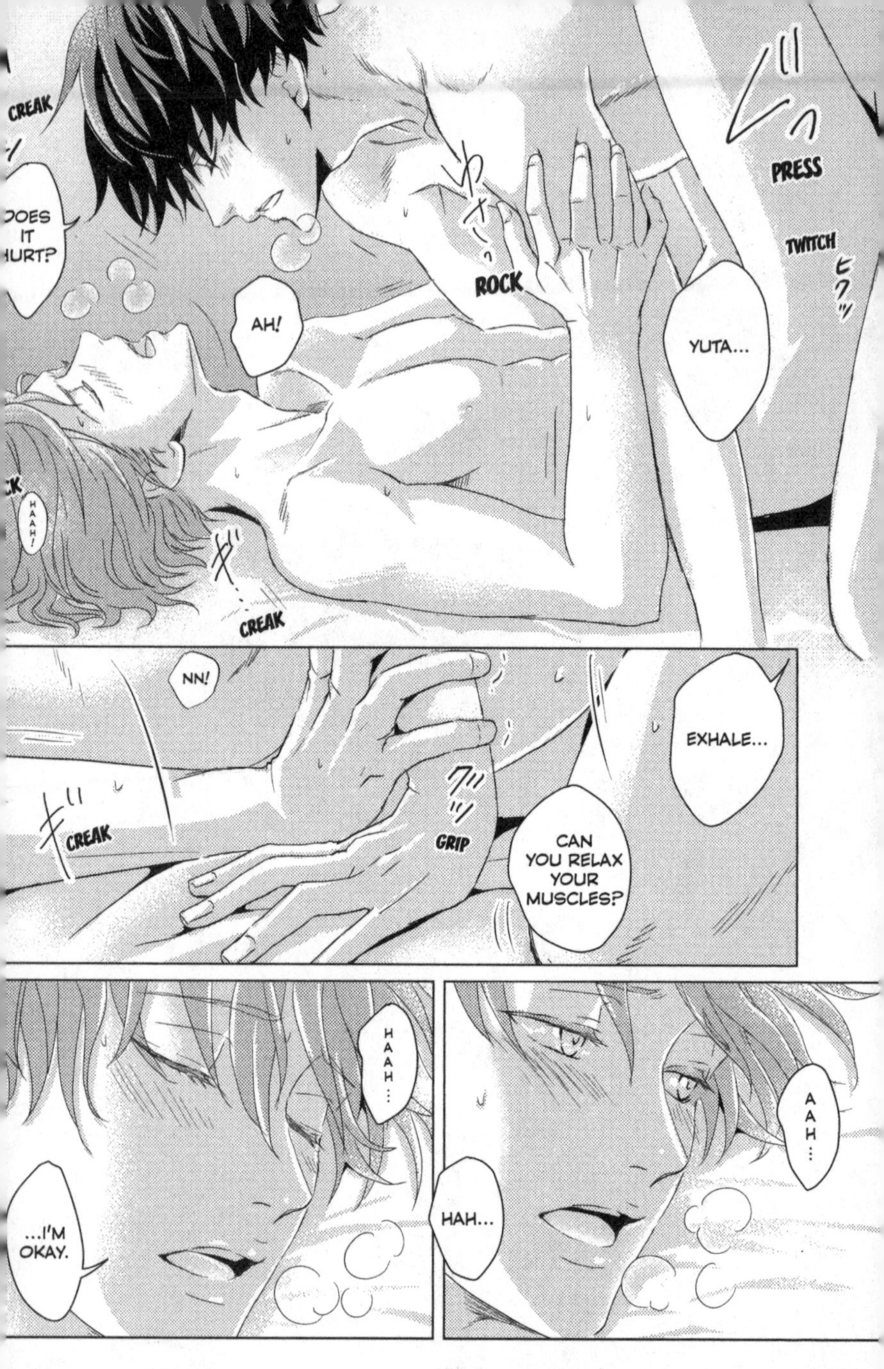
PRESS
TWITCH
YUTA...
ROCK
AH!
DOES IT HURT?
CREAK
HAAH!
CREAK
EXHALE...
CAN YOU RELAX YOUR MUSCLES?
GRIP
NN!
CREAK
AAH...
HAH...
HAAH...
...I'M OKAY.

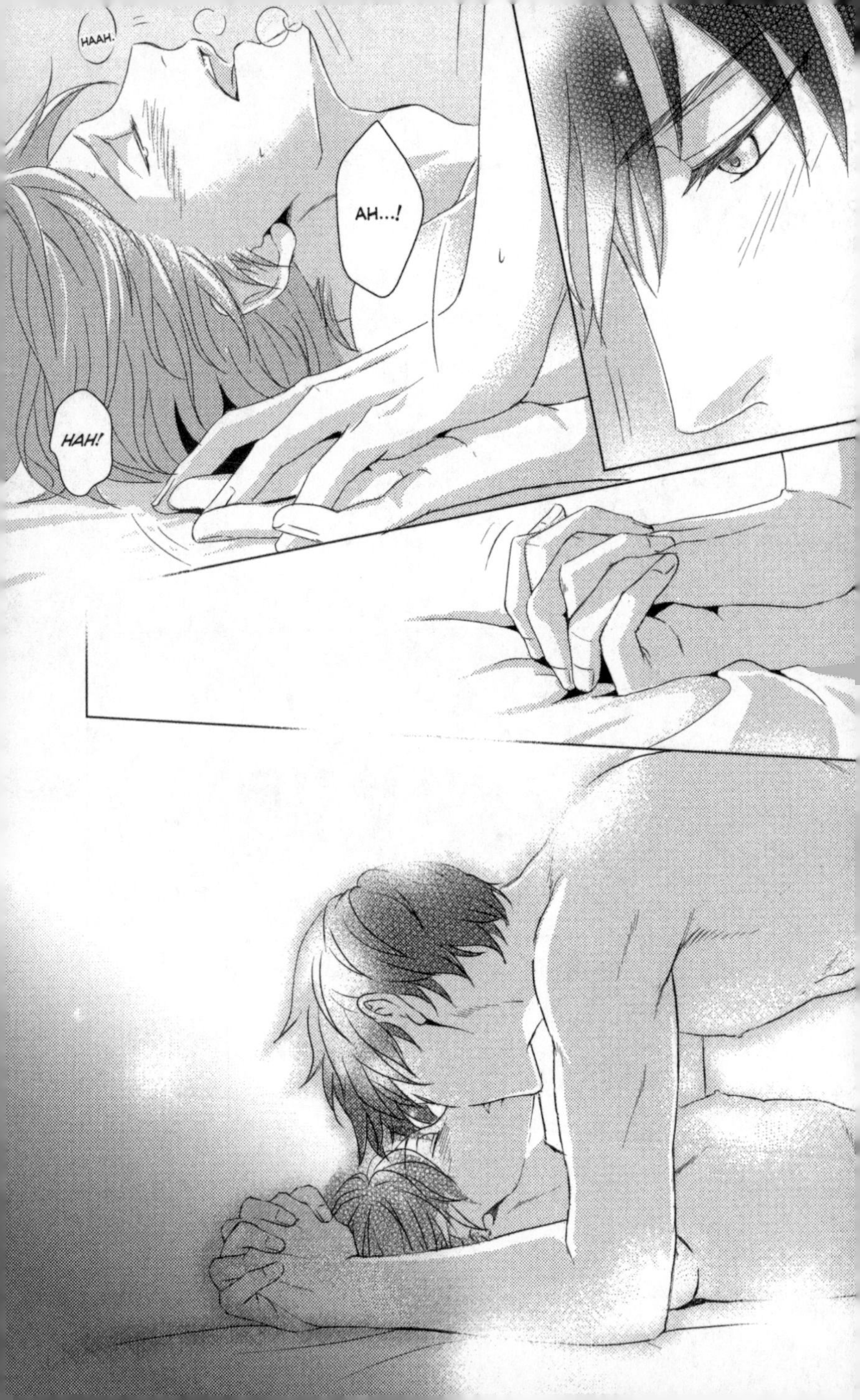
HAAH.
AH...!
HAH!

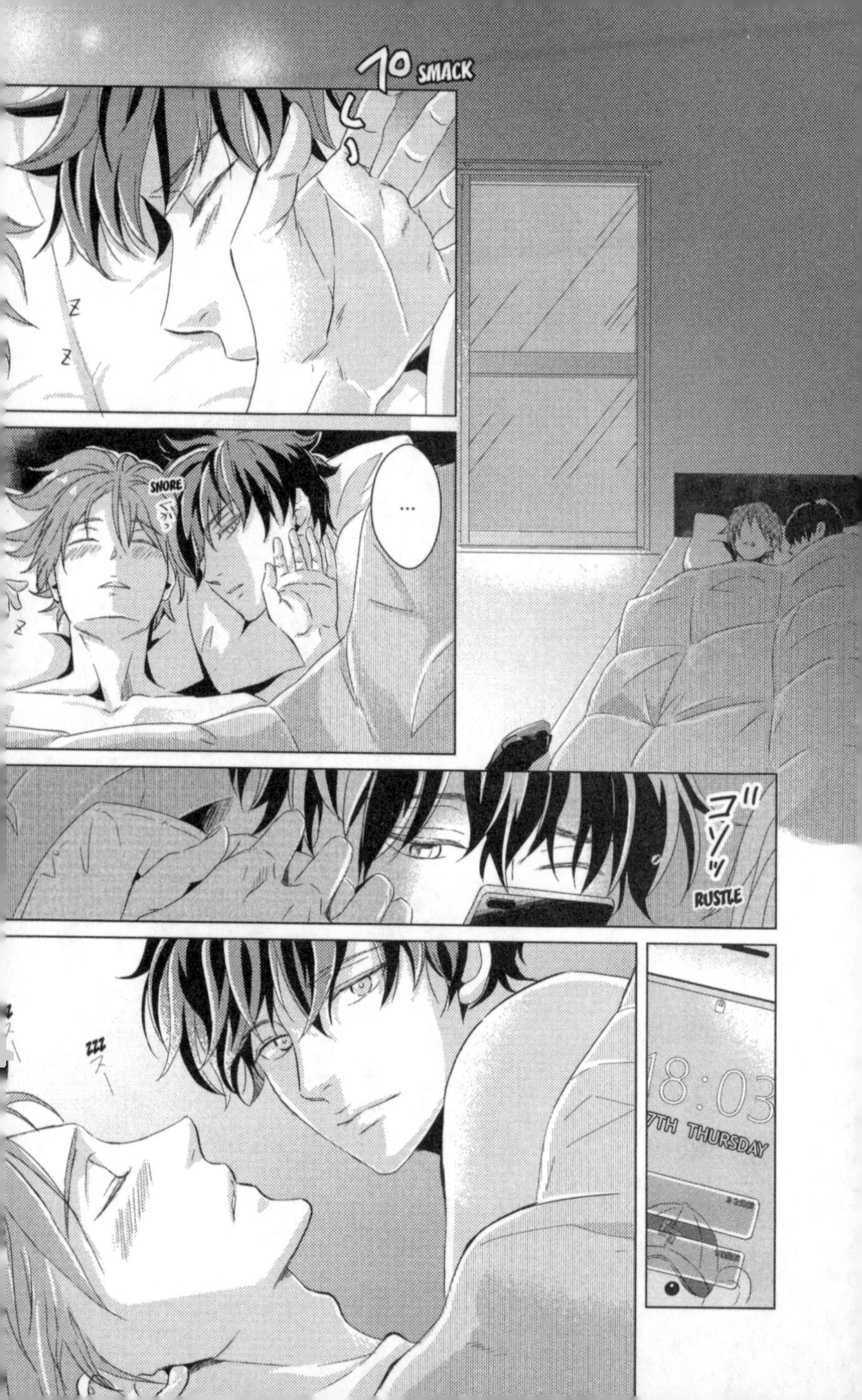
SMACK
...
SNORE
RUSTLE
18:03
7TH THURSDAY
ZZZ

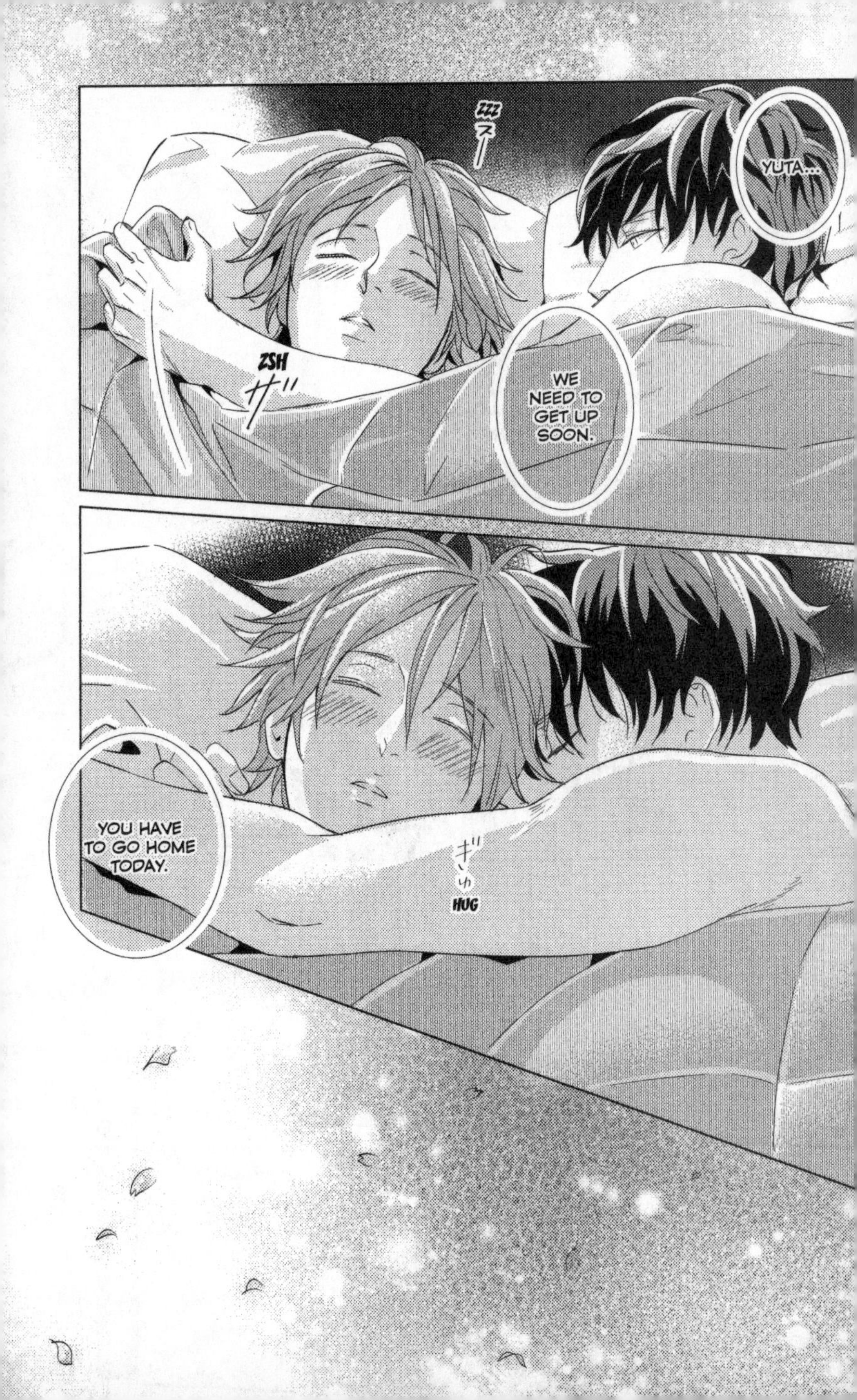
YUTA...
ZZZ
WE NEED TO GET UP SOON.
ZSH
HUG
YOU HAVE TO GO HOME TODAY.

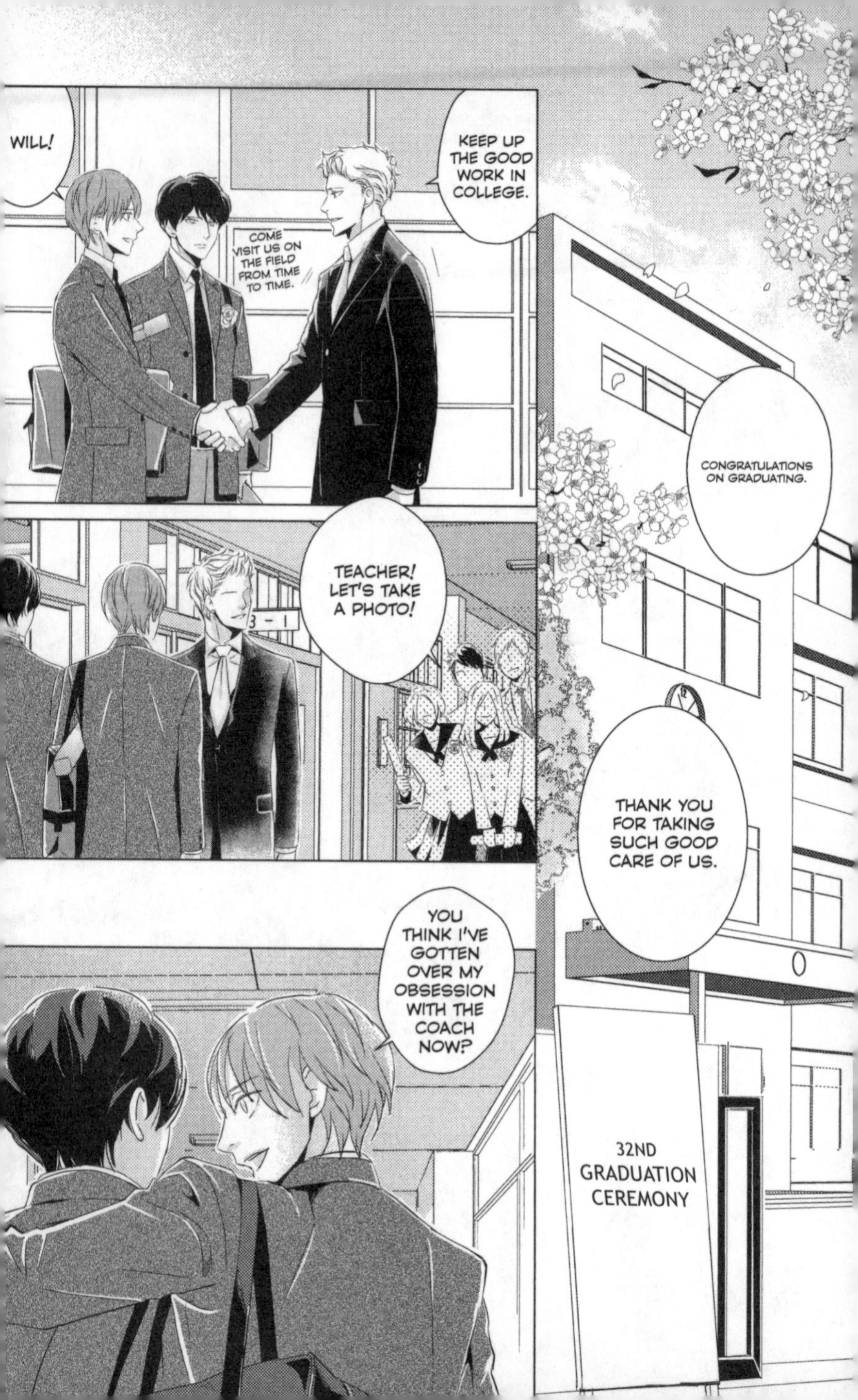
CONGRATULATIONS ON GRADUATING.
THANK YOU FOR TAKING SUCH GOOD CARE OF US.
32ND GRADUATION CEREMONY
KEEP UP THE GOOD WORK IN COLLEGE.
COME VISIT US ON THE FIELD FROM TIME TO TIME.
WILL!
TEACHER! LET'S TAKE A PHOTO!
YOU THINK I'VE GOTTEN OVER MY OBSESSION WITH THE COACH NOW?

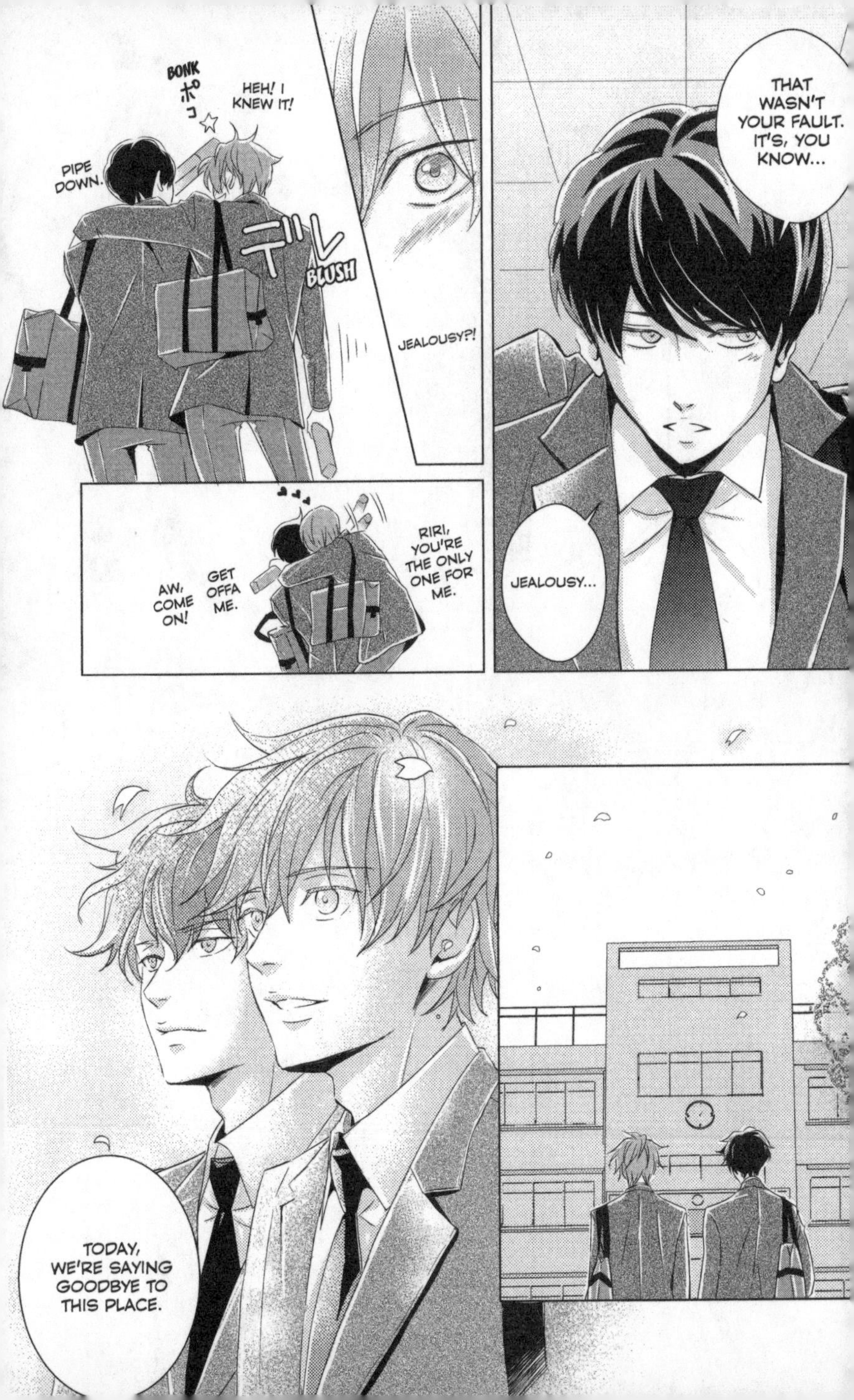
THAT WASN'T YOUR FAULT. IT'S, YOU KNOW...
JEALOUSY...
JEALOUSY?!
HEH! I KNEW IT!
BONK
ポコ
PIPE DOWN.
デレ
BLUSH
RIRI, YOU'RE THE ONLY ONE FOR ME.
GET OFFA ME.
AW, COME ON!
TODAY, WE'RE SAYING GOODBYE TO THIS PLACE.

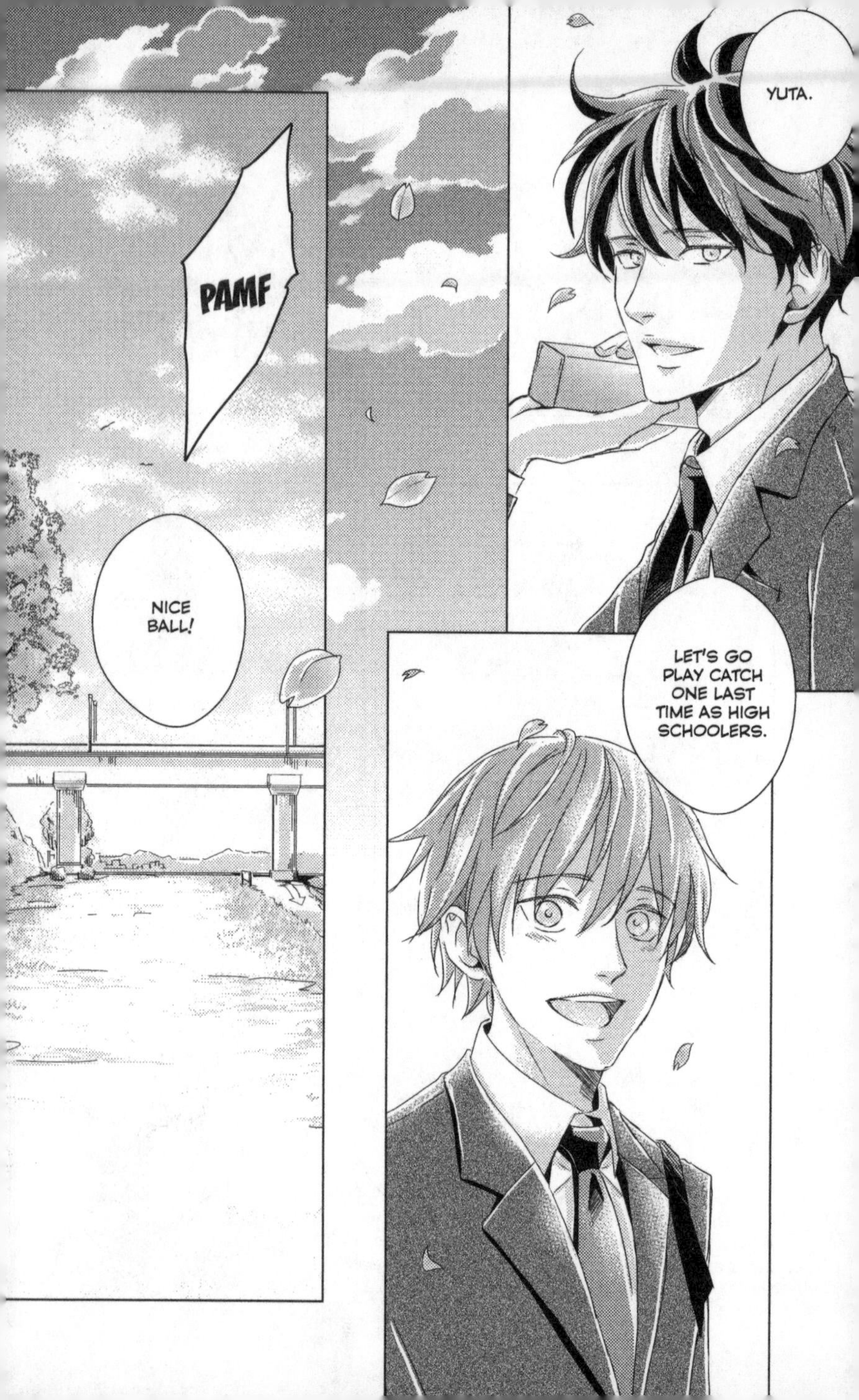
YUTA.
LET'S GO PLAY CATCH ONE LAST TIME AS HIGH SCHOOLERS.
PAMF
NICE BALL!

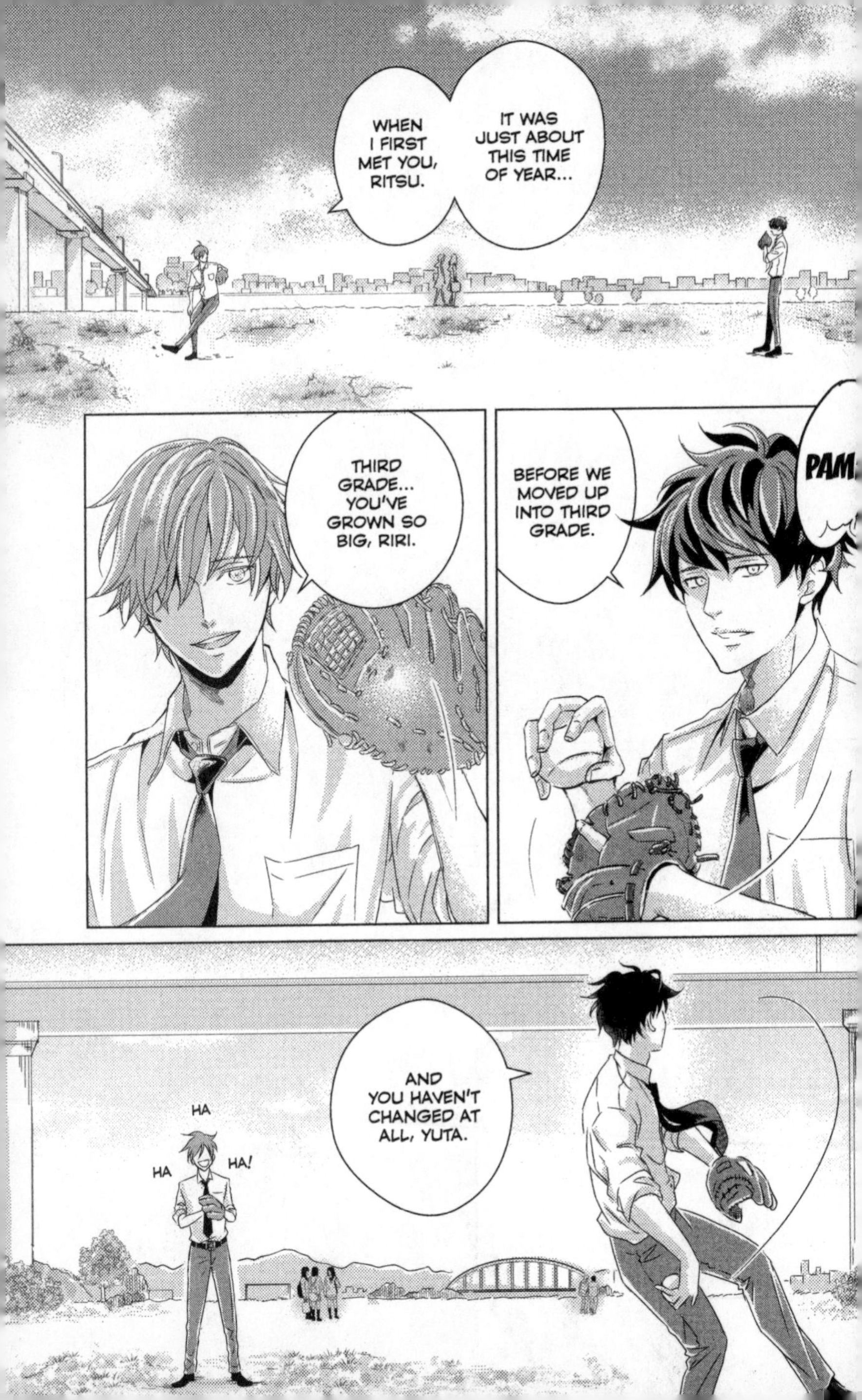
IT WAS JUST ABOUT THIS TIME OF YEAR...
WHEN I FIRST MET YOU, RITSU.
PAM
BEFORE WE MOVED UP INTO THIRD GRADE.
THIRD GRADE... YOU'VE GROWN SO BIG, RIRI.
AND YOU HAVEN'T CHANGED AT ALL, YUTA.
HA
HA!
HA

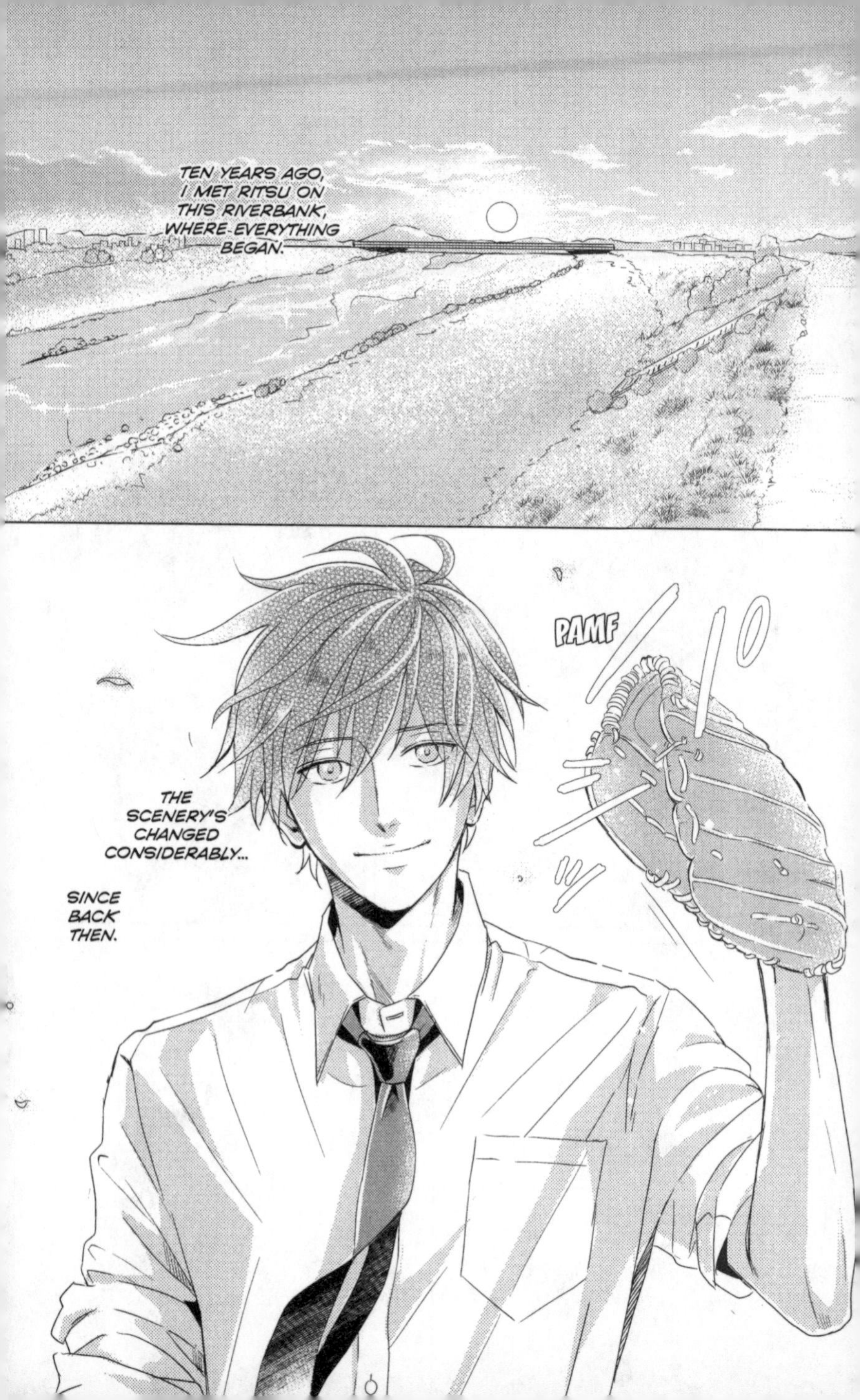
TEN YEARS AGO, I MET RITSU ON THIS RIVERBANK, WHERE EVERYTHING BEGAN.
PAMF
THE SCENERY'S CHANGED CONSIDERABLY...
SINCE BACK THEN.

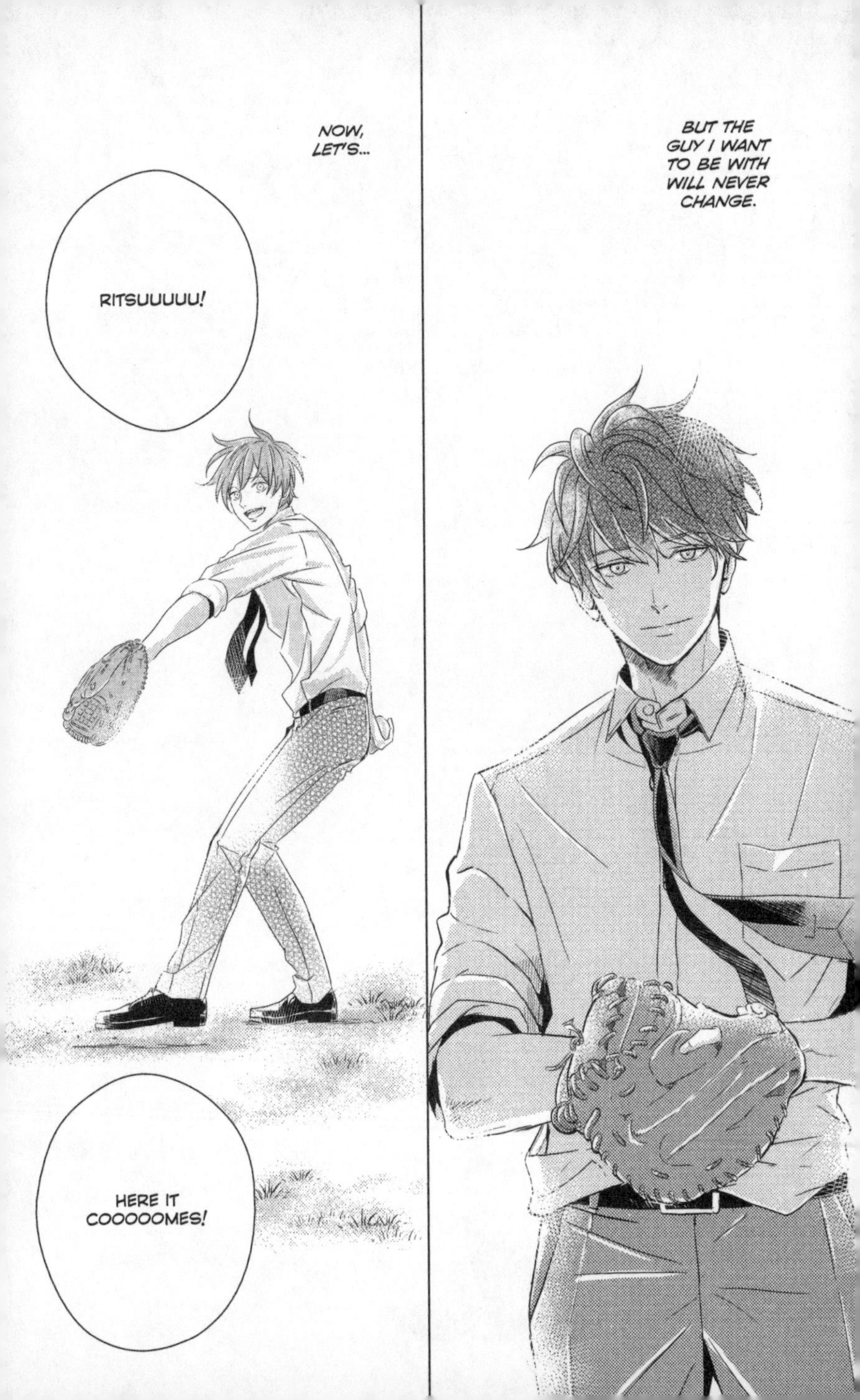
BUT THE GUY I WANT TO BE WITH WILL NEVER CHANGE.
NOW, LET'S...
RITSUUUUU!
HERE IT COOOOOMES!

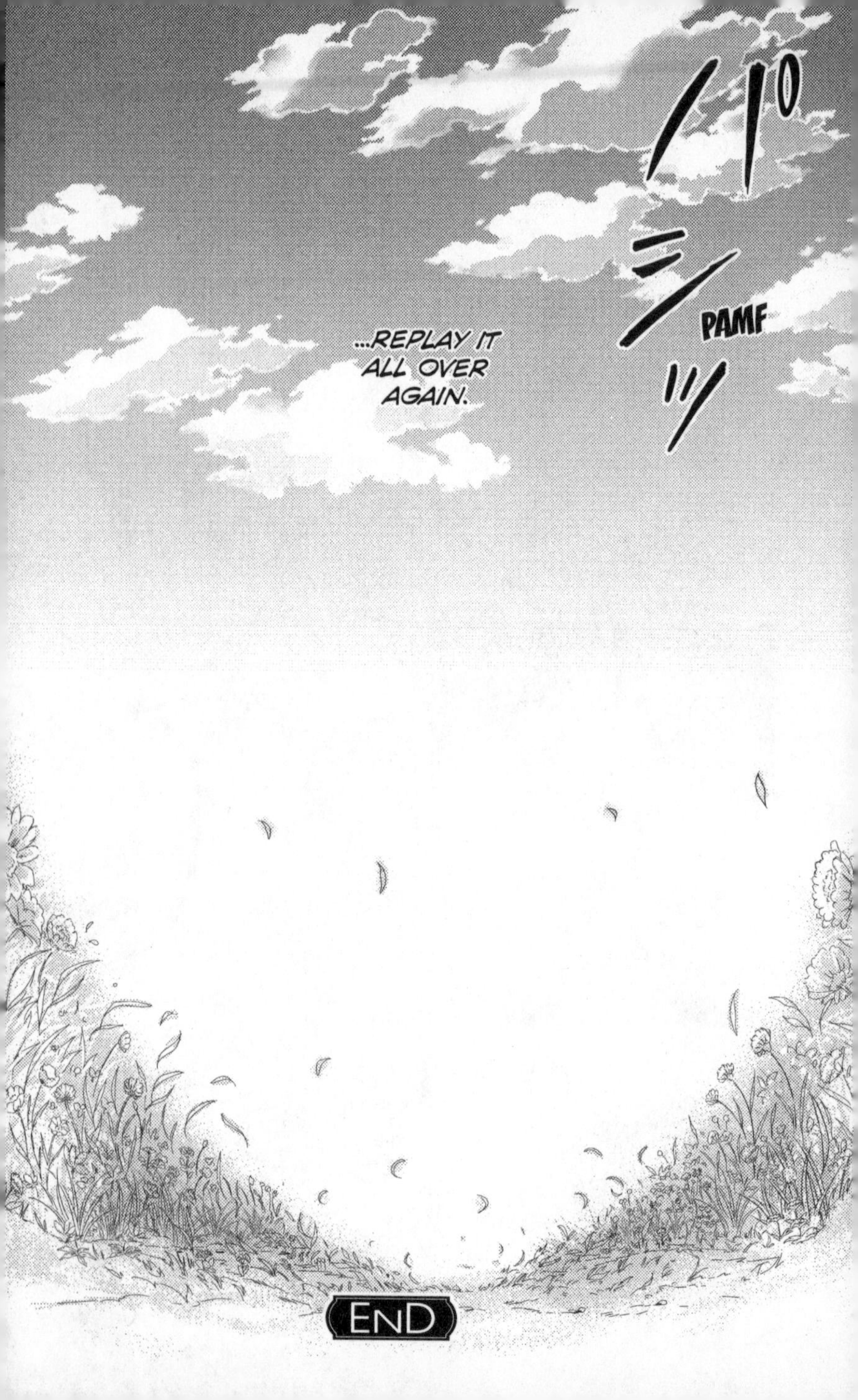
パシッ
PAMF
...REPLAY IT ALL OVER AGAIN.
END

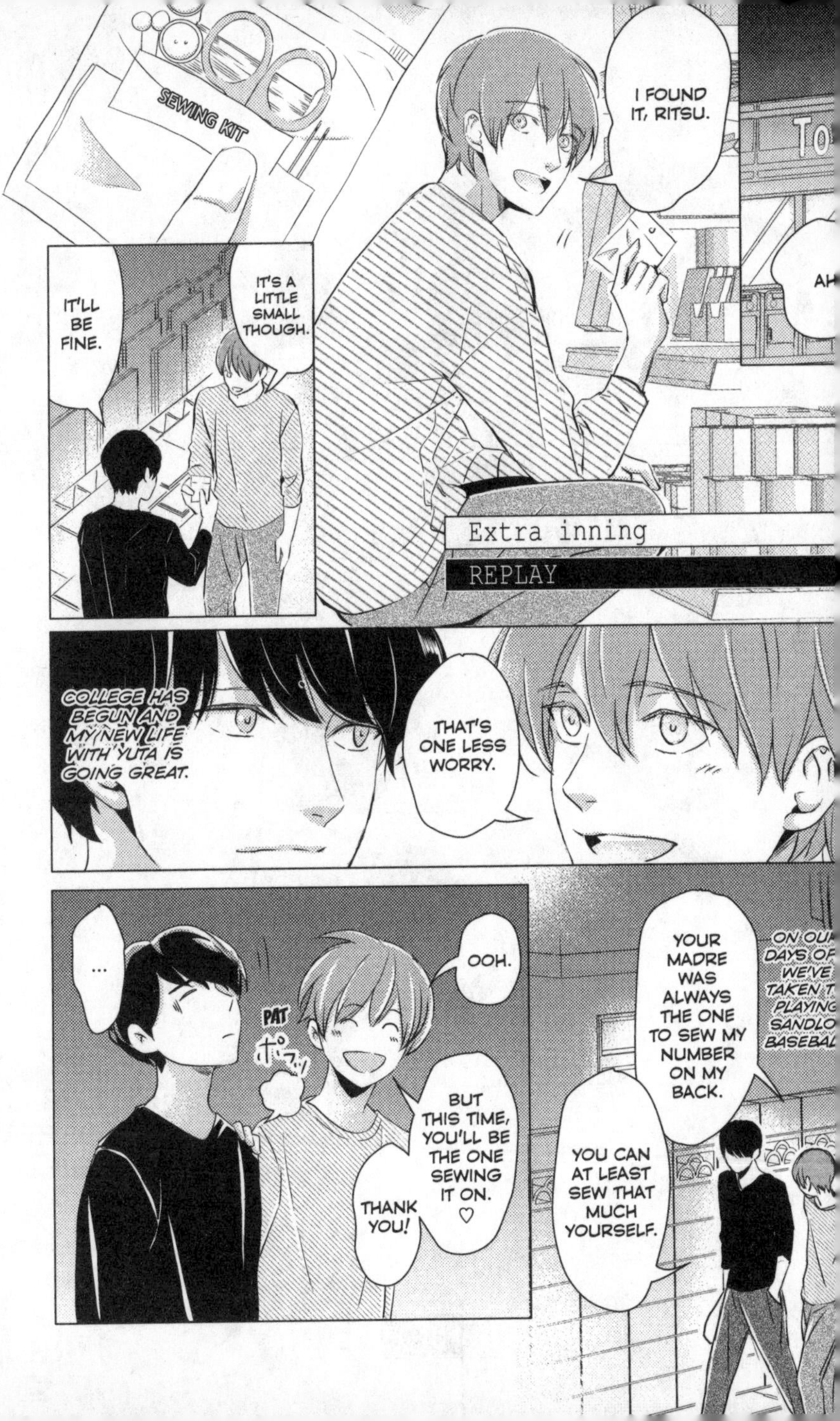
AH
I FOUND IT, RITSU.
SEWING KIT
Extra inning
REPLAY
IT'S A LITTLE SMALL THOUGH.
IT'LL BE FINE.
THAT'S ONE LESS WORRY.
COLLEGE HAS BEGUN AND MY NEW LIFE WITH YUTA IS GOING GREAT.
YOUR MADRE WAS ALWAYS THE ONE TO SEW MY NUMBER ON MY BACK.
YOU CAN AT LEAST SEW THAT MUCH YOURSELF.
OOH.
BUT THIS TIME, YOU'LL BE THE ONE SEWING IT ON. ♡
THANK YOU!
PAT
...

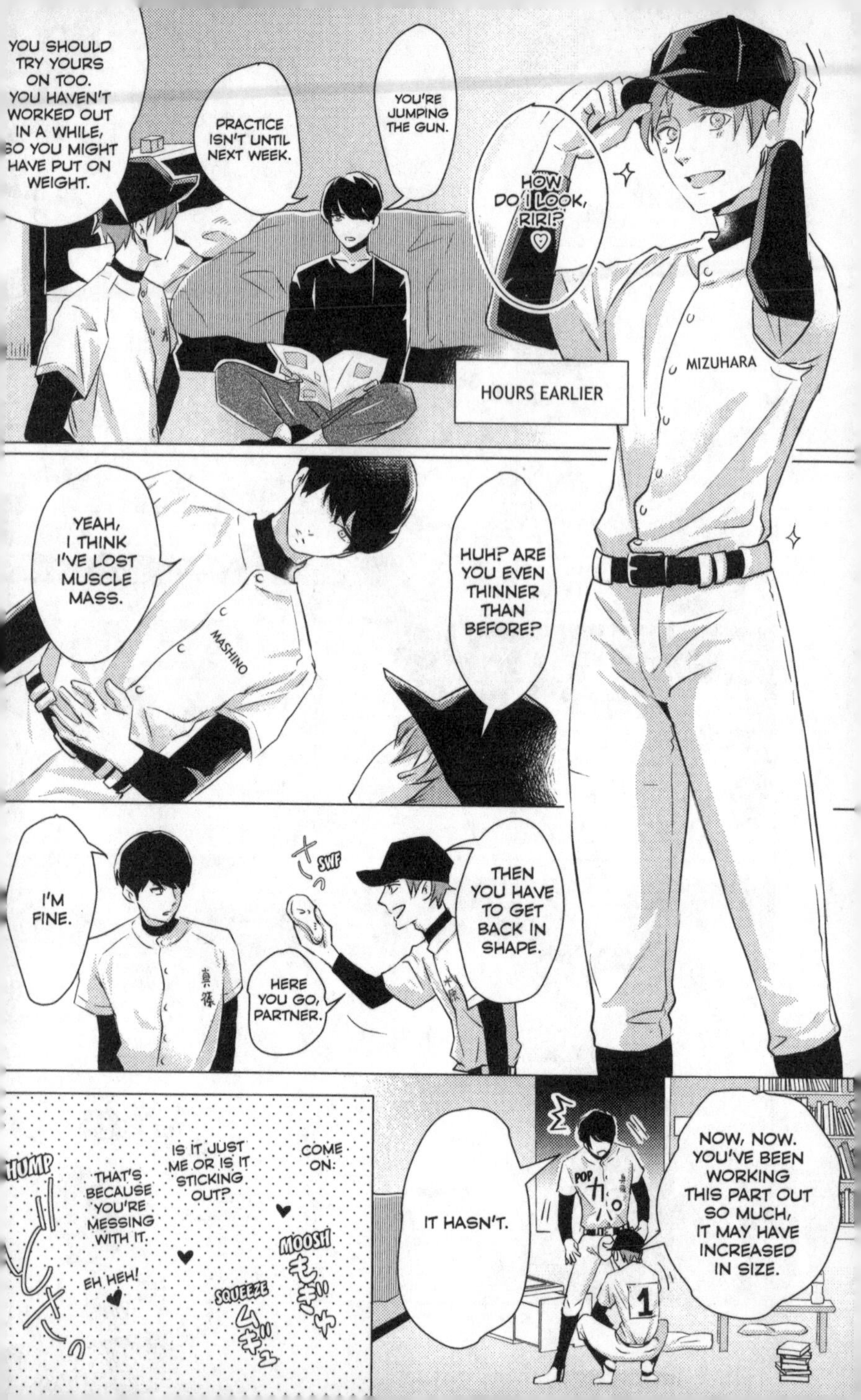
HOW DO I LOOK, RIRI? ♥
MIZUHARA
HOURS EARLIER
YOU'RE JUMPING THE GUN.
PRACTICE ISN'T UNTIL NEXT WEEK.
YOU SHOULD TRY YOURS ON TOO. YOU HAVEN'T WORKED OUT IN A WHILE, SO YOU MIGHT HAVE PUT ON WEIGHT.
HUH? ARE YOU EVEN THINNER THAN BEFORE?
YEAH, I THINK I'VE LOST MUSCLE MASS.
MASHINO
THEN YOU HAVE TO GET BACK IN SHAPE.
SWF
HERE YOU GO, PARTNER.
I'M FINE.
NOW, NOW. YOU'VE BEEN WORKING THIS PART OUT SO MUCH, IT MAY HAVE INCREASED IN SIZE.
POP
IT HASN'T.
1
COME ON: ♥
IS IT JUST ME OR IS IT STICKING OUT?
THAT'S BECAUSE YOU'RE MESSING WITH IT. ♥
MOOSH
SQUEEZE
EH HEH! ♥
HUMP

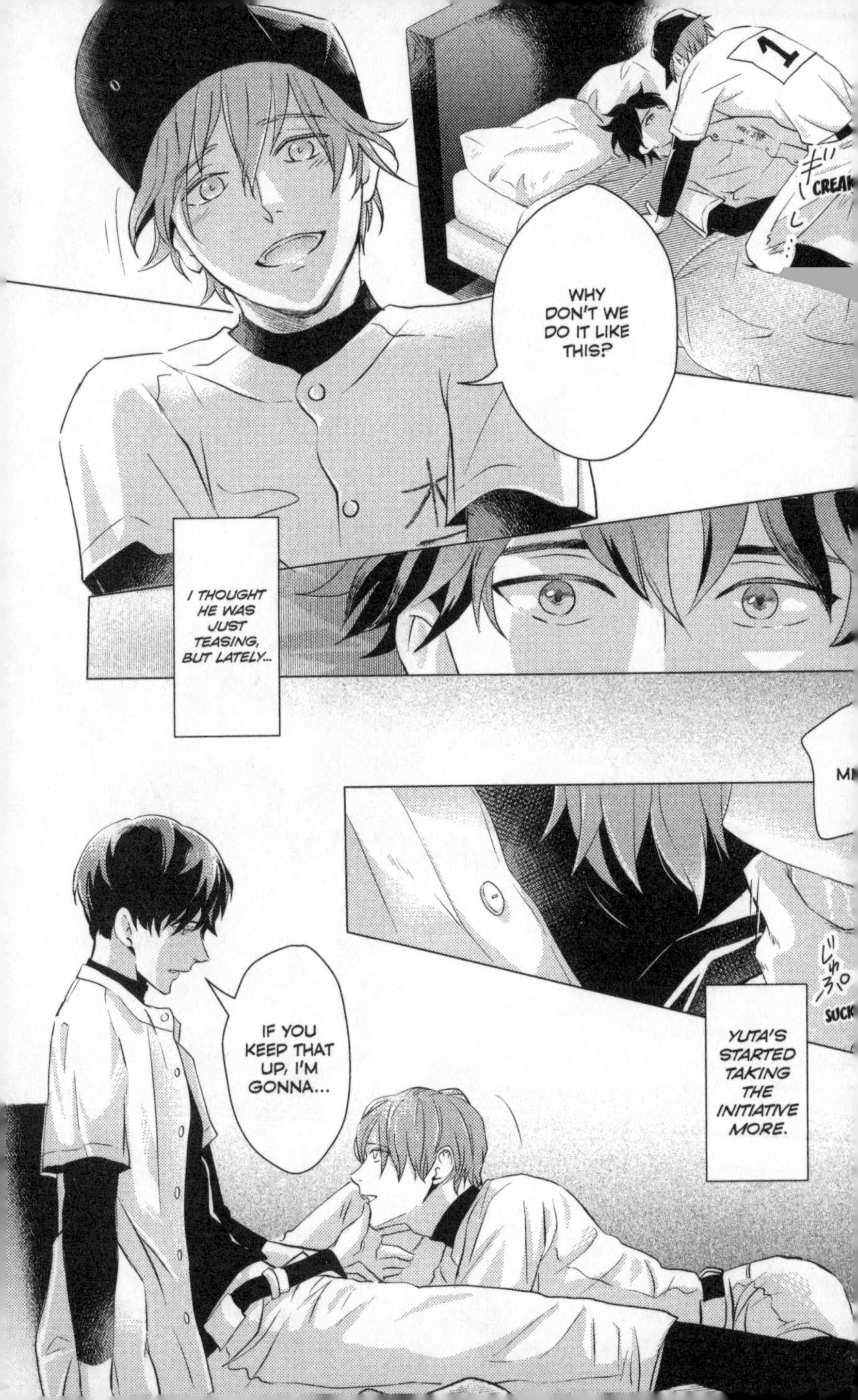
WHY DON'T WE DO IT LIKE THIS?
I THOUGHT HE WAS JUST TEASING, BUT LATELY...
SUCK
YUTA'S STARTED TAKING THE INITIATIVE MORE.
IF YOU KEEP THAT UP, I'M GONNA...

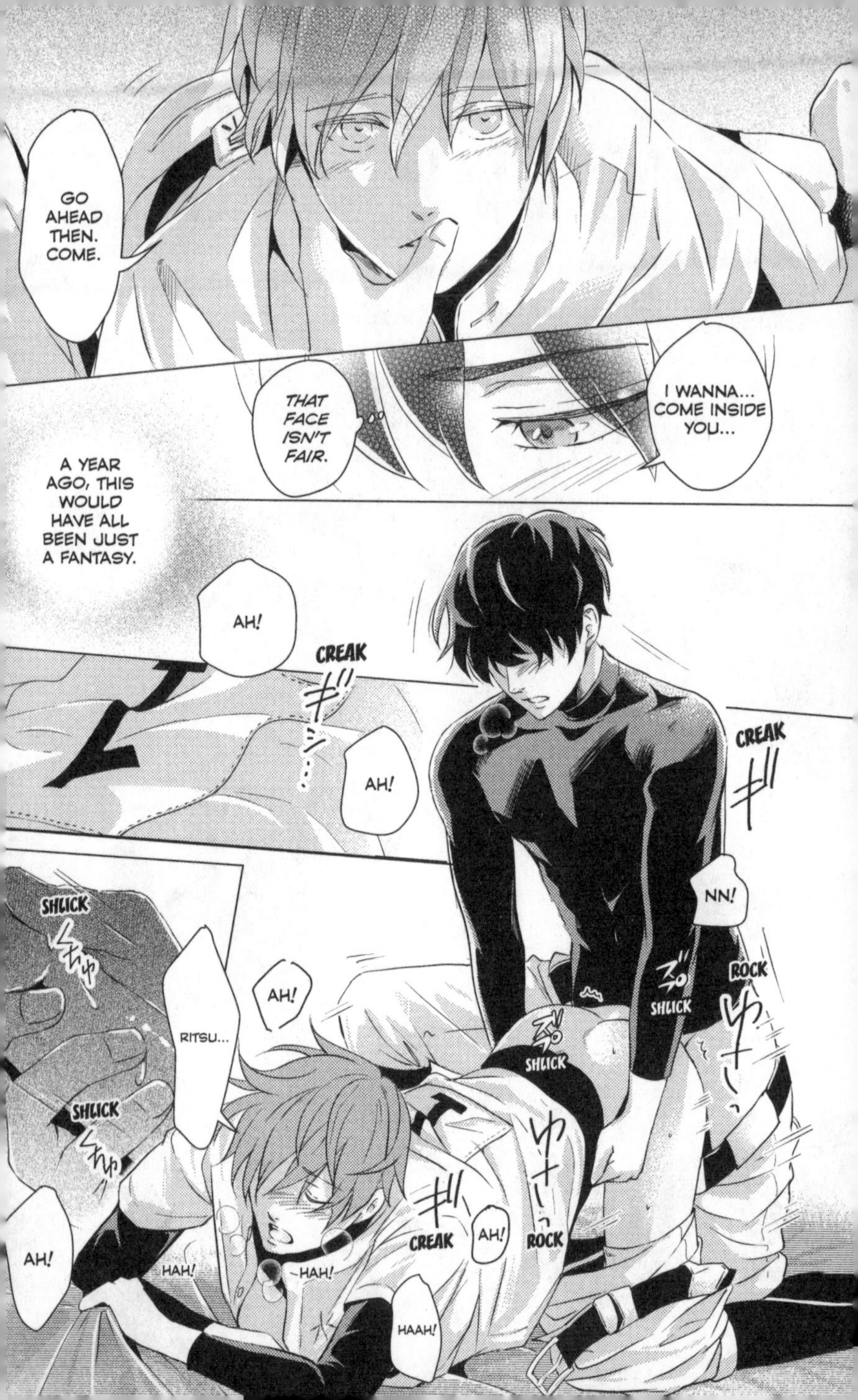
GO AHEAD THEN. COME.
I WANNA... COME INSIDE YOU...
THAT FACE ISN'T FAIR.
A YEAR AGO, THIS WOULD HAVE ALL BEEN JUST A FANTASY.
CREAK
NN!
ROCK
SHLICK
SHLICK
ROCK
AH!
CREAK
HAAH!
HAH!
RITSU...
AH!
HAH!
AH!
SHLICK
SHLICK
AH!
CREAK
AH!

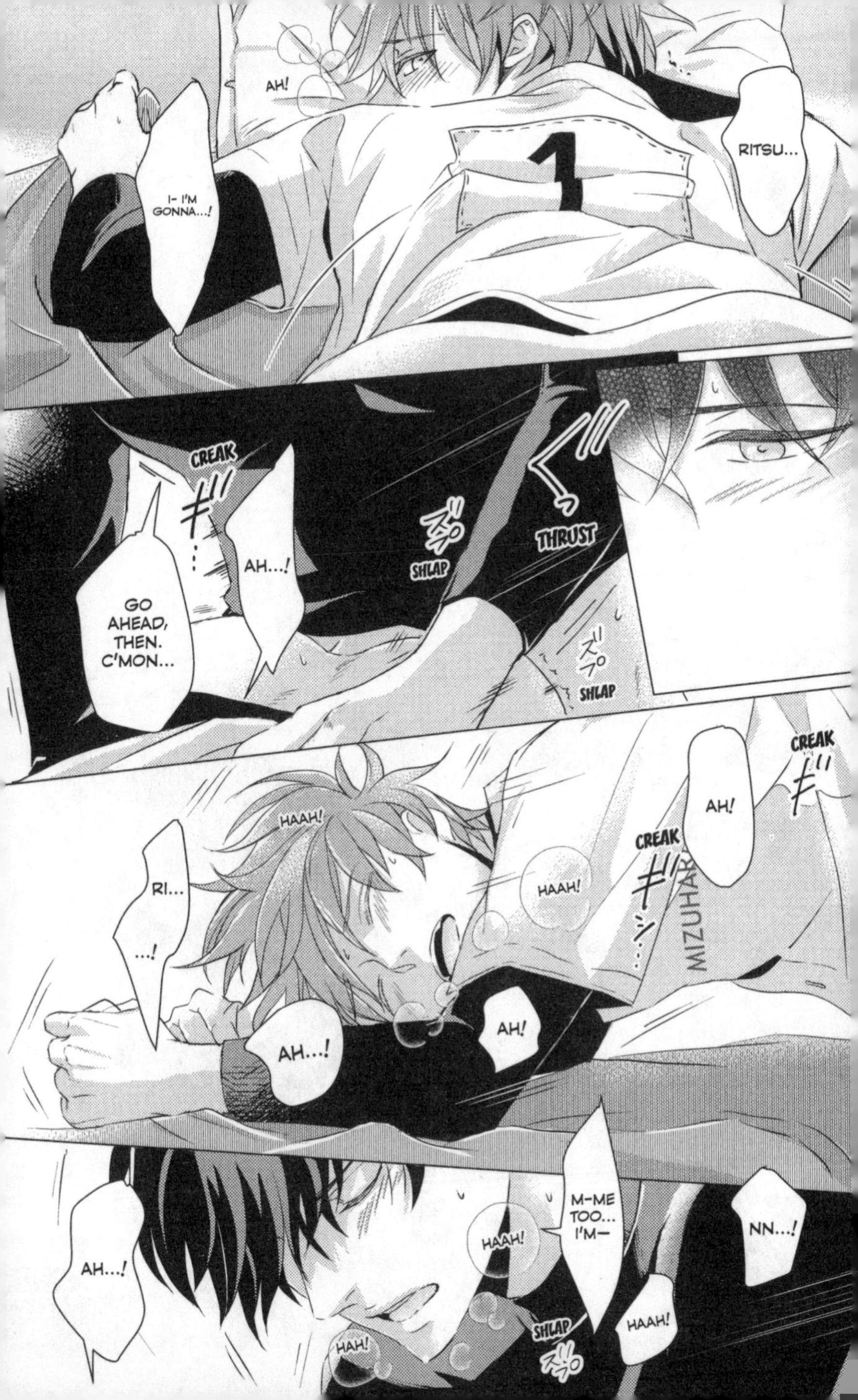

RITSU...
AH!
I- I'M GONNA...!
THRUST
SHLAP
SHLAP
AH...!
CREAK
GO AHEAD, THEN. C'MON...
CREAK
AH!
CREAK
HAAH!
HAAH!
RI... ...!
AH!
AH...!
NN...!
M-ME TOO... I'M—
HAAH!
HAAH!
SHLAP
AH...!
HAH!

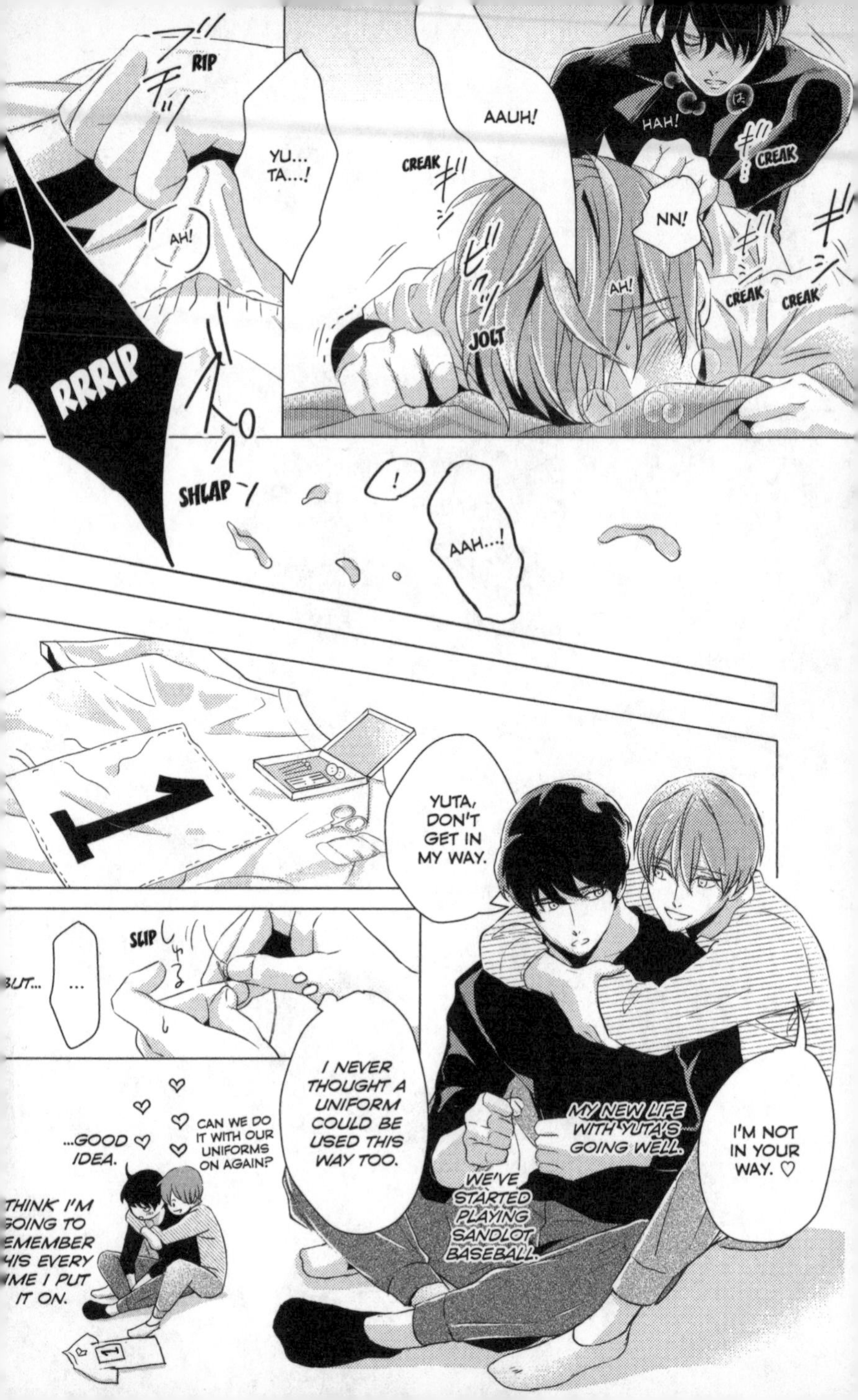
AAUH!
CREAK
HAH!
CREAK
NN!
AH!
CREAK
CREAK
JOLT
RIP
YU... TA...!
AH!
RRRIP
SHLAP
!
AAH...!
YUTA, DON'T GET IN MY WAY.
SLIP
BUT...
...
I'M NOT IN YOUR WAY. ♡
MY NEW LIFE WITH YUTA'S GOING WELL.
WE'VE STARTED PLAYING SANDLOT BASEBALL.
I NEVER THOUGHT A UNIFORM COULD BE USED THIS WAY TOO.
CAN WE DO IT WITH OUR UNIFORMS ON AGAIN?
...GOOD ♡ IDEA.
THINK I'M GOING TO EMEMBER HIS EVERY IME I PUT IT ON.

# STOP

## THIS IS THE BACK OF THE BOOK!

**How do you read manga-style? It's simple! Let's practice -- just start in the top right panel and follow the numbers below!**

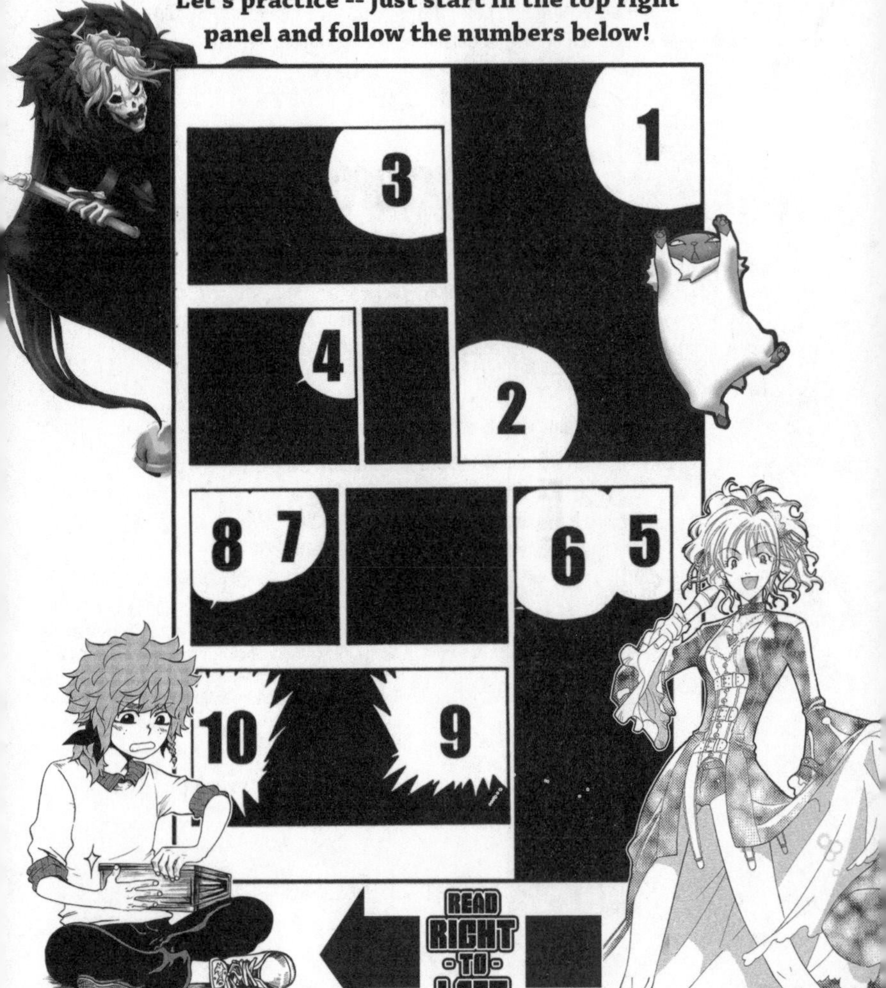
1
2
3
4
5
6
7
8
9
10
READ
RIGHT
-TO-
LEFT

Crimson from ***Kamo*** / Fairy Cat from ***Grimms Manga Tales***
Morrey from ***Goldfisch*** / Princess Ai from ***Princess Ai***

# *RePlay*
## Saki Tsukahara

Editor - Lena Atanassova
Translator - Christine Dashiell
Technology and Digital Media Assistant - Phillip Hong
Marketing Associate - Kae Winters
Graphic Designer - Phillip Hong
Retouching and Lettering - Vibrraant Publishing Studio
Licensing Specialist - Arika Yanaka
Editor-in-Chief & Publisher - Stu Levy

A  Manga

TOKYOPOP and ʘ are trademarks or registered trademarks of TOKYOPOP Inc.

TOKYOPOP Inc.
5200 W. Century Blvd. Suite 705
Los Angeles, 90045

E-mail: info@TOKYOPOP.com
Come visit us online at www.TOKYOPOP.com

f www.facebook.com/TOKYOPOP
y www.twitter.com/TOKYOPOP
p www.pinterest.com/TOKYOPOP
g www.instagram.com/TOKYOPOP

ISBN: 978-1-4278-6227-3
First TOKYOPOP Printing: February 2020
10 9 8 7 6 5 4 3 2 1
Printed in CANADA

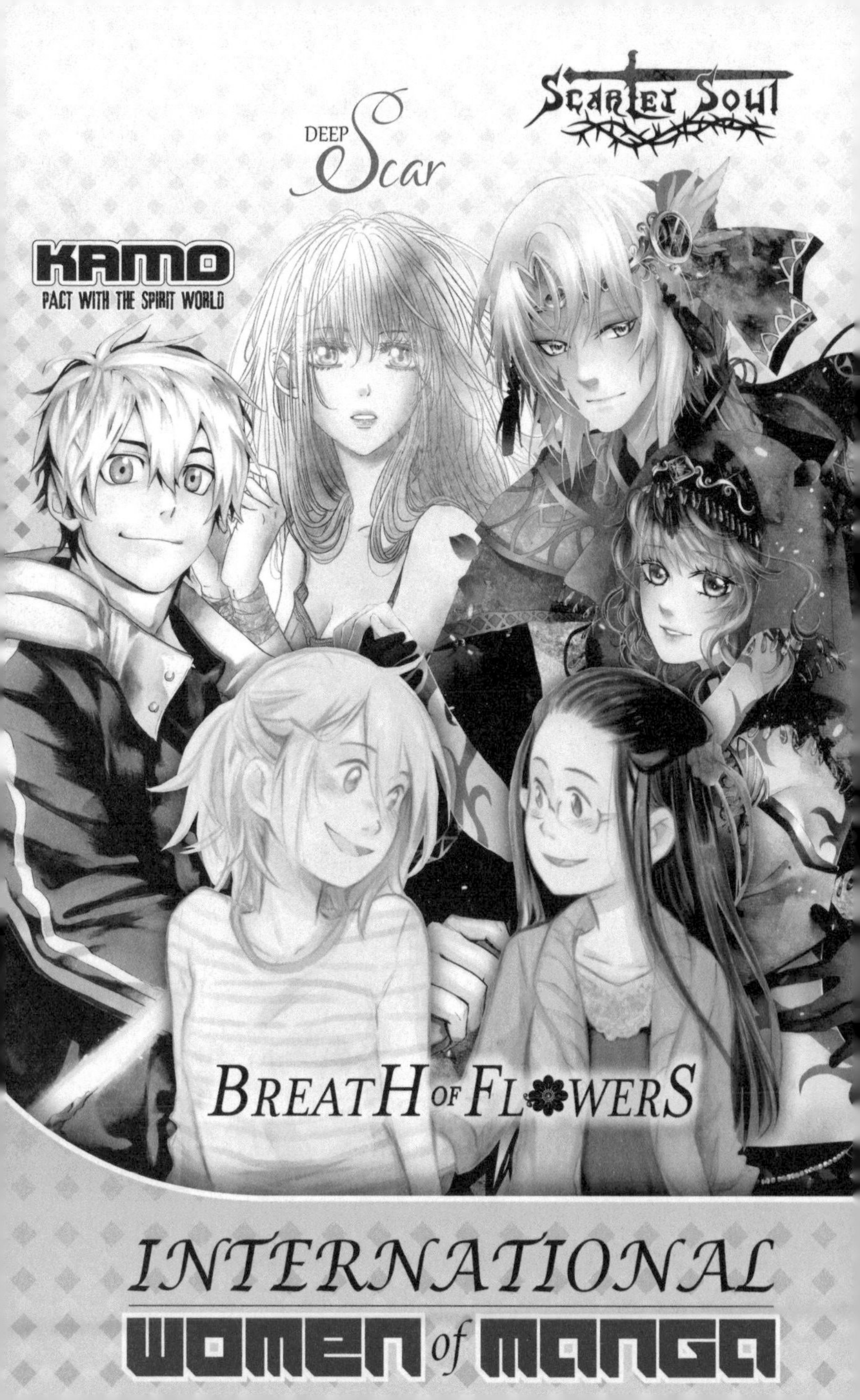

Scarlet Soul
Deep Scar
KAMO
PACT WITH THE SPIRIT WORLD
BREATH OF FLOWERS
INTERNATIONAL
WOMEN of MANGA

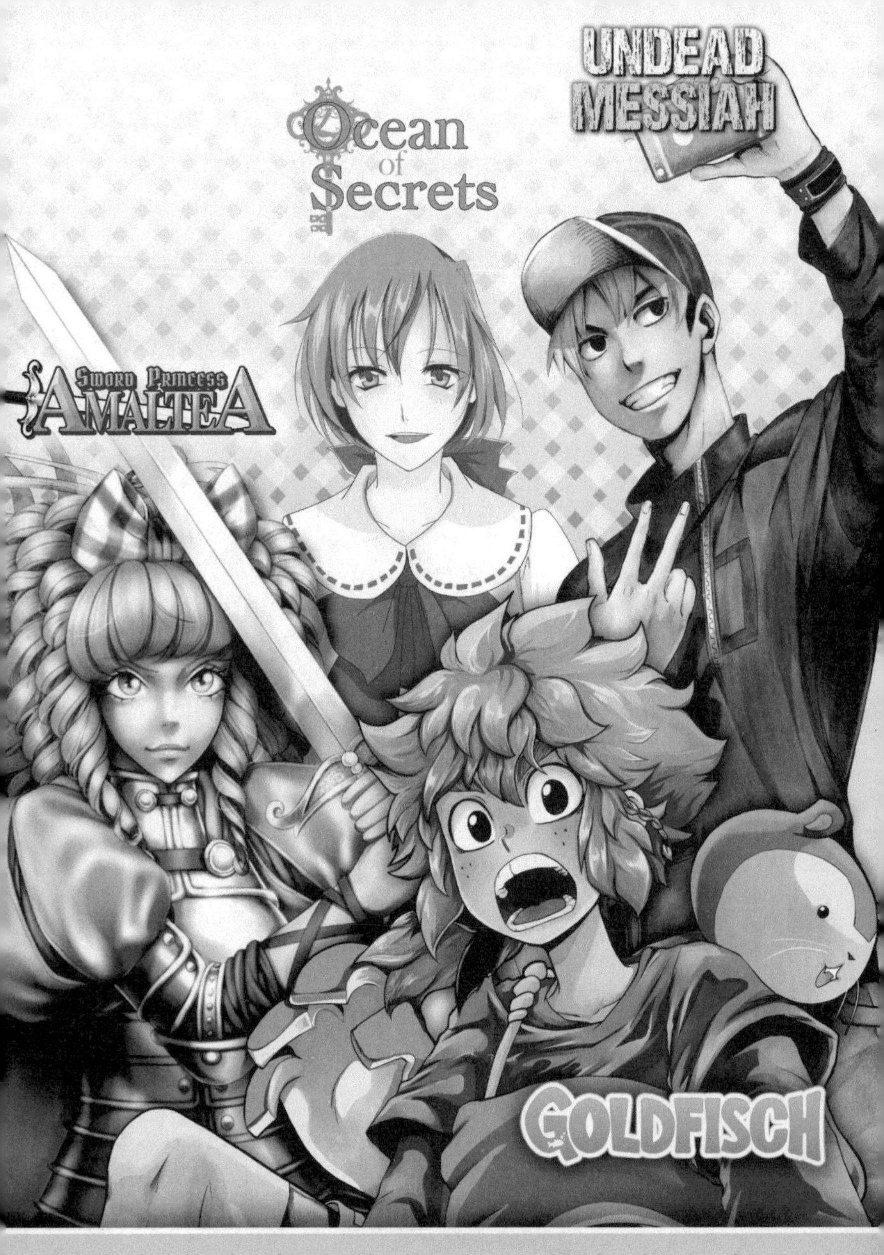
UNDEAD MESSIAH
Ocean of Secrets
SWORD PRINCESS AMALTEA
GOLDFISCH

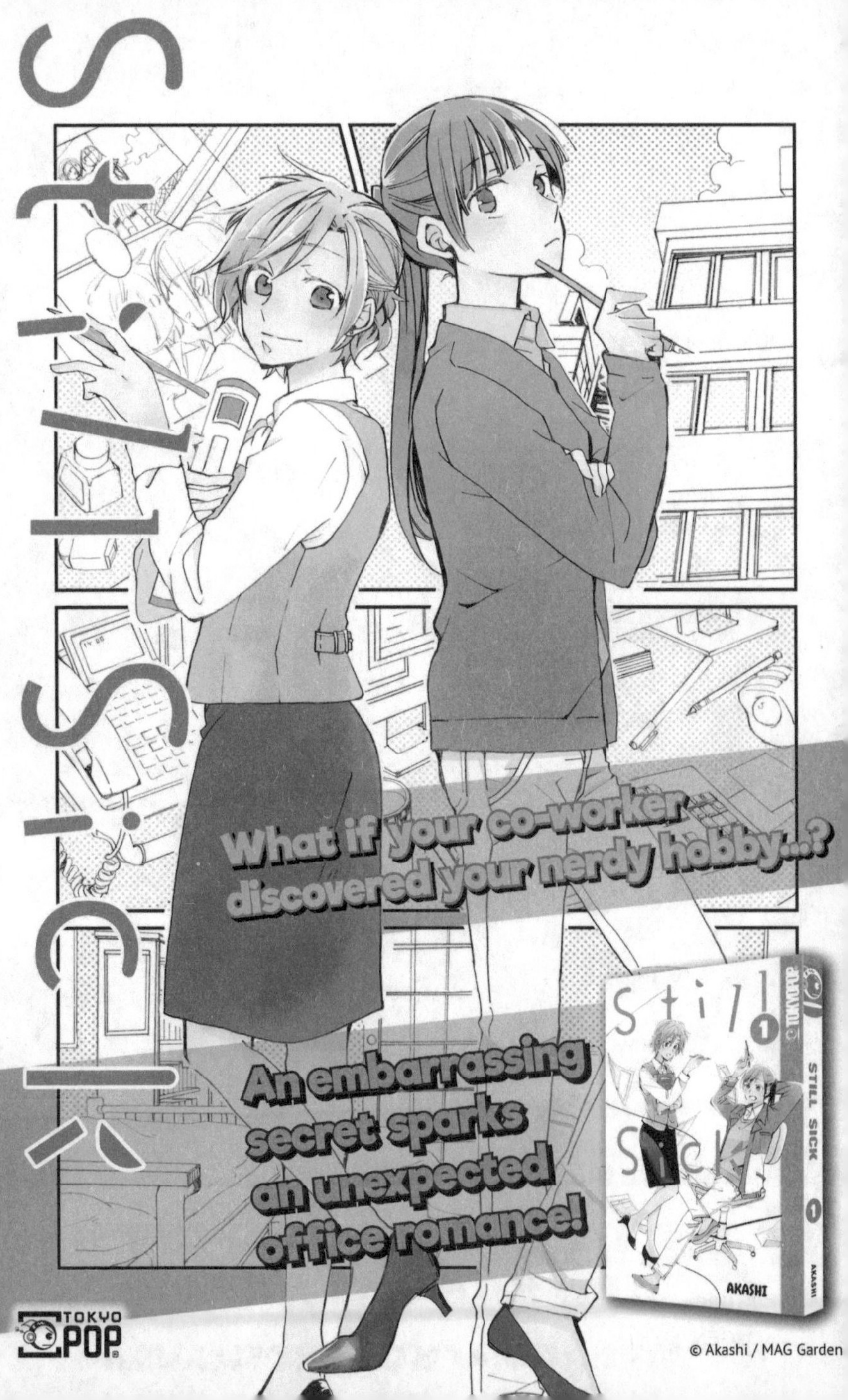
Still Sick
What if your co-worker discovered your nerdy hobby...?
An embarrassing secret sparks an unexpected office romance!
Still Sick 1
STILL SICK 1
AKASHI
TOKYO POP

# Futaribeya
## A ROOM FOR TWO

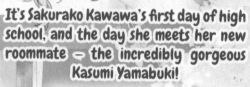

It's Sakurako Kawawa's first day of high school, and the day she meets her new roommate — the incredibly gorgeous Kasumi Yamabuki!

Follow the heartwarming, hilarious daily life of two high school roommates in this new, four-panel-style comic!

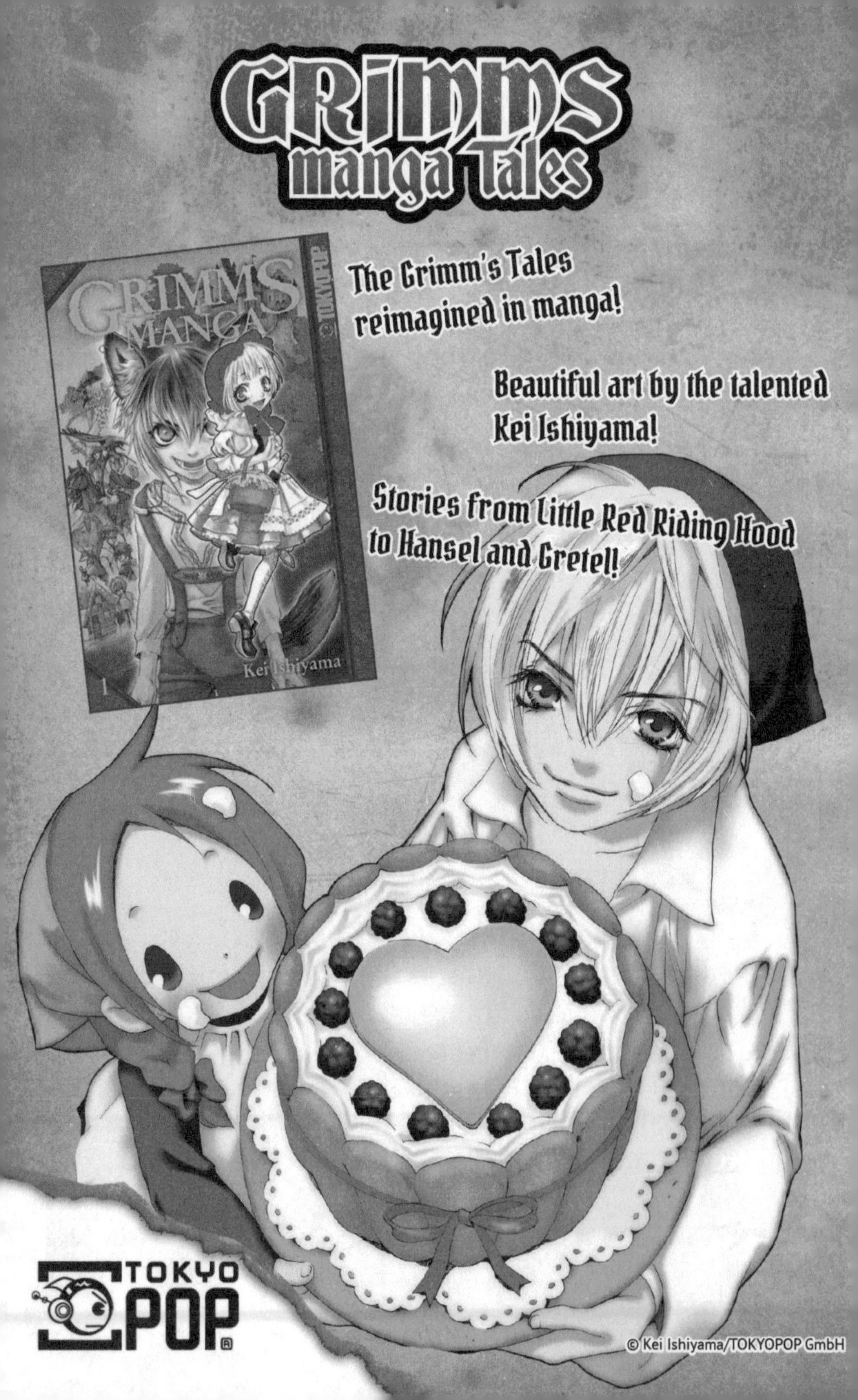
GRIMMS manga Tales
GRIMMS MANGA
TOKYOPOP
Kei Ishiyama
1
The Grimm's Tales reimagined in manga!
Beautiful art by the talented Kei Ishiyama!
Stories from Little Red Riding Hood to Hansel and Gretel!
TOKYO POP
© Kei Ishiyama/TOKYOPOP GmbH

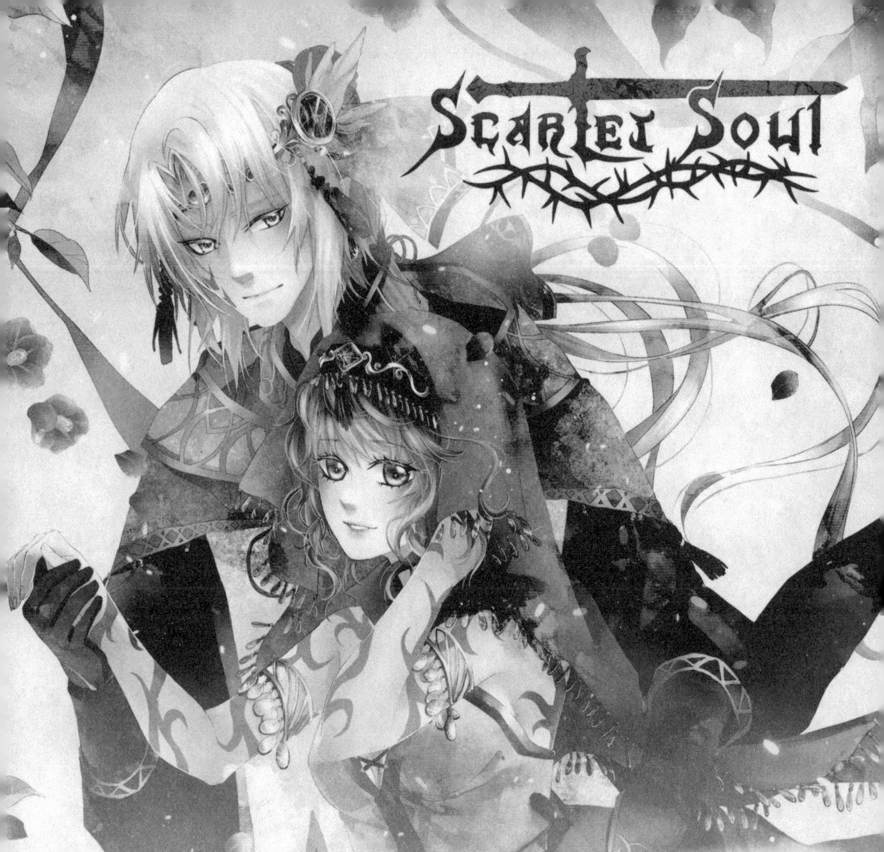
Scarlet Soul

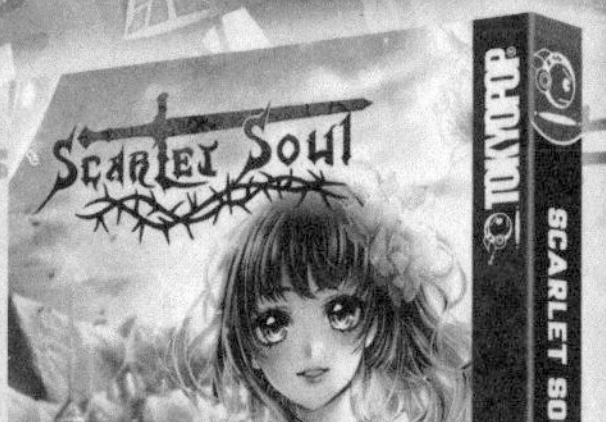
Scarlet Soul
TOKYOPOP
SCARLET SOUL
KIRA YUKISHIRO
1
KIRA YUKISHIRO
1

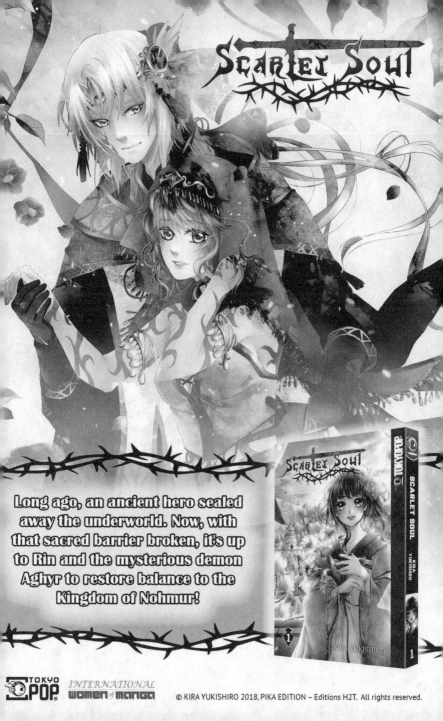

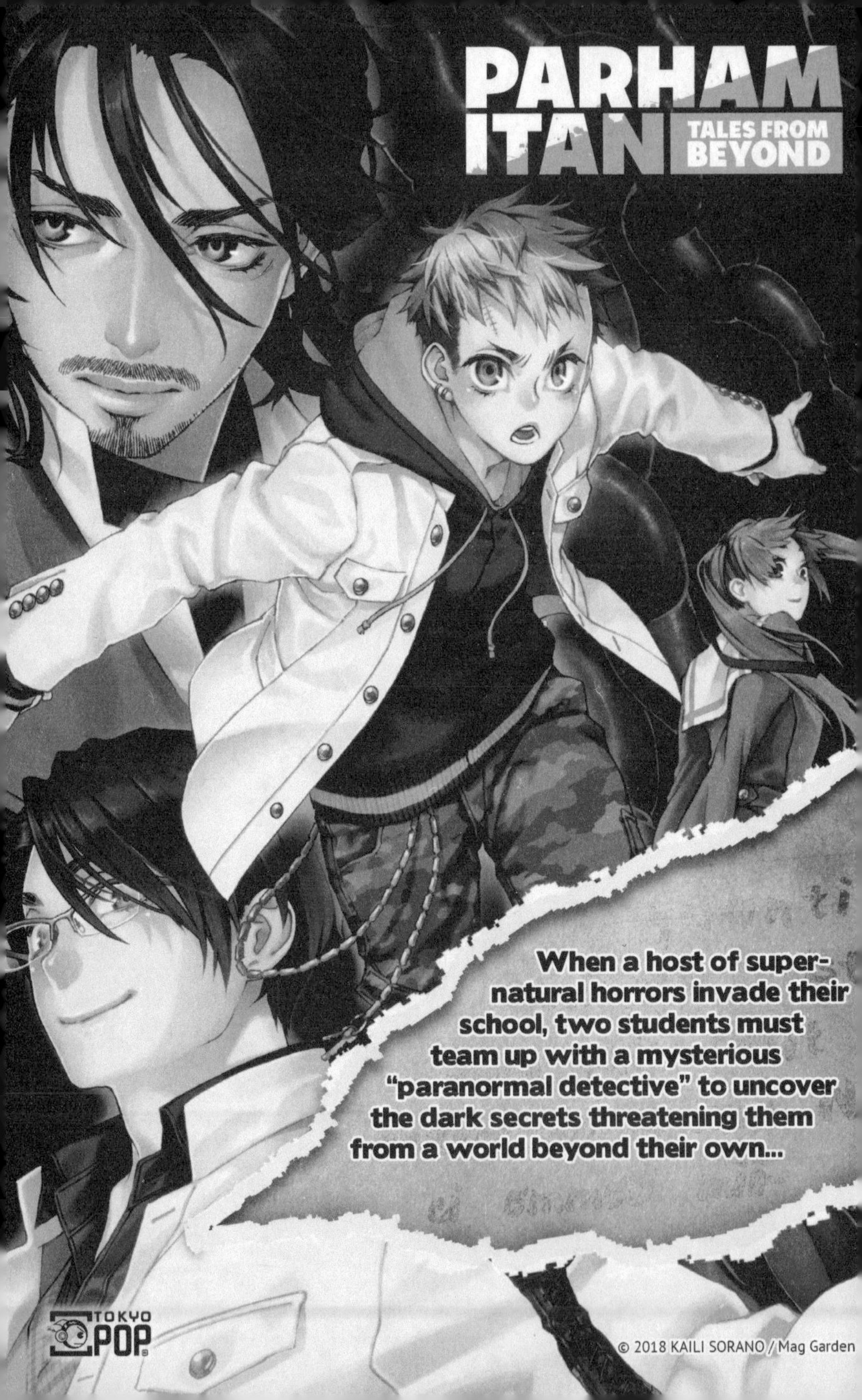
PARHAM ITAN
TALES FROM BEYOND
When a host of super-natural horrors invade their school, two students must team up with a mysterious "paranormal detective" to uncover the dark secrets threatening them from a world beyond their own...
TOKYOPOP
© 2018 KAILI SORANO / Mag Garden

# HANGER

**FROM POLICE OFFICER TO SPECIAL INVESTIGATOR —**

Hajime's sudden transfer comes with an unexpected twist: a super-powered convict as his partner!

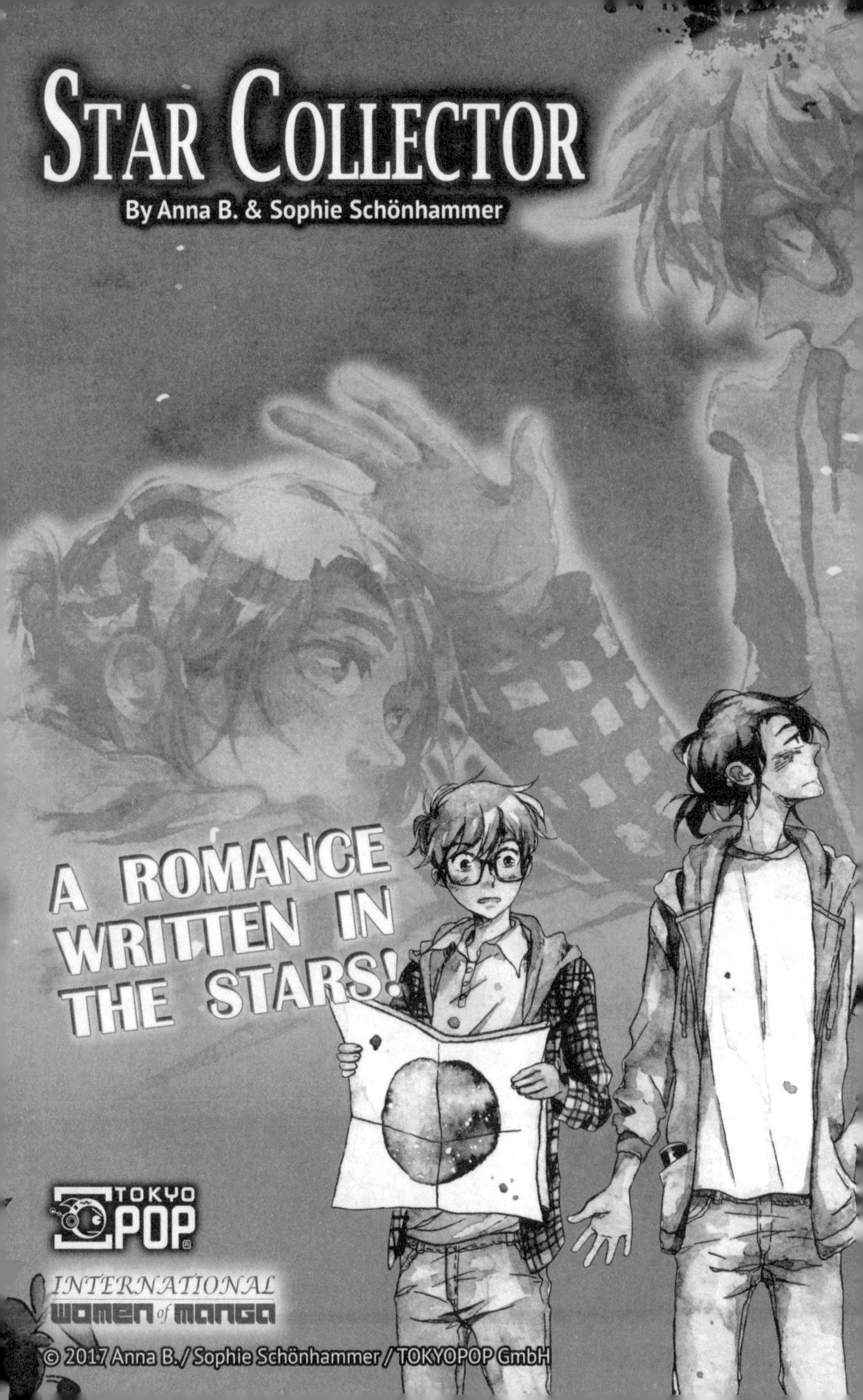
STAR COLLECTOR
By Anna B. & Sophie Schönhammer
A ROMANCE WRITTEN IN THE STARS!
TOKYO POP
INTERNATIONAL women of manga
© 2017 Anna B. / Sophie Schönhammer / TOKYOPOP GmbH

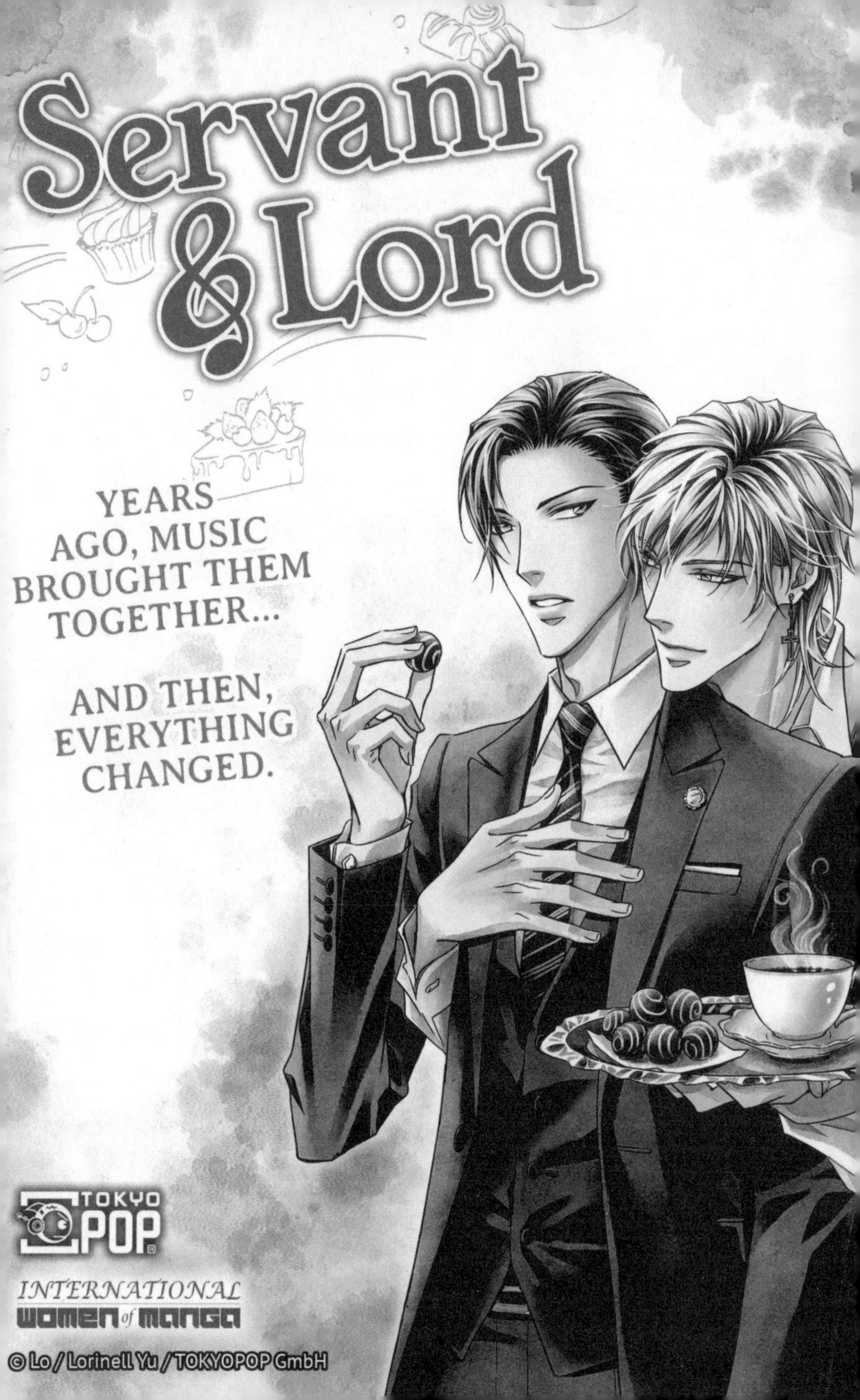
Servant & Lord
YEARS AGO, MUSIC BROUGHT THEM TOGETHER...
AND THEN, EVERYTHING CHANGED.
TOKYO POP
INTERNATIONAL WOMEN of MANGA
© Lo / Lorinell Yu / TOKYOPOP GmbH

REPLAY